A Little Solitaire

A Little Solitaire

John Frankenheimer and American Film

EDITED BY
MURRAY POMERANCE
R. BARTON PALMER

RUTGERS UNIVERSITY PRESS
NEW BRUNSWICK, NEW JERSEY, AND LONDON

LIBRARY OF CONGRESS CATALOGING-IN-PUBLICATION DATA

A little solitaire : John Frankenheimer and American film / edited by Murray Pomerance and R. Barton Palmer.
   p.   cm.
Includes bibliographical references and index.
Includes filmography.
ISBN 978-0-8135-5059-6 (hardcover : alk. paper) — ISBN 978-0-8135-5060-2 (pbk. : alk. paper)
   1. Frankenheimer, John, 1930–2002—Criticism and interpretation. I. Pomerance, Murray, 1946– II. Palmer, R. Barton, 1946–
PN1998.3.F7327L58 2011
791.4302'33092—dc22   2010045435

A British Cataloging-in-Publication record for this book is available from the British Library.

Frontispiece photograph of John Frankenheimer courtesy Evans Frankenheimer.

This collection copyright © 2011 by Rutgers, The State University
Individual chapters copyright © 2011 in the names of their authors

All rights reserved

No part of this book may be reproduced or utilized in any form or by any means, electronic or mechanical, or by any information storage and retrieval system, without written permission from the publisher. Please contact Rutgers University Press, 100 Joyce Kilmer Avenue, Piscataway, NJ 08854-8099. The only exception to this prohibition is "fair use" as defined by U.S. copyright law.

Visit our Web site: http://rutgerspress.rutgers.edu

Manufactured in the United States of America

To Evans Frankenheimer
and Gerald Pratley,
who lit our way

CONTENTS

Acknowledgments   ix

Introduction: Why Don't You Pass the Time
by Playing a Little Solitaire?   1
   R. BARTON PALMER AND MURRAY POMERANCE

Thrills

Murdered Souls, Conspiratorial Cabals:
Frankenheimer's Paranoia Films   13
   DAVID STERRITT

The Manchurian Candidate: Compromised Agency
and Uncertain Causality   29
   CHARLES RAMÍREZ BERG

Stealth, Sexuality, and Cult Status in
The Manchurian Candidate and *Seconds*   48
   REBECCA BELL-METEREAU

The Train: John Frankenheimer's "Rape of Europa"   62
   MATTHEW H. BERNSTEIN

Action and Abstraction in *Ronin*   78
   STEPHEN PRINCE

Politics

Late Frankenheimer/Political Frankenheimer   91
   DOUGLAS McFARLAND

John Frankenheimer's "War on Terror"   103
   COREY K. CREEKMUR

The Burning Season: Environmentalism versus Progress? 117
ROBIN L. MURRAY

Pictures and Prizes: Le Grand Prix de Rome and *Grand Prix* 129
VICTORIA DUCKETT

Families

Crashing In: *Birdman of Alcatraz* 145
TOM CONLEY

Walking the Line with the *Fille Fatale* 157
LINDA RUTH WILLIAMS

Live TV, Filmed Theater, and the New Hollywood:
John Frankenheimer's *The Iceman Cometh* 170
JAMES MORRISON

Ashes, Ashes: Structuring Emptiness in *All Fall Down* 184
MURRAY POMERANCE

Secrets

An American in Paris: John Frankenheimer's
Impossible Object 199
JERRY MOSHER

Shot from the Sky: *The Gypsy Moths* and the
End of Something 214
DENNIS BINGHAM

Frankenheimer and the Science Fiction/Horror Film 229
CHRISTINE CORNEA

The Fixer: A Jew Who Could Be Any Man,
Any Time, Anywhere 244
R. BARTON PALMER

Jonah 262
BILL KROHN

John Frankenheimer's Directorial Career: A Chronology 279
Works Cited and Consulted 287
Contributors 299
Index 303

ACKNOWLEDGMENTS

The editors are deeply grateful to a number of individuals whose generous assistance and warm encouragement were invaluable help in the making of this book.

We would like to thank Ned Comstock of the Cinema-Television Library (University of Southern California), Richard Dysart (Beverly Hills), Evans Frankenheimer (Beverly Hills), Christa Fuller (Beverly Hills), Kathryn Jacobi (Beverly Hills), Pamela Marvin (Beverly Hills), Chris Mason (Beverly Hills), Andrew McCarthy (Los Angeles), Jerry Mosher (Long Beach), Carl Nowotny (Toronto), Ronan O'Casey (Los Angeles), Jenny Romero of the Margaret Herrick Library, Academy of Motion Picture Arts and Sciences (Beverly Hills), Rory Sinclair (Toronto), Carol Tavris (Los Angeles), Faye Thompson of the Margaret Herrick Library, Academy of Motion Picture Arts and Sciences (Beverly Hills), Matt Thompson (Toronto), Jennifer Toews of the Thomas Fisher Rare Books Library (University of Toronto), and Evan Williams (Toronto).

Without the generous support of our families, this book wouldn't have been possible. Our heartfelt thanks to Carla and Camden Palmer, Nellie Perret, and Ariel Pomerance for their encouragement and guidance.

Our gracious and inspiring editorial team at Rutgers University Press has contributed a boundless and always delightful fountain of energy. We are particularly grateful to Leslie Mitchner, Marilyn Campbell, Ann Weinstock, and Eric Schramm.

A Little Solitaire

The journey is from nowhere to nowhere. It suits me.
The Horsemen

Introduction

Why Don't You Pass the Time by Playing a Little Solitaire?

R. BARTON PALMER AND MURRAY POMERANCE

Arguably postwar Hollywood's most politically engaged and astute writer/ director, John Frankenheimer (1930–2002) was also a powerful visual stylist, a man who learned the craft of image making both from his early years as a photographer and from demanding work in live television drama in the 1950s. In the latter he managed writing, rehearsals, storyboarding, and, as the shows unfolded, the instant editing made possible by multiple camera set-ups. It was an apprenticeship (like the celebrated years D. W. Griffith spent at Biograph) that provided Frankenheimer with the kind of concentrated hands-on training with actors and the camera that few have been lucky enough to experience.

In programs such as *Playhouse 90* and *Climax!* and working with such luminaries of the big screen as Jack Palance, Kim Hunter, James Dean, Zachary Scott, Claudette Colbert, John Carradine, Edward Arnold, Mary Astor, Joan Bennett, Charlton Heston, John Gielgud, Peter Lorre, and James Mason, Frankenheimer pushed the staging and broadcast of live drama to its existential limits. The work was still set-bound like the Broadway stage but also energized by constantly mutating camera placement that both incorporated and transcended the single-set, missing-fourth-wall convention utilized by the period's most notable playwrights. Frankenheimer's teleplays communicate the social and psychological entrapment that writers like Tennessee Williams, William Inge, and Rod Serling made their most constant theme, but, exceeding the limitations of the stage, he offered the viewer ever-emerging opportunities to see and understand. By the end of the 1950s, Frankenheimer was widely celebrated, a *wunderkind*, having become one of the true stars of the Golden Age of the medium's most prominent art, now lost beyond recovery.

With William Wyler, John Ford, and Orson Welles as possible exceptions, no American filmmaker has better understood the expressive possibilities of a carefully calculated mise-en-scène filmed from just the right angles, with the result that the story seems to film itself, creating both the meaning and emotions proper to it, a seemingly artless form of artistic creation that evokes the Renaissance concept of *sprezzatura*. As for the "universal men" of that earlier age, Frankenheimer was a director for whom competence pure and simple was an enduring, indispensable value, as exemplified onscreen by the many characters who mirror this value, demonstrating in film after film how things can be made, how action transforms raw material into meaning, how, in short, life can be lived. "He had a very fine grasp on his project," Richard Dysart reflected (Dysart). "You can't fool the camera."

The films are therefore virtual textbooks on modern life. Some memorable and characteristic moments: Burt Lancaster as inmate Robert Stroud in *Birdman of Alcatraz* (1962), rescuing and feeding his birds, then recording, like an Audubon confined to a closet by his own moral failings, his hard-won understanding of their nature and the illnesses from which they suffer. Lancaster again, as the French trainman Labiche in *The Train* (1964), spending all night in a machine shop forging and fitting new parts for his precious locomotive that has been sabotaged in an effort to prevent a shipment of priceless French paintings to Germany, an effort that Labiche will soon find his own means of halting. The trio of carnival-show parachutists in *The Gypsy Moths* (1969) practicing their complex and dangerous art. The hired mercenaries in *Ronin* (1998) checking their weapons, and, later, one among them (Robert De Niro) directing his friends in how to remove a bullet lodged in his own abdomen. The regime of plastic surgery and physical conditioning that transforms a middle-aged businessman into Rock Hudson in *Seconds* (1966). One of the long-term prisoners in *Andersonville* (1996) consuming in quick but loving bites an unpeeled onion provided him by a new arrival. In the much-celebrated *Grand Prix* (1966), we have an extended essay on the living arrangements, occupational hazards, and technical maneuvers of car racing; all the races in this film were shot on real locations and during real competitions, and the film communicates brilliantly the knowledge Frankenheimer himself gained from the experience. In these and countless other scenes, Frankenheimer's cinema opens into a bewildering variety of worlds, showing us how action looks, what it means, what it's like to *be* at work just as these characters are.

Moving into feature-film direction at the end of the 1950s, Frankenheimer successfully turned his hand to the small, adult film dramas then becoming a staple form of Hollywood filmmaking (this was an era when Hollywood often remade live TV drama, including, for example, the much-applauded *Playhouse 90* mounting of J. P. Miller's *Days of Wine and Roses*). *The Young Stranger* (1957) and *All Fall Down* (1962) are essentially family dramas that center on the discontents and disillusionment of the young men who are their central characters; they rival, and in their unremitting grimness exceed, the raw power of more noted examples of the genre, such as Nicholas Ray's *Rebel Without a Cause* (1955). *Birdman* is also a melodrama, tracing the irrepressible will of a man imprisoned for life to give meaning and purpose to his existence, however limited it has become through his own actions. But Frankenheimer was not content to work only in genres familiar to him from his years in television. In fact, he became most celebrated for a trio of political thrillers that feature the artful staging of action (*The Manchurian Candidate* [1962], *Seven Days in May* [1964], and *The Train*), a skill (or rather a set of complex skills) that Frankenheimer learned on his way to becoming a director whose recording of motion and speed exceeds even the masterwork of rivals like Peter Yates (*Bullitt* [1968]) and William Friedkin (*The French Connection* [1972] and *Sorcerer* [1977]). And Frankenheimer was anything but a conventional artist; a number of his projects, such as the screen adaptation of Bernard Malamud's *The Fixer* (1968), explore significant philosophical and religious questions, often in probing and disturbing ways that did not make them easy to like for mainstream filmgoers.

During the middle years of his career, leading figures in American film culture largely judged Frankenheimer a disappointment. This judgment of films such as *The Extraordinary Seaman* (1969), *The Horsemen* (1971), and *I Walk the Line* (1970) is eminently debatable, as Frankenheimer's talents for intimate and spectacular filmmaking are evident in all three, only the last of which (because it stars Gregory Peck) is now easily available for viewing. And yet in his end was his beginning, as Frankenheimer wrapped up his career with a productive finale worthy of any of the acknowledged great directors of the postwar era, as well as a series of fizzles that testified mostly to the failure of the critical establishment to recognize his unique talents. Indeed, if ever there were such a dismal contest, John Frankenheimer would contend closely for the title of Hollywood's most under-appreciated director. The common academic and critical view of Frankenheimer as he drifted into old age was that he was a genius somehow *manqué*, a talent puzzlingly wasted due to personal weakness or ill fortune, someone from whom more was expected, a disappointment. And yet, the contributors to this volume feel that his films cry out for another chance to work their magic and thrill viewers with their technical mastery, intellectual depth, and fervent passion. This is true not only of his most popular and famous efforts, *The Manchurian Candidate*, *Birdman of Alcatraz*, and *Grand Prix*; but of lesser known works one will find in these pages, such as *The Iceman Cometh* (1973), *The Gypsy Moths*, *Seconds*, *The Island of Dr. Moreau* (1996), *The Burning Season* (1994), *Ronin*, and many others; and also of a number of fascinating and eminently skillful productions that are not analyzed here due to space limitations: *French Connection II* (1975), *The Horsemen*, and *The Holcroft Covenant* (1985), for example; and of some films, virtually unknown today, that are discussed, such as *Impossible Object* (1973), *All Fall Down*, and *I Walk the Line*.

The reality of Frankenheimer, to be sure, easily exposes the dismissive assessment current today. Indeed, Frankenheimer ended his career with more bang than whimper, more praise from industry insiders and filmgoers than disregard. He took advantage of developments within the industry (especially the need of narrowcast providers like HBO for feature films on subjects that might not attract a large theatrical audience) and returned to work in television. In the 1990s, he enjoyed a remarkable run of success with feature films produced for the small screen. *Against the Wall* (1994, about the Attica prison riots) and *The Burning Season* (which tells the tragic story of the campaign of activist Chico Mendes against the big businesses eager to exploit and destroy the Amazon rain forest) pushed the liberal politics close to the director's heart. Unusual for TV films, even on cable, these releases engaged deeply and uncompromisingly with divisive issues and causes: the green movement, the never-ending advance of capitalism, racially unequal rates of incarceration, the inhumanity of mandatory sentencing, the deplorable health and security conditions in overcrowded prisons, and the ways in which the rich and powerful easily dispose of murder, judicial and otherwise, to solve their problems, just to name the most prominent. Made for HBO, *Against the Wall* and *The Burning Season* won well-deserved Emmys, as did *Andersonville* (TNT), which deftly engages the complex social, political, and moral issues raised by the Confederacy's notorious incarceration of Union prisoners. Both *Andersonville* and *Against the Wall* are prison movies with a distinct difference, the former also being a war movie that goes far beyond jingoistic partisanship and derring-do.

Frankenheimer stretched his string of Emmy Award-winning films to five with the political dramas *George Wallace* (1997, TNT) and *Path to War* (2002, HBO), a feat equaled only by another old industry hand, Joseph Sargent. Here Frankenheimer once again made dramatically compelling films from difficult political material resistant to the customary Hollywood melodramatization. The director's youthful apprenticeship on dramatic anthology series such as *You Are There* served him well in his effective melding of dialogue-heavy scenes with suspenseful action, reminiscent of his masterful direction of the February 1953 episode "The Capture of John Dillinger." In *Wallace*, Frankenheimer offers not only a nuanced and captivating portrait of one of postwar America's most idiosyncratic national figures, but also a detailed history of politics in the civil rights era, seen, as it were, from the other side. *Path to War* limns the other major domestic drama of the sixties, the agonies of Lyndon Johnson's presidency, as the increasingly disastrous commitment to defend the artificial division of Vietnam, with its multiplying evils (especially the several bombing offensives), undermined the president's plans to remake America into a "Great Society" of prosperity and racial justice. In all, Frankenheimer finished his career with an impressive series of successes, making effective cinema from historical subjects that, however familiar, now seemed to loom larger in social importance. His work as an industry old hand in television feature filmmaking was as thoroughly "American" (in the best national tradition of committed artistry) as that of any of his postwar contemporaries.

The end of Frankenheimer's career, however, was not free from the discontents that had haunted him ever since his extraordinary successes in the early sixties. A number of his last theatrical features, critical and box office failures, reminded many observers of the supposed decline of his artistic talents in the late sixties and early seventies. A sober reassessment of these films, however, reveals them as carefully crafted, idiosyncratic works released by an industry in crisis, striving for a viewership in the throes of disorienting changes in values and tastes. In particular, critics received Frankenheimer's last two theatrical releases, *The Island of Dr. Moreau* and *Ronin*, with scorn. The former, however, was a production so deeply troubled before the director's involvement that it was virtually unsalvageable late in the game by anyone; while the latter, majestically controlled and elegantly shaped, is one of the finest examples of the action thriller, a genre pioneered by Frankenheimer. *Ronin*'s success in DVD release has fortunately introduced Frankenheimer's considerable talents to a new generation of viewers. Even one of the few positive reviews that *Ronin* received, from Janet Maslin of the *New York Times*, although praising Frankenheimer for coaxing "hard-boiled performances" from a talented veteran cast and for treating viewers to intense "visceral excitement" (Maslin), did not note, or was not interested in, the film's other impressive achievements: its intense evocation of cinematic history, with its Hawksian exploration of male camaraderie, and its moving meditations, in the manner of Kurosawa, on the demanding moral code that mercenaries should follow. Nor did Maslin see fit to praise the spectacular automobile chase sequences in and around the old city of Nice, sequences that plainly reveal that there has never been a filmmaker who addresses the (wholly modern) automotive experience with the adeptness and visual acuity of Frankenheimer. As in *Grand Prix*, Frankenheimer shows not only his own personal love for driving, but also a serious emotional investment in placing his camera for the most intimate views of the experience of automotive speed. Behind the camera, as behind the wheel, he was an avid driver.

Further, in Maslin's constrained view, Frankenheimer was to be understood as an action director, not a moralist, a Raoul Walsh, certainly not a Billy Wilder. In truth Frankenheimer was both, though many, seduced by the wit, energy, and flash of his dynamic style, would have preferred him as more of a Walsh and to leave aside the incisive political commentary, as well as the exploration, at turns sardonic and pietistic, of existential conundra. But these were the themes that beset and structured the era in which Frankenheimer worked, notwithstanding that the critical establishment was indisposed to respond to them. To take an obvious example: in *French Connection II*, Doyle (Gene Hackman), trailing a drug kingpin in Marseilles, is kidnapped and overdosed, and so must wind his way back from the hellish torments of a near-death addiction experience—an alarming and intensive recovery that lasts well beyond the limits of most viewers' comfort (and that includes some of the most spontaneous work of Hackman's esteemed career). Why bother to explore, the chorus of reviewers whined, the psychological and physiological aspects of drug addiction at such painful length and in such disturbing detail? With his interest in the mechanics of process, however, Frankenheimer never shielded his viewers from relentless concentration upon the smallest details of human activity, suffering, accomplishment, and agony. Recollecting the shooting of *Connection*, the director's widow commented not only on Hackman's immense skill and the screen realization of his character's withdrawal from heroin addiction but also on one remarkable performance of addiction by the eighty-six-year-old (and more than frail) English actress Cathleen Nesbitt: "Wasn't that amazing, to think of those little arms with the tracks up them!" (Pomerance).

This under-appreciation and misunderstanding has been common in Frankenheimer criticism for nearly forty years. In 1968, Pauline Kael praised Frankenheimer's "talent for pace and pyrotechnics," which she summed up in the term "showmanship," qualities that had supposedly first brought him national acclaim in the wake of the thrillers *The Manchurian Candidate*, *Seven Days in May*, *The Train*, and *Grand Prix*. His work later in the decade, Kael opined sourly, put him among those "clods who think they can turn into important artists by the simple expedient of not being entertaining" (Kael, "Frightening the Horses" 208). Why do directors such as Frankenheimer, she complained, insist on making films that would allow them "to become respectable in the eyes of their old high-school English teachers" (209)?

Such flippant anti-intellectualism is common among the intelligentsia who like their popular culture unsullied by "meaning" and "significance," those who think of movies as a delightful form of slumming. It was easy enough for Kael, writing for those urban hipsters eager that the *New Yorker* should form their tastes in "movies" (never film), to link Frankenheimer with Arthur Miller and Dalton Trumbo, writers also supposedly in the thrall of "dictates-of-conscience" conceptions of human experience, and then condemn the group for shrilly promoting the "dignity-and-indomitable-spirit-of-man school of screenwriting" (209). If the "problem with Frankenheimer" was to some degree personal (such as his alcoholism, which undeniably marred his career), it was also institutional. What the critical establishment, typified by Kael and Maslin, would not recognize was plain enough: the perfectly composed optical display of personal challenge and collapse, and the dedication to showing people straining with purpose in a world that every day failed a little more to support them. We see Yves Montand's too-willful stoicism in *Grand Prix*, masked by his suave insouciance and courage in the shadow of death; Gregory Peck's equivocal morality and Tuesday Weld's conniving desire in *I Walk the Line*; Deborah Kerr's and Burt Lancaster's matching but incompatible hopelessnesses in *The Gypsy Moths*; Brandon De Wilde's slowly growing self-knowledge and Warren Beatty's slowly darkening confusion in *All Fall Down*; Gene Hackman's dissolution in *French Connection II*; and dozens upon dozens of other poignant and elegantly realized portraits of the human dream gone wrong.

The second part of Frankenheimer's career revealed a disjunction between the director's aesthetics and thematics, on the one hand, and, on the other, the sophisticated Know Nothingism of the then-regnant critical establishment.

The most prominent members of this group seemed to misread the enthusiasm of French New Wave writers for the native energy of the Hollywood system, and their resulting cinephilia strangely identified the *engagement* of directors like Frankenheimer with a despised "tradition of quality." There are now signs that this long-prevailing view is being abandoned. Stephen Charbonneau, for example, has praised Frankenheimer for his "ability to both explore complex social situations and psychological ordeals," noting that this had "made him one of the most important film-makers of the last forty years." Yet this view seems to have been purchased at the price of a disturbing amnesia, as Charbonneau wrongly observes that (with the exception of *Seconds*) "all of Frankenheimer's films during the 1960s—he made eleven of them—were critical and commercial successes" (Charbonneau 159, 160). Like his characters, Frankenheimer came to know something about the dream gone wrong, in a sharply culminating way, perhaps—he watched from steps away the assassination of his friend and candidate Robert F. Kennedy—but also more diffusely and with a slow arc of development that more or less occupied his creative life (see Pomerance).

When we look carefully at Frankenheimer's films, we can understand how in some rather important ways the sort of critical appraisal Frankenheimer received reflects upon the limitations of the critic's own experience more than on the films under review. For example, with a disarming consistency the critical consciousness has forborne to discuss the striking technical efficiency and invention visible in these films with remarkable consistency; has, in fact, neglected to consider filmmaking as a technical process that involves challenges and problems of its own. When we try to grasp what it is to dramatize a scene before a camera, with the collaboration of actors who are living participants with their own concerns and under the constraints of lighting and sound recording, not to mention scripting and budget, we can see that the achievement of aerial photography in *The Gypsy Moths* or *Black Sunday* (1977), the virtuoso dramatization of personal conflicts during Formula One races in *Grand Prix* (concentrating on character shots made inside speeding vehicles) or car chases in *Ronin*, or the use of topography for establishing narrative space in *Prophecy* (1979) are hardly negligible, decorative matters but constitute instead the very essence of intelligible filmmaking.

Critics have also tended to disregard Frankenheimer's always surprisingly expressive use of mise-en-scène, which includes many memorable bravura sequences: in *Seconds* the interview with the human recyclers sardonically staged in the meatpacking district of New York's Lower West Side; or in *Ronin* the complex gunfight that erupts in the Roman arena at Arles, all narrow passages and tunnels that lead to their starting points, and a large killing field of sand in the center—pointedly unused in the sequence by characters unwilling to reveal themselves fully; or Labiche's stroll across the marshaling yard in *The Train*, captured by a tracking camera that takes notice of a German military under great stress but still efficiently engaged with various duties, offering the visible evidence of a national predisposition toward order and an always calculating grasp of intentions, precisely those qualities that make possible on a grandly organized scale in the midst of an otherwise precipitative retreat the theft of art that constitutes the film's narrative motor. Frankenheimer "just knew exactly what he was going to do, had it all planned out, had the people around him, the camera crew and such, all knew what was going on. That's a good way to do it," Richard Dysart recollected. "Most directors are a little lax in there somewhere" (Dysart).

Further, what Frankenheimer "was going to do" was almost always a careful dissection of problematic relationships in social space—often male-male relationships, in what has come to be called the Hawksian tradition, although numerous filmmakers have seen the world as a business of interpersonality and had a special way in showing how men were with one another (Anthony Mann, Nicholas Ray, Alfred Hitchcock). We learn from Frankenheimer over and over not only what is happening dramatically but what "mechanism" of connection and balance aligns people engaged in an activity and how they work to make the changes that make for catharsis. Examples of this "technical focus" are all through the films discussed in this book: in *The Train*, detailed explorations of the railway system and its day-to-day operation, as when Labiche must decouple his engine from the cars attached to it and the camera runs into macrofocus on his hand as it operates the level that will momentarily halt forward motion, letting the next car bump up against the engine's tail so it can be loosed: the deft hand, the steam in the switch, and the sharp look of concentration in the man's dark eyes. In *Black Sunday*, as Evans Frankenheimer commented on a long sequence with Bruce Dern, "You know how to take a blimp off without stopping" (Pomerance). In *The Horsemen*, we discover the tribal customs for both goat and camel fights. In *Gypsy Moths* we find ourselves inside the skydivers' operation, hurtling toward earth at a frightening rate of acceleration. *Birdman of Alcatraz* and *Against the Wall* both reveal precise details of prison life, while *George Wallace* anatomizes the complex connections among personality, ideals, and political pressures. *Path to War* allows us the opportunity to see the workings of high power, with the president trapped between conflicting and bewilderingly articulate advisors, each of them thinking he is smarter than the executive whose career they are directing.

In that stunning and justly famous circular shot of *The Manchurian Candidate*, as we explore Bennett Marco's recurring nightmare, we learn not only some of the general effects of brainwashing hallucination but in fact penetrate to the actual process of mentality of the characters, sharing their confusion and oneiric withdrawal. In all these cases and many more, Frankenheimer's camera produces precise and detailed visions of complex interworkings, going far beyond the more lackadaisical views of filmmakers who are content to simply open a stage upon which the actors can move through their work. In *The Horsemen*, Frankenheimer realizes a stunning moment when Omar Sharif comes in upon his father, Jack Palance, dressing in his quarters in the morning, and is rebuked by the older man for looking upon him in his nakedness: a perfectly shot, perfectly lit, perfectly poised rendition not only of interpersonal tension but of cultural and traditional mores, value structure, and belief, not to say filial love.

An astute observer of the cultural scene in the first three decades of the postwar era, Pauline Kael is surely correct that there was then a group of directors (not only Frankenheimer, but Fred Zinnemann, Sidney Lumet, Stanley Kramer, Robert Aldrich, Alan J. Pakula, and Robert Mulligan, to name only some of the more prominent) who were interested in making the kind of films that would have pleased their high school English teachers, a form of filmmaking, inherited from the studio era, which quickly became an art generally lost in a 1970s film culture captivated by generic gigantism (*Jaws* [1975], *Star Wars* [1977]) and mindless wish fulfillment (the *Rocky* franchise). Those who admire Frankenheimer's filmmaking can perhaps be forgiven for thinking that this now-lost tradition of seriousness is hardly a bad thing. It may well be significant that most of those named above, like Frankenheimer, achieved their initial success directing quality small-screen drama; and, moving to Hollywood (if sometimes only metaphorically), they found unchanged in these new surroundings their commitment to the microcosmic portrayal of the human condition that, even with technical limitations, became the central concern of Golden Age television drama (as it was of the era's Broadway dramatic stage, with its diminishment of *opsis*).

But if Frankenheimer is doubtless a card-carrying member of the so-called New York School of dedicated realists and social critics, he more unusually enjoyed a career in Hollywood that saw him develop interests and skills of a very different kind. In fact, few directors (David Lean and D. W. Griffith come to mind, and that is august company indeed) have shared Frankenheimer's ability for working as ably and precisely with the small-scale aspects of human drama as with epic-sized action. His is a cinema built from both carefully meditative observation and also startling movement, a form of filmmaking that fruitfully exploits all aspects of the multifaceted and always evolving practice that is cinema. The purpose of this book is to move readers to give Frankenheimer's films, worthy testaments to his talent and visions of our condition, a second look.

Thrills

Murdered Souls, Conspiratorial Cabals

Frankenheimer's Paranoia Films

DAVID STERRITT

John Frankenheimer moved from live television to Hollywood features in 1961, and within the next five years he directed most of the pictures for which he is best remembered. The three that have come to be called his paranoia trilogy—*The Manchurian Candidate* (1962), *Seven Days in May* (1964), and *Seconds* (1966)—are cited by some critics as a point of origin for the cynical, alienated worldview found in much post-noir cinema of the 1960s and beyond. Film scholar R. Barton Palmer holds that these movies "undoubtedly inaugurated the paranoid thriller" (107). Stephen Bowie writes that *Seven Days in May* "casually perfects the formula of the paranoid thriller" and that the "unsettling and claustrophobic" imagery in *Seconds* establishes "a kind of cinematic grammar of paranoia." Along similar lines, Jay Millikan argues that post-1960s conspiracy films, such as Alan J. Pakula's *The Parallax View* and Francis Ford Coppola's *The Conversation*, both released in 1974, drew their "greatest influence" from *The Manchurian Candidate* and its "suspicion of . . . political institutions." More recent films of paranoia and conspiracy range from Robert De Niro's *The Good Shepherd* (2006) to Tony Gilroy's legal thriller *Michael Clayton* (2007) and Jonathan Demme's updated remake of *The Manchurian Candidate* (2004). A comprehensive listing might also include such topical documentaries as Michael Moore's *Fahrenheit 9/11* (2004) and Alex Gibney's *Taxi to the Dark Side* (2007).

While these movies share a fascination with conspiracies, they aren't necessarily about paranoia in the clinical sense, which involves the "insidious development of a permanent and unshakeable delusional system" related to persecution or jealousy, with "clear and orderly thinking" accompanied by emotions and behavior "consistent with the delusional state" (National). Among the traits and attributes that a paranoid personality may manifest are fearfulness, anger, hypervigilance, irrational cynicism, guardedness, rigidity, humorlessness, self-importance, self-righteousness, and self-protection (Blaney 340, 349). Any film about a hidden agenda is a conspiracy film, but only one about delusion, fixation, or fear and loathing on a grand psychotic scale qualifies as a paranoia film. And only one *with* a hidden agenda—perhaps hidden even from itself—can be called a paranoid film.

The most memorable parts of Frankenheimer's trilogy fall into all three categories—they view paranoia and conspiracy from a paranoid perspective—and this accounts for their enduring power to dig under the receptive moviegoer's skin. On their most obvious levels, the movies are against-the-grain melodramas touching on such hot ideological topics as cold war politics, military authoritarianism, instrumental psychology, high-tech media culture, mythologies of modern science, and the tension between popular perceptions of American history and the blood-stained realities they disavow. As shaped and inflected by Frankenheimer's style, these real-world subjects take on enigmatic and uncanny qualities, tapping into the political as well as the clinical meanings of paranoia.

In the 1964 title essay of his book *The Paranoid Style in American Politics*, historian Richard Hofstadter argues that clinical and political paranoids "both tend to be overheated, oversuspicious, overaggressive, grandiose, and apocalyptic in expression," but that the psychotic paranoid "sees the hostile and conspiratorial world . . . as directed specifically *against him*," while the political paranoid "finds it directed against a nation, a culture, a way of life whose fate affects not himself alone but millions of others" (4). Those clued in to the cabal live at a critical moment, moreover, faced with the knowledge that all might soon be lost: "It is now or never in organizing resistance. . . . Time is forever just running out" (29–30). Note how *Seven Days in May* evokes clock and calendar time so frequently that they become demi-characters in the story.

The continuity between Hofstadter's ideas and Frankenheimer's cinema shows that the latter had many contact points with sociopolitical realities of its day[1] Yet the dominant mood of the paranoia trilogy depends less on earthbound plausibility than on the interplay of story elements drawn from divergent, even conflicting categories—the possible and the impossible, the normal and the anomalous, the natural and the magical, the physical and the metaphysical. Their surface realism notwithstanding, *The Manchurian Candidate* and *Seconds* darkly suggest that unseen forces and cryptic energies are at work in the margins of their narrative worlds; *Seven Days in May* serves to drily contain and control a sense of conspiratorial danger that might otherwise have been too threatening in the year of President Lyndon B. Johnson's notorious "Daisy Girl" campaign commercial, which showed a little girl playing with a flower and then a nuclear explosion, implying that Johnson's defeat could mean the end of civilization itself. These are the dimensions of the paranoia trilogy that I want to explore, looking for strategies of narrative and style that destabilize 1960s-era assumptions in ways that magnify the films' cumulative power. I attribute these strategies to Frankenheimer for reasons of convention and convenience, but I don't mean to imply that he was their sole author, or that he consciously intended the particular effects they have on me and other moviegoers. Scenes that resonate so intensely, mysteriously, and enduringly must draw their inspiration from the conscious and unconscious creativity of everyone who played a significant part in bringing them to the screen.

The Manchurian Candidate

> It is difficult to resist the suspicion that behind paranoia, as behind all power, lies the same profound urge: the desire to get other men out of the way so as to be the only one; or . . . to get others to help him *become* the only one.
>
> (Canetti 462)

Paranoia surges throughout Richard Condon's novel *The Manchurian Candidate*, which scored a critical and commercial hit when it appeared in 1959. Frankenheimer's film was not so celebrated when first released on October 24, 1962, but it has gained a lofty reputation since. The story has two protagonists. One is Raymond Shaw (Laurence Harvey), a bitter man whose stepfather, John Yerkes Iselin (James Gregory), is a U.S. senator clearly based on Joseph McCarthy, the famously unprincipled anticommunist crusader who died in office two years before Condon's novel appeared. Iselin is a slow-thinking pawn controlled by his malevolent wife, Eleanor (Angela Lansbury), who has conspired with Soviet and Chinese communists to transform her son Raymond into an unwitting murderer, programmed by a Pavlovian psychologist named Yen Lo (Khigh Dhiegh) to commit murder when prompted by posthypnotic signals. The other protagonist is Bennett Marco (Frank Sinatra), an army officer who gradually figures out that Raymond's artificially induced violence is to be used in a political assassination. Musing on their scheme, the conspirators know that timing is everything: "The blow needed to be struck at exactly the right time and place, at a national emotional apogee . . . so that the selected messiah who would succeed the slain ruler could then defend all of his people from the threatening and monstrous elements at whose doorstep the assassination of an authentic national hero could swiftly and effectively be laid" (Condon 45). The time will be the climax of a political convention; the murdered hero will be a freshly nominated presidential candidate; the counterfeit messiah will be Senator Iselin, who will arise after the fatal gunshot to seize the nomination and the presidency; and his defense of the realm will take the form of never-ending totalitarian rule.

Condon's novel expresses his opinion that Americans have been "brainwashed" through an "unrelenting conditioning to violence," meaning not only the violence of war but also (as he explained in a 1973 memoir) such routine manifestations as cigarette marketing, brutality in popular culture, and dishonesty in government (Westcombe). Sharing this view, Frankenheimer and screenwriter George Axelrod crafted an adaptation so steeped in paranoia that it's tempting to diagnose all the major characters—and, for that matter, the movie itself—with that condition, in either its clinical or political form.

Ben definitely has paranoid symptoms: he is plagued by anxiety and foreboding, which visit him by night in horrible recurring nightmares and by day in obsessive thoughts that something is profoundly wrong with Raymond, even though another part of his mind insists that Raymond is his finest friend. His fears are entirely justified, however, and only when he learns their origins and decodes their meanings can he take decisive action to more or less save the day. Ben's intuitive awareness of the looming danger points to a well-known idea in social science. As sociologist Erich Goode writes, "To some observers of contemporary society, paranoia is a healthy, not a delusional, perspective" (208). Or, in William S. Burroughs's pithier formulation, paranoia is "having all the facts" (E. White 476).

Things aren't actually so simple, however. Raymond's fear and anguish are as justified as Ben's, yet he emerges as the story's most tragic figure. One reason for his unhappy end is that the fates (i.e., the storytellers) don't allow him to understand the evil forces that beset him; unlike Ben, who slowly grasps the outlines of the conspiracy and manages to mitigate its outcome, Raymond never gets farther than a dim intimation that unseen enemies have stolen his mind. A deeper reason is that Raymond's chronic instability has at least two distinct sources. One is Yen Lo's hypnotic conditioning, which retooled crucial areas of his mind, leaving enough tinges and traces for him to know he is warped without knowing why. The other source is the long-term, slow-motion psychological mangling he has endured at Eleanor's hands.

"My mother, Ben, is a terrible woman. A terrible, terrible woman," Raymond says to his (only) friend during a Christmas Eve get-together. As a child, he "only kind of disliked her," but later, when she sabotaged his romance with the daughter of a liberal senator, he "began to hate her," and he fervently hates her still. More insight regarding this dysfunctional pair arises in one of the film's most disturbing scenes, when Eleanor gives Raymond her side of the story, making the explicit claim (probably true) that she didn't know the communists would use her own son as raw material for the psychiatrically constructed killer, and the implicit claim (outrageously false) that she wasn't such a bad mother at heart. She then covers his forehead and cheek with kisses, finishing with a passionate kiss on the mouth that Lansbury partly covers with her hand, veiling but not obscuring the act's incestuous import, which Frankenheimer underscores by framing it in a claustrophobically close profile shot. Far from being impulsive on Eleanor's part, this is the culminating deed in a life of all-devouring narcissism that has treated Raymond as nothing more than a pathetic stooge. While the movie eliminates some of her most unsavory characteristics—in the novel she is a heroin addict who grew up in an incestuous relationship with her father—it hardly reduces the barbed-wire viciousness of her repellent personality.

Soul Murder

> If you can't trust your mother, whom can you trust?—Victim of soul murder
>
> (Shengold, *Revisited* 108)

In his 1903 autobiography *Memoirs of My Nervous Illness*, German jurist Daniel Paul Schreber introduced the term "soul murder," reporting that "a plot was laid against me . . . the purpose of which was to hand me over to another human being . . . in such a way that my soul was handed over to him," while his body, transformed into that of a female, would be given over for sexual abuse and then "simply 'forsaken,' in other words left to rot" (63). Raymond might say something similar had he survived his ordeal; the first part of Schreber's passage fits his case exactly, and although his body is not transformed into that of a female, Eleanor has systematically eroded his masculinity, and he meets his death wearing (as disguise) the garb of a (celibate) Roman Catholic priest. Sigmund Freud used Schreber's text as the basis for a lengthy treatise on paranoid psychosis, finding (among many other things) that the judge's fantasies had transfigured his father into a God worthy of both "reverent submission and mutinous insubordination" (52). This captures Raymond's clashing reactions to his mother, an aspiring deity and soul-murdering matriarch if ever there was one.

The incestuous kiss that Eleanor plants on Raymond's mouth puts a seal on what the film strongly suggests (and the novel spells out) was a malign child-rearing program that included deliberate "instances of repetitive and chronic overstimulation, alternating with emotional deprivation," which psychoanalytic theorist Leonard Shengold posits as the necessary condition for soul murder, defined as "actual killing of the spirit" caused by experiences that the victim was "unable or forbidden to register and react to" (*Soul* 16–17, 310, 311). Raymond's affective responses, or rather his lack of them, testify to the damage he has undergone. He is "a counterfeiter of emotions," Condon writes; the closest he can come to displaying an authentic mood is to "remember how other people looked" and mimic what he saw, always unpersuasively (181–82). In a sense, Yen Lo's psychic operations on Raymond complete what Eleanor began years earlier, since "one of the common effects of child abuse is brainwashing—the cultivation of denial of what has occurred and the suppression of what was experienced" (Shengold, *Revisited* 11). Despite his own rocky spells, Ben has maintained enough baseline sanity to wrest critical advantages from the suspicion and knowledge that his paranoia brings. But the paranoia that arises from the kind of life inflicted on Raymond has no advantages, however marginal, to give. His rage is omnipresent and ineluctable, and his last-minute inkling of the facts brings no relief to anyone, including him.Raymond's dismal paranoia and Ben's useful paranoia are drastic in their different ways, and the film's own fears and phobias are equally extreme, springing from the cultural unconscious of the filmmakers who produced it and of the society—our society—that produced *them*. The notion of brainwashing crystallizes this anxiety. Explaining the deluded state of the prisoners he has manipulated, Yen Lo tells his communist guests, "I have conditioned them, or 'brainwashed' them, which I believe is the new American word." To prove this, he has Raymond strangle a fellow soldier to death, showing no more emotion about it than the onlookers in the audience do. One needn't have a paranoid disorder to believe that brainwashing, hypnosis, and posthypnotic suggestion are overwhelmingly potent instruments that no human will can resist. But a paranoid mentality would be extra-receptive to the idea, which the movie presents with deadpan wonderment, appealing to the paranoid elements in *our* minds.

The popular belief that many American soldiers had succumbed to brainwashing in the Korean War[2] heightened the fear quotient of *The Manchurian Candidate* in the 1960s by linking it with supposedly real events.[3] Its paranoid aura is further boosted by its contradictory discursive positions: world communism is a ghastly and immediate threat, able to control even the American presidency through conspiracy and violence; yet public proclamations of this danger, by Iselin as by McCarthy, are so grotesquely false that crucial details (e.g., the number of infiltrators in the U.S. government) fluctuate like mad. If nobody seems to notice this, it's because the media are as susceptible to trickery as the public. If one wonders how Iselin got into the Senate to begin with, the answer lies in Eleanor's skill at exploiting the American electoral system—a hyperbolic exercise of political savvy, but plausible enough from a paranoid perspective. While the movie is a fiction, its overlaps with reality lend it undertones of truth, or rather "truthiness," to borrow journalist-comedian Stephen Colbert's coinage. One might call the film a truthy fiction, much as *Time* magazine called Condon's book one of the "best bad" novels. Paradoxes and oxymorons come with the conspiratorial territory that *The Manchurian Candidate* surveys.

Seven Days in May

The screenplay for *Seven Days in May*, written by Rod Serling (a household name in America for his 1959–1964 television program *The Twilight Zone*), closely follows the eponymous novel published by Fletcher Knebel and Charles W. Bailey II in 1962. The story centers on a marine colonel named Martin "Jiggs" Casey (Kirk Douglas), who stumbles on a scheme by top military brass to depose American president Jordan Lyman (Fredric March) because he is bargaining away the country's nuclear arsenal in negotiations with the Soviet Union, undeterred by public protests and his historically low standing in opinion polls. The ringleader of the proposed coup is James Mattoon Scott (played with icy power by Burt Lancaster), the powerful general who chairs the Joint Chiefs of Staff and believes that Lyman's liberal statesmanship rests on nothing but gullibility and weakness. (In a marvelous irony for twenty-first-century viewers, Lyman's humiliatingly low public-approval rating—a miserable 29 percent—is the same as George W. Bush's approval score throughout the last portion of his presidency. The fictional president has risked his reputation in the name of peace, however, while the actual one lost his in the name of war, torture, and mendacity.)

As its title suggests, *Seven Days in May* has a deadline plot, with Lyman, Casey, and a handful of trusted colleagues racing the clock to expose the conspiracy and save the nation from a military takeover. Perhaps because it conveys a political message through a suspense-based narrative, this picture was a favorite for Frankenheimer, who selected it above all his other productions to open "Directed by John Frankenheimer: The Television and Film Work," a sweeping retrospective presented in New York by the Museum of Modern Art and the Museum of Television and Radio in 1996. This notwithstanding, I find *Seven Days in May* less original in style, less gripping in story, and less inventive in visual storytelling than the other films of the paranoia trilogy. Why did the most conservative of these pictures hold such a special place in the director's heart? I interpret it as a sign of conservatism within his creative personality— not political conservatism (he was an everyday liberal Democrat in that area) but psychological conservatism, impelling him to shore up his bona fides as an all-American storyteller after having jolted his audience (and probably himself) with the disruptive pleasures of *The Manchurian Candidate*. As clipped and constipated as its military characters, *Seven Days in May* reflects an artistic unconscious that is afraid of its own grim imaginings. Here the dark enjoyment that surged through Frankenheimer's previous picture comes up against a cinematic superego that errs in the opposite direction, warily policing itself lest its scary and plausible plot displease audiences even more than the 1962 movie, scary but *im*plausible, had done.

The superego, Slavoj Žižek tells us, comprises "fragments of a traumatic, cruel, capricious, 'unintelligible' and 'irrational' law text." This phantasmal law determines the tone of *Seven Days in May* as surely as the id's anarchic energies propel *The Manchurian Candidate*, and this dominance accounts for the film's excessive self-surveillance. For the paranoiac, Žižek further states, the superego's secret knowledge takes on a presence that is almost palpable, since in paranoia the "agency that 'sees all and knows all' is embodied in the real," causing the symbolic order of cultural meaning to be perceived as "a plot staged by some evil persecutor" (*Looking* 152–53). *Seven Days in May* envisions such plots several times over: General Scott feels persecuted by obtuse civilian leaders who are imperiling his country; President Lyman feels persecuted by military industrialists and their reckless bomb building; Colonel Casey feels persecuted by clandestine cadres and their traitorous plans. The conspirators here don't act in the name of sadistic gratification, as in *The Manchurian Candidate*, but in the name of national security. The movie's mission, aligned with that of Lyman and Casey, is to condemn the subversive plot, preserve the liberal status quo, and reaffirm Hollywood's faith in the sacred text on which the existing order can forever stand secure—the

Constitution of the United States of America, which majestically fills the screen during the opening and closing titles. To achieve these ends the movie conspires against itself, subordinating vision and spontaneity to its Important Message: that the convictions of patriotic Americans like us must be vigilantly held apart from the convictions of patriotic Americans not like us.

With its sanctimonious moral tone, the right-wing militarism represented by General Scott resembles the cultural conservatism of right-wing Christians in the age of televangelists and megachurches. While the film doesn't explicitly connect these ideologies, Scott's belief in the inerrancy of his ideas does link up with religion near the end, when he resentfully asks Casey if he knows who Judas was. A brief consideration of this moment will illustrate Frankenheimer's use of cinematic style to indicate the paranoid style of the American military as Scott understands it. The episode begins when Lyman confers with Casey and three others about the arrival of a written communication that provides irrefutable proof of the conspiracy; he immediately orders that Scott and the other joint chiefs get copies without delay. The camera films Lyman and his confrères in one lengthy take from a conspicuously low angle, stressing the importance of the moment and reinforcing the narrative ranks of the characters, with Lyman and Casey in the foreground and the others grouped between them farther back.

The next scene begins with a similarly symmetrical shot of the Joint Chiefs of Staff office lobby: four flags in the foreground, marking pomp and patriotism; a pillar at dead center near the far end of the space, marking firmness and stolidity; a security guard's desk even farther back, providing little sense of security at such a distance; and farthest away of all, General Scott walking in the direction of the lobby (and the camera) with his unmistakable stride. After passing through a door that opens for him with military precision, he comes face to face in the middle distance with Casey, who has entered from the opposite direction. They face each other at attention, crisply framed by flags to the right and left. Casey hands the fateful document to Scott, who takes it as the camera cuts to a close-up. The scene continues in alternating close-ups of the men's faces as Casey describes the document's contents and Scott listens with grim concentration; behind Casey we see the carefully arranged flags (patriotism) and behind Scott we see a sculpture representing an atom (military might, cold war paranoia) in schematized, semi-abstract form.

SCOTT: You're a night-crawler, Colonel, a peddler. You sell information. Are you sufficiently up on your Bible to know who Judas was?
CASEY: I suggest you read that letter, sir. It's from the President.
SCOTT (commandingly): I asked you a question!
CASEY: Are you ordering me to answer, sir?
SCOTT: I am!
CASEY: Yes, I know who Judas was. He was a man I worked for and admired—until he disgraced the four stars on his uniform.

The camera then returns to its long-shot position as Casey walks past Scott, through the automatic door, and down the corridor into the distance, leaving Scott meaningfully framed alongside the pillar, which mirrors the stiffness, stasis, and inflexibility that are visible in the general's obdurate and unyielding pose. Scott then walks out of view on the right side of the screen as Casey proceeds down the corridor into the extreme background of the shot, finally free (at least for the moment) of the crushing burden that's been imposed on him throughout the film by the quasi-religious zealotry of Scott's self-righteous militarism.

The film is interested in Scott less as a religious zealot, however, than as a political *renegade* in Hofstadter's sense—a person "who has been in the secret world of the enemy" and brings forth evidence that "might otherwise have been doubted by a skeptical world." Scott's tenure as chairman of the Joint Chiefs of Staff has placed him in the most elevated government circles. To those he conspires against he is a traitor, but to his co-conspirators he is living proof that "in the spiritual wrestling match between good and evil . . . all the conversions are not made by the wrong side" (Hofstadter 35). This wrestling match is familiar game to the paranoid, who shares with other political fundamentalists an "apocalyptic style of thought" that is readily transformed into "a curiously crude and almost superstitious form of anti-communism," in Hofstadter's words (72–73).

Scott's willingness to trash the electoral process with a military coup bespeaks the extremity of his hatred for the Soviet Union and his suspicion that "the whole American political system, with its baffling ambiguities and compromises, is too soft and equivocal for this carnivorous world" (Hofstadter 101). Like other paranoid figures in modern conservatism, from Richard M. Nixon to George W. Bush, this American archpatriot holds the American system in contempt. In his finicky telling of Scott's rise and fall, Frankenheimer fights paranoia with paranoia—the liberal kind against the conservative kind—privileging the former by means of overdetermined narrative structure, moralizing dialogue, and humanistic performances by Douglas and March that make Lancaster's villain seem robotic by comparison, thanks partly to Frankenheimer's wide-angle lenses and low-angle camera positions looking up at Lancaster's looming torso. Mounting a primal challenge to the symbolic authority of the presidency, Scott is a threat to sociopolitical meaning itself. The film's single-minded enmity toward him indicates the importance it sees in vanquishing what he represents.

Seconds

> I want to speak to the despisers of the body. I would not have them learn and teach differently, but merely say farewell to their own bodies—and thus become silent.
>
> (Nietzsche 34)

Like the other films in the paranoia trilogy, *Seconds* is based on an eponymous novel, this one published by David Ely in 1963. A bored, burned-out bank executive named Arthur Hamilton (John Randolph) receives cryptic phone calls from an old friend, urging him to contact a company that can offer him an entirely new lease on life. Visiting the business and meeting the folksy old gent who runs it (Will Geer), Hamilton is whisked through a rapid-fire enrollment process that makes him a client before he fully realizes what he has contracted for. He soon learns the details: "The Company" will fake his death by staging an accident with a mutilated corpse in his place; then multiple surgeries will change his appearance and voice beyond recognition; and finally he will be given a new identity, a new home, and new friends in a new community. He emerges from this process as Antiochus "Tony" Wilson (Rock Hudson), a handsome and young-looking artist. But although everything has gone as The Company promised it would, Tony can't adjust to his unfamiliar new surroundings and radically altered persona. Complaining that The Company has botched his case, he starts breaking its strict policies of secrecy and discretion, angering other "reborns," who turn out to be all around him all the time. Ultimately he makes his way back to the firm's offices, hoping for a second rebirth but doomed instead to become the substitute corpse in the bogus death of some other, perhaps luckier client.

Frankenheimer was clear about the message he wanted *Seconds* to convey: "that an individual is what he is [and] he has to live with his life. He cannot change anything, and all of today's literature and films about escapism are just rubbish because you cannot and should not ever try to escape from what you are." Additional themes were in the mix as well. Frankenheimer wished to oppose "all this nonsense in society that we must be forever young, this accent on youth in advertising and thinking." He wanted the film to be "a matter-of-fact yet horrifying portrait of big business that will do anything for anybody providing you are willing to pay for it." And he aimed to speak "against 'The Dream,' the belief that all you need to do in life is to be financially successful" (Pratley, *Films* 58). *Seconds* effectively communicates these ideas, but they are not very original; rather than generating the movie's power they *catalyze* it. The uncanny resonance of *Seconds* derives less from the thoughts it wants us to think than from the emotions it forces us to feel. It is best illuminated not by the psychoanalysis of Freud and Žižek but by the schizoanalysis of Gilles Deleuze and Félix Guattari, which gravitates toward cinema favoring "chaos, 'wild' connections, immersive overload of the senses, ambiguity, confusion and affect," and toward films where "affect touches us *as affect*" (Pisters 112, 110), triggering haptic, erotic, and synesthetic responses in the spectator's embodied mind. In schizoanalytic theory, desire is "machinic" and the individual subject, properly conceived, has "no fixed identity" but is "forever decentered, *defined* by the states through which it passes" (Deleuze and Guattari, *Anti-Oedipus* 20). Schizoanalysis is a means of exploring one's libidinal investments in the social realm, learning how one's "infinity of . . . flows" are either crammed into stifling cultural categories or liberated into torrents of "natural and sensuous" desire (350, 353, 311). The goal is to advance existence from a steady state of *being* to an enduring action of *becoming*.

Faces

Seconds premiered six years before Deleuze and Guattari introduced schizoanalysis in *Anti-Oedipus: Capitalism and Schizophrenia*, but the film is a schizoanalytical project *avant la lettre*, destabilizing and deterritorializing the aspects of the social realm that Frankenheimer saw as the movie's main concerns—the nature of selfhood, the cult of youthfulness, the suffocating power of business, and the ruthless allure of capital. When he identified these matters as evils of society and targets of his film, Frankenheimer acknowledged the antipathy they aroused in him; when he made them the story's propulsive elements, he instilled it with a sadomasochistic energy that constantly envelops the protagonist, whose feelings of persecution are evident throughout. Yet the film *as a film* puts a double spin on paranoia, rendering it in terms so hyperbolic that psychological drama and cultural critique morph into autotelic visions of delirious intensity.

This process culminates in the film's last portion. By cooperating with The Company, Hamilton has sought to rejuvenate himself and revitalize his life. Yet what he discovered as Tony Wilson was more of the dead-end displeasure that plagued him before his transformation, and he must recognize that a second try (or a fifth, or a tenth) would simply bring repetitions of the same, ensnaring him in a bleakly bourgeois version of Friedrich Nietzsche's eternal return. Realizing this, Wilson might agree with Deleuze and Guattari that sometimes it would be better "if nothing worked, if nothing functioned," if the pieces of his inadequate new self were to fall apart and he could dissolve into "a free state, flowing without interruption" over what schizoanalysts call the body without organs—a metaphorical body that "designates the human potential for freedom" from the cultural categories that circumscribe desire (Holland 58).

Tony craves freedom but remains stuck in the order of determination, glimpsing the unfettered body without organs only in a fleeting vision at the instant of his death, when the last feeble flicker of his brain conjures up a vision of a man and child on a beach[4] that becomes illegibly distorted and fades into oblivion almost as soon as it is born. Although he eventually rebels against The Company, he is too confused and obtuse to be called a hero, and when, in the penultimate scene, an envoy from the firm comes to take him away for ambiguous and perhaps sinister reasons, he gives in as resignedly as Josef K. and Gregor Samsa submit to their fates in *The Trial* and *The Metamorphosis*, the great works by Franz Kafka that *Seconds* parallels in intriguing ways.[5] As a schizoanalytical film, *Seconds* displays not a shred of interest in old Hamilton's childhood, parental relationships, or other psychoanalytical matters; nor does it show the slightest curiosity about what causes the depression that engulfs his outwardly comfortable life, apart from a generic liberal assumption that worldly success is its own worst enemy. As noted earlier, the movie communicates most forcefully by means of unadulterated affect, conveyed via visual distortion (as in scenes where Hamilton/Wilson is drugged or drunk, photographed with anamorphic

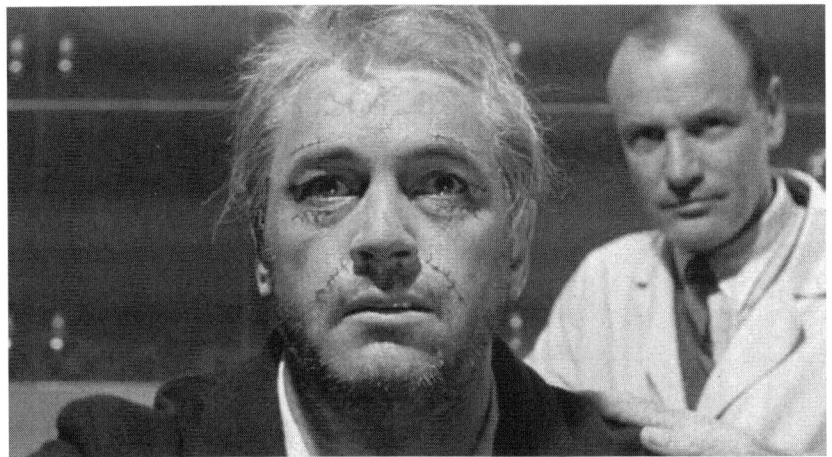

The reflective face: Wilson (Rock Hudson) in *Seconds* (Gibraltar Productions, 1966) after surgery—a field of virtuality, a template of possibilities.
Digital frame enlargement.

lenses and bizarre camera placement); shots of atypical length (as when Hamilton first talks with The Company's founder and the conversation goes on as though forever in a single unedited take); and skewed facial close-ups (as when we see Hamilton for the first time and Wilson for the last). A brief look at the latter device will illustrate the film's schizoanalytic ingenuity.

Seconds uses facial close-ups in the form that Deleuze calls the affection-image, which emphasizes affect over story and character per se; what's important in such shots are "the tendencies and trajectories of the face, the *direction* of the thoughts, feelings, and affects that energize the face, rather than the thoughts, feelings, and affects that the face expresses" (224, 228–29). This ably captures the most potent facial images in *Seconds*, starting with those behind the opening titles, which distort parts of an unidentified face through extreme proximity and anamorphosis. The first scene then begins with weirdly unstable shots of a Company messenger (filmed with a camera attached to his body) stalking Hamilton in a railroad station; his identity and purpose are disturbingly out of whack, but his *presence* and *portentousness* are inescapably clear. A different affect emanates from the close-up of Tony's face after his physical transformation; his scars and sutures hint at a Frankenstein-like unnaturalness, yet his features are a field of pure virtuality, exemplifying what Deleuze calls the *reflective* face, "an externalized template of possibilities" (Rushton 229). During the awkward dialogue between Tony and his old friend Charlie Evans (Murray Hamilton) in The Company's dayroom, Wilson's features are more concentrated with earnest thought than at any other time in the film, while Charlie's face appears to be straining against some mysterious tension battering it from within.[6] And

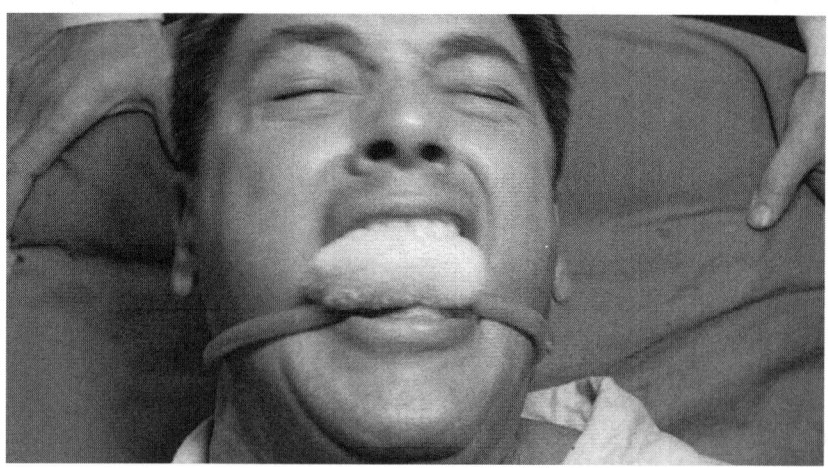

The intensive face: Wilson struggling against death—his features pulsate, twist, and creep as the parts lay siege to the whole.
Digital frame enlargement.

finally there are the long, agonizing shots of Tony being wheeled to his death at the end, strapped to a gurney as terror, helplessness, and despair erupt from him in animalistic screams—a stunningly pure specimen of the *intensive* face, which "pulsates, bends, and creeps around its own surface" as "the parts lay siege to the whole" (Rushton 230) and the whole lays siege, savagely and schizophrenically, to the spectator.

Anarchic Pleasures

The chief interest of *Seven Days in May* lies in its obsessive limning of superego energies as a body of unconscious law that is irrational, illogical, and unintelligible to its core. This law's hard strictures and erratic demands give rise to the conspiratorial schemes that fuel the narrative, afflicting the characters with persecution complexes and the filmmaker with a need for cautious self-surveillance. The result, as I suggested earlier, is a battle between clashing modes of paranoia—the "good" traditionalist kind versus the "bad" militaristic kind—with the symbolic authority of the American sociopolitical order hanging precariously in the balance. The film's argument in favor of "good" paranoia is rigged, but there's a stolid pleasure in watching its gears click meticulously along.

The pleasures of *Seconds* are more radical, anarchic, and exciting. Remarkably for the Hollywood cinema, which has worshiped at the shrines of materialism and physicality from its beginnings, this unique film uses narrative and stylistic means to inveigh *against* those limited paradigms, and to do so in a rigorous way that locates the body itself—as opposed to its social and cultural conditions, those standard-issue scapegoats of contemporary theory—as the cause and nexus of its own spiritual failures, psychological blind alleys, and existential dreads. One thinks of Nietzsche's "despisers of the body" (34), meaning those who place their trust in temporal gratifications—the "things" that Tony speaks so passionately against during his last conversation in the dayroom—but then feel betrayed by the transience and inadequacy of what they have obtained or failed to obtain, turning their bitterness inward until it attacks their own souls. The protagonist of *Seconds* gets a reinvigorated body to replace the one he's come to despise, and a rejiggered lifestyle into the bargain, but when his Wilson existence proves as spirit-killing as the Hamilton one did, all The Company can give him is a lecture about what a shame it is that his (botched) rebirth didn't work out, and what a fine cause his (actual) death will now serve by replenishing the Cadaver Procurement Section's dwindling supplies. All he can do is rage, rage against the dying of the light, in chthonic synchrony with the unsparing film itself.

Seconds enriches the horror genre even as it breaks the mold, and *The Manchurian Candidate*, conventionally tagged as a political thriller and/or social satire, does the same. Film scholars Matthew Frye Jacobson and Gaspar González have linked it with *Strangers on a Train* (1951) and *North by Northwest* (1959), which also show conversations on trains during the cold war, but there is an Alfred Hitchcock movie that *The Manchurian Candidate* resembles a great deal more: *Psycho*, released just two years earlier. On an obvious level, each picture makes use of psychiatric discourse; each has a climax illuminated by a bare

The body without organs: Wilson glimpses the potential for unfettered freedom in a fleeting vision at the instant of his death.

Digital frame enlargement.

light bulb; and each concludes with a psychologically fraught monologue. (Each also features Janet Leigh in a substantial role.) More important, both films are haunted by an all-controlling mother who has colonized her son's mind to such a totalitarian degree that he kills for her without recollection or remorse. The instrumentalities at work in the two films are different, to be sure. The mother is dead in *Psycho*, kept mentally alive by her son's psychotic dependency, while in *The Manchurian Candidate* she is a vigorous presence, empowered by malevolent scientists (the term "alienist" never seemed more appropriate) from hostile nations. Yet the similarities are strong, especially when we become aware of Eleanor Iselin's incestuous attachment to her son, and of the destructive force this attachment has unleashed.[7]

That twisted maternal force takes on its most mesmerizing contours when, speaking with Raymond for the last time, Eleanor transfixes him (and the moviegoer) with a recital of her lust for power. Thus unveiled, her political fanaticism is so obsessive and all-consuming that it takes on a quasi-supernatural glow. After the assassination, she gloats, she and her husband will be swept "up into the White House with powers that will make martial law seem like anarchy." What would such awesome powers consist of, one might reasonably ask? It is impossible to imagine, and therein lies the mystical force of this extraordinary moment. What makes *The Manchurian Candidate* so spellbinding is that it's a film *about* spellbinding, with a doomed wayfarer (Raymond) trapped by an evil enchantress (Eleanor) so baleful that not even a resolute hero (Ben) can readily break the chains her pitch-black magic has forged. This underlying scheme holds true from the opening sequence, with its night-cloaked violence, to the climax, when Raymond, dressed in the attire of a priest, puts on his Medal of Honor talisman before committing suicide. And it continues to the final shot, when nature itself grieves with cracks of thunder as Ben desolately chants, "Hell. Hell," in Frank Sinatra's indelible voice.

Ben has most of the movie's charisma, and Eleanor has some of its best lines. But the heart of the story is Raymond, a victim destined for destruction as clearly as any character in myth or legend; and Hamilton/Wilson is equally lost in *Seconds*. These figures exemplify that categorically tragic figure, the paranoid who does have enemies, and whose fears become more justified the more the facts are known. "The true zero point," Žižek says of paranoia, "is where your whole universe disintegrates. Paranoia is the misdirected attempt to reconstitute your universe so that you can function again. If you take from the paranoiac his paranoiac symptom, it's the end of the world for him" ("Superego"). The powers operating on these protagonists are complex and cruel enough to strain even Žižek's extravagant theories. But the violent affects radiating from the films—the remorseless harshness of their mood or *Stimmung*, in Martin Heidegger's terminology—carry their own dark wisdom about the existential fear and trembling we fitfully repress but can't fail to recognize when it is expressed so powerfully in art.

NOTES

1. However fantastic the plots of *The Manchurian Candidate* and *Seconds* are, Frankenheimer regarded realistic storytelling as one of his strong suits. He told me in 1975 that he "hated" a comedy he had made the year before, *99 and 44/100% Dead*, and planned a permanent return to "semi-documentary realism" (Sterritt, "Films" 26).
2. "When, in May 1952, two American airforce [sic] men corroborated Chinese propaganda claims that U.S. forces had engaged in germ and bacteriological warfare in Korea, many Americans believed that brainwashing explained their 'confessions' and other 'anti-imperialist' propaganda that followed. Such alarmism was heightened at the end of the war when twenty-one U.S. POWs refused repatriation to the United States in favor of a new life in Communist China—a decision so perverse, in the opinion of many Americans, that it could only have been the result of brainwashing" (Carruthers 47).
3. Viewed today, the film's brainwashing theme foreshadows the George W. Bush administration's uses of torture, aka "enhanced interrogation techniques," in the so-called war on terror. Unlike brainwashing as commonly imagined in the 1950s, moreover, the Bush gang's policies unquestionably existed.
4. Frankenheimer took the footage from a scene he trimmed out of the final cut.
5. Like the Kafka characters, Hamilton/Wilson embodies "a [neurotic] desire that is already submissive and searching to communicate its own submission" (Deleuze and Guattari, *Kafka* 10).
6. Of all the unsupported, impressionistic, and ill-advised remarks in Greil Marcus's book on *The Manchurian Candidate*, one of the most feckless is his dismissal of *Seconds* as "a *Twilight Zone* episode blown up to big-picture scale and starring a confused-looking Rock Hudson" (35). The film is stunningly inventive in a host of ways, and Hudson's performance is the most skillful and courageous of his career.
7. See my review of Jacobson and González ("*What*").

The Manchurian Candidate

Compromised Agency and Uncertain Causality

CHARLES RAMÍREZ BERG

Nearly fifty years after its release, and more than two decades since it resurfaced after lingering in obscurity, John Frankenheimer's *The Manchurian Candidate* (1962) is now generally regarded as a classic American film of the late studio era. The tale it tells, about communist agents infiltrating the highest levels of the American government, comes right out of cold war paranoia—but with a twist. The Sino-Soviet plot to seize control of the U.S. presidency is coordinated not by the liberal left, but by communist agents masquerading as the ultraconservative right.

Critics have analyzed the film from various perspectives in essays treating it as an expression of cold war–era anxieties (Kirshner; Coates), as a reflection of the Kennedy presidency (Hoberman), as a depiction of gender relations (Jackson; Wildermuth), as a film with a gay subtext (Ohi; Bell), as a movie about presidential assassinations (Hampton), and as a distillation of the fears surrounding brainwashing (Carruthers "Redeeming"; Carruthers "Candidate"; Seed). Two monographs, one by Greil Marcus and another by Stephen Badsey, have dissected *The Manchurian Candidate*, trying to get a handle on what exactly makes it memorable. A still more detailed analysis is found in Matthew Frye Jacobson and Gaspar González's *What Have They Built You to Do?*, a comprehensive discussion of the film that places it within a number of contexts: social, sexual, historical, political, cultural, industrial, and critical.

As of yet, however, no systematic neoformalist reading of the film has surfaced to break down its visual style and dramatic structure to shed some light on its canonical status, its enduring popularity, and its strangeness. A few forays along these lines have looked at Frankenheimer's style and the narrative of *The Manchurian Candidate*, but they are incomplete (see for example Armstrong; Rhys and Bage; Pratley *Films*; Champlin). The director's commentary on *The Manchurian Candidate*'s DVD is helpful. And crucial to any investigation of Frankenheimer's career and style is an in-depth interview on his television work,

"John Frankenheimer—Archive of American Television Interview," a detailed, six-hour interview conducted by Michael Rosen on March 21 and April 13, 2000 (available for viewing on YouTube).

After its first run and its subsequent television broadcast, *The Manchurian Candidate* was out of circulation and difficult to see, but this was the case with all but the most successful films released in an era before the rise of ancillary media markets such as videotape, cable television, DVDs, and the Internet. In the case of *The Manchurian Candidate*, one factor keeping it off the revival circuit was a justifiable skittishness about exhibiting a film whose similarities to the assassination of President John F. Kennedy, which occurred a year after the release, were uncomfortably prescient. There may have been legal and financial haggling between the studio and star Frank Sinatra, who gained the rights to the picture in 1972, although Sinatra later disavowed such stories.[1] Whatever the case, the film was on the whole fondly remembered but little seen after 1962. It began its comeback and its critical reevaluation in 1987 when it was shown at the twenty-fifth New York Film Festival. It was so well received that United Artists made plans to release it on VHS the following year. To help promote the video release, the film was rereleased in selected cities (New York, Los Angeles, Atlanta, San Francisco, Boston, Washington, D.C., Seattle), where it performed well enough that exhibition was expanded to four dozen more markets (Robertson; Harmetz). A new generation of critics discovered and acclaimed it, initiating a cascade of accolades and honors that continues to this day.

The fact that *The Manchurian Candidate* is still a classic, fifty years after the cold war frenzy and the paranoia that spawned it has ended, and more than two decades after the fall of the Berlin Wall announced the death of the Red Menace, suggests that it touches something more troubling than the fear of a communist takeover. The film endures because its style and storytelling are different and because it disturbs, effectively and entertainingly presenting the ultimate American nightmare: the loss of agency, free will, and individualism. If the film were just the story of Raymond Shaw (Laurence Harvey), a brainwashed Medal of Honor winner transformed into a communist assassin, it would simply be a spy movie with an interesting variation in villainy. What makes *The Manchurian Candidate* unique and singularly terrifying is its unrelenting portrayal of life without agency. As a brainwashed pawn of the communist conspiracy, Raymond is obviously bereft of self-determination. The challenge facing this thriller's ostensible hero, Major Bennett Marco (Sinatra), is whether he can rescue Raymond, restore his free will, and thwart the villains. Marco fails at the first task, and it is unclear whether he succeeded at the other two.

The film's bold and eccentric formal characteristics are at the heart of what make it special and strange. The visual style and narrative structure add a disturbing thematic dimension. Put all the formal elements together and *The Manchurian Candidate* raises some dark, even despairing questions about American individualism, which, I think, is what makes it a masterful oddity, at once memorable and existentially spooky.

The Poetics of Frankenheimer's Visual Style: Dialectical Narration

The Manchurian Candidate's visual style stood out from run-of-the-mill Hollywood movies in 1962, and is still striking today. As Frankenheimer says, his style was developed as he worked his way up from assistant director to head director of dozens of live dramatic TV programs like "You Are There," "Danger," and "Climax" in the 1950s:

> Let me make this real simple for you. Everything I've ever done in film is directly a result of my live television experience: the way I move the camera, the way I frame a shot, the way I work with actors, the way I work with writers, and the rhythm at which I work. Everything. I owe everything to live television. (Frankenheimer, "Archive Interview" part 11)

Frankenheimer's style was honed and polished in the more than fifty *Playhouse 90* dramas he directed at the tail end his television career from 1956 to 1960. Live television dramas in the 1950s were competing with those on rival networks for viewership, of course, and one impetus of Frankenheimer's pursuit of a special style was his acknowledged competitiveness in trying to set his shows apart from the work of other television directors ("Archive Interview" part 6).

At the same time, television as a medium was competing with the movies, trying to give viewers a compelling reason to stay home and watch TV rather than spending a night at the pictures. TV was beginning to be recognized as a serious medium, and Frankenheimer was its *wunderkind*. He was awarded the Radio and Television Daily Award for best director in 1956 and for six years running, from 1955 to 1960, was nominated for best director Emmys (Badsey 5). Television critics for *The Hollywood Reporter* and the *New York Times* in the mid-1950s used superlatives like "superb" (Lubin) and "magnificent" (Gould, *Watching* 51) to describe his direction, and the *New York Journal-American* declared him "TV's best director" in 1957 (O'Brian). Aiming to direct the best live dramas on television, be live television's best director, and generate shows that rivaled the movies, Frankenheimer originated and refined an unmistakable visual style.

The Frankenheimer style reached its fullest, boldest expression in *The Manchurian Candidate*. He would never go so far stylistically for the rest of his forty-five-year career in the movies. Reflecting on it later, he said it was

the first film I really instigated and had complete control over. . . . This is
the film I did exactly as I wanted. . . . If you look at some of the plays like
The Comedian, which I did on television, you'll see the same kind of style
that I used in *The Manchurian Candidate*. It was the first time I'd had the
courage, the assurance and self-confidence to go back to what I really had
been good at in television. (qtd. in Pratley, *Films* 38)

Indeed, Frankenheimer's characteristic style is one reason the film is idiosyncratic. In the following breakdown, I describe its key components, tracing them back to his work in live television in the 1950s, using "The Comedian" (1957), an award-winning *Playhouse 90* drama, as an exemplar of his TV work. I illustrate his stylistic choices by presenting examples from both that TV drama and *The Manchurian Candidate*. I have chosen "The Comedian" for comparison because the director himself cites it as a notable example of his television direction and because it is a well known, commonly acclaimed landmark of "the Golden Age of Television."[2] For me, as for many television critics and professionals of the era and since, "The Comedian" holds roughly the same position in Frankenheimer's television output as *The Manchurian Candidate* holds in his film *oeuvre*, that is, as an acknowledged masterwork. Many of the stylistic choices he made in his TV work were made for practical as well as aesthetic considerations. In film, however, where a different set of production standards applied and there was more time and money for postproduction, choices were made mainly for aesthetic reasons. More important, all four components operate dialectically. That is, each one contraposes elements that deepen and enrich the narrative: foreground versus background, past versus present, fact versus fiction, actual versus mediated.

Composition-in-Depth

Frankenheimer favored shooting with great depth of field. He achieved this by combining wide-angle lenses (in the 18 mm to 24 mm range; he said the 18 mm was his favorite lens) with abundant light that allowed him to stop down to apertures of f 11 to f 16 (Frankenheimer, "Archive Interview" part 8; Rhys and Bage). Screen sizes of TV sets in the 1950s ranged from ten to twenty-one inches in diagonal measurement. Thus the wide angle/deep focus look clearly enhanced production value for his live TV dramas by making small studio sets appear bigger on those little home screens ("Archive Interview" part 8), and by giving some much-needed depth to television's 4:3 or 1.33:1 aspect ratio. (The frame's dimensions are usually referred to as a ratio of width to height. The film frame, from the silent era to the coming of sound in 1927, was standardized at an aspect ratio of 4:3 or, as it is sometimes expressed, the Academy ratio [Bordwell 284]. Television adopted film's 1.33:1 aspect ratio.)

Aesthetically, the composition-in-depth style added dynamism by stretching out the drama from foreground to background. Furthermore, deep focus had the potential of "doubling" the drama because the foreground narrative plane could be juxtaposed against the background one: "two stories going on at the same time," as Frankenheimer put it ("Academy Interview" part 8; *Ronin* DVD commentary). At its most effective, this technique heightened the tension between the two planes. But Frankenheimer expanded his depth of field further than most TV directors by placing the foreground subject, most often a character's face, extremely close to the camera lens, aggressively accentuating it and highlighting the distance between it and the middle ground and background. David Bordwell calls this kind of staging "recessive" composition (Bordwell 297), as the action within the frame recedes from foreground to background; Frankenheimer simply referred to it as his signature "big head" shot (*Ronin* commentary).

Composition-in-depth in "The Comedian" (1957), one of Frankenheimer's most honored and best-known dramas for *Playhouse 90*, and a good example of depth of field creating a tension-packed "double narrative." At the play's climax, the domineering TV comic Sammy Hogarth (Mickey Rooney, *rear*) calls for his timid brother, Lester (Mel Tormé), to attend to him. Next to Lester in the foreground is his wife, Julie (Kim Hunter), who begs Lester to quit belittling himself by submitting to Sammy's abusive, disrespectful treatment.

Digital frame enlargement from kinescope original.

In *The Manchurian Candidate* (M. C. Productions, 1962), Frankenheimer's most extreme use of the "big head" shot comes near the end of the film, in the scene where Major Marco (Frank Sinatra), in the background, berates himself for losing contact with—and control over—Raymond during the political convention. In the foreground his commanding officer, Colonel Milt (Douglas Henderson), listens to his rant. Compositionally, the low-key lighting darkens the mood and Marco's placement in the distance diminishes his importance and illustrates his minimized agency. Frankenheimer was daring enough to attempt this technically difficult shot and include it even though the foreground focus wasn't sharp. Digital frame enlargement.

The Extended Montage Dissolve

In Frankenheimer's live television work, form often followed function. The dissolve was a common live TV scene-to-scene transition, following the tradition established by classical Hollywood filmmaking to indicate shifts in time and/or space. But occasionally it served another purpose: as a sleight-of-hand technique that allowed his actors time to get from one set to another and perhaps, if need be, to change their costumes and maybe even make-up, too. Another way Frankenheimer used long dissolves was as a narrative device to compress time within a sequence, following a method commonly used in Hollywood movie montage sequences. Frankenheimer's TV montages, however, sometimes added a new wrinkle: the depiction of concurrent actions by superimposition. In "The Comedian" (February 14, 1957), for example, Sammy Hogarth's (Mickey Rooney) live broadcast is compressed into a series of slow dissolves in which Frankenheimer stacks images of simultaneous events. One remarkable triple superimposition, for example, includes all of a long shot of the audience watching Sammy's show live in the theater; Sammy's performance being captured by a television

The extended montage dissolve in "The Comedian" condenses almost the entire Sammy Hogarth comedy show into 125 seconds. Throughout the montage sequence, Frankenheimer superimposes two or three simultaneous actions at once. Shown here are three stacked images: a long shot of the audience, a medium shot of Sammy performing for the TV camera (in the top half of the frame, camera on the left and Sammy on the right), and a close-up of Sammy's head writer (Edmond O'Brien) watching from backstage.
Digital frame enlargement.

camera in a medium shot; and a close-up of the head writer (Edmond O'Brien) watching from the wings.

In film, of course, one no longer needed dissolves to solve on-air logistical problems, but Frankenheimer nevertheless retained the long montage dissolve technique. He used it in *The Manchurian Candidate* in the slow transition from the fitfully sleeping Marco to his recurring garden party nightmare. Later he used it more extensively in the intricate overlapping dissolve of Raymond's flashback of his summer romance with Jocie (Leslie Parrish). The sequence, which runs forty-nine seconds, combined two types of shots. The first, a medium close-up of Raymond narrating, remained in the frame throughout; at a second visual level a series of slowly overlapping long shots portrayed the romance. It was an unusual montage sequence because it combined three rather than the usual two images onscreen at once. It was even more out of the ordinary because the image of Raymond narrating remained constant while the others appeared

Raymond's falling-in-love-with-Josie summer montage from *The Manchurian Candidate*, which Frankenheimer used to convey multiple incidents in different times and places. Here three separate images relate the present and two parts of the past, a sort of cinematic present-pluperfect tense. In medium close-up on the left side of the frame, the present-day, "unlovable" Raymond remains constant, narrating the story of his love affair. Concurrently, several past episodes with Josie appear in longer shots as a series of extended overlapping dissolves. A typical Hollywood version of this montage sequence would have contained a succession of shorter, quicker dissolves without the shot of Raymond narrating; his speaking presence would have been confined to a voiceover. By seeing him in the past and seeing and hearing him in the present, Frankenheimer contrasts two times and two moods: Raymond's melancholic present and his happy past. Digital frame enlargement.

and faded. Standing out from standard Hollywood montages, it was devilishly difficult to achieve. Frankenheimer remembered having "to send that sequence back [to the lab] fifteen times" to get it just right (Pratley, *Films* 38). This technique was an extension of the multi-layered storytelling he achieved with deep focus, but now he juxtaposed three different spaces and contrasted two times: Raymond's melancholy present with a happy, carefree past.

Complex Mise-en-Scène

Mise-en-scène, everything placed in the frame for the viewer to behold, may be simple (an Ingmar Bergman character in a sparsely decorated room) or complex (the newspaper party scene in Orson Welles's *Citizen Kane* [1941]). Frankenheimer preferred complex. From the time of his TV work, he delighted in complicated staging accompanied by carefully choreographed camera moves. At the conclusion of Sammy's show in "The Comedian," for example, Frankenheimer's mobile camera follows the television director as he bolts out of the control booth, then races across the crowded set to congratulate Sammy for turning in a great performance. He pushes his way through the pandemonium—production assistants running around, camera crew moving floor cameras this way and that, actors and extras rushing about—finally arriving at the door to Sammy's dressing room. Beyond displaying Frankenheimer's technical virtuosity—once again, all this was done live-to-air—the elaborate staging serves a narrative function, providing a professional's perspective on Sammy's show. What appeared to be a disaster (Sammy and his brother come to blows on the air) is regarded as a sensation. The director's animated response cues viewers to reevaluate what they've just seen, and to consider the seemingly improbable possibility that what looked like Sammy's downfall might turn out to be, by virtue of its very outrageousness, a show-biz triumph.

Dazzling shots like this displayed Frankenheimer's command of the medium, added production value, and prepared him for shooting the bravura set pieces in *The Manchurian Candidate*, most famously the film's tour-de-force garden club sequence. As anyone who has seen the film knows, this is a technically breathtaking piece of mise-en-scène magic: ladies attending a garden club meeting in New Jersey turn into an assembly of communist officials in Manchuria right before our eyes. But beyond the impressive unedited substitution of one set—filled with extras—for another, there are even more levels of subtle mise-en-scène trickery at work here. Watching the sequence in its totality, which includes the nightmares of two of the surviving soldiers, Marco and Corporal Melvin (James Edwards), each one depicting a different murder, reveals Frankenheimer, good showman that he is, building the bizarre shared nightmare very gradually, adding one surprising, incongruous, and perplexing ingredient after another.

With Marco's dream, he carefully assembles an increasingly dense and disquieting mise-en-scène collage. To begin, why are the uniformed soldiers sharing the stage with the speaker in her flowered dress and hat? Why is Raymond playing . . . solitaire! . . . with an invisible deck? Then there's that remarkable single-take, 360° pan in which an audience of women in a hotel lobby on a rainy Saturday afternoon, politely listening to a dreary lecture entitled "Fun with Hydrangeas," transforms into a gathering of communist officials in a steeply pitched lecture hall being addressed by a bald, twinkly-eyed Chinese scientist, Dr. Yen Lo (Khigh Dhiegh). Then, Dr. Lo calmly asks Raymond to strangle one of his fellow soldiers—a task he promptly and dutifully completes. The second part of the sequence, Corporal Melvin's nightmare, begins right where Marco's left off. Adding another wrinkle to the mise-en-scène, however, is the fact that since Melvin is African American, in his dream the garden club ladies are black. Moreover, there is the disconcerting tone throughout the paired sequences, an unsettling mixture of Lo's perverse sense of humor with Raymond's calm, serene demeanor as he murders two servicemen. (I'm not completely sure about this, and it's always dangerous to make claims about firsts, but I think the second killing is Hollywood's first use of the now-familiar blood-on-the-wall spatter shot.) By its end, Frankenheimer has packed the mise-en-scène to overflowing with eerie, unexpected elements.

The stitched-together nightmare scenes also serve a narrative function, planting clues that will help viewers decipher the communists' plot: that all of the soldiers have been brainwashed by the communists as part of a larger conspiracy; that Raymond murders two fellow soldiers; that a game of solitaire is somehow, yet mysteriously, involved; and that the nightmare is shared by at least two of the survivors. Having seen the nightmare, viewers share it, too. Technically, this is very adroit exposition, because these are details the writer and director want the audience to remember. In a way, Frankenheimer is engaging in cinematic brainwashing since, like Marco and Melvin, viewers now have those same images implanted in their brains and share a memory that will be impossible to forget (even decades later).

This virtuoso sequence is the film's through-the-looking-glass moment, disclosing not the brainwashing itself but its chilling effects. It is viewers' first glimpse of what *lack of agency* looks like. The communists made Raymond a cold-blooded killer and rewired the others to block out what their eyes told them and remember instead a fantastic fiction, encapsulated in the sentence they have been programmed to recite automatically: "Raymond Shaw is the kindest, bravest, warmest, most wonderful human being I've ever known in my life." More than technical showboating, Frankenheimer once again puts technique in the service of another dialectically doubled narrative. Like the summer romance montage, this one concerns memory, and similarly contrasts past with present. But these memories riddle fiction with fact. The surviving soldiers were brainwashed to remember an innocuous garden club meeting, but in their recurring dreams the repressed memories of murder keep returning.

The Media Metanarrative

A special case of Frankenheimer's complex mise-en-scène was his reveling in elaborate media set pieces that double the narrative in yet another way. Beyond showing how he can incorporate his technical knowledge of television production into the film, he uses his techniques to comment on what might be called reality relativity: events look one way on the scene and another on the screen, that is, as captured and packaged by the media. The narrative dialectic at work here is the opposition between the actual and the mediated. Frankenheimer played with this throughout "The Comedian," placing it at the heart of the play's concluding irony: an on-air fistfight between Sammy and his brother is understood "out there in TV land" (to use the catchphrase of the era, later parodied by Rocky and Bullwinkle) as boffo, socko entertainment.

The best example in *The Manchurian Candidate* is the Defense Department press conference. The scene demonstrates the difference between the unmediated event (the totality of what happened) and its mediated version (where selected portions of it are recorded by cameras and furnished for viewers to see).³ It is essentially a scene about media narration, Frankenheimer's commentary on the story-making, meaning-producing quality of television in particular and media in general. He illustrates how the medium organizes raw material and shapes it into a consumable narrative by determining the lead characters, identifying conflict, and establishing the stakes. But he also shows how the obvious story selected by the media may be at best incomplete and at worst a lie. Frankenheimer contrasts the events transpiring in the room with the bits of the confrontation selected by the TV cameras. Interrupting a press conference, Senator Iselin (James Gregory) accuses the secretary of defense of harboring communist spies within the Defense Department. Television, film, and still cameras swing into action to catch the accusation as reporters jot notes, and we see Iselin's purposive, jowly face grimacing to fill the TV screen. Although Senator Iselin has been presented to us as a mindless buffoon, his televised image could be read as just the opposite: a forceful, assured, seemingly knowledgeable crusader and patriot. What the TV cameras miss—but Frankenheimer's shows, in the extreme foreground—is the senator's wife (Angela Lansbury) choreographing the whole thing. In the rush to report events, the media get the apparent story but overlook the deeper one, something smart media-manipulators like Mrs. Iselin rely on.

Composition-in-depth, complex mise-en-scène, and the media metanarrative. In the background Senator Iselin (James Gregory) brandishes a list of what he claims are 207 communist spies at work in the Defense Department. In the foreground is the televised close-up of the senator making his allegation under the watchful eye of his wife (Angela Lansbury). The media immediately identify the narrative's antagonists, conflict, and stakes, but overlook Mrs. Iselin's orchestration of the entire event.
Digital frame enlargement.

The Frankenheimer Style and Its Disappearance

Much of what constituted the Frankenheimer style had been done before. Parts of it—the deep focus compositions, aggressive foregrounding of subjects in the frame, complex mise-en-scène, and moving camera—constituted the deep-focus style described by André Bazin in his discussion of Jean Renoir, Welles, and William Wyler (23–40). It enjoyed a limited Hollywood vogue in the late 1930s and 1940s and was especially favored by Welles and Wyler, but could also be seen in films directed by John Ford, Joseph H. Lewis, and Alfred Hitchcock, among others. But its use declined after that (Bordwell 295–301). Interestingly, Frankenheimer claimed that he developed his style independently, without knowledge of Welles's work (Rhys and Bage).

Whatever the case, the extended, multi-layered montage sequence was innovative. And his style was certainly distinctive for television in the 1950s, and likewise for a film made in 1962, two decades after it had made such a splash in *Citizen Kane* and Wyler's *The Little Foxes* (1941). What's more, to a younger generation of filmgoers unfamiliar with those films or Welles's and Wyler's 1940s style (at a time when older films were much more difficult to see) and who were the first generation of moviegoers who grew up watching television, Frankenheimer's style *looked* new. For its time, then, *The Manchurian Candidate* was a novel-looking film compared to most Hollywood releases. Furthermore, as we have seen, the dialectical dynamics operating beneath its stylish surface enhanced the film immeasurably. Never again would Frankenheimer achieve such a perfect balance of form and content.

Paradoxically, Frankenheimer's television successes indirectly helped cause his cinematic demise. During the 1950s and 1960s, movies were struggling to compete with television, which was luring audiences away from filmgoing in large part due to the outstanding work of directors like Frankenheimer. Hollywood responded with two major formal innovations, both of which restricted deep focus (see esp. Bordwell chap. 10). First, beginning in 1954, Hollywood began abandoning the 1.33:1 screen aspect ratio in favor of a wider frame. Eventually the standard would expand to 1.85:1 (give or take: in actual practice it depends on each theater's individual projection set-up), but some widescreen processes originating at the time were wider still. CinemaScope, for example, was between 2.66:1 and 2.35:1, and Panavision was 2.35:1 (Bordwell 284–86). Second, movies switched to color. The first year that color films accounted for more than half of Hollywood studio output was 1961 (51 percent); by 1968, when 100 percent of released studio films were in color, the transition was complete (Finler 369). As fate would have it, Frankenheimer broke into the movies just at the time Hollywood was adopting technical developments—shallower-depth widescreen lenses and low-ASA color films—that would hamper his style by severely limiting deep focus, which in turn hindered composition-in-depth and mise-en-scène complexity.

One has only to look at Frankenheimer's first color film, *Grand Prix* (1966), shot in Super Panavision 70 (2.2:1 aspect ratio), to see how widescreen and color neutralized his style. Depth of field was greatly reduced and as a consequence Frankenheimer's favored composition-in-depth shots, particularly those stretching from a big foreground figure to those in the middle- or background, are almost entirely absent. Furthermore, the shallow depth of field evidently curtailed attempts at complex mise-en-scène, resulting in routine Hollywood staging and camera coverage.

One bright spot was the montage sequences. Visual designer Saul Bass assisted on the long montage dissolves, which were retained to a degree. Bass added something that hadn't been used much since Dziga Vertov's *Man with a Movie Camera* (1929): split-screen imagery, producing frames containing two, three, four, six, twelve, twenty-four, even sixty-four images at a time. As graphic art they are impressive, though they are frequently multiplications of the same image; as the film wears on, the technique loses its effect, lapsing into a gimmicky variation on the standard montage. There are some extended dissolves, shorter than the long one in *Candidate*, but they tend to be blurry and distracting. On occasion, Frankenheimer and Bass do employ split screens to further the narrative, depicting different times and spaces (the past and present of several romantic relationships, for example). More often than not, however, despite their snappy new look, the montage sequences remain a rather conventional means of compressing time.

The Manchurian Candidate's Three-Act Structure

> The problem with *Candidate* was that it had no third act, if you wanted to observe the codes. In the book, Marco orders the execution of the mother and father. Now we couldn't have a film that advocated killing people. We couldn't get around it, until at last we hit on the idea that he doesn't know what Raymond is going to do, that Raymond is going to shoot them down.
>
> John Frankenheimer (Higham 93)

The typical Hollywood film tells the story of a single, usually male, protagonist striving to achieve a goal. A film's dramatic structure can be illustrated by a graph, a modification of Gustav Freytag's pyramid, which charts the escalating degree of a protagonist's physical, emotional, and psychological stakes as he or she works toward the goal. The line represents the protagonist's progress and also the film's causal structure. The narrative is divided into three acts, roughly marking the beginning (introduction), middle (complication), and ending (resolution) of the film. Acts 1 and 3 generally run approximately thirty minutes in length, while act 2 can range from thirty minutes in a shorter film to sixty minutes or more in a longer film.

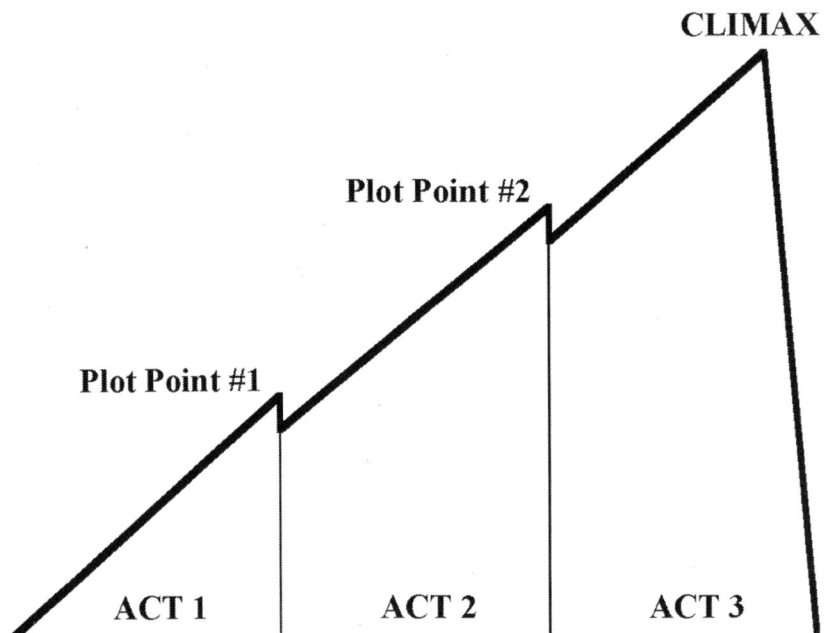

The shape of Hollywood's three-act structure. The line represents the protagonist progressing on his or her quest toward a goal as tension increases, difficulties mount, and stakes escalate. The climax, the protagonist's Big Decision, occurs just before the end. The plot points are mini-climaxes ending acts 1 and 2.

The climax is the Big Decision that the protagonist makes near the end of the film in order to accomplish his or her goal. The downward line after the climax is the dénouement, the speedy conclusion resulting from the climactic decision that releases the tension. One more important element worth noting is the plot point, a mini-climax that concludes each of the first two acts. As such, it is the biggest decision made by the protagonist up to that point. Each of these mini-climaxes significantly escalates the stakes for the protagonist, propelling the action forward by raising a question (What will the effect of this cause be?) that is answered in the next act.

With *The Manchurian Candidate*, the book's ending makes perfect dramatic sense—Marco takes control of the communists' killing robot and turns it on the villains. And the bloody killing of the antagonists is the ideal spectacle to conclude a thriller, in a novel or on the screen. But Frankenheimer was right in saying that he and screenwriter George Axelrod couldn't produce a Hollywood film that advocated killing, nor could they have a Hollywood hero acting in such a bloodthirsty and immoral way. According to the Hollywood paradigm, movie heroes obey a strict moral code, resorting to violence only as a last resort, and when provoked, in order to save others, or in self-defense.

Frankenheimer and Axelrod were backed into a corner: they needed a climactic action set piece, preferably a shootout that cuts down the baddies, but Marco couldn't order it without having his virtue and moral superiority compromised. The solution they came up with is the film we know. However, the ending they devised—keeping Marco unaware and on the sidelines—fixed one problem but introduced a number of ambiguities, chief among them determining who the protagonist is. Hollywood heroes are active; their actions dictate the ending. But because of Marco's inadequacies at the climax it's difficult to identify him as the protagonist. Either Marco or Raymond could be considered the hero, creating yet another way in which *The Manchurian Candidate* is strange.

Usually, spotting the protagonist in a film is easy: the biggest star plays the hero. Additionally, the protagonist is usually the character who dominates the bulk of the film's time, who is the most developed, whose cause-and-effect goal quest drives the story and structures the plot's three acts, who has the most pronounced character arc (the correcting of a personality flaw that allows him or her to achieve the goal), and who is directly opposed to the antagonist (an opposition that inevitably leads to a showdown finale). At first glance it would appear that Marco is *Candidate*'s protagonist: he is played by Sinatra, the film's big, bankable star, whose participation assured that the film got made.[4] Moreover, Marco's search for the meaning of his recurring nightmare launches the narrative. In addition, Marco is the film's chief investigator, unearthing clues as he tries to uncover and undo the conspiracy.

But Marco's absence and Raymond's active participation in the climax muddy the water. As a consequence, there are several ways that Raymond's prominent presence throughout the film and particularly at the climax thrusts him into the spotlight and shoves Marco aside. First, there is the stature of the actor playing him. Possibly lost on viewers today is the fact that Laurence Harvey was a considerable screen presence at the time. Not, to be sure, as big, well known, or bankable as Sinatra, but still an important movie actor who had made a successful transition from English cinema to Hollywood films and was at the height of his popularity. He had recently received third billing behind John Wayne and Richard Widmark in Wayne's *The Alamo* (1960) and was billed just below Elizabeth Taylor in *Butterfield 8* (1960), the film in which she won her first Oscar.

Next, the film devotes more screen time to Raymond's character than to Marco's. If we leave out the scenes that Marco and Raymond share, including the political convention finale that cuts back and forth between them and the events on the stage, their rounded-off screen time favors Raymond by ten minutes (forty-one to thirty-one). Had Marco been actively and decisively involved in the climax this wouldn't have mattered, but as it stands it could be argued that Raymond's character is more developed than Marco's. But even if, for the sake of argument, we say that the film develops both characters equally well, this still breaks the rule that the protagonist is always the most developed character.

Further, although Marco's nightmare is the narrative's opening mystery, Raymond's journey organizes the film's three acts. Curiously—though logically, for a film about brainwashing—the film's plot points are actions decided by others, rather than marking Raymond's decisions: the murders he commits as a programmed assassin. Plot point number one (at minute 36; the film's total running time is 126 minutes) is Raymond's test-run killing of his boss at the behest of Dr. Lo. Plot point number two (at minute 99) is Raymond's murdering his new wife and father-in-law at the command of his American operator, his mother.

This sets up act 3 as the battle fought for Raymond's soul between Marco and Raymond's mother, Mrs. Iselin. But the fact that the obligatory final confrontation between Marco and Mrs. Iselin (or any of the principal communist villains) never occurs raises still another difficulty with Marco as protagonist. In the Hollywood paradigm, the hero confronts and ultimately vanquishes the villain; in *Candidate*, that's what Raymond does. Indeed, the film's climax is a rapid series of Raymond's—not Marco's—decisions and actions: his assassinating his stepfather, murdering his mother, and killing himself.

Finally, Raymond possesses the greater character arc, something usually associated with the questing hero. Marco has a noteworthy character arc, overcoming his nervous breakdown by discovering the source of his nightmares. Two signs of his healthy recovery are his deepening romantic relationship with Eugenie Rose (Janet Leigh) and his being put in charge of the joint CIA-FBI unit focused on Raymond. In a more traditional film, this evolution would clear the way for him to save the day. But by limiting Marco's knowledge, Frankenheimer and Axelrod blunted his agency, the crucial defining trait of Hollywood male heroes. Action film protagonists and Hollywood heroes in general are champions because they can make independent decisions and impose them on the world. Marco's agency is debatable because it's unclear what if anything he caused to happen. In the end, then, he is overshadowed by Raymond, whose actions during the climax decisively demonstrate that he overcame a much more serious flaw—*his* loss of agency. Raymond's transformation from automaton to autonomy is in fact the film's climax.

Genre, Narrative, and *The Manchurian Candidate*

The Manchurian Candidate is a thriller, a genre whose protagonists try to unravel a convoluted conspiracy that threatens theirs and usually others' lives. As in the detective genre, the hero is necessarily a reactive protagonist for much of the film, responding to events managed by a shadowy villain while frantically collecting and making sense of clues. At some point, however, the hero pieces the puzzle together and sees the big picture. Then he or she becomes proactive, anticipating the villain's actions and enacting a strategy to outwit and defeat the antagonist. But in *Candidate*, because Axelrod's script kept him in the dark, Marco never gets ahead of the curve.

Furthermore, in most thrillers and mysteries, viewers generally know roughly what the hero knows. From Roger O. Thornhill in *North by Northwest* (1959) to Jason Bourne, from Sam Spade in *The Maltese Falcon* (1941) to J. J. Gittes in *Chinatown* (1974), audiences gather clues and hypothesize solutions to try to solve the mystery along with the heroes. This conforms to orthodox Hollywood dramaturgical practice for thrillers. Viewers and protagonists generally share more or less the same knowledge (even if protagonists may trump us with their skills); the fact that screen characters make more from information we possess with them is one of the things that makes them seem heroic. We may temporarily know more than the hero (there's a bad guy hiding in the shadows!), but that's usually a short-lived plot device used to build suspense. *Candidate* breaks this rule because we know more than Marco for almost the entire film.

True, Marco (finally) catches up to us when he realizes that the queen of diamonds is the trigger activating Raymond, and then seemingly de-programs him. Normally this would have been the thriller turning point where the hero gains the upper hand and controls the narrative. But due to the filmmakers' alteration of the novel, the hero's advantage is quickly nullified. Shortly after the de-programming scene, viewers are made privy to the conspirators' plan, once again jumping ahead of Marco. Worse, Marco botches the thriller genre's trademark last-minute chase/rescue, arriving too late to influence the ending and powerless to save Raymond. For an action hero, Marco is remarkably uninformed, tardy, and impotent.

The problem surrounding the climax is that the film is vague about ultimate causes and effects, something uncharacteristic of Hollywood. It may be because Marco's de-programming worked that Raymond killed his mother and stepfather (the Manchurian candidate), but the film never conclusively specifies that. By actively defeating evil, Hollywood heroes confirm their agency and certify that they are the determining cause of the resulting Happy Ending. Here Marco is absent at the climax, doesn't pull the trigger, and is never indisputably identified as the cause of Raymond's actions. He may well have been the cause, of course. But if he was, then Marco in effect killed the villain in cold blood, which is exactly what Axelrod and Frankenheimer were trying to avoid in the first place. Furthermore, if Marco caused those killings, isn't he partly responsible for Raymond's suicide, too? It's also possible that Marco's de-programming didn't "take." Or that Raymond's mother counteracts it in next scene, when we can assume *she* programs him. After all, we see the queen of diamonds trigger she used: Jocie's costume draped over the sofa. In that case, Raymond reversed his brainwashing independently and killed his mother, her husband, and himself of his own volition.

As opposed to typical Hollywood's heroes who prove their heroism beyond a doubt, the degree of Marco's involvement is unclear. His causality is possible, perhaps probable, but uncertain. His climactic impotence together with Raymond's abrupt, unexpected, and unexplained metamorphosis culminate in a bizarre closing to a most unusual film. Raymond's death deprives the film of a conventional Happy Ending. Marco's failure to save him—or do anything unambiguously heroic—contributes to making the film's ending such a downer, exactly the sort of moment that could inspire Marco, turning away from Eugenie Rose and staring at the formless gray sky, to mutter, "Hell!, . . . Hell! . . ." This melancholy conclusion plus the confusion about causes and effects makes *Candidate* an unorthodox variant of the Hollywood paradigm.

Conclusion: Compromised Agency and Uncertain Causality

One ideological function of the thriller is to provide a triumphant endorsement of the rugged-individualistic American ethos. Taken for granted in such stories is the assumption that their protagonists possess qualities—resourcefulness, self-reliance, autonomy, independence, self-determination—that allow them to persevere and prevail. *The Manchurian Candidate* is a far less mythic, even antimythic, case, more akin to Graham Greene than Hollywood. Like many a Greene protagonist, for much of the film Marco doesn't know what to do. When he finally acts, it's debatable whether he made a difference or not.

The things we should know for sure about Marco are vague. We should be certain that he caused the deaths of Senator and Mrs. Iselin (or otherwise prevented the Manchurian candidate from becoming president). We should be certain that he did not cause Raymond's suicide. On the other hand, the things we do know for sure are damning. He is absent from the climax. He is late for the rescue. And he fails to save Raymond. His late-in-the-game error in judgment results in the murder of Jocie and her father. "It wasn't Raymond that really did it," Marco says of those killings; "in a way, it was me."

At this level, it's a film about the lack of agency, the difficulty of taking effective actions, and connecting causes and effects. Since causality is the basis of Hollywood storytelling, *The Manchurian Candidate* is an atypical, baffling viewing experience. For American audiences accustomed to reassuring repetitions of confident, competent heroes saving the world, the film can be existentially chilling. Rather than providing a rousing affirmation of heroic individualism, the ambiguity surrounding the cause or causes of the film's ending instead raises unsettling questions about some foundational American beliefs: What if you don't control your destiny? What if you're not the master of your fate? What does it mean if the good guy—with God, morality, brains, good looks, the beaming smile of Frank Sinatra, a beautiful blonde, and the full might of the U.S. government on his side—fails? Does it mean he didn't matter?

And, most terrifying of all, if the good guy doesn't matter, do you?

NOTES

1. There are a number of accounts as to why the film was difficult to find and hard to see during this time. See, for example, Harmetz; Hinson; Dirks; Menand; and Levy.

2. "The Comedian" was awarded an Emmy in 1957 as the best single show of the year. It was selected as one of the programs to be included in a 1981 PBS series, *The Golden Age of Television*, produced by Sonny Fox. It has also been included in two DVD collections: *The Golden Age of TV Drama* (2006, Passport Video), as well as the Criterion Collection DVD, *The Golden Age of Television* (2009).
3. Eileen McGarry calls this the profilmic event, which she defines as that "which exists and happens in front of the camera" (McGarry 50).
4. According to Frankenheimer, several studios passed on making *The Manchurian Candidate*. "But George [Axelrod] got Sinatra" (Champlin 67), and "as soon as Sinatra said he wanted to do it, we could have shot it at any studio in town. After that, the rest was easy" (Pratley, *Films* 38).

Stealth, Sexuality, and Cult Status in *The Manchurian Candidate* and *Seconds*

REBECCA BELL-METEREAU

John Frankenheimer's *The Manchurian Candidate* (1962) and *Seconds* (1966) feature mind manipulation, torture, and kinky sex, topics with a visceral punch for 1960s viewers and an eerie resonance for post-Abu Ghraib audiences. Richard Condon's novel of *The Manchurian Candidate* (1959) describes clearly how a domineering mother uses and seduces her own son, and Frankenheimer's film adaptation depicts this unhealthy sexual relationship as explicitly as possible, given the censorship restrictions of the era. In an interesting shell game, the domineering mother becomes the face of the Communist Party and her assassin son becomes a suicidal hero, a transference that is paralleled in *Seconds*, when a dissatisfied middle-aged banker has plastic surgery to take on a second life as an artist in the physique of Rock Hudson—an actor eventually known in Hollywood as a sexually bi-curious figure. Both narratives displace anxieties about ambiguous sexuality onto safer political and philosophical targets. The violation of visual and proxemic rules highlights the transgression of sexual boundaries in these groundbreaking films, while the gay, closeted personal lives of the two stars, Laurence Harvey and Rock Hudson, add layers of irony to their roles. This combination of formal and topical innovation, along with serendipitous and dramatic events that mirrored key plot elements of both films, contributed to their complexity and eventual achievement of cult status as two of the films in what David Sterritt calls Frankenheimer's "Paranoia Trilogy."

Militarism and Momism: A Recipe for Paranoia

John Frankenheimer's adaptation of *The Manchurian Candidate* was groundbreaking in its evocation of post-fifties paranoia, suspicion of government conspiracies, and anxiety about mind manipulation and implanted memories, explored in a film that inspired imitations for years to come. Frankenheimer expresses the anxious spirit of the post-McCarthy era by questioning the value of memory in an age that uses science and psychology to shape both personal and public history. If James Naremore argues that "the ironies in *The Manchurian Candidate* are in fact so numerous that one cannot be sure whether Frankenheimer and his collaborators were purveying old myths or making fun of them" (134), the film was certainly taken seriously at the time. *The Manchurian Candidate*'s release coincided with the Cuban missile crisis in October 1962, followed by the assassination of John F. Kennedy in November 1963. It was quickly pulled from circulation, an accident of timing that was initially unfortunate, but which eventually contributed to the film's aura of prescience and unattainable mystery. Frankenheimer's skeptical portrayal of political and military tactics was perfect for 1962, appearing two years after President Dwight Eisenhower's famous farewell address, in which he advised constant vigilance:

> In the councils of government, we must guard against the acquisition of unwarranted influence, whether sought or unsought, by the military industrial complex. The potential for the disastrous rise of misplaced power exists and will persist. We must never let the weight of this combination endanger our liberties or democratic processes. We should take nothing for granted. Only an alert and knowledgeable citizenry can compel the proper meshing of the huge industrial and military machinery of defense with our peaceful methods and goals, so that security and liberty may prosper together. (Eisenhower 1037)

The kind of suspicion Eisenhower called for came into vogue during the early 1960s, as Hollywood and the nation were beginning to emerge from the era of Joseph McCarthy, blacklists, and the House Un-American Activities Committee. The intelligentsia was becoming increasingly aware of the Office of Strategic Services and the Central Intelligence Agency's brainwashing and drug experimentation, torture methods, and other questionable covert operations, but people were torn over how to feel about these revelations. When it came to massive electroshock treatments, drugs, and hypnotism, according to John Marks, "for career CIA officials, exceeding these limits in the name of national security became part of the job," while "most academics wanted no part" at this point of techniques that might cause death or madness (Marks 35). The history surrounding the production of *The Manchurian Candidate* is as fraught with anxiety and paranoia as the film itself. Discrepancies abound even in the account of how the film first came into existence, then became practically unavailable for exhibition, and finally reemerged in an uncut DVD version with the director's commentary track.

It was clear that Frank Sinatra's involvement was key to the initial development of the project. According to Jacobson and González, "From the moment of its inception—certainly from the time Sinatra went to John F. Kennedy to secure his blessings—the project seemed tied to the larger world, to its cultural and sociopolitical moment, in quite exceptional ways" (171). As an entertainer who was deeply enmeshed in politics, Sinatra was so taken with Condon's cold war thriller that he lobbied for the part of Major Ben Marco, much to Frankenheimer's and screenwriter George Axelrod's delight. When the studio cautioned that the film's portrayal of the Soviet Union might interfere with Kennedy's future relationship with the Russians, Sinatra told them that he had just come from discussing the idea with Kennedy, who professed great enthusiasm for the project, even asking who was going to play the mother. This image of a powerful maternal presence would soon dominate both the plot of the film and the consciousness of the nation, as it agonized over momism and women's liberation.

The intersection of art and real life would also eventually color Sinatra's handling of the film version. After rumors that Lee Harvey Oswald had seen the film before assassinating Kennedy, the film disappeared from circulation for a while. Although some conspiracy theorists suggested that "the coincidence in names [Lee Harvey Oswald and Laurence Harvey], which unsettles the observer, may also have taken possession of Oswald," Michael Rogin asserts that "no doubt Oswald was neither stimulated nor alerted by *The Manchurian Candidate*" (18). Despite claims to the contrary, "it is true that [the film] was eventually pulled from circulation, but not because of its explosive story line or any role it might have played in the assassination of the president. The motive, according to both Frankenheimer and Axelrod, was money. . . . The film would make a remarkable cultural (and financial) comeback" (Jacobson and González 174). Far from damaging the film's ultimate reputation, this kind of speculation and the film's relative unavailability eventually heightened its cult appeal. Frankenheimer, Axelrod, and the Sinatra family clearly exploited this fact, if their cagey handling of the property is any indication. Despite competing claims, it seems fairly clear that, while the justification for pulling the film initially might have come from a combination of respect and fear, the reasons for keeping it unavailable for so long were primarily financial.[1]

Frankenheimer describes how he and Axelrod were the first to incorporate a critique of Senator Joseph McCarthy's anticommunist tactics into a mainstream film, along with positive references to the American Civil Liberties Union. He also notes with some pride their inclusion of the African American actor Joe Adams in a role that had not been specifically designated for a black man (DVD commentary), that of a psychiatrist who consults with Marco. Although critics disagree on the extent to which Frankenheimer successfully critiques anticommunist hysteria, all agree that one of the most innovative elements of the film was its depiction of "brainwashing." Hypnosis and psychological torture had gained notoriety during the 1950s as powerful methods of mind manipulation. In order to capture the disoriented fugue state that was typically produced in brainwashing, Frankenheimer used a sound stage equipped with a 360° camera set-up to film an opening dream sequence from the perspective of Major Marco. The major's company sits at a tedious garden club meeting populated by a group of middle-aged white women discussing hydrangeas in the lobby of a southern hotel. We travel in a circle, from the yawning soldiers and the wispy chairlady (Helen Kleeb) into the audience (attentive women in chiffon dresses and hats, including Madame Spivy) spread under dappled sunbeams from a skylight; and when we return to the soldiers, there is a bald Asian man on the platform, lecturing about brainwashing techniques. As we continue to rotate, we find that a military audience has replaced the other one, uniformed officers sitting in elevated ranks in a sterile lecture theater (including Reginald Nalder). Frankenheimer cleverly did this shot in one take, with the scenery and actors being silently moved when out of shot. Thus, the women of the first part of the shot and their frowzy hotel setting represent the captor/brainwashers in their lecture theater from the mesmerized soldiers' point of view. The chief brainwasher, Dr. Yen Lo (Khigh Dhiegh), demonstrates to the Russians how he has hypnotized Sergeant Raymond Shaw to be an assassin, by having him calmly kill one of his own men. Marco awakens from this nightmare screaming. As the film progresses, his investigation eventually reveals that the "dream" was in fact a reality, and uncovers the plan to put in the presidency a "Manchurian candidate" who will be under communist control.

Like a bored schoolboy, Laurence Harvey yawns during a brainwashing session, while Frankenheimer's mise-en-scène reveals a matronly figure in the background. *The Manchurian Candidate* (M. C. Productions, 1962).

Collection Rebecca Bell-Metereau.

While this political plot churns along, the issue of identity and sexuality arises repeatedly, beginning with the initial appearance of Shaw's domineering mother, bustling in as he arrives to receive his congressional medal of honor. She engineers the public reception of her war-hero son, ordering around the press, the military, her husband, and Raymond himself. Further, in the first brainwashing dream sequence, male figures are replaced by middle-aged matriarchs, and the soldiers reply, "Yes, ma'am" to their captors, thus suggesting a link between totalitarian communism and female domination. Later on, when Shaw comes to kill his boss and mentor, newspaper columnist Holborn Gaines (Lloyd Corrigan), the old man is in bed, wearing his deceased wife's feathered dressing gown. "Don't get any silly ideas about this ridiculous-looking bed jacket," he cautions Raymond. "It was my wife's. It's the warmest thing I have." When Raymond moves closer to the bed to kill him, the frame goes black, as Raymond destroys the threatening feminized version of this fatherly figure. Contrary to Gaines's disclaimer, the feminine bed jacket actually calls our attention to inverted gender roles from this and other scenes throughout the film.

Hatred of the feminine resides at the emotional core of the film, and at a more profound level rests fear and hatred of the feminized male. To compound Raymond's mother's obnoxious personal behavior, her traitorous allegiance as a secret operative causes her to send him off to the Korean War and thereby make him an unwitting tool of the Soviet state. Through hypnosis, he becomes the perfect sniper who will kill a presidential candidate so that his own pitifully dominated stepfather, Senator John Yerkes Iselin (James Gregory), may take over as the title's "Manchurian" candidate for president of the United States. Under the influence of brainwashing, Raymond cannot remember the murders he has committed, but he does remember that he hates his mother, and this stubborn remnant of memory is significant even beyond its necessity in the plot. His indestructible loathing for her reflects the larger culture's suspicion of a particular type of mother, as captured in Philip Wylie's famous description of "Momism," and the film's trope plays on precisely this kind of anxiety about frustrated, ambitious women who emasculate men. As Wylie puts it in *Generation of Vipers*, "The Oedipus complex had become a social fiat and a dominant neurosis in our land. It was past time somebody said so. As a way of life, it is shameful in grown-ups of both sexes; as a national cult, it is a catastrophe" (194).

The film narrative's portrayal of psychological issues is resolutely Freudian in its concept of repressed memories and a man's subconscious sexual desire for his mother as a primary source of abnormal and antisocial behavior. James Naremore explains, "Like a good many classic films noirs, *The Manchurian Candidate* subscribes to Sigmund Freud's theory that male homosexuality is caused by a son's unresolved romantic attachment to his mother—indeed, it alludes to Freud and to Greek drama during an extended flashback sequence when the brainwashed son tries to explain his evil mother to Frank Sinatra" (133). With Raymond's rather pitiful admiration for the manly character of Ben Marco, both the novel and Frankenheimer's film code him as an unlikable repressed homosexual. Condon's novel questions Shaw's sexuality early on, with one of his men on the Korean battlefield wondering, "You think he's a fairy, or very religious?" (21). In the film, the audience gradually learns that Raymond's mother had thwarted his attempts to establish a heterosexual relationship with Jocie Jordan (Leslie Parrish), daughter of his mother's political rival. The novel goes one step further by having Raymond's mother tell Jocie's father "that his daughter was far too fine a girl to be hurt or twisted by her son, that Raymond was a homosexual and in other ways degenerate" (103–04).

Frankenheimer's film establishes Shaw's indeterminate sexuality in more subtle ways, at the same time diminishing masculine influence over Raymond's psyche and culpability for his behavior. Throughout the film, Raymond's mother treats him in a condescending yet seductive manner, forcing him to remain in a pre-adolescent sexual limbo. Frankenheimer maintains Condon's psychoanalytic and misogynist core, even though he is at great pains to establish his work's left-wing and anti-establishment credentials. In spite of pinning blame for this conspiracy on communism in a conventional way, Frankenheimer wishes to aim most of his critique at McCarthyism and the fifties Red Scare. It can be argued that Frankenheimer portrays the faults of the mother with fewer layers of irony. In his DVD commentary, Frankenheimer offers positive comments about the American Civil Liberties Union, but he transfers any overt animus in the narrative onto the character of Raymond's mother.

It is not surprising that Kennedy's first question about the adaptation was who would play the mother, for she is the emotional linchpin of the tale. Beneath the scapegoat of the communist menace, the film's covert message is a negative depiction of "mother" as the true culprit and cause of Raymond's stunted heterosexual development. Hidden in plain sight is the threat of female domination as expressed through incestuous intimacy between mother and son, a memory so traumatic that characters and viewers must forget it, even as it drives the plot. Despite the film's overdetermined emphasis on the villainous mother, she is not the most important focus for anxiety; rather, it is the homosexually coded figure of Raymond himself who must be destroyed in order to restore sexual equilibrium. Beyond the narrative of the film, an important factor that supports a queer reading of the film resides in the star identity of Laurence Harvey, "who exaggerates his prissy, slightly effeminate mannerisms, as if to suggest a young man struggling to maintain a hold on his sexuality" (Naremore 133). Harvey's notoriously cold and effete persona was a perfect match for the character of Raymond, described by Marco as "not just hard to like; he's impossible to like." This confluence of Harvey's personal life and career persona is essential, for "the private is public, as commentators like J. Edgar Hoover suggested, because sexuality and the domestic arrangements of the family will invariably radiate outward to affect those spheres more typically identified as 'public' or 'civic'" (147). Laurence Harvey's ruthlessness and bisexuality were no secret to a coterie of influential actors—including Judy Garland, Elizabeth Taylor, and Sinatra—who often collaborated on projects. These personal details add to the mystique of the film and blur the line between fiction and real life in Harvey's convincing portrayal of this cold-blooded and sexually conflicted character.

At the film's end, as Raymond shoots his mother and stepfather and then points the gun at himself in front of the only man he considers his friend, the narrative simultaneously slides blame away from government, military, and political conflict and onto the domineering, ambitious mother. For viewers suspicious of government, this conclusion may seem to evade the real issues of unethical manipulation and control, but more traditional viewers may take comfort in the notion that, with hegemonic order restored, patriarchy is back in charge and heroism is still possible. The death of Raymond Shaw may be seen to represent the death of a weakened version of masculinity, with Marco's coda of praise (which was not in Condon's novel) signifying the reassertion and reinscribing of "normal" masculinity. In this Hamlet-like tale, Marco stands in as Fortinbras, who eulogizes and promises eventual restoration of political stability.

Futurism and the Disappearing Past: A Recipe for Crisis

A pattern of destroying the weakened and insufficiently "masculine" hero also emerges in Frankenheimer's less commercially successful, even more innovative work, *Seconds*. This adaptation sticks closely to David Ely's tale of a dissatisfied banker who takes on another man's face and a new identity as the artist he always wanted to be. This transformation is accomplished through surgical procedures that only slightly exaggerate the capabilities of modern medicine, placing the film on the borders of science fiction and fantasy.

Simon Spiegel claims that "apart from the opening sequence, *Seconds* is (for the most part) filmed in a sober, rather flat black and white," with no "special effects" (379). Aside from the inaccuracy of his assessment of the visual look of *Seconds*, which actually made extensive use of unusual lenses and other distortions, this description also misses the numerous other ways in which Frankenheimer manages to "make strange" the characters, perspective, and narrative of *Seconds*, all of which contributed to the film's ultimate success as a cult favorite. Frankenheimer prided himself on his daring, both in terms of content and formal choices, and in *Seconds* he pushed the boundaries of his own creativity and audaciousness. His concept for *Seconds* was to have the audience feel immediately that this was "not a straightforward tale" (*Seconds* DVD commentary). In the title sequence, Saul Bass used a metal mirror to warp Rock Hudson's classically handsome face, and cinematographer James Wong Howe chose a 9.7 mm extreme wide-angle lens to further skew the image. Howe's inventiveness in filming *Seconds* (for which he was nominated for an Academy Award) reinforced his reputation as an innovative cinematographer, famous for using unusual mounts and filming in awkward situations.

In the midst of this expressionist approach to filmmaking, Frankenheimer also tried to take advantage of real surroundings insofar as possible, and this cinéma vérité approach is another feature that gives *Seconds* its disquieting impact. Jerry Goldsmith's music sets an ominous tone as it moves from the title segment into the opening scene set in Grand Central Station, a difficult filming location. The production crew couldn't close down the station, yet they wanted to keep people from looking into the camera as they naturally would in this busy setting. In order to distract passers-by, Frankenheimer set up a phony camera and megaphone in another location where crew members pretended to film a male model and Playboy Bunny making love. Meanwhile, Frankenheimer and Howe did the real filming with a little-known actor wearing a camera on a harness and another camera on a suitcase rolling along the ground. Howe did his own handheld camera work on the next sequence, shot on the train from New York to Scarsdale, violating the 30° rule, showing two slightly different views out the train window, intercut with shots of the anxious protagonist, Arthur Hamilton, in queasy close-ups of actor John Randolph's sweating face.

The creepy funhouse atmosphere continues once Hamilton decides to check out The Company's offer of a second life, posing as "Mr. Tony Wilson," as he has been instructed. Upon arriving at the designated rendezvous, a tailor's shop, he receives curt instructions to go instead to a slaughterhouse, a location that contributes to the grotesque atmosphere and underlying motif of human flesh as just another piece of meat, with human existence a meaningless process of aging and dying. This disquieting imagery is reiterated in the plastic surgery sequence, again shot on location in an actual operating room. Six members of the crew fainted during the filming of this scene, and Frankenheimer himself eventually had to help shoot, with Howe instructing him to "just hold the wide-angle lens camera" (DVD commentary). In these and other sequences, Frankenheimer uses real-life settings to create a strange hyperreality that causes viewers to confront the issue of existential angst. And in keeping with the spirit of cinéma vérité, Frankenheimer shot a number of scenes in long takes, a technique that required multiple rehearsals and seemed to bring out a truly authentic performance from Hudson, who had not previously had the luxury of this method.

Given the director's desire to make the fantastic second-life plot believable, Frankenheimer had to carefully finesse the transition from the shorter, older John Randolph to the hulking, handsome Rock Hudson. First, we see drawings that show how Randolph's facial structure will be altered, and then the initial shot of Hudson after surgery makes him look puffy and bruised, with sutures and scruffy gray hair. A montage sequence shows the new "Tony Wilson" exercising and beefing up, as his physical transformation takes shape. In what Frankenheimer calls an "homage to me," Khigh Dhiegh plays Davalo, the postoperative therapist, just as he was the brainwashing psychiatrist in *The Manchurian Candidate*. Like many an auteur director, Frankenheimer admits, "I have a tendency to use the same actors again and again" (*Seconds* DVD commentary), but he also acknowledges a profound debt to his writers. In the same way that he stuck closely to Condon's dialogue for *The Manchurian Candidate*, Frankenheimer relied on his screenwriter for *Seconds*, explaining that he changed very little from Lewis John Carlino's relatively faithful adaptation of David Ely's novel. In addition, he had Carlino on set so that he could approve any minor adjustments as they occurred.

Seconds questions the ethics of the era, which glamorized the role of the lone masculine hero: Davalo explains to him, "You are accepted. You will be in your own dimension. You are a bachelor. You are alone in the world, absolved of all responsibility except to your own interest. Isn't that marvelous?" This rather Ayn Rand–ish statement takes on ironic weight as this new version of masculinity turns out to be no more marvelous than the original stodgy, traditional role from which the character escapes. Frankenheimer offers his take on the film's meaning: "This movie says something that I firmly believe. In life you are the result of your experiences, the result of your past. . . . If you take away your past, you don't exist as a person. By your past I mean your mistakes as well as your triumphs. That's what this movie really says; that's what it's about" (*Seconds* DVD commentary).

The director strives to make statements about the past of his actors on several levels, from their personal lives to their political identities, in part by using previously blacklisted artists to play minor but significant roles. John Randolph had been blacklisted when Frankenheimer wanted to work with him for television, and this was the director's first opportunity to finally hire him. Jeff Carre, the man from The Company who interviews Wilson, had also been blacklisted. Will Geer, another actor who had been blacklisted, plays the fatherly figure who runs The Company, in a creepily homey scene shot in one long take. Another actor in the cocktail party scene was Nathan Young, a blacklisted writer who wrote and rewrote *Seven Days in May* and *The Train*. In an echo of the McCarthy hearings, the penultimate scene shows The Company worker grilling Tony to "name names" of others who might be likely "clients" for a second life, a request that Wilson refuses. Frankenheimer comments: "The whole business of blacklisting was just so shocking. It's amazing to me that I lived through it." Aside from making a political statement, Frankenheimer was able to recruit a number of highly skilled artists desperate to work after years of exclusion or only minimal or covert participation in the film industry.

Seconds was groundbreaking in several other ways, including its violation of audience expectations for the genre and the film's star, Rock Hudson. At first Frankenheimer did not want Hudson to play the lead, but he bowed to studio pressure to include a major box-office draw, based in large part on Hudson's work with Douglas Sirk in the famous women's melodramas *Magnificent Obsession* (1954) and *All That Heaven Allows* (1955). Hudson's earlier triumphs, however, did not prepare viewers for his offbeat role in *Seconds*, and the resulting mismatch between fan expectations for the star and genre expectations for an arty horror fantasy produced an abysmal box office failure. At Cannes, audiences even booed at the end of the film.

As Frankenheimer later observed, however, the film went from failure to cult status, in part for reasons the director himself may not have fully appreciated: the choice of Hudson playing against type. In this regard, Frankenheimer's focus on blacklisting takes a backseat to the closeted, parallel world of gay Hollywood. Hudson's biography echoes the events of the film in a number of ways, including the fact that he changed his name and identity to become an artist, of sorts. Under the management and tutelage of the "fairy godfather of Hollywood," Henry Willson, Hudson went from a working-class kid with chipped teeth and limited prospects to a glamorous star, famous for playing the lead in light romantic comedies with Doris Day. As Robert Hofler observes, Willson "took full credit for Rock's name, his grammar, his clothes, and everything else that took Roy Fitzgerald from truck-driver to 'bobby-sox idol'" (188). Willson was also involved in the careers of other closeted gay stars, such as Tab Hunter, Roddy McDowell, and Anthony Perkins, in an era when the California scene of Hollywood Hills and Sunset Boulevard was "an alternate universe of great sexual fluidity, and one which Rock often referred to as a 'secret society' with its own language and code of behavior. 'It was a club back then,' Rock said of gay Hollywood" (Hofler 227). But Willson, unlike his famous protégés, did little to hide his homosexuality, and by 1966, "Henry had turned into a major liability. 'Every time Henry Willson sucks some cock, I get blamed for it,' Rock complained.... Henry's very representation branded Rock as a homosexual not only to the Hollywood community but to the cognizant world beyond" (Hofler 389). It is no wonder, then, that in *Seconds*—what Hudson and others have called his best acting job—Hudson displays a keen sensitivity to the plight of a character living a lie in order to achieve his dream.

Beyond connections to Hudson's gay lifestyle, which was well known in some Hollywood circles, other factors contribute to a queer reading of *Seconds*. Key details of plot, dialogue, and blocking point to a homoerotic subtext, beginning with the central character's peculiar fascination with the old college buddy who convinces him to give up his stodgy existence as an unhappily married banker in favor of a new second life. In order to convince Hamilton that he is not dead but has been reborn into a new identity, Hamilton's friend calls him and tells him to look at the inscription on the bottom of a college tennis trophy, which reads "fidelis eternis," ever faithful. A photograph on the mantle shows two young men in their tennis garb, arms around each other, smiling into the camera. Later that night, instead of making love with his wife, who tries to interest him in having sex, he turns a cold shoulder to her and frets nervously, apparently recalling the phone call from his friend. The next day, he takes the fateful step to have himself "die" as Mr. Hamilton and enter a new life in a plush California bachelor pad as Tony Wilson, "artist."

Translating this complicated transformation into filmic terms called for Frankenheimer's creativity and resourcefulness. As in *The Manchurian Candidate*, the substance and process of the film were entangled with the real lives of the director and actors, sometimes with negative results. Not all of Frankenheimer's attempts at realism were as productive as his use of real trains and actual surgical procedures. For example, he managed to get a Boeing 707 from TWA for one scene in which he agreed to use the wardrobe man's girlfriend as a flight attendant. In their futile attempts to get usable footage from the nervous actress, they flew to the Canadian border and back to Los Angeles four times. Frankenheimer notes that they only "ended up with two close-ups we could have gotten in a bathroom." He also used his own home for the setting for Wilson's new house. Frankenheimer had to move out and go to a motel, and he worried that the crew would wreck his house. He made this sacrifice because he thought it would be a good fit for the character of Wilson, who tries in vain to become the artist he has always dreamed of becoming. Ultimately, Frankenheimer concluded that the set was probably needlessly elaborate. In this modern, isolated setting, we see Wilson trying to adapt to his new identity, painting and discarding his work, with Goldsmith's melancholy sound track playing and his fussy butler John (Wesley Addy)—another ambiguously gendered character—hovering in the background.

Tony Wilson tries his hand as an artist but finds himself hopelessly lost and unhappy, a situation that may have paralleled Rock Hudson's own experience in learning to become an actor. *Seconds* (Gibraltar Productions, 1966).
Collection Rebecca Bell-Metereau.

When Wilson decides to emerge from the cocoon of his house, his first encounter with a female love interest is almost as grim as his artistic endeavors. Wilson first sees Nora (Salome Jens) outdoors on the beach in overcast lighting as a black form, a huddled figure, staring at the sand. Offering to read tea leaves for him, she says, "Somewhere in the man there is still a key unturned." This "key unturned" is never made explicit, but given his dissatisfaction with the marriage of his former life and his apparent inability or unwillingness to consummate his relationship with Nora, it is not unreasonable to infer that repressed homosexuality may be the hidden key to his unnamed dissatisfaction.

The next important turning point occurs at the cocktail party, where Wilson learns the truth about his supposed friends—that they, too, are "seconds" living a lie. Frankenheimer got Rock Hudson very drunk for this scene and used the highly mobile Arriflex cameras, which made so much noise that they had to loop the dialogue in post-production. Frankenheimer notes that in those days they didn't have silent handheld cameras, but this method gave him a great deal of freedom to capture the actor behaving spontaneously. In this freewheeling scene, Wilson repeats the pattern of rejecting a heterosexual experience, choosing instead to hang, quite literally, with everyone but Nora—again and again, he drapes himself over the male figures in the scene. He talks with one rather chubby woman (Elisabeth Fraser), who tells him she is part of a secret organization, and he says, "I hope it isn't anything subversive," to which she replies that they "change sects." For a moment he misperceives her words, thinking she has said that they change sex, an error she laughingly corrects. Although he has promised to get rid of guests at his cocktail party so that he can make love to Nora, instead he becomes increasingly drunk, falling all over his male companions, until he is carried out and surrounded on his bed by a circle of men. His butler informs him that these men are all "like you—reborns," and that Nora was simply paid by The Company to ease his transition into a new life.

In Hudson's final scene in the film, the fatherly head of The Company sits on his bed and leans into his body, a hand on Hudson's shoulder and the other on his stomach, again in a position of intimacy ordinarily reserved for romance. He wistfully tells him, "I sure hoped that you'd make it, find your dream come true." After this, Wilson is forcibly wheeled out to become one of the fake dead bodies of a new "second." Frankenheimer recounts how, as they strapped the actor down, with his mouth gagged and a camera mounted on the gurney, they had to have "two professional football players to keep Rock Hudson on this gurney. Nobody could hold him down" (*Seconds* DVD commentary). The character's failure in the end of the narrative seems to parallel the actor's decline in his career after *Seconds*. Although Hudson was proud of his work for the film, he had to face a critical and financial disaster.

Like *The Manchurian Candidate*, *Seconds* makes the most of a performer not particularly noted for his acting ability, by depicting a character whose situation parallels the actor's life in almost uncanny ways. Similarly, in both films,

Rock Hudson embraces another "reborn" during the cocktail party scene of *Seconds* (Gibraltar Productions, 1966), in a pose of unusually intimate male proximity. Collection Rebecca Bell-Metereau.

Frankenheimer translates almost directly two rather unexceptional novels into films that uniquely capture the anxious spirit of a decade in which secrets were revealed, new identities were born, and a nation lost its illusion of innocence. Through formal innovation and an almost instinctive exploitation of the ambivalent sexual personas of his lead actors, Frankenheimer created complex and peculiarly haunting and tragic characters. One is the stereotype of the effete momma's boy and the other is the hypermasculine gay pinup, but both characters have a second life, a hidden identity, which seemed to speak to the actors who embodied them. Through Frankenheimer's ability to plumb this emotional connection, take artistic and substantive risks, and exploit chance circumstances, *The Manchurian Candidate* and *Seconds* took their place in the pantheon of paranoid cult favorites of the 1960s.

NOTE

1. Easily confused with *The Manchurian Candidate* in this regard, another Frank Sinatra vehicle, Lewis Allen's *Suddenly* (Libra Productions/United Artists, 1954), was similarly pulled from circulation at the same time, for a protracted period, and for the same reason, namely, that Lee Harvey Oswald had seen it and been inspired by Sinatra's performance as a would-be presidential assassin. The story has been told that Sinatra was uncomfortable with that legacy and wanted the film pulled (see also Pomerance). (With thanks to Eric Schramm.)

The Train

John Frankenheimer's "Rape of Europa"

MATTHEW H. BERNSTEIN

While most critics hailed John Frankenheimer's *The Train* (1964) as a superlative action film upon its initial release, it earned only $9 million ($6 million abroad, $3 million in the United States) off its $6.7 million budget (Balio 279). Moreover, the film had its detractors. Some singled out the way in which Burt Lancaster's distinctive, patented acting mannerisms and star image disrupted an otherwise thoroughly realistic mise-en-scène—that, in short, it was impossible to accept the casting of Lancaster as the hardy, ingenious French yard master Paul Labiche who is also a Résistance fighter during the German occupation. Others found the brief relationship between Labiche and the pacifist railway hotel owner Christine (Jeanne Moreau) a highly conventional concession to the box office in the middle of what was otherwise a male-oriented super-action film. Most significant, still other critics ridiculed what they saw as the film's posing of a facile moral dilemma faced by Labiche and his allies: choosing between preserving human life and recovering France's artistic legacy of painting masterpieces from the clutches of a determined Nazi colonel, Von Waldheim (Paul Scofield). Most critics were surprisingly tolerant of what seems a remarkable flaw to contemporary eyes—the atrocious dubbing of major French actors such as Michel Simon (as the aged, Nazi-hating train engineer Papa Boule) into English.

I think it worth addressing these criticisms. Far from the paranoid fantasy of *The Manchurian Candidate* (1962), *The Train* represents Frankenheimer's extraordinary effort to realize a realistic drama that he and his collaborators constructed from the kernel of a historical incident. The director put every technical tool at his disposal to work in this project: location shooting in French rail yards and stations, the use of actual locomotives and real dynamite, long takes, tracking shots, deep focus cinematography, careful cutting that provides all the pertinent views of a scene's action, and a sound effects symphony of railroad whistles and track rumbles. The keynote of Frankenheimer's commentary on the DVD of the film is this effort: to persuade the viewer that what they see in the film could and did happen (unless otherwise noted, all my quotations from Frankenheimer come from this source).

History and Inaccuracy

In the early 1960s, screenwriters Franklin Coen and Frank Davis (later aided by the blacklisted Walter Bernstein, uncredited) wrote a script on spec, taking inspiration from three and a half pages in a French memoir (sometimes inaccurately described as a novel) by a painting curator named Rose Valland, entitled *Le Front de l'art: Défense des collections françaises, 1939–1945*.[1]

One gets a brief introduction to Valland in Lynn H. Nicholas's 1995 *The Rape of Europa* (especially chapters 5, 6, and 10); and in the 2006 documentary adapted from it by Richard Berge, Bonni Cohen, and Nicole Newnham (produced by Actual Films, Argon Arts and Entertainment, and Oregon public Broadcasting). Both book and film provide an exhaustive account of the Nazi plundering of thousands of artworks in western and eastern Europe and Russia (from France alone, more than 22,000 paintings, many of them Jewish-owned) as well as the Allies' efforts to carefully recover what was stolen or sequestered as they reconquered the continent. Reichsmarshall Hermann Goering personally abducted works both for himself and for Hitler's planned grand museum in his hometown of Linz. The Einstatzstab Reichsleiters Rosenberg (or "E.R.R.") was the Nazi agency placed in charge of this operation—led by one Colonel Von Behr. According to Nicholas, even while in hiding in his bunker as late as March 1945, Hitler still hoped the museum would be built (315). It never was.

Characterized in the film *The Rape of Europa* as France's "most unlikely spy," and by Louvre archivist Isabelle le Masne de Chermont as "a little gray mouse creeping around the building all the while observing and listening to everything that happens there," Valland is further described by art historian Kenneth Lindsay: "Nobody knew that every night when she went home, she kept a secret diary of what French paintings, owned publicly or privately, were taken by whom, sent where." One can see Valland's notebook entries in a few close-up shots in *The Rape of Europa* film.

In her *Le Front de l'art*, Valland recounted how the Nazis knew that they could also resell "degenerate art" to fund their war machine. In three and a quarter pages, Valland described Colonel Von Behr's attempt to transport Impressionist and Cubist masterworks by some of France's greatest painters as the Allies approached Paris from the west. One hundred and forty-eight crates were loaded onto trucks on August 1, 1944. Within twenty-four hours, they were packed onto five train cars with "a special military guard." Their departure from the Paris rail yards was delayed for nearly two weeks by the greedy Germans' own plodding, awkward attempts to stow plundered furniture on an additional 137 cars. The "Germans themselves" blocked the tracks as they retreated from

The middle of Frankenheimer's sequence-shot long take, discovering Colonel Von Waldheim (Paul Scofield) in the middle of "controlled chaos" at Nazi headquarters in Paris as they prepare to retreat from the Allied advance in *The Train* (Dear Film Produzione, 1964).
Collection Matthew H. Bernstein.

France, creating further delays for the art train's departure. By mid-August 1944, the art train sat in the station at Aubervilliers, northeast of central Paris. Valland informed the Société Nationale des Chemins de fer français (S.N.C.F. [the French National Railway]) about the train and the need to keep it from leaving France. One of their Résistance groups did the rest.

Let Valland take up the story from here:

> It was now time to take action! The S.N.C.F. did it with flexibility and cleverness.
>
> Colonel Von Behr was redoubtable. The man stopped at no decision, he was still an authority and he had an armed guard, which was certainly impatient to leave the station in which it was staying for a dozen days. . . .
>
> The signal for departure was finally given. Von Behr could believe in the success of his mission. In fact, the convoy had simply been taken away from his control.
>
> The famous colonel didn't plan that technical accidents could easily happen with (and be explained by) a train so heavily overloaded. . . .
>
> A first breakdown stopped the convoy for forty-eight hours in Bourget. Forty-eight hours at this time could change everything [i.e., as the Allies marched on Paris]. . . . Then it was moved to a spur line in Aulnay [further northeast of Paris] to wait for a new locomotive.

At the end of the forty-eight hours the real departure seemed inevitable. This is when the miracle happened. Leclerc's army, which was already in the Parisian region, reached Aulnay on the 27th. Being told of this urgent task by the S.N.C.F., it immediately sent a detachment to catch the cars and get rid of their German guard, always there.

. . .

Thus, a few of the most authentic masterpieces of modern art remained in France. Among them, some paintings by Cézanne, Gauguin, Modigliani, Renoir. I was very proud to bring back to the museum, without a single one missing and about a month after their departure, 24 Dufy, 29 Braque, 25 Foujita, 4 Degas, 3 Toulouse-Lautrec . . . 64 Picasso . . . etc. (Valland 184–87; trans. Violaine Boutet de Monvel)

For protecting the art as Paris was liberated, Valland was regarded as a collaborator but would eventually earn the Légion d'honneur and the Medal of the Résistance for her heroic efforts in keeping track of the art and locating most of it after the war (Nicholas 292–94, 440).

Rose Valland would also earn the honor of having her story dramatized in a major Hollywood film; she has a featured role early on. In the opening scene, the curator of the Jeu de Paume, Valland, here named Mlle. Villard (Suzanne Flon), joins the Von Behr character, here named Colonel Von Waldheim (Scofield), as he gazes quietly and appreciatively at some French Impressionist paintings hung there—Renoir, Picasso, and Gauguin. Their subdued conversation in the dimly lit gallery reveals Von Waldheim's unexpected appreciation for the paintings that the Third Reich had denounced as "degenerate." But this perception of him is upended when Von Waldheim abruptly orders his subordinates to crate up the canvases for shipment by train to Germany the next morning. Villard is shocked that he is doing this, arguing that the paintings are safest in Paris, which is now an open city. Maurice Jarre's martial theme music (heavy on drums and horns) starts up as the credit sequence ensues, during which the art is crated, the crates are stenciled with the names of the painters ("2 Manet," "4 Degas"), and various works are shown to the champagne-sipping Von Waldheim for approval.

A few scenes later, Villard asks yard master Paul Labiche and his fellow Résistance train workers to protect the art train and prevent it from leaving the country without blowing it up. They turn her down, and only gradually find themselves protecting it in the course of the film.

Villard/Valland, that is, sets the narrative of *The Train* in motion. Yet as *Newsweek* pointed out,

> to have followed [Valland's] modest story would have been to unmake the movie. Imagine Burt Lancaster as an assistant bookkeeper with a green eyeshade and snappy sleeve garters. There was bravado and action on

Rose Valland, turned into Mlle. Villard in *The Train*, and portrayed by Suzanne Flon. Here, she consults her notebook on looted paintings, while asking Labiche (Burt Lancaster in the foreground) for his help in stopping the art train.
Collection Matthew H. Bernstein.

the railroads during the Resistance—but with munitions trains and shipments of vital materiel. And it was this kind of incident upon which Frankenheimer grafted the exotic story of the art shipment. ("Big-Bang" 112)

Many incidents of "bravado and action" had already been dramatized in René Clément's rapturously received but now overlooked 1945 film, *La Bataille du rail*, a straightforward, reenacted documentary shot on location and using S.N.C.F. workers for the cast, in the style of John Grierson's British documentary film movement (critic Adrian Danks compares it briefly with Humphrey Jennings's *Fires Were Started* [1943] ["Border Crossings"]). As if in homage to these actual episodes of resistance, *The Train* includes an extended, bravura sequence involving the delay and bombing of a German munitions train, while the art train is fortunately driven to safety outside of Paris. Coen and Davis's original script, however, simply followed Valland's description of events. *Their* train, in Frankenheimer's words, "went on a straight line out of Paris and was stopped by the Résistance . . . and then captured by the Americans." (Frankenheimer has one detail wrong here: it was in fact a division of the French Army that recovered the art train, led, by coincidence, by the son of one of the Jewish collectors from whom the Nazis had stolen some of the paintings.)

So, not surprisingly, the creators of *The Train* added characters, incidents, and explosions to this outline in accordance with Hollywood action moviemaking. The result is a film full of narrative incidents and action sequences centering on Labiche's seemingly endless, almost Sisyphean struggle against the evil Von Waldheim. Frankenheimer and his team added the Allied bombing raid involving the art train. They created the blustering, artless character of Papa Boule, Labiche's father figure who is caught and summarily executed for jamming the gears in the oil works of the art train engine using a franc coin. They invented the attractive, widowed rail station hotel manager, Christine, who briefly helps Labiche. The filmmakers thought up painting the train car roofs white to signal the Allies not to bomb it. They structured their script around the one-on-one struggle between Labiche and Von Waldheim, and they kept the Americans out of it. Most complexly of all for the story, Frankenheimer ensured the addition of the Résistance workers' scheme of disguising various French towns in and around Paris as Alsatian and German cities (a conspiracy that is planned almost entirely offscreen) to deceive the Germans on board the art train into thinking they are approaching Germany—another delaying tactic until the Allies can arrive. As Valland's biographer puts it, "There was no death during the operation (the delay of the train), contrary to the scenario of 1964 John Frankenheimer's movie, *The Train*." Nicholas peremptorily characterized the film as telling Valland's story "rather inaccurately" (440).[2]

National Identity, National Character

The Train effectively exploits what Lynne Kirby has called "parallel tracks"—the visual and narrative affinity of moving pictures for trains. This is based on certain crucial analogies between them: the immobility of the spectator in the theater and that of the passenger on the rail car. There is also the similarity between the dynamic, moving images on the screen (Kirby calls this "instability") and the rapid movement of the train as well as the view of the passing scenery. In making the train a special object of the drama, Frankenheimer's film heightens this kinship—much as Buster Keaton's *The General* (1926) had done nearly forty years earlier. *The New Yorker*'s review stressed this connection: "Not since Buster Keaton's perfect comedy 'The General' has the camera surrendered itself more eagerly to the steamy, sooty, black-and-silver, hissing-and-hooting world of rolling stock, signal towers, yards, shops, cranes, tunnels, bridges, and track" (Gill 152). Of course, Keaton's film had no "hissing and hooting." *The Train* is full of them.

Yet *The New Yorker* was overlooking a crucial intermediary film, Clément's *Bataille du rail*. Like Frankenheimer's, Clément's film staged a scene in which a stationmaster is tied up to deflect suspicion from the Germans. The film also includes a sequence featuring the bombardment of trains and, even more impressively, the actual derailment of a moving train, sabotaged by the S.N.C.F. workers who ply their furtive and inventive trade from the time of the Normandy invasion until the Allies liberate France. The sequence in which a series of train workers are slowly executed one by one is incredibly moving, as is a futile firefight with the Germans on a munitions train. Yet, as Alan Williams notes, perhaps because of the non-professional actors used, "the film almost always directs the spectators' interest toward overall situations rather than to the lived experiences of people in them, and provides little individualization or development of characters (or even simple background information about them)" (303). Still, the film was shown to terrific acclaim and received multiple awards. In reviewing *The Train*, Bosley Crowther repeatedly referred to "that sizzling French war film" ("Burt Lancaster"), and commented in a later think piece that *The Train* "is so boldly and bluntly assembled and so dynamically engineered that it isn't at all disturbing to note that it cribs a lot from old silent jobs and especially from René Clément's famous French film of the resistance, *Battle of the Rails*" ("Familiarity Breeds Content").

In the final endnote to her book (which focuses on silent films), Kirby notes that Clément's *La Bataille du rail* provides "the literal sense of controlling the train as controlling national destiny" (Kirby 303n2). She could be writing of Frankenheimer's film, only now the nationalist stakes are doubled down, as it were, because the art itself is "the heritage of France," asserting French character in an entirely different dimension. Mlle. Villard's speech to Labiche and his colleagues (in their only scene together, early on in the canal boat) articulates this in the strongest terms:

> Those paintings are part of France. The Germans want to take them away. They've taken our land, our food, they live in our houses. And now they're trying to take our art. This beauty, this vision of life borne out of France, our *special* vision, our trust, we hold it in trust, don't you see, for everyone. This is our pride, what we create and hold for the world.

It is striking in this regard that *The Train* does not emphasize the fact that the paintings the Nazis gathered in the Jeu de Paume during the war were looted from Jewish collections. Villard refers to "the Clouvet collection" in discussion with Von Waldheim in the film's opening scene. But that is as far as *The Train* goes toward explicitly acknowledging the deportation and dispossession of France's Jews. By contrast, *La Bataille du rail*'s first image is of a sign in German and French forbidding Jews to cross the line of demarcation.

The French paintings on French trains being abducted by the Germans only intensifies the French desire to retain them, even if, in one of the film's great ironies, the railway workers have never seen the paintings and do not know their value. Moreover, the film's assertion of French nationalism is compromised by the success of the Résistance's ruse of disguising French towns as German; this suggests, as does Jean Renoir's 1937 *La Grande Illusion* (not least in the final scene in the snow-covered mountains), that national boundaries are social constructions. (It is equally striking that, at least according to the sample in Frankenheimer's personal scrapbook, French film critics had high praise for this film written, co-produced, and directed by Americans. On the other hand, no Americans are shown to have any role in liberating the art train. This is portrayed as entirely a French operation.) Overall, Frankenheimer's film conveys the idea, phrased quite directly by Archer Winston in his review of the film for the *New York Post*, that "the Germans are ruthless and determined and that the French match them with equal determination and an ingenuity continuing into self-sacrificial dedication" (20).

Close as *The Train* comes to retracing the steps of *La Bataille du rail* in terms of international struggle and even visual style (Clément uses deep space and at times deep focus to show the viewer the disposition of the trains, the resistance fighters, and the Germans), the achievements of Frankenheimer's film are equally well illuminated in comparison with *The General*. The characterizations of the antagonists in each film certainly differ. The Union spies who steal "The General" in Keaton's film have very few distinctive traits; their function as agents in the plot is far more important than their particular personalities. Frankenheimer and the screenwriters were able to develop Von Waldheim's character to create the driven aristocratic Nazi elitist who outsmarts his superiors, much as Labiche outsmarts him, in order to get control of the art train. Novelist Harlan Ellison described Von Waldheim well: "He is a dedicated man, a man with lofty motives, serving a beast master, and himself part-beast. . . . He is a man doing the wrong thing—for the right reason" (48). Von Waldheim's high-mindedness resides solely in his paradoxical appreciation for art (Valland described him as charming and speaking very good French [qtd. in Bouchoux 34–35]). His beastliness is apparent throughout, notably through the execution of various Frenchmen and most of all in the gratuitous slaughter of innocent villagers tied to the train at the end of the film.

Von Waldheim regards everyone who gets in his way—the German high command and his enemies, especially Labiche—with contempt. This is never more apparent than at the conclusion of the film. Unarmed, and facing an armed Labiche, Von Waldheim tells him:

> A painting means as much to you as a string of pearls to an ape. You won by sheer luck. You stopped me without knowing what you were doing or why. You are nothing, Labiche. A lump of flesh. The paintings are mine. They always will be. Beauty belongs to the man who can appreciate it. They will always belong to me or a man like me. Now—this minute—you couldn't tell me why you did what you did.

Von Waldheim is wrong on several counts, not least of which being that Labiche and his allies triumphed over the Nazis through an act of the mind: their superior knowledge of trains. But he is also right: Papa Boule's successful preservation of the art train during the British bombing of the rail yard *was* in good part a matter of luck; and Labiche has never seen the paintings he fights to protect, nor understood their worth.

Von Waldheim's love of fine painting remains the film's chief example of the contradictions of National Socialist ideology: ruthless elitism combined with a love of artistic beauty. As Dr. Leonard Malamut, an American veteran of the 11th Armored Division, comments in the film version of *The Rape of Europa* about finding the largest Nazi cache of looted art in a salt mine: "All of this accumulated beauty had been stolen by the most murderous thieves that existed on the surface of the earth. How they could retain the nicety of appreciation of great art and be exterminating millions of people nearby in concentration camps I couldn't understand then and I can't understand it today."

Malamut here articulates that central paradox surrounding the Nazis. As Lester D. Friedman has written, they "emerged from one of the most civilized nations in Europe. . . . How could it be that the Third Reich sprang to life in the land of Goethe and Mann, of Bach and Handel, of Nietzsche and Kant?" (Friedman 261). The pistol whipping of Jacques the station master and the indiscriminate killing of innocent French citizens throughout the film, and especially those tied to the art train as shields, only reinforce our sense of Nazi ruthlessness (although Frankenheimer admits on the DVD commentary that he had some of the secondary French characters shot by the Germans because those actors had other film sets to report to before he had completed filming).

Von Waldheim further embodies a not-infrequent characterization of the German officer as upper class, immoral, and even decadent. In this, his portrait partakes of a resentful attitude toward the European aristocracy in connection with the advent of World War II. Pitting the cultured and corrupt Von Waldheim against Labiche and his compatriots only cements the viewer's sympathies with the working class. Paul Scofield's performance throughout the film (down to his huge strides as he walks across the screen, his left arm swinging and his right arm still, or the way he stands with his legs spread far apart) allows Von Waldheim to come alive.

The focus on the Von Waldheim–Labiche conflict is another shift in emphasis away from historical fact, made to order for Hollywood storytelling: Valland emphasized the S.N.C.F. as a whole delaying Von Behr's train; Clément's *La Bataille du rail* emphasizes the teamwork involved in sabotaging German trains. *The Train*, while showing extraordinary cooperation among the rail workers, centers on Labiche as a defiant, shrewd, and worthy working-class opponent to the aristocratic Von Waldheim—and a charismatic leader as well. Labiche's power and authority are asserted the first time we meet him. Early on, Von Waldheim has asked his officers, "Who cancelled my train?" in the yard; the answer comes in a quick dialogue cut to the next scene from Labiche in his office: "I did."

Resolutely opposed to this nonsensical assignment, especially since the Allies are expected in Paris any day, Labiche must be persuaded to take on the protection and recovery of the art train by small increments: the endorsement of DeGaulle's leadership, aka "London," when Labiche first refuses the request; the Nazis' execution of Papa Boule on the train platform, for jamming the oil works on his engine; the constant urging of his colleagues Didont (Albert Rémy) and Pesquet (Charles Millot) to prevent the art train from getting to Germany after Boule is killed; and, finally, the near bombing of a French train on a practice run by the Allies who do not recognize it (an action scene shot after principal photography and added to the film at the request of United Artists for $500,000). Unlike in *The General*, it takes nearly an hour of *The Train*'s running time for the hero to sign on to the cause. Once Labiche does sign on, however, he is unstoppable.

As portrayed by Lancaster, Labiche is nearly as acrobatic as Keaton's Johnny Gray, running aboard and jumping off moving trains (with Lancaster performing his own stunts). Frankenheimer lavishly praises Lancaster's performance: "He is such a good actor. I believe him *completely* as a French railroad worker." Unfortunately, many film reviewers in March 1964 did not. *Newsweek*'s film critic, praising the film as a whole, wrote: "All right, so Lancaster leaps around, doing ridiculous acrobatics (lest anyone forget he used to be in the circus!), climbing mountains even though shot in the leg, grimacing and gesturing like a Kabuki player—but let it pass" ("The Right Track").

Harlan Ellison was even more cutting, writing that the film "offers us Burt Lancaster as Labiche. Correction. It offers us Burt Lancaster as Captain Marvel."

> He can act, certainly, but on what level above that of swashbuckling, I cannot conceive. The usual Lancasterite mannerisms—the unclenched teeth, the balled first swing across the body, the spread-legged stance and the furiously shaken arm, the tossed head, all so damnably predictable and cliché, so useless and needless here, in a setting of purest gold—the same mannerisms of Elmer Gantry once again, for the millionth time restated. The intrusive personality of Lancaster the acrobat, doing his special parlor tricks down ladders, over garden walls, superbly muscled and annoying as hell when they tell us over and over, 'I'm not really Labiche, I'm Lancaster.' Singly, he deadens suspense. It is to Frankenheimer's credit that he has been able to direct around this more-than-minuscule handicap. (48)

The mannerisms Ellison decries are undeniably there, and Labiche is truly superhuman.

Yet Lancaster's physicality was integral to the visual design of the film, a given. It was for this reason that Frankenheimer was called in to replace Arthur Penn, another alumnus of live TV drama, after shooting on *The Train* had begun. *Newsweek* reported, "Penn didn't satisfy [producer Jules] Bricken, who said he never 'got at the essential point in the film—its physicalness.' Lancaster's, however, was the more crucial disapproval. The star, with a 50 percent share in the profits, did not like the way Penn wanted him to play the part of Labiche . . . and he had Penn dismissed" ("Big-Bang" 112). So Lancaster asked Frankenheimer—who had previously directed him in *The Young Savages* (1961) and in an Oscar-nominated performance in *Birdman of Alcatraz* (1962)—to join the production in Paris in August 1963 ("Frankenheimer Replaces" 1). In *The*

Train, everybody—offscreen and on—is meant to admire Labiche, Von Waldheim excepted.

Moreover, Frankenheimer's admiration for Lancaster and Labiche melds with the director's fascination with the sheer process of work expertly performed, that is, his Hawksian admiration for characters who are good at what they do and for the skilled actors who play them; and his fascination with the way things work. In *Birdman of Alcatraz*, this is manifested in the montages of John Stroud (Lancaster) crafting wooden bird cages without glue, or his trial-and-error process for creating antidotes to bird diseases, and even the long take (actually two shots linked by a jump cut) featuring the long, slow, but exhilarating process by which a chick hatches from an egg and new life is paradoxically born in a prison.

In *The Train*, we see how sticking a Nazi officer's pipe in the gears of a track switcher blocks it. We see how throwing track switches alters the course of a train. We see Papa Boule place a coin in the engine gears to cut off the oil supply (something the rail resistance workers actually did). We see Labiche working with liquid metal to create a new bearing on the crossbar destroyed by Papa Boule on the art train's engine. As Frankenheimer says: "I think the audience likes to know how things work." This belief applies not only to his scripting, staging, and shooting scenes, but his own DVD commentary. He explains how everything in the film worked and discourses upon his love of the 25 mm wide-angle lens. One reason Von Waldheim and his men lose their fight, in spite of his obsessive focus on the art train, is that they have little idea, beyond Papa Boule's coin sabotage, how the French train system works. In this, too, he resembles Johnny Gray's antagonists, the Union military officers who steal The General. (Von Waldheim's ignorance about French trains equals in this sense the rail workers' ignorance about great French painting.) *The Train* affirms French nationalism by dramatizing the inherent technical advantage the French rail workers hold over their foreign occupiers. This advantage is also dramatized repeatedly in Clément's film.

Visual Style in *The Train*: "Superreal"

The Train and *The General* also share a signal visual style. It is here most of all that we see Frankenheimer's desire to overcome the stylization and fictional inventions of the script to create a realistic, believable film world, much as he used an utterly realistic, even hyper-realistic visual style to compensate for the surreal outrageousness of *The Manchurian Candidate*'s scenario. As Frankenheimer says on his DVD commentary, in particular of the "roundelay" of French train stations disguised as German stations, "We made this stuff up. I suppose it's believable. When you look at the movie it *is* believable. But I always dreaded that it wouldn't work. So we had to make it superreal." While intentionality does not equal realization, it's hard to argue otherwise in the case of *The Train*.

Frankenheimer (and his cinematographers Jean Tournier and Walter Wottitz) accomplished his goals in several ways, not only with the location shooting but with their penchant for camera movement during a shot, long takes, deep focus, and, in a number of scenes, quick cutting, all effectively orienting the viewer to the overall action at every moment.

Virtually all the scenes in *The Train*—except the opening in the Musée du Jeu de Paume and the scene in the Nazis' Parisian headquarters—were shot using actual locations. With the S.N.C.F.'s permission, Frankenheimer was able to stage the Allied attack on the train yards, destroying a "surplus" train station using more than twenty cameras in bunkers around the yard, three of them with camera people in them (Lenoir; J. O'Neill). Photographs of train station destruction appeared in American newspapers, and articles compared the scene to the famous burning of Atlanta in *Gone with the Wind* (1939). Publicity detailed the amount of explosives and the cost of the sequence (estimated at $3,000 per second, or $150,000) ("Big-Bang" 112). The S.N.C.F. company also allowed Frankenheimer to stage and film the derailment of a train at the Rive-Reine station (only one camera buried beneath the ground surviving to record it, because the stunt man drove the engine too quickly off the rails) and the smashing of a second engine into it and yet a third into the art train. The director discusses this on the DVD commentary; at the time, he told William Millinship of the *Washington Post*, "One locomotive crashed on its side just five feet from where I was standing. It smashed three cameras, but a small automatic camera got the whole sequence. Just as well: we couldn't do it twice" (Millinship G1).

Yet other examples of realistic mise-en-scène combined with elaborate camera movement and precise cutting are sequences before and during the Allied bombing of the French rail yard. The camera cranes up repeatedly from switching tracks to show where the munitions train and the art train are going (Pesquet and Didont ingeniously stall the movement of the munitions train for a few seconds—Pesquet by scalding the Nazi soldiers with engine steam, Didont by jumping out of his cab to see what is going on). We see both trains from high angles, from ground level angles, and from reverse angles. In one reverse-angle shot, Labiche slides down the ladder, runs, jumps on the train, and is kicked off. As Frankenheimer says in his commentary on the bombing scene in the Paris train yard, "We had to set this up logistically so you knew where each train [i.e., the munitions train and the art train] was."[3] Long shots during the allied attack show the bombs exploding behind the art train and then a montage shows train cars and yard buildings being blown up (in this case by real dynamite). As Jean-Pierre Coursodon and Pierre Sauvage write of the director's films, they "are primarily distinguished by their visual impact. . . . They enhance reality, impart people and objects with a disquieting presence" (139).

The same principle of orientation and persuasion motivated the film's extensive long takes, often in crisp, deep focus, as are many shots in this and other Frankenheimer films. The best example is probably the sequence in the

Rose Valland, whose book inspired *The Train*, in one of the few photos of her that survive (from *The Rape of Europa*, dir. Richard Berge, Connie Cohen, and Nicol Newnham [2006]).
Collection Matthew H. Bernstein.

Nazi Paris headquarters, where Von Waldheim goes to the Commandant de Paris in order to get permission to requisition a train for the art. The camera tracks and cranes back from the Nazi flag, tracks along, Renoir-style, with officials pushing papers between offices, and picks up Von Waldheim as he enters the second floor, tracking back with him as he approaches his superior's office. Frankenheimer aptly described this sequence shot as showing the "controlled chaos" of the Nazis preparing to abandon Paris. Von Waldheim is the one character in this sequence shot who has a strong, steady sense of purpose. He is almost oblivious to the frantic activity that surrounds him. But the point about Frankenheimer is that he shows the Nazi chaos in an entirely methodical and unchaotic way.

In *The Train*, Frankenheimer creates the "visual intelligibility" that Noel Carroll ascribed to Keaton's classic, "a situation which one comprehends at a glance in terms of its causal processes. . . . [Keaton's style] promote[s] visible intelligibility about physical relationships and physical processes," and "sensitizes the audience to key physical variables in the situations being portrayed" (95–96). We see not only "what" Labiche and his cohort are doing but "how"—as with Johnny Gray in the 1926 film and the French rail workers in Clément's film—by virtue of all these techniques and all the additional resources with more advanced technology (cranes, wide angle lenses) at Frankenheimer's disposal. The *Hollywood Reporter* described *The Train* this way:

> Manipulating trains for action is somewhat like getting elephants to dance. If it can be done it is impressive . . . the action is sometimes

intricate. Since it must fool the Nazis, since it must look like one thing but be another, there is a possibility of the audience being bewildered, too. This does not happen. Better, the action is able to proceed without dialogue or explanatory scenes, before or after. . . . It is perfectly clear as it happens and the audience is involved. (untitled review, n.p.)

Critic Stephen Bowie cites cinéma vérité as a considerable influence on Frankenheimer's tendency toward physical and visual concreteness, a "documentary-styled mise en scène," that is combined with a sense of the surreal in *The Manchurian Candidate*. *The Train* lacks any sense of the surreal (except perhaps when Von Waldheim goes off the deep end near the film's conclusion). But it certainly does not lack a sense of the absurd.

Frankenheimer's film (like Clément's) does not question the rail workers' desire to sabotage Nazi efforts, but through the character of Labiche it ambivalently invokes the aura of traditional art embodied in the paintings (famously theorized by Walter Benjamin) and pits it against the equally unique value of every human life. When Villard pulls out her list of paintings on the canal boat while she is talking to Labiche and company, Labiche asks her if the paintings are worth human lives: "[The Nazis] would shoot a few hostages, but that's the price you pay. Are your paintings that important, Mademoiselle?" Speaking of the loss of his colleagues in the Résistance (from the eighteen trainmen who committed sabotage against the Germans since the start of the Occupation to the three we saw early on in the canal boat scene), he tells her, "Like your paintings, Mademoiselle, we couldn't replace them. For certain things we take the risk. But I won't waste lives on paintings." This is the basis of his initial refusal to save the art train. Villard eloquently positions the paintings as invaluable in and of themselves, and the art train as the last outrage among many that Nazis have committed against the French: "There are worse things to risk your life for than that." Yet when Labiche's ally Didont innocently asks her about the paintings, "Don't you have copies of them?" Villard gives up her pleading and leaves.

As mentioned earlier, *The Train*'s meditations on whether the saving of art treasures is worth human lives was one source of critical disapproval of the film. The film restated the issue in its final sequence: Frankenheimer cuts together shots of crates of paintings alternating with shots of the bodies of villagers shot by the Germans, all spread out beside the train. The film's ending shot is desolate: in a high-angle long shot, as a solo harmonica reiterates Maurice Jarre's signature theme music, Labiche limps along the road above the train tracks, as the bodies of the French villagers lie alongside the track in the foreground and the painting crates rest in the background. We do not see the painting crates reloaded and shipped back to Paris. We do not see Villard thank Labiche for saving them. There are no celebrations of Labiche's victory, no scenes of awarding medals to Villard and Labiche for their work in recovering the art. To William Millinship of the *Washington Post*, Frankenheimer was explicit about his ideas on the subject: "He told me that he was trying to say two things. First, that no art is worth killing people for. Secondly, that a succession of small incidents can induce people to make sacrifices their common sense would reject." We might argue that the exhilaration of watching Labiche and his allies outsmart the Germans implicitly contradicts Frankenheimer's explicit moral.

The Rape of Europa (both the book and the film) proves that there was in fact a debate over preserving European art treasure at the cost of human lives during World War II. Prior to the declaration of war against Nazi Germany, the Roberts Commission, a gathering of National Gallery officials and academics, "warned President Roosevelt of the grave problem facing the Allied armies: how to save Europe without further destroying its historical buildings and cultural treasures in the process." General Eisenhower even ordered field commands to "respect monuments so far as war allows" in Italy (qtd. in *The Rape of Europa* film). While advancing through Europe, Allied commanders often had to choose whether to use overwhelming force to dislodge the Germans or to use lesser force in the hope of saving entire locales or the artworks contained therein. The latter strategy, often chosen, saved monuments and buildings at the risk of soldiers' lives. As Nicholas details, a key focus of such arguments was the 1,400-year-old Abbey of Monte Cassino; the issue of bombing it caused heated debates in the House of Lords; "the *Times* letter columns overflowed with missives from angry parents declaring that their sons should not give their lives for a building" (246). Such arguments may not have been addressed to art trains or paintings in Paris, but they were a reality in liberating Europe from the Nazis' grip. The Roberts Commission ultimately persuaded the army to allow (fewer than 200) art experts, later dubbed "The Venus Fixers" and "Monuments Men," to go on the front lines to work on salvaging works of art.

Frankenheimer and his collaborators had to build up and elaborate upon Valland's episode and the original script's narrative; their positing of the difficult choice between masterworks and human life was not one of their fabrications. Furthermore, the combination of Nazi immorality and ruthlessness with trains inevitably evokes associations with the "final solution," particularly as the film ends with shots of innocent victims of German carnage. Valland's biographer writes that Frankenheimer's film "systematically raises the same question among its viewers: could we not have thought about an analog operation that, instead of saving works of art, would have saved the deportees of the last convoys in August 1944 from death?"

The Train succeeds as a tribute to the French resistance in the S.N.C.F., as a tribute to the special skills and intelligence of the railroad workers, as an imaginative and visually compelling dramatization of their ingenuity used against an excessively oppressive foe. It is also testimony to Frankenheimer's extraordinary skills as an action director. We may be distracted by Lancaster's performance into appreciating him as a star, but one cannot help but watch the film without compulsive admiration for Frankenheimer's inventiveness.

Perhaps one final tribute to the achievement of *The Train* resides in the fact that although contemporary Hollywood filmmakers have contemplated remaking it, they have realized that the special effects and computer-generated imagery required would not measure up to the concreteness of Frankenheimer's staging. Perhaps you can fake stuff like this, but it wouldn't be the same.

ACKNOWLEDGMENTS

I thank Eric Garfinkel, R. Barton Palmer, and Lee Tsiantis for supplying me with research materials, Violaine Boutet de Monvel for her translations of French writings by and about Rose Valland, and Murray Pomerance for his editorial acumen.

NOTES

1. Screenwriter Frank Davis had had a fairly successful career in Hollywood, extending back to the 1920s. His scripts included *Dance, Girl, Dance* (1940), *Remember the Day* (1941), *A Tree Grows in Brooklyn* (1947), *The Woman on the Beach* (1947), *Jim Thorpe—All American* (1951), *Springfield Rifle* (1951), the 1952 remake of *The Jazz Singer*, and *Night of the Quarter Moon* (1959). Franklin Coen had been far less successful, but among his writing highlights were *Night of the Quarter Moon* with Davis, the western *Alvarez Kelly* (1966) and *Black Gunn* (1972).
2. One astonishing detail in the historical record that Valland discusses but the film leaves out: among General LeClerc's liberators was an officer named Rosenberg, who upon opening some of the painting crates realized the contents had been looted from his father's collection.
3. Frankenheimer makes a similar comment about Labiche's walk through the train yards where the Nazis prepare the munitions train on his way to the canal boat, where he meets Mlle. Villard—he might have started the scene on the boat, but he wanted the audience to see where the boat was relative to the train yard.

Action and Abstraction in *Ronin*

STEPHEN PRINCE

In 1997, John Frankenheimer explained the difference between an amateur and a professional filmmaker. The former works only on projects that he or she likes while the professional may be compelled to do work not of his or her choosing (Pratley, *Films* ix). In making this distinction, Frankenheimer seemed to be alluding to the doldrums that had afflicted his career following that extraordinary run of pictures in the sixties—*Birdman of Alcatraz* (1962), *All Fall Down* (1962), *The Manchurian Candidate* (1962), *Seven Days in May* (1964), *The Train* (1964), *Seconds* (1966), and *Grand Prix* (1966). In the decades that followed, his career faltered badly. While he continued to do strong work such as *52 Pick-Up* (1986), critics focused on the poor and mediocre films—*Prophecy* (1979), *The Challenge* (1982), *The Island of Dr. Moreau* (1996), *Reindeer Games* (2000)—to which he put his name. His late career triumphs mostly came from television movies produced for HBO and Ted Turner, which included *Andersonville* (1996) and *George Wallace* (1997).

But near its end his career as a feature filmmaker yielded one magnificent return to form in *Ronin* (1998). Along with his made-for-television movies, *Ronin* vindicates Frankenheimer as a still-major filmmaker even in the midst of his late career downturn. He never stopped knowing how to make a movie, and *Ronin* is a splendidly filmed production, finely crafted and calculated as an exercise in pure cinema. By that I mean its narrative content is highly abstracted, is conveyed obliquely and tangentially, mostly through subtext and back stories parsed in a severely parsimonious way. At the same time, the filmmaking—the scriptwriting, cinematography, editing, sound and production design—is assertive, muscular, and acutely conscious of deploying cinematic elements for a maximum of dramatic tension and narrative momentum. This formal expressiveness generates its own plenitude and pleasure. *Ronin* is an extremely entertaining movie, and its balance of elaborated formal designs with an oblique and recessive content provides a splendid model of a kind of action filmmaking that is rarely practiced in today's American cinema.

Less Is More

David Mamet's spare, reticent script for *Ronin* gave Frankenheimer an ideal template for staging a series of outstanding action scenes that are threaded together along a narrative line focused on issues of honor, duty, and obligation as faced by a band of mercenaries when they tackle a dangerous and enigmatic job. Mamet's dialogue was so superbly economical that it obviated the need for lengthy exposition. One of the best examples of the terseness comes in a scene between the two mercenaries whose friendship forms the emotional spine of the film, Vincent (Jean Reno) and Sam (Robert De Niro). Vincent asks Sam how he knew a money-for-guns exchange inside a Paris tunnel would be an ambush. (This scene furnished the first test for our heroes and the film's first action sequence.) Sam replies, "Whenever there is any doubt, there is no doubt. That's the first thing they teach you." Who taught you? Vincent asks. "I don't remember. That's the second thing they teach you." The dialogue provides an elliptical, spare, and poetic resolution to Vincent's question; a more conventional film and filmmaker would have furnished a tiresome explanation and motive for Sam's having foreseen the ambush.

The other mercenaries in the group include Gregor (Stellan Skarsgård), Larry (Skipp Sudduth), and Spence (Sean Bean). They are all hired by Deirdre (Natascha McElhone) to snatch a briefcase from a group of armed men who are transporting it. This is the set-up, as spare and abstract as it can be, and the characters are delineated through their behavior and through the subtext that surrounds their actions. This subtext—never overtly explained—is that the end of the cold war has left numerous covert agents stranded without employment. Sam has been with the CIA, a fact that is confirmed obliquely by Vincent and Deirdre (along with their knowledge of it) when they press him to use his old network of contacts to track a cell phone signal. Vincent, too, has been a player in East-West intrigue. When a Russian thug gets the drop on Vincent and prepares to shoot him, the thug pauses, realizing that he has seen Vincent somewhere before. "Vienna," Vincent tells him. Nothing more is said, the one-word reference providing Vincent with his cold war credentials. Gregor is former-KGB, and in one of the late narrative twists, he betrays the team, steals the case for himself, and plans to sell it to the Russians, who are former colleagues but not friends. Deirdre is with the IRA and is fronting for a rogue operative, Seamus O'Rourke (Jonathan Pryce), who is being hunted and cannot show himself publicly.

What is in the elusive metallic case? What are its contents that so many players will die for and fight over? Frankenheimer and Mamet know that the contents of the case are totally unimportant for the film. The case is what Hitchcock called a MacGuffin, an object that is terribly important to the characters in a movie but about which the audience cares not a bit. Thus, in *Ronin* the audience never learns what the case contains. Deirdre and Seamus know, as do the

Russians and Gregor. Sam, too, seems to know because the final narrative twist reveals that he has remained a CIA operative and has been hunting Seamus. Sam is the one who finally captures the box. As in *Kiss Me Deadly*, the case contains "the great what's-it," the thing that everyone wants and whose existence is important only insofar as it motivates the action of the movie.

As Frankenheimer has said, the narrative and characters are designed in terms of "less is more."[1] They are defined by their attitudes and their behavior, as these are revealed in action rather than in messages. In this, *Ronin* is like *The Train*, Frankenheimer's earlier masterpiece about efforts by the French underground to stop a Nazi train laden with French art treasures. Frankenheimer wanted that movie to get across the idea that no artwork was worth a human life. But he distinguished between action and messages and suggested that cinematic truth resides more in the former:

> To say that the film is a statement of a theme like that is really being unfair to the film because in my opinion it is also a significant action movie. . . . What people do and how they think, feel and behave, is important in itself . . . and you can show this in a film which is on the surface an action story. Honesty and reality are reflected in people's attitudes. (Pratley, *Films* 52)

A filmmaker can show honesty and reality without needing to have characters proclaiming great messages about life.

This is very much the way that *Ronin* works. We know Vincent and Sam and the others through the way they behave. For example, Spence's drinking and boasting tell us that there is disgrace in his past and he is adrift because of this and not merely because the cold war has ended. In their pursuit of narrative abstraction, Frankenheimer and Mamet jettison one of the major story conventions found in films about professionals banding together to undertake a dangerous mission. That convention details how the group is recruited, and, as found in such films as *The Magnificent Seven* (1960), *The Professionals* (1966), or *The Dirty Dozen* (1967), it provides colorful vignettes serving to introduce each team member. *Ronin*, by contrast, begins *in medias res*. The group has already been recruited and is assembling in the first scene to meet Deirdre in a local Montmartre bar. Mamet and Frankenheimer allude to the method of recruitment in their typically oblique way. Sam is the cautious member of the group, and he pretends not to be in the bar for anything other than a casual visit, wanting to case the place and its occupants before revealing that he is part of the team. But Deirdre is impatient with his evasiveness and tells him he's here because "the man in the wheelchair" called him. This "man in the wheelchair"—the one who was responsible for rounding up all these professionals—remains an undefined character throughout the film. We never learn any more about him, nor need we, because like the contents of the case, he is a plot contrivance, a necessary mechanism for the action but one that possesses no real content.

Vincent (Jean Reno, *left*) and Sam (Robert De Niro, *second from left*) join the rest of the mercenaries to learn about their mission in *Ronin* (FGM Entertainment, 1998). Frankenheimer's deep-focus designs throughout the film create shots that are uncommonly rich, as numerous things co-occur within the frame.
Digital frame enlargement.

Frankenheimer was advised during the production to define this character more clearly, but he felt that it was more interesting for viewers not to know.

There are only two devices in the film that run counter to this drive toward narrative abstraction. One is the news broadcast that Frankenheimer brings in at the end, in what he acknowledges was an afterthought, to give the story a larger dimension and a political frame. In it, we learn that the capture of Seamus has enabled peace negotiations to progress between the IRA and the Protestant government in Northern Ireland. The other device is the analogy from which the film derives its title, the likening of Sam, Vincent, and the others to *ronin*. These were samurai in Japan's middle centuries (1185–1868) who had become unemployed through battlefield losses, economic dislocation, or other misfortune. With no lord to serve, the ronin wandered town and country, searching for work or excitement. Ronin are figures of legend and folklore in Japan, somewhat comparable in their mythic stature to the gunfighter of the American western. The film's conceit is that these unemployed spies, cast adrift in a post–cold war world, are contemporary ronin, skilled at violence but with no honorable employer to serve. The substitution proposed by the ronin metaphor—of the CIA and KGB for the lords served by samurai—introduces an irony that the film's abstract narrative design precludes it from exploring. Are we to take these spy organizations during the cold war as honorable employers? The question turns out to be moot. Samurai honor lay in service to the lord, regardless of whether the warrior's master was wise or foolish, honorable or corrupt. And it is service to an ideal that Sam and Vincent believe in as the organizing principle of their lives. Within Japan's samurai culture, ronin were figures of disgrace; they had fallen from high status. Sam, Vincent, and the others are men down on their luck, with hard times etched in their faces, and one of them—Spence—has so completely fallen apart that he can no longer work as a professional.

Samurai Ethics

The film opens with a title card briefly relating the history of Japan's ronin for the audience. To reinforce the metaphor, midway through the film Frankenheimer and Mamet bring in a mysterious but sophisticated old character named Jean-Pierre (Michael Lonsdale). Sam has been wounded by gunfire and needs a secure place to tend to his wound. Jean-Pierre is a friend of Vincent's and has some unspecified connection with the world of intrigue and violence that the other men inhabit, not to say the world of medicine. Jean-Pierre's hobby is miniatures, and he has been working for what seems to have been a very long time on a tableau depicting the loyal forty-seven ronin. As Sam recovers, Jean-Pierre explains the legend of the forty-seven, which is one of samurai culture's most sacred stories (epitomized by Hiroshi Inagaki in his *Chushingura* [1962]). Early in the eighteenth century, a feudal lord (daimyo) named Asano assaulted another daimyo, Lord Kira, in the Shogun's palace. For breaking the law, the Shogunate condemned Asano to death and made him commit *seppuku*, ritual suicide. His loyal samurai retainers resolved to revenge themselves on Kira, and for a year they resorted to elaborate schemes of trickery and dissimulation to disguise their intentions. They then broke into Kira's compound, killed him, and, having upheld their obligation to Asano, committed ritual suicide, bringing the episode to closure in a way that acknowledged their transgression and that kept their honor intact.

Jean-Pierre patiently explains the legend to Sam and says that he knows Sam understands this concept of duty and of obligation to something that is larger and that lies outside of oneself. Earlier, Jean-Pierre had questioned Vincent about whether Sam had really left the CIA. Vincent believed he had, that Sam was adrift like the rest of the group. But Jean-Pierre cannily suspects otherwise—hence, his discourse on the loyal forty-seven. By introducing this historical parallel into the narrative, Frankenheimer and Mamet deepen the film's thematic core by raising questions about how the codes of honor that are in play relate to Sam, who is running his own game on the others. Like the loyal forty-seven, Sam remains bound by his ties of obligation to the CIA. He in fact still works for the CIA, and his posing as a drifter is a scheme like the one the forty-seven employed to allay Kira's suspicions. It enables him to blend in with the other mercenaries and to surreptitiously track and apprehend Seamus, but all of this is unknown to Vincent and the others. Thus, though he and Vincent part as friends, in no small way Sam has betrayed Vincent's trust. Sam continues to serve his lord and master, but Vincent is a true ronin, a man left at the end with no answers, only questions, and with no lasting allegiances.

The poetic analogy with Japan's masterless samurai built into the film pays dividends and is not gratuitous. It raises issues of service, honor, and obligation in complex ways by showing that service may entail betrayal and that honor may be measured according to disparate terms. Sam maintains a duplicitous relationship with Vincent because doing so allows him to serve CIA goals. Vincent, by contrast, is the person he claims to be. Vincent has retained his honor at film's end. Has Sam?

Mamet's oblique and highly condensed dialogue is a familiar feature of his other plays and scripts—*House of Games* (1987), *Glengarry Glen Ross* (1992), *Wag the Dog* (1997), to name but three—but Frankenheimer did not need to wait for this collaboration with Mamet to discover the virtues of indirection and minimalism. As noted, *The Train* already moves in these directions with its insistence on defining character through action rather than through expository dialogue. And *The Gypsy Moths* (1969) is a remarkably spare, existential portrait of a band of skydivers who make a daily choice between life and death and of one member, Rettig (Burt Lancaster), who feels the lure of crossing the boundary. *The Gypsy Moths* and *Ronin* do not state openly what they are about. They are all subtext, and an attentive viewer has to look for the meaning. Their spareness in this respect is akin to the films of Jean-Pierre Melville, a director with whom Frankenheimer had become friends when he was in Paris to make *The Train*. The poetic template furnished by Japanese samurai culture had also been of interest to Melville, most notably in his existential portrait of a hit man, *Le Samouraï* (1967). Frankenheimer acknowledged that Melville and *Le Samouraï* were probably an influence on *Ronin* (Amos). Frankenheimer, then, already had an affinity for the spare punchiness that Mamet could bring to the table, and this collaboration seemed to release Frankenheimer's energy in ways that his feature film projects had not done in many years.

Thus he is not simply illustrating ideas and a style that are in the script. Frankenheimer knows how to make a movie, and he returns here to his bedrock preferences, which include an aesthetic of hyper-realism and wide-angle cinematography. In Frankenheimer's pursuit of a heightened and stylized realism, Gillo Pontecorvo's *The Battle of Algiers* (1966) influenced him more than any other single film because of the ambiguities of perception that it induced in the viewer. Was Pontecorvo filming things as they happened or staging things for the camera? The latter condition, of course, was the true one, but it is difficult when watching the movie not to feel that his cameras caught events in Algeria's rebellion against French colonial rule on the fly, as they were happening. Frankenheimer has always preferred an aesthetic of realism, of staging events live (his career began in live television), as they happen in front of the cameras, rather than taking advantage of cinema's many trickeries, which today include the powerful arsenal of greenscreening and digital effects. *Ronin* was shot nearly a decade into Hollywood's digital effects revolution, which got under way with

James Cameron's *The Abyss* (1989) and accelerated with Steven Spielberg's *Jurassic Park* (1993). Digital tools were therefore available to Frankenheimer, but they were inconsistent with his aesthetic preferences for staging things live on camera. He often described his approach as semi-documentary, and as *Ronin*'s cinematographer, Robert Fraisse, reported, "John wanted this movie to appear onscreen almost like reportage, as if we had shot things that were really happening" (Magid 37).

High Performance

Ronin is a car chase movie boasting three extraordinary chase sequences, and Frankenheimer was an aficionado of high performance driving and himself a race car driver. He made *Grand Prix* without using a single process shot—he was especially proud of this—and with the actors actually inside the speeding cars that he filmed. In *The Train* and *The Gypsy Moths* he used a similar approach, staging events live for the camera and minimizing the use of process photography. An elaborate train crash in the former film was done with real trains, not models, in a small village, and town officials worried that the shock wave of the impact would demolish nearby buildings. Except for a few process inserts, the skydiving scenes in *Gypsy Moths* were shot by a cameraman in free fall. On *Ronin*, Frankenheimer resolved to place the actors inside cars speeding along the narrow streets of Montmartre, Arles, and Nice and used many of the same camera set-ups that he had employed on *Grand Prix*. The actual drivers were professional Formula One drivers, but specialty rigs—some with right-hand driving mounts and others that were an automobile cutaway towed by a professional driver in a high performance car—enabled De Niro, Pryce, and the other actors to be inside the vehicles as they sped through narrow French streets at more than 100 miles per hour. The actors had attended professional racing classes, but the fear and anxiety registering on their faces is often less a matter of performance than of an immediate response to the situation.

Moreover, Frankenheimer avoided using long lenses to shoot the car chases from afar, relying instead on short focal lengths, which made capturing the vehicles harder for the cinematographer since they crossed the frame much faster in this lens perspective. As Fraisse reported, "When you shoot car chases with long focal lengths, you can shoot for 20 seconds, because you see the car far into the depth and you can let it come toward the camera. But with very short focal lengths, the cars cross the frame very fast, which I think is a very strong effect" (Magid 39). Frankenheimer's success at working in this realist style, avoiding special effects trickery, places the car chases in *Ronin* in the same rarefied class as the celebrated chase in *Bullitt* (1968), where the road duel between cop Steve McQueen and two thugs—everyone driving muscle cars—shows nothing that couldn't be actually performed under the conditions shown. The chase scene in *Bullitt* avoids employing a music score—as do most of the chases in *Ronin*—and

Frankenheimer insisted on placing the actors inside the speeding vehicles. Specialty rigs, like this cutaway towed by a professional race car driver, create the illusion that the actors are doing the high performance driving.
Digital frame enlargement.

the sound effects are produced by the vehicles seen onscreen, as in *Ronin,* with Frankenheimer post-recording the sound on a race track using the vehicles that had been before the camera.

Frankenheimer distinguished a realist aesthetic from a stylized one, acknowledging that realism is, in its way, a style but not one pushed to baroque extremes. "To me, stylization is deliberately exaggerating action and costumes and performance—taking it away from realism—and hyper-realism is bringing it as close to reality as you can but not forgetting the fact that there's dramatic content to it" (Amos). On *Ronin,* he said, "I was trying to create a heightened reality, which is the opposite of a stylized approach" (Magid 35). Hyper-realism for him entailed more than making the effort to stage the car chases in a physically real way. It also entailed shooting according to his long-standing preferences, which include reducing color saturation, using wide-angle lenses, and composing shots in terms of a choreographed depth of field. He employed Deluxe Color Contrast Enhancement (CCE), a silver-retention method of processing film that deepens blacks, reduces color, and heightens the visible appearance of film grain. In terms of camerawork, he has criticized the tendency for contemporary directors to shoot close-ups of people talking and then cut them together to create a movie. Thus, in *Ronin* he composed his shots according to deep-focus aesthetics, which privilege group relations, since we can see multiple members of the team in the frame at any time, and in terms of location, since the depth of field can retain the actor and the surroundings in sharp focus. Frankenheimer shot the film in Super 35 mm, rather than anamorphic widescreen, because that format's spherical lenses provided sharper depth of field.

Camera movement extended these principles. Frankenheimer has noted his preference for staging action in depth *and* according to a mobile perspective. "With the semi-documentary type of movie that I do . . . where I didn't want the shot to be absolutely perfect . . . I would use the Steadicam. If I wanted to do a shot establishing locale and I had to stop and see this object, I would crane up and see this, down here to see this, come across, very tight across a person's face, then dolly with that person to somebody else, and the whole scene depended on that shot" (Pratley, *Cinema* 274). As in the films of Jean Renoir, this kind of camera movement renders a world in fluid motion and suggests a richness of activity that the boundaries of the frame only imperfectly capture. An example of this fluidity occurs when Vincent, Deirdre, and Sam find themselves stranded in Vieux Nice, after Gregor has betrayed them and taken the case. Vincent and Deirdre pressure Sam to use his CIA contacts to track Gregor's cell phone. The scene opens with a deep-focus shot of Vincent in the extreme foreground, with the road and shoreline behind him. As Vincent moves out of the frame, the Steadicam operator moves across the road to reveal Sam at the shoreline and then follows him as he crosses the road to the bars and restaurants on its other side. The camera move pivots around Sam 180° as he turns and looks at the cars parked along the shoreline and then focuses on a man walking in the background of the shot to one of the vehicles. The camera operator follows Sam as he walks on a converging diagonal to meet this individual as he gets into his car, and the two converse for a moment before the cut occurs.

The shot is an elaborately choreographed but not ostentatious move through the space of the scene, connecting Vincent, Sam, the location, and the new, unknown man in a manner that exemplifies visual storytelling, that is, Frankenheimer's ability to narrate story information according to the plastic properties of cinema rather than through the expository dialogue that many,

With his wide-angle aesthetic, Frankenheimer characteristically places objects and actors very close to the lens of the camera.

Digital frame enlargement.

if not most, filmmakers employ. The shot is carefully and expansively planned and executed, but it does not advertise itself. It enmeshes viewers with the characters in the unpredictable exigencies of the narrative moment. It is realistic because nothing is faked, and it is hyper-realistic because the calculation of the cinematic design is intended to heighten the emotional payload of the narrative moment.

In a similar fashion, Frankenheimer's transitions are calculated to plunge viewers aggressively into rapidly unfolding story situations and make them viscerally experience the narrative's progression. He cuts according to the audio-visual logic of formal design. Blood spatter against a car window from one of Gregor's victims forms a chromatic and poetic link to the following shot, an extreme close-up of the red sweater of skater Natacha Kirilova (Katarina Witt), the red a blur as she spins away from the camera on the ice of an arena. She will be shot dead by a sniper later in the film. When, early in the film, Deirdre slams a car trunk prior to the money-for-guns exchange that turns into an ambush, the thudding trunk forms a subliminal audio transition to a boat horn on the river next to the tunnel where the ambush will occur. Much later, when Vincent and Sam track Gregor to Arles, a slow but relentless dolly-in to a crowd of pedestrians shows them moving forward as an ensemble toward their bus, all except for Seamus, who stands motionless reading his newspaper. It's a splendidly visual way to reveal a plot twist—the viewer has not suspected that Seamus is in Arles, nor that he would be so deeply involved in efforts to seize the case. The camera movement and the blocking of the actors create a startling visual flourish, a hyper-realist element of style.

With *Ronin*, Frankenheimer vindicated his cinematic talents and aesthetic preferences. The film is stylistically bonded with the principles of his work as found in the earliest and best period of his career. Its aesthetic of realism places it with *Grand Prix*, *The Train*, and *The Gypsy Moths*, and its minimalist conception of character and narrative detail bonds it to those productions as well. Frankenheimer had not lost his touch as a filmmaker, far from it. *Ronin* is smart, sharp, and witty, and it shows a greater facility for visual storytelling than most films made today, by younger directors, can muster. The film industry is often unkind to aging directors whose best work tends, all too often and too easily, to be seen as behind them. Industry demographics skew young (and therefore older filmmakers tend to be seen as faded and less relevant). When Frankenheimer went into the hospital for a routine operation and suddenly died of a stroke, cinema lost a great director, though not the kind of filmmaker that scholars and critics tend to prize. His work was too idiosyncratic and too varied in subject matter to land him in a critical pantheon. But in his late-career television work for HBO and Turner, he returned to his origins as a director, having cut his teeth in live television in the 1950s. Above all in *Ronin*—his end-of-career masterpiece—Frankenheimer vindicated his talents by showing they had endured. In an era of green screens and digital fakery, he reclaimed his belief that action staged live for the camera has an integrity and truth that makes it the essential heart of cinema. This claim to truth and for cinema is Frankenheimer's and *Ronin*'s most elegant gambit.

NOTE

1. Unless otherwise sourced, Frankenheimer's remarks about *Ronin* and about filmmaking derive from his commentary on the DVD edition of the film.

Politics

Late Frankenheimer/ Political Frankenheimer

DOUGLAS McFARLAND

Robert Kennedy spent the final day of his life at the Malibu home of John Frankenheimer, awaiting the results of the 1968 California presidential primary. When it became clear that he had defeated Eugene McCarthy, a weary and reluctant Kennedy agreed to appear before his supporters on national television at the Ambassador Hotel on Wilshire Boulevard. Frankenheimer drove the senator to the hotel and accompanied him to an upstairs suite. After Kennedy had come down and uttered the rallying cry, "On to Chicago and let's win there," the director went ahead to bring his car to the side entrance of the hotel. Here he would wait in vain for Kennedy to emerge, since the senator had been shot to death by Sirhan Sirhan as he made his way through the hotel's kitchen. Frankenheimer's personal investment in Kennedy was deep and heartfelt. He had traveled with the candidate through much of his eighty-two-day campaign for the presidency in the spring of 1968, compiling footage for political ads and a planned documentary. Because of his personal involvement in the campaign, his closeness to Kennedy, and his physical proximity to the assassination itself, Frankenheimer was profoundly affected by the senator's death. Thurston Clarke goes so far as to claim in *The Last Campaign* that in the aftermath of the assassination, "Director John Frankenheimer ... developed a drinking problem that crippled his career for two decades" (Clarke 8). Thirty years later, Frankenheimer would still refer to the night of the assassination as a devastating turning point in his life: "All his [Kennedy's] clothes were in my house.... I really had a nervous breakdown after that" (Simon).

By the early 1990s, after a series of artistic and commercial failures, Frankenheimer's career had, in fact, reached a dead end. In an American Film Institute interview in 1997, he recalled that when he was asked in 1994 to direct *Against the Wall* (1994), an HBO docu-drama on the Attica prison riots of 1971, with a small budget and a six-week shoot, he called a friend to ask if he should accept a project that he considered beneath him. His friend wryly told him that he should turn it down and then sit next to his telephone, awaiting a call from a major studio. Frankenheimer immediately called the producers to tell them he would accept. He went on to direct four more television docu-dramas and several major films. The opportunity to do the film allowed him not only to revitalize his career but also to exorcise the demons that had haunted him since the assassination in 1968. For Frankenheimer, *Against the Wall* marked a turning point in his professional and personal life and opened a path to a future in which he would produce some of his best work.

Attica

On September 9, 1971, a group of inmates in the Attica State Penitentiary in upstate New York overcame prison guards in a walkway between the central communication post and the prison yard. The ensuing riot quickly spread to the other cell blocks and in a few hours approximately 1,300 prisoners had moved to D Yard along with the hostages they had taken. Here they would remain until the morning of September 13, when the yard was forcibly retaken by order of Governor Nelson Rockefeller. In the assault led by New York state troopers, twenty-nine inmates and ten hostages were killed. Contrary to initial reports, all the deaths were attributable to the troopers, guards, and sheriff's deputies. Before order could be fully restored, guards carried out violent and sadistic reprisals against the prisoners. All participants were stripped naked and many were beaten and sexually abused before order was restored.

What distinguishes the Attica prison riot from others are its deep social and political underpinnings. The riot was in large measure a response to the deplorable conditions in the prison. In a facility originally built to house 1,600 prisoners, Attica held 2,300. Sanitary conditions were particularly appalling. Toilets were often overflowing. One shower and one clean pair of socks were provided per week. One bar of soap and one roll of toilet paper were allowed per month. But in the minds of both inmates and authorities, the violent takeover of the prison was more of a political uprising than a protest over conditions. In their sociological study of prison violence, Bert Useem and Peter Kimball point out that in the aftermath of the initial violence, prisoners created their own society: "Within the next couple of hours the inmates in D Yard laid the foundations of an inmate counter society, with a degree of formal organization, articulation of political principles, democratic participation, and law enforcement unprecedented in prison riots" (34). Moreover, perhaps because the majority of the prisoners were African American, the authorities reacted to the inmates as if they were inner-city insurgents. The head of the New York prison system claimed the authorities "were dealing with a very sophisticated and determined coalition of revolutionaries who were trying to exploit public sympathy to achieve their political objectives, to trigger a chain reaction undermining authority everywhere" (Useem and Kimball 51). The belief that the uprising went beyond the immediate issues of prison life at Attica was held by many inmates. As one prisoner told Tom Wicker, "the Brothers" are demanding what "oppressed people are advocating all over the world" (Wicker 96–97).

Montage and Opening Credits

The events at Attica generated multiple responses: personal testimony, political manifesto, investigative exposé, commission report, sociological study, lawsuit, and jazz improvisation. The complexity of Frankenheimer's own historical reenactment of the events comes from the interplay between multiple narrative typologies, none of which becomes dominant until the end of the film; and multiple sociopolitical allusions, which reach beyond the immediate events depicted. Frankenheimer's approach to Attica is established in the first seven minutes of the film through two formal devices: an opening documentary montage and an extended sequence of parallel edits.

Frankenheimer prefaces *Against the Wall* with footage drawn from events of the late sixties and early seventies. Pieced together and out of chronological order are shots of the lunar landing of July 20, 1969, a chanting Allen Ginsberg, the assassinations of Martin Luther King Jr. and Robert Kennedy on April 4 and June 5, 1968, respectively, inner-city rioting, a defense of violence by Malcolm X, the Tet offensive of January 1968, Henry Kissinger's announcement that "peace is at hand," napalm falling on the jungles of Vietnam, Tricia Nixon's wedding reception in the White House Rose Garden on June 12, 1971, draft card burners, and the shootings at Kent State University on May 4, 1970. The series ends with footage from a rally by construction workers in New York City protesting antiwar demonstrations. For those who lived through the times, the impact of the montage is visceral and traumatic. For those born later, it is revealing and instructive. The montage dramatically and economically depicts the turbulence, the hope, the despair, the anger, the hypocrisy, the deep divisions, and the self-indulgence of the era. By prefacing his film with these images, Frankenheimer makes it clear that his depiction of the Attica riots will fall into the political and sociological context of the civil rights movement, the Vietnam War, the youth culture of the sixties, and the working-class backlash against student protests and racial violence. Moreover, the three prominent shots of the Robert Kennedy assassination suggest that for Frankenheimer the events at Attica provide the opportunity to address a personal as well as a collective trauma. Frankenheimer may have been influenced by a similar montage that opens Martin Ritt's *The Front*, a 1976 film about the blacklisting of writers and actors in the fifties who were perceived as communist sympathizers. Ritt includes shots of Joe McCarthy, the Rosenbergs, Joe DiMaggio, Marilyn Monroe, the MacArthur ticker-tape parade, a family entering a backyard bomb shelter, Korean War veterans, and the crowning of Mrs. America. Over these images, Frank Sinatra can be heard crooning "Young at Heart." With a few images,

Ritt captures the paranoia, the casualties, the icons, the complacencies, and the contradictions of post–World War II America. In *Against the Wall*, Frankenheimer does something similar for the sixties.

The final shot of the montage moves seamlessly into a narrative in progress. The flag carried by construction workers in their counter-rally dissolves into a flag in a barber shop in Attica, New York. The camera pulls back and away from this flag to a medium close-up of Michael Smith (Kyle MacLachlan), a young man whose shoulder-length hair is about to be shorn. The immediate function of the close-up is symbolic. The shoulder-length hair and the resignation in his face as it is being cut reflect the generational culture wars of the 1960s. He is the "hippie" son who has returned home to be absorbed back into his father's uptight world. Then we quickly learn that Attica is that world. The father, now retired, was a guard there, and now the son will follow in his footsteps. Michael clearly has been a member of the counter-culture movement, a bohemian and largely urban response to the middle-class conformity of suburbia, the working-class patriotism of the World War II generation, the corporate leadership behind the Vietnam War, and the racism of white America. One minute into the film Frankenheimer has made it clear that the Attica riots will be depicted in the context of the primarily white generational conflicts of the 1960s and within an overarching narrative typology of the return of the prodigal son. The choice of a biblical paradigm, a traditional cultural form which is immediately recognizable to a vast range of viewers, reflects the reduction of complex historical forces to a most reassuring "narrativity." Frankenheimer signals, at least at this point, that he will eschew destabilizing modernist techniques of narration with which

Upon his return to working-class America, Michael Smith (Kyle MacLachlan) prepares to shed his shoulder-length hair, an emblem of the counterculture movement of the sixties and early seventies. *Against the Wall* (HBO, 1994).

Digital frame enlargement.

he had experimented earlier in his career in films like *The Manchurian Candidate* (1962) and *Seconds* (1966), in favor of a narrative of containment. Hayden White argues that modernist narration is a response to the inability of traditional forms to contain a traumatic event. "Modernism," he argues, " . . . marks the end of storytelling" (24). At this moment in the film, Frankenheimer seems to have retained his faith in "storytelling."

The camera follows Michael as he leaves the barber shop and drives to Attica Prison for his first day on the job as guard. His bright red Mustang convertible passes through downtown Attica and then through rural countryside before arriving at the prison. Our first view of Attica prison is a point-of-view shot from Michael's car, confirming his role as the dominant perspective of the film. What follows, however, is a significant complication to that expectation, one that provides a political point of view and a second narrative typology. As Michael makes his way to the entrance, he passes an African American grandmother and her grandchild leaving the prison, the first African Americans to appear in the film. The implication is that the father of the child is in Attica and that his mother has brought his child for a visit. It has already been established that Attica prison is located in the countryside, seemingly far from any urban center from which most of the prison population has been drawn. On the other hand, prison guards are literally at home in Attica. The audience is meant to wonder, in contrast to Michael's mobility, how the grandmother and grandchild got to Attica prison in upstate New York, virtually on the Canadian border. Does she have a car? Is there public transportation? This is the first political statement expressed in the film and speaks to one of the underlying causes of prisoner dissatisfaction that contributed to the riot. Tom Wicker writes, "When criminals were banished from society in New York State, most were effectively removed from their communities and jobs . . . as if they had been swallowed by the sea" (33). As a result, "families and friends had difficulty visiting during the limited hours when it was permitted" (34). From New York City, round-trip bus and taxi fare would come to approximately $55.00 (and almost ten times that in today's dollars). In short, most of the inmates of Attica found themselves isolated in a rural white enclave far from the world they had known. As one inmate later recalled, upon arriving at Attica, it seemed as if he were entering a "concentration camp" (Wicker 329).

In one fluid movement, the camera now pans to the arrival of another vehicle, a bus transporting prisoners into Attica. Frankenheimer cuts to a medium close-up of one of the prisoners, Jamaal (Samuel L. Jackson), peering through the dirty window of the bus and making eye contact with Michael. What follows is an extended sequence of parallel editing that links together the two primary characters as they simultaneously enter the prison system. Frankenheimer uses the set piece to deepen the political subtext and complicate the narrative structure. We quickly learn that Jamaal is a repeat offender. One prison guard welcomes him back as if he had been waiting for his return. This gives the impression that he may be caught up in the self-perpetuating cycle that John Hersey describes in *The Algiers Motel Incident*, published in 1968, just three years before the Attica riots. Hersey asserts that "white society confronts every black youth in this country with a fork in the road. . . . One path takes him on through some schooling, to some job, to living more or less 'straight'" (Hersey 167). The other path leads the black youth to a "hustling life," part of an underground economy of crime and drugs. Once that second choice is made, he has "no stake in the social arrangements of life" (Hersey 324) and inevitably becomes the repeat offender, in and out of prison for most of his adult life.

However, the physical appearance of the prisoner who steps off the bus suggests that he has taken a third path. By his neatness, his Malcolmesque goatee, and his horned-rimmed glasses it is strongly suggested that this African American is a Black Muslim. Indeed, this is confirmed later in the film. He will prove to be an activist working for prison reform but also intent upon bringing a sense of discipline and self-respect to the prisoners through the ethical standards of Islam. The characterization of Jamaal is given an additional political component as the sequence progresses. The captain of the prison guards slips easily into the role of drill sergeant. He treats the new prisoners as if they were raw recruits who need to be broken. (He is a Vietnam veteran and continually makes reference to Vietnam during the film.) In a somewhat subtle way, Frankenheimer links the incarceration of a black underclass with their exploitation in the Vietnam War. Largely because it was to college students that draft deferments were granted during the Vietnam War, the burden of fighting fell disproportionately upon those whose socioeconomic status precluded the possibility of attending college. A great many of those who found themselves in that category were African American.

In addition, the parallel editing charting the entry into Attica of the two characters, one a prisoner and the other a guard, also suggests another narrative typology, a variation on the interracial "buddy film," very popular at the time thanks to *Silver Streak* (1976), *48 Hrs.* (1982), and the *Lethal Weapon* series (1987, 1989, and 1992). Although multiple political and social allusions have been made, these allusions are ready to be subsumed by an apolitical narrative. The film, in short, may very well become a drama of character, one that is concerned with the relationship between these two figures, with Attica functioning only as scenic context. Sumiko Higashi has pointed out something similar in the narrative strategy of *Mississippi Burning* (1988), in which male camaraderie contextualizes and contains racial violence: "The film achieves narrative closure by encoding a pattern of social organization based on male bonding that cuts across class and racial lines" (226). For Frankenheimer, the narrative pattern is less about "social organization" than about character. In *Birdman of Alcatraz* (1962), Frankenheimer's focus had been not on reform of the prison system but rather on the struggle of one individual, Robert Stroud (Burt Lancaster), to maintain hope and self-respect. At this point in *Against the Wall*, Frankenheimer signals a similar strategy. The question remains whether the bonding of these two figures, Michael and Jamaal, each crossing over into an alien space, will provide a model for interracial justice and hence the resolution of racial violence represented in the montage, or will simply transcend politics.

Revolution

The prison riot that led to inmate control of Attica is a generic cinematic set-piece drawn from the prison movie, a staple of American film narrative from *The Big House* (1930) to Frankenheimer's own *Birdman of Alcatraz*. Frankenheimer displays his own virtuoso technique in his depiction of the Attica riot, employing a rapid series of cuts, parallel editing, tilted camera angles, and blurred images. Moreover, although the uprising at Attica was sparked by abusive conditions at the prison in 1971—and by degradation and unacceptable conditions in the American prison system more generally—Frankenheimer invokes African American unrest from the early 1960s and 1990s. As the inmates set fire to the cell block, Frankenheimer cuts to a medium close-up of a prisoner who screams, "Let it burn!" an allusion to "Burn, baby, burn!" which was allegedly shouted by Dick Epton, a Marxist activist, during the Harlem riots of 1964. Epton was charged with "criminal anarchy" for using this phrase, and the words took on a life of their own as a symbol of the Black Power movement of the late sixties and early seventies. Frankenheimer therefore connects Attica to the unleashing of repressed black rage of inner-city America. This is qualified, however, by the characterization of the inmate who screams the words in the film. He is a borderline psychotic, irrational and unbalanced, whose rage is directed not only to guards but to fellow inmates as well.

The white paranoia this invokes is reinforced by an allusion to a more recent event. In 1992, just two years before the airing of *Against the Wall* on HBO, widespread rioting occurred in Los Angeles after the acquittal of four white police officers who had been videotaped beating Rodney King. One particular incident was repeatedly played up by mainstream media. Reginald Denny, a white truck driver who happened to be in an African American neighborhood when the riots broke out, was pulled from his cab at the corner of Florence and South Normandie and viciously beaten by a group of black youths. Frankenheimer shot *Against the Wall* shortly after this incident, and images of white prison guards being overpowered, dragged to the ground, and beaten invoked the Denny attack and powerfully spoke to the fears of the predominately white audience. Moreover, this kind of racial fear is specifically expressed by a character in the film. When the warden is informed of the riot, he remarks, "Is this it? Is this the big one?" His words dramatize the anxious anticipation of the eruption of repressed black rage.

However, the introduction of another narrative type qualifies these fears. At the same time as the warden learns of the takeover a siren goes off, notifying

A rioting African American inmate (Clarence Williams III) shouts, "Let it burn!" echoing the cry often associated with the Black Power movement of the sixties, "Burn, baby, burn!"
Digital frame enlargement.

the townspeople of the riot. Frankenheimer shows us the anxious and stricken faces of the relatives of the guards reacting to the alarm. For a moment, *Against the Wall* becomes John Ford's *How Green Was My Valley* (1941), a film that chronicles the travails of a coal-mining family whose lives are centered on the town's industry. Women and children live in the unspoken fear of an accident that might claim the lives of their husbands and fathers. This genre depicts the working class exploited by powerful class and economic interests. By invoking this type of narrative in *Against the Wall*, Frankenheimer suggests that Attica is a company town and that the guards and their families, as well as the inmates, are victims of powerful forces. It is fitting that the governor of New York at the time of the takeover was Nelson Rockefeller, a member of one of the most powerful families of early twentieth-century America. This sequence looks back to the concluding images of the opening montage and suggests that those construction workers rallying against antiwar protests are, to paraphrase Bob Dylan, only pawns in someone's game. But any sympathy the audience feels for these families is almost immediately undermined by betrayals amongst the normally self-protective "family" of guards during the riot. In one striking moment, a guard who had been particularly demonstrative in his contempt for the prison population closes off D Block before all his fellow guards can get out, in order that he might save himself. Not only does the audience witness class exploitation, in which power is exercised routinely by one group over a disenfranchised other; it is also privy to the corruption and hypocrisy of the controlling class.

This set-piece demonstrates in a concentrated form the salient characteristic of the film: the interweaving of multiple social and political references in the context of multiple generic forms. Frankenheimer alludes to the counterculture movement of the sixties, the Black Power movement of the sixties and early seventies, and contemporary urban violence. He places these in the context of the traditional prison picture, the story of the prodigal son, the interracial buddy film, and the working class exploitation film. The density of *Against the Wall* is not intended to problematize historical narration, but to clearly express the forces at play under, in, and around the event of the riot. While Oliver Stone in *JFK* (1991) "is engaging with American history in ways that make manifest its ultimately unknowable nature" (McCrisken and Pepper 148), Frankenheimer is interested in exploring how Attica embodies a matrix of cultural forces of the period.

Attica Nation

The takeover of Attica prison constituted something more than a violent response to inhumane conditions. Although negotiations with officials primarily focused on the conditions of Attica and amnesty for the rioters, for some the uprising offered an opportunity to create a new society. In a larger context, the takeover of Attica prison reflects a pervasive utopian impulse of the sixties and seventies. Frankenheimer shares this understanding. On the night of the third day of the occupation, rain fell heavily, reducing D Yard to a muddy field, very much like the rain-drenched scene on the second day of Woodstock. Many viewed the Woodstock Music Festival as a pastoral utopia, affording the opportunity, as Joni Mitchell sang it, to "get ourselves back to the garden."

The most prominent reference to the utopian agenda is Jamaal. When he hears the sounds of rioting, he carefully emerges from his cell to assess the situation. All along there has been the suggestion that Jamaal has returned to Attica on a mission to convert inmates to Islam. Now, perhaps naively, he senses the opportunity to create a society based on a politics of participation and an Islamist ethic. At the onset of the riot he stops prisoners from beating and killing the guards and begins to organize the rioters into a political and social system. Formal divisions of labor, a security patrol, guards to protect the prisoners, and an assembly through which group decisions could be made were all established at the onset of the takeover. Near the end of the standoff, however, he must confront his failure. He brings Michael Smith, now one of the hostages, inside the prison to show him the bodies of inmates who had been killed by other inmates in reprisals. The bodies bear graphic witness to his inability to create a new social order among the prisoners. The failure at reform is powerfully expressed earlier in the film by a non-actor playing an older prisoner. He tells an assembly of inmates that he is himself a "lifer" and that his son is currently in prison as well. There is, in short, nothing but prison. He and his son are part of a black underclass who have given up, to use Hersey's phrase, on the "social arrangements of life" (Hersey 324).

Within Attica Nation, Frankenheimer inserts another political reference and another narrative form. Michael and the other hostages form their own enclave inside D Yard, and suddenly *Against the Wall* becomes a POW film, perhaps looking ahead to *Andersonville* (1996), Frankenheimer's depiction of Union prisoners in the notorious Civil War stockade. The hostage with the highest rank is also a Vietnam veteran who demands that his fellow prisoners adhere to the strict code demanded of POWs. The Attica uprising has become in his eyes Vietnam redux. Concurrently, Michael reverts to his pre-Attica role as protester of the war and refuses to join in with the other hostages. Moreover, the separation of Michael from his peers parallels Jamaal's failure to organize the inmates. This suggests the possibility, first raised at the beginning of the film, of a bond growing between these two outsiders.

The Turkey Shoot

On the morning of Monday, September 13, the decision was made by Russell Oswald, the commissioner of prisons, and Governor Nelson Rockefeller to break off negotiations with the prisoners and to retake the yard by force. As Oswald later asserted, this would reestablish the "sovereignty and power" of the state. Rockefeller claimed that because of the action of the state, "coercion was rejected, and the necessity of preserving a lawful society was upheld" (Useem and Kimball 51). Oswald handed over the planning of the assault to the New York State Police. Joining them were correction officers from Auburn Prison and members of the Genesee County Park Police force. Although the assault team had been told not to make this a "turkey shoot," it did in fact turn into one (Bell, *Turkey* 1). After tear gas had been dropped into D Yard, rifle squads that had been positioned above the yard began firing. The barrage lasted for fifty seconds. In the aftermath it was determined that ten hostages had been killed by friendly fire.

Frankenheimer's filming of the assault follows his earlier practice of making multiple political allusions. That the assault represents something more than the retaking of a public facility by the state is explicitly made clear by a state trooper who declares that a stand must be made against the forces that threaten traditional American values, from hippies and student protesters to feminists and Black Panthers. He makes this announcement with the same fervent right-wing anger shown by the construction workers in the final clip of the opening montage. What ensues is a frenetic outpouring of indiscriminate rage. The tear gas dropped into the prison yard literally creates the fog of war as hostages and inmates are shot down. The assault echoes the Chicago police riots at the 1968 Democratic Convention, as well as the My Lai massacre of March 16, 1968 (in which some four hundred South Vietnamese women, children, and elders were killed by the U.S. Army).

On the morning of September 13, state troopers fired indiscriminately into the crowd of inmates and hostages occupying D Yard. When the shooting ended, twenty-nine inmates and ten hostages had been killed in what became known as the "Turkey Shoot."

Digital frame enlargement.

The relationship between Michael and Jamaal now begins to override political and social perspectives. As anticipated, each man steps out of his group to bond with the other. The traditional "buddy" form that had been established in the beginning of the film now takes precedence over the events being depicted. In what is intended as a poignant moment, Michael and Jamaal, perhaps mortally wounded, vow to one another to contact the other's family if he did not "make it." Although, as I have shown, Frankenheimer repeatedly politicizes the narrative, as he reaches the conclusion of the film he offers the characters a chance to find meaning in a bond that transcends race, class, and the divisive vicissitudes of the world.

Michael Smith and John Frankenheimer

In his final gesture, Frankenheimer further depoliticizes the film in a movement toward melodrama and, arguably, sentimentality. The director abandons the buddy narrative to return to the first shot of the film: a close-up of Michael. In the aftermath of the "turkey shoot," and after Michael and Jamaal have made their pledges to one another, Jamaal is erased from the film. We learn nothing more about him, neither whether he suffered reprisals nor whether he was convicted for his participation in the takeover, nor even whether he survived. We most certainly learn nothing of the family that Michael has promised to contact. (Jamaal is a fictional character very loosely based on Richard Clark

X, a Muslim leader who sat on the prisoner committee negotiating with the state and who wrote his own highly critical version of events. Michael Smith was a hostage at Attica, however, and served as the historical consultant for the film.) At any rate, the film now turns to a reunion of the Smith family, a reconciliation of marital and generational conflict. Michael is taken away from the prison yard on a stretcher to an ambulance while the Black Muslim continues to lie on the ground. Outside the prison, father, son, and daughter-in-law are united in the aftermath of violence, as if Attica had brought them together and redeemed the family. At one telling moment, the film shifts into slow motion as the father races to climb into the ambulance already holding Smith and his wife. The slow motion provides a kind of lyricism to his movements, countering the violent forces that had been unleashed in the prison yard. As to the unspeakable acts of reprisals against the inmates, which have already begun as the ambulance pulls away—the film is oblivious. To put it differently, the film ends with a disturbing sense of disloyalty to the prisoners of Attica and abrogation of a commitment to political and social change.

The extent to which Frankenheimer is complicit in this ending, the extent to which he participates in this disloyalty, is difficult to ascertain. It is clear to me that *Against the Wall* provided him with a much-needed vehicle to address the politics of the 1960s. Like many others, he had not come to terms with the bitter disappointments and traumatic failures of the era. Twenty-five years after the assassination of Robert Kennedy, Frankenheimer was given the chance to reengage the political and social forces that informed that moment in history. The film expresses the overlapping complexities of those forces while avoiding a specific political point of view. But at the end of the film that avoidance becomes an abandonment of political perspective altogether. The film proved to be one of the most significant in the track of Frankenheimer's career. *Against the Wall* brought him the Emmy that had eluded him throughout his early years in television, and propelled him into a late flowering of creativity. He went on to make four more very ambitious docu-dramas, each dealing with Kennedy in direct and indirect ways. In *George Wallace* (1997) and *Path to War* (2002) he goes so far as to reconcile himself with two of Kennedy's adversaries: George Wallace and Lyndon Johnson. So let us forgive Frankenheimer's lapse in the final moments of *Against the Wall*. Let us think that if he momentarily lost sight of others in the release of Michael Smith from the conflicts and disappointments of his life, Frankenheimer felt his own release. At the climactic point in *Birdman of Alcatraz*, Robert Stroud is asked by an embittered inmate of Alcatraz, "What's wrong with dying?" Stroud responds, "Life is too precious a gift." I suspect that in 1994, when Frankenheimer found himself at a professional and personal dead end, these words came back to him.

John Frankenheimer's "War on Terror"

COREY K. CREEKMUR

> Today's violence, the violence produced by our hypermodernity, is terror. A simulacrum of violence, emerging less from passion than from the screen: a violence in the nature of the image. Violence exits potentially in the emptiness of the screen, in the hole the screen opens in the mental universe. So true is this that it is advisable not to be in a public place where television is operating, considering the high probability that its very presence will precipitate a violent event. The media are always on the scene in advance of terrorist violence.
>
> Jean Baudrillard (85–86)

The violent, unanticipated division of contemporary American history into pre- and post-9/11 has depicted the latter as a era of incomplete mourning and inadequate memorialization, with the advantage of hindsight offering small comfort for the lack of foresight that, had it been available and exercised, may have prevented or at least better prepared Americans for the traumatic assaults that became the watershed event of our time (see Simpson; Butler; Engle). However, our admission that we "didn't see it coming" has been consistently challenged by the common claim, made immediately following the attacks and persistently thereafter, that the massive destruction on September 11, 2001, uncannily resembled spectacular special-effects sequences from big-budget Hollywood action films we had been enjoying for years. The regular production and consumption of such films in the decades before 9/11 suggested that the "unexpected" attacks had actually been anticipated, perhaps even unconsciously desired, at least within the seemingly secure, fantastic realm of popular entertainment. In perhaps the most provocative of such claims, Slavoj Žižek declared that "the unthinkable which happened was the object of fantasy, so that, in a way, America got what it fantasized about, and that was the biggest surprise" (*Welcome* 15–16).

More recently, film scholars have returned to pre-9/11 films in order to carefully reconsider the significance of the popular cinema that the destruction of the World Trade Center was so often said to recall. Among the dozens of books devoted to 9/11 and the subsequent "war on terror" that the attacks were claimed to justify, Lawrence Wright's *The Looming Tower: Al-Qaeda and the Road to 9/11* (2006), a best-selling, Pulitzer Prize–winning account of the historical events leading up to the attacks, is emblematic of the retroactive desire by both film scholars and historians to recover the previously neglected recent past in order to belatedly attempt to comprehend the present, the new age of "terror" we hadn't seen coming, still blinded as we were by the residual scenarios that had been generated by the increasingly irrelevant cold war. As many enthusiastic reviewers also noted, Wright's nonfiction book reads like a popular thriller, which is unsurprising once we recall that the author had already been one of the screenwriters of *The Siege* (1998), a film that, viewed in retrospect, seemed to anticipate terrorist attacks on American soil before real events rendered such speculative fantasies unnecessary.

If *The Siege*, a minor hit that had been quickly forgotten despite its major stars, only looked prescient in retrospect, the events of 9/11 also rendered an even earlier film, John Frankenheimer's *Black Sunday* (1977), even more disturbingly prophetic, instantly rescuing the film from two decades of easy dismissal as ludicrous given its story of a massive attack by Middle Eastern terrorists, launched from the air (hijacking the Goodyear Blimp) against the backdrop of a densely populated, iconic American event (the Super Bowl) certain to be fully covered by the mass media. The postmodernist theorist Jean Baudrillard's provocative claim that "the media are always on the scene in advance of terrorist violence" does not cite Frankenheimer's film—which portrays its attack during the event that regularly generates one of America's largest television audiences—as popular evidence for his assertion. He could have done so, however, since *Black Sunday* is one of the first films to acknowledge terrorist acts as spectacles carefully staged for the greatest possible mass media exposure, unlike crimes or acts of espionage (typical in earlier cold war films) that their perpetrators wish to perform in secrecy, ideally to remain forever undetected. In other words, *Black Sunday* vividly anticipates both Baudrillard's claim and its evident confirmation given the 9/11 attack's successful capture of the world's media: terrorism is an assault on the world's screens as much as an attack on human beings, who are viciously reduced to "collateral damage" when terrorism finds its actual targets.

The goal of this essay is to again take advantage of (admittedly impotent) hindsight in order to recover a single director's regular yet largely unacknowledged anticipation of the "war on terror" in his films. Looking back in order to see John Frankenheimer looking ahead, I hope to demonstrate that *Black Sunday* is not the unique and rather isolated work recent critics returning to it have suggested: if the film indeed has the dubious distinction of being, as Jack G.

Shaheen finds, "the first feature film to display Palestinian terrorists on American soil" (104), it nevertheless occupies a pivotal position within its director's oeuvre and one neglected by recent critics. In fact, *Black Sunday* is conveniently located between the films (and era) with which Frankenheimer remains largely identified (the 1960s) and our present condition, which he—perhaps more fully than many others—saw coming.

My repositioning of a number of Frankenheimer's later films in relation to a historical period that follows his own last feature film (*Reindeer Games*, 2000) may seem forced, if only because the director remains justly acclaimed for—yet, given the span of his career, too narrowly associated with—films that now define the cold war. *The Manchurian Candidate* (1962), as well as *Seven Days in May* (1964), are considered two of Hollywood's most significant engagements with their era's politics in a popular form. In *American Politics in Hollywood Film*, Ian Scott typically identifies *The Manchurian Candidate* as "the definitive Cold War conspiracy thriller of the Kennedy era" (113). At least three book-length studies of that single film attest not only to its still-dazzling cinematic style but especially to its status as one of the quintessential cultural artifacts of its historical period: for Stephen Badsey, "Above all, as a political thriller of its time, *The Manchurian Candidate* is a historian's film. It belongs not only to the history of Hollywood and the movies, but also to the wider political and social history that gave it life and shaped its reception. It is text, but even more it is context" (8). The stated goal of the most recent book devoted to the film, by Matthew Frye Jacobson and Gaspar González, is to provide "an analysis of the ways in which this text opens out onto larger questions and themes of American politics and culture in the Cold War years" (x). While *Seven Days in May* remains, perhaps like all of Frankenheimer's subsequent films, overshadowed by its unprecedented predecessor, it also now functions as a condensation of its historical moment, vividly depicting a world divided into politically antagonistic superpowers threatening one another with nuclear annihilation. While the ongoing appreciation of the central importance of Frankenheimer's cold war films is justified, the emphasis on them tends to reduce his later work not only to minor status within his own long career but to a kind of historical irrelevance in light of the keen ability of the earlier films to so fully capture the zeitgeist of their cold war context. Like the best-selling, contemporaneous spy novels of John Le Carré, Frankenheimer's cold war films achieve a rare balance between incisive critique of sociopolitical reality and thrilling entertainment in their summary of (at the time of their production) something like the paranoid national consciousness. Now, the earlier works of both popular artists function as historical documents of a rapidly fading era.

However, Frankenheimer's secure status as a major cold war filmmaker hasn't yet allowed for a full appreciation of a similar, prescient shift in his later work toward a focus on terrorism rather than the state-sponsored nuclear threats central to cold war politics and popular culture. Yet a number of

Frankenheimer's films from the 1970s through the 1990s find themselves, in Doug Davis's term, "telling war-on-terror stories before there was a war on terror" (17). In an illuminating post-9/11 essay reconsidering films made before 9/11, Davis traces the shift from cold war techno-thrillers (including *Seven Days in May*) to "stories that pitted cold-war military and intelligence institutions against terrorists," the latter now appearing to both anticipate the attacks of 9/11 and, in their details, miss the mark (often by continuing to rely on cold war myths and stereotypes that appear suddenly irrelevant). As Davis argues, however, "Changing enemies did not change the genre," and so many of the formulaic elements of the techno-thriller have remained in place in spite of wrenching changes in our view of global politics and violence (17). Davis analyzes *The Peacemaker* (1997) and *The Sum of All Fears* (released in 2002, but produced before 9/11), and effectively demonstrates their reliance upon earlier, increasingly anachronistic cold war models despite their new terrorist villains. Popular films produced in the wake of 9/11 and the war in Iraq have since adapted many of the thriller's generic conventions to reflect a world redefined by the actual, recent past rather than fantasized future terrorism, the "future-war" plots that, Davis argues, drove the cold war nuclear thriller: after 9/11, films no longer need to imagine nightmarish future terrorist attacks, but can draw upon the audience's vivid (even if mediated) memory of the real thing. Unlike the films Davis analyzes, most post-9/11 films now ignore any ongoing threat of nuclear terrorism, instead recognizing that improvised explosive devices, suicide bombers, and hijacked airplanes, while promising something less than total war and planetary annihilation, nevertheless possess their own, previously underestimated ability to terrorize audiences.

I would like to consider the ways in which some of Frankenheimer's later films anticipate what might be identified as the increasingly conventionalized "style of terrorism" now employed by popular films after 9/11. Instead of emphasizing the shifting thematic concerns that direct Frankenheimer's better-known cold war narratives toward the "war on terror," my emphasis will be on visual strategies that perhaps even more decisively mark historical changes in contemporary thrillers, whether directly engaged with contemporary events, like *Syriana* (2005), or dramatizing the war in Iraq, like *Redacted* (2007). In fact, the new cinematic texture of the "war on terror," available at the level of style as well as content, is dispersed through many more commercially successful thrillers that often only engage with current events obliquely or allegorically. Whether set amidst real or imaginary top-secret security agencies or military units, or often within the everyday world that now includes ubiquitous cell phones, global positioning system units, and computer screens, such films are marked by their almost continual representation of the post-9/11 world through virtual images or the pervasive mediation of electronic communications, often replacing the conventionally overlooked frame of the movie screen with images emphatically derived from digital cameras, industrial surveillance video, the internet, interactive video games, or camera-equipped military hardware (the latter often offering a "bombs-eye-view"). Such increasingly common images, whose sources are foregrounded (often by onscreen "information") rather than obscured when incorporated into fiction films, seem to announce the full arrival in popular cinema of the virtual distance from unmediated vision that theorists like Paul Virilio and Peter Sloterdijk (or the experimental filmmaker Harun Farocki) have traced through the development of ever-advanced technologies of war. As Rey Chow emphasizes:

> As a condition that is no longer separable from civilian life, war is thoroughly absorbed into the fabric of our daily communications—our information channels, our entertainment media, our machinery for speech and expression. We participate in war's virtualization of the world as we use—without thinking—television monitors, remote controls, mobile phones, digital cameras, PalmPilots, and other electronic devices that fill the spaces of everyday life. (34)

Working before many of these now everyday devices were widely and visibly available, Frankenheimer's films nevertheless often anticipate the "virtualized" world that critics such as Chow have sketched. Gerald Pratley, for instance, notes what he calls "the Frankenheimer television touch" in the ending of *Year of the Gun* (1991), a recourse to an emphasis on mediation within his narratives that Frankenheimer himself identifies as a means to bring characters "together—and to keep them apart" (209, 211). The critique found throughout Frankenheimer's work of the power and alienation made possible by mass media—a concern frequently acknowledged by critics as well as the director himself in interviews—is in fact among the most perceptive means by which he traces the shift from cold war paranoia among national leaders to the increased experience of the "war on terror" in everyday life.

Televising Terrorism after the Cold War

Revisiting films produced before 9/11 in his comprehensive study *Firestorm: American Film in the Age of Terrorism*, Stephen Prince identifies *Black Sunday* as an example of the once-popular "disaster film" that "morphed in a way that gave us the first prominent disaster spectacle that was also explicitly and emphatically about terrorism" (25). Moreover, Prince emphasizes how in this depiction of "terrorist acts carried out on American soil" it is clear that "what in 1977 seemed like outlandish fantasy has been overtaken by events" (27). Prince credits *Black Sunday* for its reliance on a rare "blowback theory of terrorist violence," which, unlike most other popular depictions of terrorism as simply "evil" or "crazy," acknowledges terrorist violence as often deriving from the "unintended consequences of foreign policy," including in this case U.S. support for Israel and anti-Palestinian policies (27). Prince notes that by providing its terrorists with political motives, Frankenheimer's film "is relatively singular among Hollywood movies about terrorism" (28). At the same time, that the Palestinian actions in the film stem from the desire for national liberation rather than Islamic fundamentalism distances the film historically from post-9/11 perspectives (28). In another extended critical discussion of *Black Sunday*, Tim Jon Semmerling provides a politically valid but often critically awkward analysis that devolves into rather risible psychoanalytic interpretation (viewing the hijacked blimp as breast-like, and thus itself a *femme fatale*, for example). I am entirely sympathetic with his recognition that the film, like others of its era, relies upon crude stereotyping of Arabs and Muslims (in this case mired with the gender anxieties created by an unconventional female terrorist), but his treatment of the film as relatively unique also unnecessarily isolates it from the director's career, and the analysis relies on descriptive plot summary to the near exclusion of the film's stylistic features. However, Semmerling does recognize that *Black Sunday*'s "use of real events . . . specific dates, real people . . . [and] real commercial labels . . . blends fiction and fantasy with the real world in order to create the fear that this just might happen in real life" (122–23). In interviews, Frankenheimer emphasized his unusual efforts to obtain realism in the film, which included securing an actual Goodyear Blimp (with its logo constantly visible), despite the nefarious use to which it would be put, and "getting the rights to the Super Bowl," which included filming action sequences during the actual event but without marring the game or its television broadcast (most remarkably when actor Robert Shaw ran the length of the field for a shot made during the actual game) (Pratley, *Films* 163–64). In some sense, *Black Sunday* acknowledges its own losing battle as a widescreen major motion picture against the pervasive power of broadcast television as the dominant medium of the postwar era (a cultural status to which Frankenheimer himself of course contributed significantly): the television broadcast of the Super Bowl obtains an audience that only the few, newly defined "blockbuster" films could dream of addressing, so terrorism is staged for television coverage, with whatever representation it finds in cinema increasingly irrelevant to its aims.

Beyond Frankenheimer's close association with cold war cinema, he is commonly identified as one of the key American filmmakers to have emerged from the first generation of artists trained in live television drama. In addition to their political context, his cold war films are simultaneously, and often emphatically, located in the period in American culture when television threatened to displace the important role that cinema had played in the lives of Americans for the previous half-century. Unsurprisingly, then, a number of the most prominent sequences in *The Manchurian Candidate* emphasize the role of television, a subject about which Frankenheimer had much insider knowledge, in the representation and manipulation of political reality. In his innovative television work, Frankenheimer had already experimented with complex framing that included television screens within his images, dramatically suggesting through framing alone the gap between reality and representation that might be opened up even across the unified space of a single room, between source and transmission. This recognition is intensified in *Black Sunday*, even though it centers on an ostensibly "unpolitical" sporting event. Nevertheless, Frankenheimer's bid for realism—freely mixing his actors with actual athletes and sportscasters "playing themselves," and fully intertwining his staged event with footage documenting an actual sporting event—points toward the key later shift I have already noted in popular films following the events of 9/11, when frightening predictions of the future could be immediately replaced by terrifying memories (and footage) of the actual past. Terrorism, we have come to realize, brutally stages our destructive fantasies—perhaps our nightmares—in reality, secure in the assumption that reality is now always recorded and replayed, immediately mediated. One of the many ironies of the "war on terror" has been to introduce even more cameras into the world: their aim to provide pervasive security also ensures that any future attacks will receive the media attention their perpetrators seek. The 9/11 attacks dared to presume—rightly, it turned out—that cameras would be ready to capture the first strike of the World Trade Center on film: the first strike then ensured that the second strike would be recorded by hundreds of cameras. Almost twenty-five years earlier, Frankenheimer's *Black Sunday* already imagines similar conditions, with the terrorists counting on network television coverage to highlight and magnify their own production. In its construction, the film blurs the ever-evaporating distinction between dramatization and documentation. One might even suggest that Frankenheimer's film anticipates post-9/11 "reality television," which is widely understood and readily accepted as a staged, manipulated representation of "reality" for savvy or cynical audiences who no longer believe in the possibility of raw, unfiltered reality.

In addition to its prescient shift from a basis in cold war nuclear anxieties to terrorism with sources in Middle Eastern conflicts, and its perhaps even more significant recognition of the spectacular aims of terrorism to capture the attention of the media, *Black Sunday* also anticipates some of the conventions of later cinema usually thought to derive from more recent historical contexts. Viewed today, it also shows its age: the opening sequence, in which a terrorist cell in Beirut watches the confession in Vietnam of the American prisoner of war Michael Lander (Bruce Dern), whom they will recruit (exploiting his disaffection with the United States) to pilot the deadly Goodyear Blimp, is screened as a 16 mm print, a relic that the compactness, ease, and low cost of video would soon replace as the medium of choice for terrorist communication (facilitating the unprecedented genre of martyr videos recorded by terrorists before a suicide mission). However, the following sequence, in which Black September member Dahlia Iyad (Marthe Keller) makes an audio recording of the sort Osama bin Laden would later call his "messages to the world," does emphasize the sort

The culture of surveillance in *Black Sunday* (Paramount, 1977).
Digital frame enlargement.

of inexpensive but highly effective media that would be used by international terrorists for decades to come. After the terrorist cell is attacked by Israeli commandoes, an establishing shot in the Israeli embassy in Washington is careful to include a bank of five glowing television screens linked to surveillance cameras before cutting to an extreme close-up of the tape recorder that will repeat her message. As Israeli intelligence team leader David Kabakov (Robert Shaw) warns the officials around him, "This tape is not a threat: it is to be used after the attack." In general, the film relies upon the high-tech trappings of most modern thrillers, including numerous shots of both news cameras and the audiovisual tools of various police and intelligence agencies.

In its frequent use of aerial shots (especially of Miami and its Orange Bowl stadium), *Black Sunday* also inherits the long tradition traced by Paul Virilio and others of the close relationship between war and cinema, with the view of the earth from above increasingly treating the world below as a target. Eventually such images, now common in popular cinema, would no longer require a cameraman to go aloft in a balloon or airplane but would be made by remote-controlled satellites or other devices (including cameras fitted onto missiles), or would render the earth virtually rather than through actual views of the ground—the ground again understood as a target for attack rather than simply a space to be observed from an increased distance. Viewed after 9/11, the conclusion of *Black Sunday* functions less as classically constructed suspense (in which we are privy to escalating violence in the air while a large crowd remains oblivious to the danger fast approaching them) than as a cross-cut sequence that offers competing media spectacles: the regulated violence of football against the threat of large-scale terrorism. Kavakov's suggestion that the Super Bowl be cancelled is rejected as not just difficult but unthinkable, and so the two activities will vie for audience attention until the attack eventually overwhelms any remaining interest in the game.

"Terrorism from the Inside"

Black Sunday has recently compelled critics to reconsider it as a fictional precursor to 9/11, but they have not relocated it in relation to Frankenheimer's own return to the topic of terrorism in subsequent films. Historians of terrorism have often noted that the concept, after 9/11, has become misleadingly narrowed to an almost exclusive application to Arab and Muslim political violence, obscuring the practice of terrorism by other groups and cultures (including "homegrown" American terrorism without any "international" component). Frankenheimer's *Year of the Gun* is located very specifically in Italy (primarily Rome) in early 1978, and depicts the events leading up to the kidnapping of former prime minister and Christian Democrat Aldo Moro on March 16 (his murdered body was discovered almost two months later). Its neglect in recent accounts of terrorism and film perhaps stems from its focus on a place and time that no longer command the attention of terrorism scholarship. In the film, two American journalists, writer David Raybourne (Andrew McCarthy) and photographer Alison King (Sharon Stone), are caught up in the drama, in part through their personal connections to Professor Italo Bianchi (John Pankow) and Lia (Valeria Golino), David's lover, who are both affiliated to the Red Brigades through personal rather than political ties. Although there are continual suspicions that both David and Alison must have CIA connections, simply because they are Americans, they are in fact both attempting only to record the events they witness, David by writing a novel, Alison through her up-close photographs of Red Brigade bank robberies. Rather than later films centered around terrorism, the film resembles the vogue for films in the previous decade depicting intrepid white (usually American) reporters attempting to cover volatile international politics and failing to maintain their neutrality, such as *The Year of Living Dangerously* (1982), *Under Fire* (1983), and *Salvador* (1986). When Alison discovers that David is writing a book about the Red Brigades (depicting, she says, "terrorism from the inside"), she wishes to collaborate by providing accompanying photos, but David demurs that his work is simply a travel book. The plot later hinges on his depiction of the kidnapping of Aldo Moro in his novel, a scenario suggested by his newspaper editor boss, which inadvertently reveals the actual plans of the Red Brigades. At one point, David suggests one of his (and the film's) models, Frederick Forsyth's 1971 best-selling novel *The Day of the Jackal* (filmed by Fred Zinnemann in 1973), which wove the historical Charles De Gaulle into its thriller conventions much as *Year of the Gun* incorporates Aldo Moro into its fiction. Except for Alison's camera (whose viewfinder at times becomes our screen as well), and a device that distorts a character's voice when he speaks on the phone, the film is notably low-tech: David even writes on a manual typewriter. Frankenheimer indulges once again in his penchant for including shots of televisions, when a press conference at the airport (taking place as Lia and her son arrive) is shown later on the television in Lia's apartment, a blending of an event and its representation that seems coincidental until Lia is much later revealed to be a part of the Red Brigade faction that is planning to kidnap Moro.

Only in an ironic, somewhat surprising ending does Frankenheimer's film suggest the stylistic traits of later "war on terror" films. Having barely escaped with their lives (Alison is called upon to photograph the murdered Lia, whom the Red Brigades have executed as a traitor, and David is badly beaten), the journalists are depicted sometime later on a TV talk show (hosted by Dick Cavett), promoting their collaborative best-seller, *The Year of the Gun*. Asked uncomfortable questions about the fine line between reporting on terrorism and promoting it, David and Alison show that they are obviously somewhat pained by their success. However, Frankenheimer stages the sequence in his distinctive style: David is in the studio (where the next guest is, suggestively, the United Nations ambassador from Iran), but Alison appears on a TV screen in the studio via a live feed from war-torn Beirut, presumably the next hot spot in her career (she earlier recounted witnessing a harrowing event in Vietnam).

When David and Alison seem to exchange grim glances following the interview, they do so only through media, bridging the international space as well as whatever emotional gulf now isolates them. After Frankenheimer's camera moves toward the television screen containing her, so that its borders and

David (Andrew McCarthy) and Alison (Sharon Stone) isolated and connected by mass media in *Year of the Gun* (Initial Films 1991).

Digital frame enlargement.

those of the film we are watching align, a single shot of Alison looking directly at the camera (which editing alone suggests allows her and David to look at one another directly) is visibly distinct from the images of her on a monitor in the television studio, briefly slipping out of the explicit mediation that both isolates the couple in space and defines their own silently acknowledged distance from the events they now represent professionally following their emotional involvement in them. As the feed from Beirut is cut, the television monitor and Frankenheimer's film both end with electronic static filling each screen. From an art cinema director like Jean-Luc Godard working in the same period, the image might suggest the continually predicted "death of cinema" at the hands of video, but it also resembles dozens of shots of assaulted video cameras and corrupted videotapes or hard drives in contemporary cinema, the illegible images of "digital disintegration" that Garrett Stewart has recently defined as a persistent feature of films that openly acknowledge their failure to represent the war in Iraq (46).

The Virtual Style of the "War on Terror"

Although it follows *Black Sunday* by twenty years and *Year of the Gun* by almost a decade, *Ronin* (1998) still seems like a transitional film, insofar as its heist conventions and concern with "the Russians" and "the IRA" obtaining the mysterious silver case at the narrative's center—for the entire film a McGuffin of unrevealed content—still suggest residual cold war narratives, with the French setting providing a geographical mid-point between older Western and Eastern European interests. Unlike the earlier films, *Ronin*'s references to terrorism are perfunctory and even cautious. In the film's final moments, one of its principal villains, Seamus O'Rourke (Jonathan Pryce), is identified by a CNN reporter as an "Irish terrorist," albeit a "rogue breakaway operative" denounced by the IRA, a qualification encouraging us to understand that personal profit rather than group politics really drives the film's characters. If O'Rourke is in fact a "rogue," no longer affiliated with the IRA, his casual identification as a "terrorist" might even be misplaced: in any case, this is the film's sole invocation of the designation, now common in popular cinema for identifying villains of all stripes.

Like *Black Sunday* and *Year of the Gun*, however, *Ronin* also includes a sexy and perhaps traitorous European woman, here as mysterious leader of a band of international mercenaries. With the sort of self-reflexivity familiar from his earlier films, Frankenheimer also fills this film with the high-tech tools central to spy films and cold war thrillers. Sam (Robert De Niro), the American thief, frequently relies on binoculars and a camera, used surreptitiously when he masquerades as a common tourist, to plan the heist that drives the first part of the story. A few shots mimic Frankenheimer's extensive use of television in his earlier films: a doomed Russian ice skater, the victim of an assassin hidden in the rafters of an arena, is briefly glimpsed in a frame that includes her as well as her television image, and her violent death is yet another moment in the director's work that brings together violence and its capture on live television. But the film's reliance during a key sequence on the traitorous ex-KGB computer expert Gregor (Stellan Skarsgård) most fully updates the film for its contemporary audience, even if his bulky equipment nevertheless now dates the film as well.

For its first third, *Ronin* is vaguely contemporary, with its Paris setting initially providing few cues to its time period; only the quiet arrival of computers and cell phones into the narrative fully locates the story in the present, defined by cutting-edge technologies rather than the global conflicts this film keeps largely offscreen. While the small team of assembled mercenaries undertakes its plan to retrieve the case, Deirdre (Natascha McElhone) drives a van with Gregor in back, monitoring the action as it unfolds on his computer screen. In verbal communication with the others, he guides the operation through his superior, but mediated, vantage point. Although he is literally on the ground along with his colleagues, his perception takes the position of an omniscient overseer, and the sequence is constructed by cross-cutting between the action seen directly onscreen and indirectly, on the computer screen onscreen, with frequent high-angle shots providing an intermediary distance reminiscent of *Black Sunday*'s ominous aerial point of attack.

Although it is located in a "heist" or "caper" film, the sequence anticipates a future in which "war" will be waged increasingly if not exclusively through video-game-like technology, in the sort of scenario now commonly played out not only within but across the entire length of recent popular films. Indeed, no sequence in Frankenheimer's work anticipates the style of post-9/11 cinema more fully than this one, which tellingly begins with a fade in and Gregor's offscreen announcement, "System activated," as a rapid series of maps on a computer screen resolve into a grid of the space in Monaco where the ensuing sequence will take place. Echoing the concluding shot of *Year of the Gun* that collapses the film screen and a dead television channel, the computer screen and film screen here are briefly indistinguishable until a cut allows us to see the computer as an object within Frankenheimer's larger frame. Gregor's sophisticated electronic maps now replace earlier, crudely drawn maps or simple diagrams with still photos attached, typically inspected in the planning scenes of heist films. Soon, a direct cut from Gregor's map of Nice to a traffic sign reading "NICE" renders the latter, although placed in the actual geographical location, only a severely limited perspective on the space compared to Gregor's virtual, global view. Gregor's simulated view of the sequence that follows will continue to be intercut with the events he directs (much like a filmmaker) from his semi-omniscient perspective, a position that allows him to anticipate and control the moves of his colleagues and their prey.

This sequence fully anticipates the increasingly elaborate but commonplace scenes that Garrett Stewart describes in recent cinema: "Regular intercutting from strategic control centers to war zones is stretched at times, beyond the

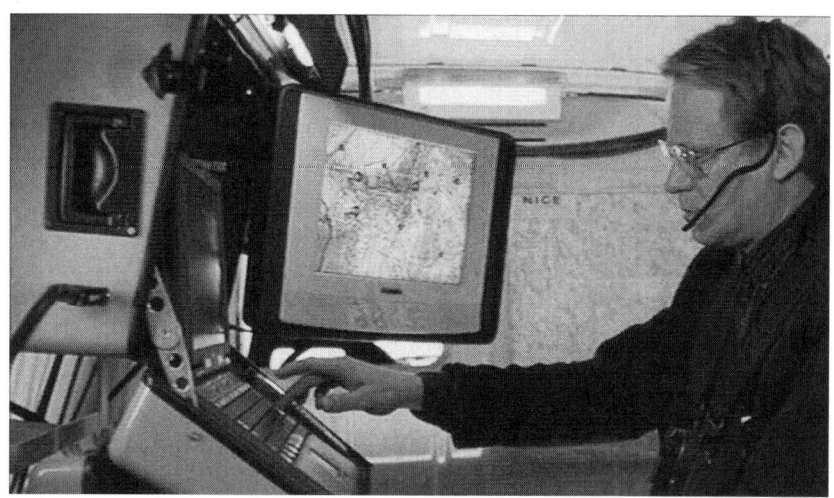

Gregor (Stellan Skarsgård) directs a scene on the computer screen, on Frankenheimer's movie screen, in *Ronin* (FGM Entertainment, 1998).

Digital frame enlargement.

immediate span of telecommunication, to full-blown parallel editing across hemispheric distances . . . in what amounts to a geopolitics of montage" (47). More recent thrillers, such as *Syriana* (2005), *Body of Lies* (2008), *Eagle Eye* (2008), or even the willfully outrageous *Crank* (2006), in which spatial transitions are unnecessarily announced with animated shots of GPS mapping, provide the perspective occupied by *Ronin*'s Gregor regularly, and in some cases almost continuously: shots identified as derived from satellites or surveillance cameras are nearly as frequent as "neutral" shots from an unobtrusive camera in *Eagle Eye*, for instance, and the bravura sequence in which Jason Bourne negotiates the cameras that monitor (almost) every inch of London's Waterloo Station in *The Bourne Ultimatum* (2007) can serve as a representative example of what has become a dominant trend in recent cinema. As in the Nice chase sequence in *Ronin*, but now greatly extended, we shift between perspectives that place us at the center of furious action (often reinforced in *Ronin* by point-of-view shots through car windshields) and what is understood to be a global view, extending the bird's-eye, aerial shots with which Frankenheimer introduces Nice and later Arles. We swoop into Arles, indeed, through a slow descent toward an open-air arena that cannot help but invoke the director's attack on Miami's Orange Bowl from *Black Sunday*.

Frankenheimer's aerial shots—which are repeated throughout the film, although not always in scene-setting panoramic views—still imply a human perspective, achieved through the standard technologies of airplanes, helicopters, or even blimps, whereas the global perspective glimpsed on Gregor's computer in *Ronin* and dominating more recent films removes the requirements of human scale and origin. A later, even more spectacular car chase in the film, however thrilling, reverts to the norms of similar sequences in earlier films in seeking to place us within rather than above, or in virtual relation to, the action.

John Frankenheimer's long career as a filmmaker ended just as the post-9/11 era of the (spuriously named, dubiously engaged) "war on terror" began. Although direct representations of that "war" and the more conventional conflicts it has led to in Afghanistan and Iraq have generally failed to attract audiences, the slight displacement of the virtual technologies associated with security and surveillance into more popular thrillers and actions films has perhaps permanently obscured the once-significant difference between the movie screen and the screens of laptop computers, cell phones, and other forms of new media (this at a time, of course, when the computer screen as a venue for motion picture presentation has markedly intensified). Perhaps fated to be remembered as one of the key chroniclers of the cold war rather than the "war on terror," some of Frankenheimer's films produced before 9/11 nevertheless anticipated the world to come, first through his keen awareness of the complicated interaction between television, politics, and violence, which he chose to represent on movie screens, and eventually through his extension of that critique to include the onscreen computer screen, which now threatens to render television as antiquated as cinema. Now part of our past, the "war on terror" that Frankenheimer in some measure foresaw, is an element of this visionary filmmaker's career that demands another look.

The Burning Season

Environmentalism versus Progress?

ROBIN L. MURRAY

According to a 1969 interview with Gerald Pratley, many of the films of John Frankenheimer "concern the individual trying to find himself in society and trying to maintain his individuality in a mechanized world" (qtd. in Ecksel). In the interview Frankenheimer explains, "I do feel that society wants everybody to be exactly the same. It's so much easier. I think the theme of the indomitability of the human spirit is very much there, and the fight against regimentation" (qtd. in Ecksel). That indomitability of human spirit certainly underpins the narrative of *The Burning Season* (1994), a biopic of Chico Mendes (Francisco Alves Mendes Filho), the leader of Brazil's Rural Workers' Union, who from 1977 to 1988 fought to preserve the livelihood of Amazon rubber tappers and develop their standard of living and educational prospects. In *The Burning Season*, Mendes (Raúl Julia) heroically battles corrupt businessmen, politicians, and ranchers to provide a better life for rural workers, who tap rubber trees for their latex. Saving the rainforest means saving the tappers' jobs, jobs Mendes strives to equate with communal progress.

As a hero, Mendes resembles a pioneer who sacrifices himself for the good of his people and their wild frontier. Pioneers in western culture are associated with both progress and sacrifice. According to American mythology, for example, American pioneers cultivated a wild frontier for either personal gain or community development or both. Richard Slotkin explores the significance of this frontier myth in American history and culture, viewing America's westward expansion and search for new frontiers as violent transformations based in a drive to develop and settle the "wild." Once the frontier closed in 1890 (see Turner), Americans sought new frontiers to exploit, especially those rooted in industry and technology. But, as Slotkin asserts, "Within the purlieus of a commercial and increasingly industrialized popular culture, the genres that carried the Myth of the Frontier became the site of a cultural contest between two different schools of American ideology" (22): "progressive" and "populist."

Martyrdom opens *The Burning Season* (HBO, 1994).
Digital frame enlargement.

Slotkin's definition of the "progressive style" lines up with corporations like those supporting the burnings for both roads and ranches that we see in *The Burning Season*.

According to Slotkin, "The 'progressive' style uses the Frontier Myth in ways that buttress the ideological assumptions and political aims of a corporate economy and a managerial politics" (22). The populist view, on the other hand, "values decentralization, idealizes the small farmer-artisan-financer, and either devalues (or opposes) the assumption of a Great Power role or asserts that the nation derives both moral and political power from its populist character" (22–23). Both styles, however, draw on "the relevance of something called 'the Frontier' as a way of explaining and rationalizing what is most distinctive and valuable in 'the American way'" (23–24).

Pioneers, however, may also align with either tragic or comic narrative structures and the narratives of the natural world on which theories of evolution have been built. According to Joseph Meeker, humans typically embrace a tragic evolutionary narrative, as in *The Odyssey* (162), a position that may cost humanity its existence: "We demand that one species, our own, achieve unchallenged dominance where hundreds of species lived in complex equilibrium before our arrival" (164). Meeker believes humanity has "a growing need to learn from the more stable comic heroes of nature, the animals" (164).

The evolutionary narrative of *The Burning Season* explores what might happen if humanity did learn from these more stable comic heroes, since, according to Meeker, "evolution itself is a gigantic comic drama, not the bloody tragic spectacle imagined by the sentimental humanists of early Darwinism. . . . The evolutionary process is one of adaptation and accommodation, with the various species exploring opportunistically their environments in search of a means to maintain their existence. Like comedy, evolution is a matter of muddling through" (164). For Meeker, successful evolution encourages communal action, to ensure survival, rather than formation of a tragic hero.

The figure of Chico Mendes complicates definitions of a tragic hero. Although Mendes does fight to the death to preserve his community's way of life, he fights without weapons or violence, using words and collective non-violent demonstration to advance his union message, and fails to fit in categories of tragic or comic heroes. Mendes sacrifices himself not as a solitary pioneer but as a leader of a group, and he ultimately builds a durable community where the goal is survival of all rather than, as with the tragic heroes described by Joseph W. Meeker, "destruction of all our competitors and . . . achieving effective dominance over other forms of life" (162). For Meeker, ecological pioneers are "the loners of the natural world, the tragic heroes who sacrifice themselves in satisfaction of mysterious inner commands which they alone can hear" (161).

Mendes sacrifices himself not as a solitary pioneer but as a leader of a group, and he ultimately builds a durable community where the goal is survival of the community rather than, as with tragic heroes, "survival through the destruction of all our competitors and [. . .] achieving effective dominance over other forms of life" (162). Mendes, then, connects the martyrdom of the tragic hero with the more communal aspects of the comic, and ultimately contributes to a vision of sustainable development that moves beyond progressive and populist styles and the violence that "regenerates" them both. In an interview with Alex Simon, Frankenheimer clarifies this focus on political themes or sociopolitical overtones. According to Frankenheimer, "It stems from the fact that when I was in high school, I started disagreeing with my father on politics because he was really very conservative. He really wanted the status quo. I didn't want the status quo." This same inclination seems to inspire the hero of *The Burning Season*. Implicitly acknowledging traditional Marxist visions of the hero, Andrew Revkin writes in the preface to the 2004 edition of his book that inspired the film, "With all Mendes's successes, the central lesson of his life may well be that the vigilance and resolve of the individual must be passed to the community, and then down from one generation protecting an environmental legacy to the next" (xxi).

Chico Mendes (Raúl Julia) fills the screen as a hero of the people. Digital frame enlargement.

Chico Mendes: Martyr and Tragic Hero

Before this vision of community connects tragic and comic, however, *The Burning Season* first establishes Mendes as a tragic hero. After explaining, "This is a true story," the film highlights Frankenheimer's use of Steadicam as it opens on a statue of a martyred Christ figure, rotating through 360 degrees around its pierced torso and tormented face. However, when the film's narrator asserts that for generations workers who harvested rubber treasured the forest and lived in fear of the men who enslaved them and exploited their labor, the film connects that Christ figure with its hero (Raúl Julia), turning "truth" into myth: "Finally a man was born who would fight back," the narrator exclaims. "His name was Chico Mendes."

From the film's beginning, then, Mendes is constructed as a tragic hero, a lone male figure who must "fight to the end" and sacrifice himself for the greater good, the livelihood of Amazon rubber tappers threatened by corporate ranchers and their greed. According to Ken Tucker, "The script by Ron Hutchinson and the direction of John Frankenheimer cast the subject as nothing less than Brazil's naïve but noble savior. We rarely see him doing anything but making grand pronouncements about justice; the occasional scenes with his wife, Ilzamar (Kamala Dawson), are trite" (Tucker n.p.).

The Burning Season constructs Mendes as a "naïve and noble savior," a hero who stands apart from the status quo, from a childhood in which he learns the rubber trade from his father until his murder by the "thugs" he seems to have defeated. As a boy in 1951, in Cachoeira, Brazil, for example, Chico accompanies his father to the estate boss's rubber weighing station and watches the man (Luis Guzmán) move the needle on the scale. The boss declares a weight of forty kiloliters, in spite of the initial weight of seventy on display. A stranger, later revealed to be union organizer Wilson Pinheiro (Edward James Olmos), looks on and asks the boss if the weight is accurate, but when the boss shows his strength, Pinheiro acquiesces, admitting he is new to the Amazon. Chico sets himself apart from his family when he smiles at the stranger while he and his father are leaving, but he also registers his questioning of the boss and asks his father whether or not the weight the boss provides is accurate. "If he says it's forty, it's forty," the father answers. "It's bad business, but it's all we've got. Maybe life will be better in the next world." But Chico seems unconvinced, and, perhaps because he notices Chico's dissatisfaction, Wilson Pinheiro joins the boy and his father in the rainforest, providing Chico with a mentor for the union work that serves as the catalyst for his roles as both tragic and comic hero.

Wilson's arrival in the forest also seems to ignite Chico's desire for an education, what he later sees as the path to his people's freedom. When Chico teaches Wilson the rubber trade in exchange for reading lessons, however, he also demonstrates his connection with the forest and his strength as the Amazon's advocate. Chico teaches him to tap rubber but tells Wilson not to dig too deep in the trees. A montage of shots of the pristine forest illustrates the lessons Wilson learns about tapping rubber. Chico teaches him not to take too much, or the little man of the forest "won't like it" and will "swallow you up."

Also in exchange, Wilson gives Chico math lessons so he can be canny about the price of rubber in relation to the greed of the area bosses. While Chico prepares Wilson to lead the Rural Workers as one of their own, Wilson teaches Chico how to lead the union and ensure that its members will have a better life built on an education that will protect them from the greed of the bosses.

To illustrate both the power of the bosses and the consequences faced by tragic heroes who defy their greed, the film bridges to a procession lit by burning torches when Wilson lights a match with his thumb after explaining the true price of rubber to Chico. The procession is leading a rubber worker to his death because, we later learn, he attempted to form a union. Peasants watch as a boss burns the rubber tapper to death. Still a child, Chico watches, not allowing his father to cover his eyes. The boss exclaims, "He knew the punishment when he tried to form a union. He knew this would happen." As a witness to this torture, Chico seems to dedicate his life to the cause of the Rural Workers Union, setting himself apart from his father—who looked on without acting—and from the rest of his community as a tragic hero-pioneer willing to sacrifice himself for the greater good.

Yet it is not only because he dedicates his life to the union that Chico is established as a tragic hero in the film. Although Camilo Gomides argues that it erases the connections with Christ established in Revkin's book, the film also carefully aligns Chico with martyred Christ figures, from the opening shot till the ending. The opening view of the martyred Christ statue returns in several scenes in the film. A martyred Christ at the front of the village's Catholic church connects with both Wilson and Chico, and with their work for the union. In a nod to the church and another reference to martyrdom, Wilson asserts during a first union meeting, "Christ would put his body between the chainsaws and the rubber trees." The assassination of Wilson literally establishes him as a martyr for the union members he supports.

But Chico's martyrdom is graphically presented, not only during his own assassination but also while, and after, the federal police torture him in retribution for union members' murder of Wilson's assassin. Before Chico's future wife Ilzamar (Kamala Dawson) heals his wounds, Chico is constructed as a martyred Christ figure with camera shots panning down and around the martyred statue that opened the film before revealing his figure in a hammock, bloodied and immobile like the statue. At Chico's son's funeral, too, the martyred-Christ image is evoked again through the crucifix carried to the grave. And the martyred-Christ image is on display in the church when Chico is summoned to stop the ranchers from destroying the rainforest for roads and ranch land.

Most powerfully, however, Chico is martyred by his assassins when they kill him to avenge their loss of land. Chico's funeral procession ends the film. Now that he has become a martyr, his face literally replaces that of the Christ figure on the cross that leads the procession. The Christ figure that opened the film has been replaced by Chico's fallen body and face on the cross. The implication is that, as Christ redeemed us, Chico Mendes saved at least part of the rainforest and preserved the rubber tappers' livelihood.

Complicating the Hero: When Progressive and Populist Views Are Thwarted

On the surface, *The Burning Season* follows the narrative pattern of a typical classic American western film like *Shane* (1953), in which the "little guy" triumphs over the corporate "big guy" with help from a mythic tragic hero. In fact, a businessman flying over the burning Amazon even proclaims that there will be ranch land from horizon to horizon, once the territory is cleared and the road is built, and refers to American western themes as an explanation: "That's how the American pioneers did it," he declares, "and that's how we're going to do it. . . . When I see fire, I see the future." Businessmen like this represent a fair-use view of the environment, which sees environmental laws and regulations as diminishing the value of land by limiting its use.

Revkin also associates the Amazon with the American Wild West in his book *The Burning Season*. Describing the local rancher Darli Alves da Silva (Tomas Milian), one of Chico's "most dangerous foes," Revkin asserts that "Darli was confident he could act with impunity" once he moved to the Amazon. As Revkin explains, "His brother worked in the Xapuri sheriff's office, just forty paces from Mendes's front door, and the sheriff was a good friend of the family." According to Revkin, "The main reason Darli had moved to the Amazon was that it was one of the last places where might still made right" (10). For Revkin, such a perspective connected the Amazon to the American West: "In that sense it differed little from the American West of the nineteenth century, as described in 1872 by Mark Twain in *Roughing It*: 'The very paradise of outlaws and desperadoes'" (10).

But *The Burning Season* moves beyond the conflict between progressivism and populism foregrounded in most western films to illustrate a way to provide for both human and nonhuman nature: sustainable development through nonviolence rather than, as Richard Slotkin explains, regeneration through violence. Even though the film dilutes Mendes's attempt to maintain an interdependent relationship with nonhuman nature with its push toward conservation, Julia's performance reinforces Mendes's goal: sustainable development as an environmentally friendly means to build a better life for himself and his community.

Although Chico Mendes and members of the Rural Workers Union seem at first to draw on the populist style that Slotkin describes, their protection of the Amazon rainforest for a sustainable livelihood conflicts with visions of the frontier as a source of economic development. Instead of exploiting resources as do corporate ranchers, rubber tappers like Chico Mendes preserve the forest and its trees, if only to stave off the mythic "little man" who protects the Amazon from the fires deliberately set to destroy the forest for both road and ranch.

Sequences of fires dissolving into more fires serve as a bridge to the year 1983, when the destruction of the rainforest has escalated the conflict between progressive businessmen and ranchers on one side and populist union workers on the other. The individual progressive perspective illustrated by these images of burning rainforest is contrasted with the populist perspective represented by the Rural Workers Union leader, Wilson, who is organizing the rubber tappers. In the front of a church sanctuary, Wilson explains, "Together we're united," as he demonstrates how much stronger a bundle of twigs is than a single twig. According to Wilson, they have the law on their side, since the law says they can keep land they have made productive. They also have the strength of the collective and its populist goals to support their battle with the corporate ranchers. To illustrate the strength of that collective, Wilson leads members of the Rural

Workers Union, Chico, and other rubber tappers in a demonstration against the Amazon Road builders and their chainsaws. But it is Chico who effectively stops the destruction by telling the road builders they need a union more than the rubber tappers do. Here Frankenheimer emphasizes Chico's powerful presence with a wide-angle shot that nearly fills both foreground and background with extreme depth and focus, a signature camera move.

Chico's methods set him apart from both Wilson and the ranchers he defies, since he relies on his wits rather than on a demonstration of collective strength to stop the chainsaws. After the demonstration, Chico moves beyond Wilson's perspective on the collective when he takes steps toward sustainable development that will ensure both human and nonhuman nature will thrive. When Wilson asserts that the rubber tappers need to organize before they can succeed, Chico disagrees, arguing that first they need a school and the education it will provide: "What good is an organization without education? An educated man is the beginning of a movement." Chico wants his community to both preserve the forest and develop culturally and economically, while Wilson concentrates on economic development. Chico begins to work full-time for the union to support his goals.

The conflict between the tappers and the businessmen who seek to clear the rainforest for profit escalates as the union gains power. The businessmen now have a politician to back their plans, Galvao (Tony Plana), who is running for state deputy. According to Galvao, the road is "a matter of national security" and has his support. He and the businessmen will do what it takes to ensure the rubber tappers are destroyed. In metaphor, they even illustrate their plan to assassinate Wilson, saying that if there is "no queen, there's no nest. No nest, no termites." Darli Alves accomplishes the assassination. Now, Wilson has been martyred, passing his leadership role on to Chico.

Chico's first duty as the union leader is to announce Wilson's death on the radio, but as a peaceful demonstrator he tells the union members, "Don't fight back. That's what they want." When one of the rubber tappers seeks revenge, Chico and other union members are arrested and tortured. The torture scenes are graphic and both establish Chico as a martyr and highlight the violence of a progressive view. The police assault Chico with electrodes, hang him upside down and beat him, and then throw him out of their jeep into the street where children find him and take him to Ilzamar for help.

The scene first establishes Chico as a martyr, but it also highlights the work Chico must do to sustain both the forest and the rubber tappers he represents. He nearly leaves once Ilzamar heals him, but when he sees the convoy of Borden Company trucks and equipment go back to destroy the forest for the Amazon highway, he leaves the bus and goes back to the union office to rebuild and reignite the work Wilson began. When he looks at the photographs of dead tappers, he declares, "No more widows. No more orphans."

In contrast, Galvao, vying against Chico for the State Deputy post, advocates for a progressivist view with support from ranchers, businessmen, and even the military police. After the police band introduces him, for example, Galvao broaches his ideals in support of his campaign: "Why shouldn't we have what everyone else has? . . . We have wide open pastures . . . resources . . . space enough. . . . Amazonia will feed the hungry world and make each of you wealthy men." He argues that Chico and his union "are going against progress. They want you to stay poor, as if there were something wrong with developing the land that God has given us." The struggle between progressivist and populist views is unmistakable during this campaign, and "the big guys" strike a devastating victory, Chico losing the race with only 10 percent of the vote. Galvao and his supporters offer chainsaws in exchange for votes.

Environmentalism versus Progress?

The film both foregrounds Frankenheimer's use of the Steadicam and connects Chico's work with a global environmental movement at the point when a documentary filmmaker, Steven Kaye (Nigel Havers), arrives to document the workers' struggle. According to Frankenheimer, "Seventy-five percent of *The Burning Season* was on steadicam" (Rhys and Bage). The Kaye character introduces a second conflict to the film, that between the deep ecology represented by radical environmentalists and the sustainable development supported by Chico and his Rural Workers Union. According to an article in *Environment*, development is sustainable when "it meets the needs of the present without compromising the ability of future generations to meet their own needs" (Kates et al. 10). Chico's work for his union depends on sustainable development principles, connecting rural workers with their environment to sustain both. Deep ecologists, on the other hand, believe that "the environmental movement must shift from an anthropocentric to a biocentric perspective" (Guha 232) and accordingly separate humans from nonhuman nature. According to Guha, deep ecologists also "focus on the preservation of unspoiled wilderness—and the restoration of degraded areas to a more pristine condition—to a relative (and sometimes absolute) neglect of other issues on the environmental agenda" (233). The environmentalists Chico encounters in Miami, Washington D.C., and New York City support principles of deep ecology, especially the preservation of an unspoiled wilderness. Ultimately, however, his work for sustainable development effectively fuses with deep-ecology politics, providing a viable solution for himself, his people, and the Amazon—if only temporarily.

Steven Kaye's documentation of Chico's work gives a broader voice to Chico's message to ranchers and other developers. Kaye arrives immediately before what seems like a failed attempt to stop another effort to cut down the forest for the road. Chico and Rural Workers Union members demonstrate against the destruction but cannot stop the chainsaws. In fact, one of the union members is cut by a chainsaw, and Alves and his cattle block Chico's truck when he races the union member to the hospital. Since the wounded union member loses his arm, however, the rainforest destruction halts temporarily. Even though the Borden Company behind the road construction claims it is departing because of seasonal rains, Kaye asserts that the boss doesn't know what to do about Chico and declares the departure a victory. Chico disagrees: "This road . . . the ranchers need it to make their investment in the land pay off. They'll be back." Chico pledges to stop the road and preserve the rainforest for the rubber tapping that sustains them. When he and Kaye share a cigarette, however, Frankenheimer uses the fire from his match as a bridge to fires four years later that illustrate the return of the road construction forces.

To combat the fires and the road they represent, Kaye documents smoke and fires to share with environmental groups and invite Chico to go to Miami for a World Bank Conference. When Chico's race for the state deputy position fails, he agrees to go, since it is now evident that to save the forest for his community of rubber tappers and their way of life he must build global support. After his election loss, Chico asks a boy from Alves's ranch, Genesio (Jonathan Carrasco), "How do you know when to give up?" The boy tells him, "You don't. You go down fighting." That fight takes him to Miami for the Inter-American Development Bank Conference, where he confronts excesses like uneaten food and the contempt of an Italian banker, who declares, "You are bad for business."

In a sudden shift, however, the seemingly insurmountable conflict between deep ecology and sustainable development is resolved. In a speech broadcast over television, Chico claims his union and environmentalists around the world "can work together" because they "have the same goal." If things don't change, Chico explains, they won't have a forest but a desert.

Conclusion

When Chico returns to Brazil, the road building has stopped, and he is greeted with cheers. A final battle is fought between the ranchers and union members, however, when Alves is given a deed for 15,000 more acres of the very land the tappers are trying to protect. Chico cannot talk Alves out of building a road, so he organizes a large peaceful demonstration to stop him. Alves's henchmen and local police incite violence, and while women, children, and union members leave peacefully, the ranchers' henchmen fire rounds from the forest, killing a child. The next day, as one of union members, Jair (Esai Morales), taps for rubber, a henchman kills him, shooting nine bullets into his body.

Because Kaye and his allies have spread Chico's message widely, with newspapers around the world giving front-page coverage to the violent attack on the union, Galvao betrays the ranchers to save his political position and travels to the union headquarters to negotiate with Chico, who explains his demands: "We want the rights to the land. We want to save the forest. . . . Give us the land. Take away the chainsaws. . . . Give our people back their fathers, sons, and brothers." When the townspeople gather outside the union hall the next morning, Galvao relents.

Galvao designates the land as one of the first extracted preserves, asserting, "From this moment forward, the forest belongs to you." The police now protect the land for the rubber tappers and evict the ranchers. Alves seeks revenge, ultimately assassinating Chico and, perhaps, continuing a legacy attached to an extracted reserve mission.

In December 2008, however, Andrew Revkin argued that "extractive reserves never became self-sustaining, much less capable of generating the billions Brazil needed to service its gargantuan $500 billion debt" ("The Uncertain Legacy"). Although Revkin sees these extractive reserves as a failure, the film highlights their difference from the deep ecology approach that mainstream environmentalists propose. And Revkin would agree that steps toward more environmentally sound approaches to development require an interaction with nonhuman nature, not a separation from it—the message of sustainable development.

It is Frankenheimer who brings life to the story of Chico Mendes and the plight of the rainforest. Even though Frankenheimer claims in an interview with Tim Kring that he doesn't look for some sort of political or sociopolitical vein in his script, his search for "a good story, really good characters, and serious subject matter" (Tobias) has led him to tackle environmental issues in several of his films: *Seven Days in May* (1964), *Prophecy* (1979), *The Burning Season*, and *The Island of Dr. Moreau* (1996). For Frankenheimer, however, ecological disaster is a "societal, political evil" that he likes to "deal with in a movie" (Rhys and Bage). In fact, he asserts, "The environment to me is the most important thing we've got going for us. And nobody seems to really give a shit; it's not in vogue anymore. We're ruining the world we live in for generations to come. I've dealt with this issue in *The Burning Season* and again in *Moreau*" (Rhys and Bage).

The film version of *The Burning Season* became possible only because Frankenheimer and HBO were willing to tackle what David Puttnam called "a political film, especially one about an unreconstructed Marxist like Mendes" (qtd. in Svetkey). Mendes's widow first sold the rights to her husband's story to the Brazilian JN Filmes. They resold the rights to Warner Bros., but when the studio bailed out of the project because of rising costs, the film seemed doomed. Then, as Frankenheimer explains, "HBO saved it." Yet it is Frankenheimer who really saves the film, winning both an Emmy and a Golden Globe for his deft direction. Frankenheimer describes *The Burning Season* as "the sort of movie that studios aren't making anymore" (qtd. in Svetkey), but it is very much the sort of film Frankenheimer made.

Chico Mendes replaces the martyred Christ.
Digital frame enlargement.

Chico's death ends the film, but it does not silence his support for sustainable development or Frankenheimer's call to action. During a procession led by the Rural Workers Union members and their families, a voiceover explains that the Chico Mendes Reserve saved 2.5 million acres of rainforest and warns that destruction of the rainforest continues. But the film ends with a clear focus on Chico's face imprinted on the cross that leads the procession, highlighting his continuing significance even in death. Chico Mendes's message of sustainable development continues despite the film's move toward deep ecology. As the credits roll, Chico's voice explains, "We have work to do."

Pictures and Prizes

Le Grand Prix de Rome and *Grand Prix*

VICTORIA DUCKETT

By the second half of the twentieth century, American film had not only usurped the spectacle and popularity of the traditional fine arts, it had also adopted many *beaux arts* practices and institutions, prime among which was the Grand Prix de Rome. While this was a competition historically associated with the international renown of the French fine arts, by the time of John Frankenheimer's *Grand Prix* (1966) it was instead Hollywood, with its studio system, its Academy, and its annual awards, that could claim international and artistic prestige. *Grand Prix* was conceived, produced, and celebrated within the logic of this system. Emerging at a moment when the Grand Prix de Rome was being changed, the film provides a case study of the way in which new Hollywood adapted and claimed the practices and privilege of the French *beaux arts* for its own.

It is unusual to argue that a Frankenheimer film might return us to seventeenth-century France. As we know, *Grand Prix* is usually contextualized in a very different fashion. A film that forms part of a larger oeuvre, it is Frankenheimer's racing car epic that followed the bleakness of his *Seconds* (1966) and that preceded the comedy of *The Extraordinary Seaman* (1969). *Grand Prix* has also been grouped with those other Frankenheimer works that "feature athletes and sportsmen who pursue physical challenges with intense enthusiasm" (Armstrong 69). Hence Stephen B. Armstrong considers it part of "The Physical Challenge" and positions it as antecedent to *The Gypsy Moths* (1969), *The Horsemen* (1971), and *The Challenge* (1982) in his book *Pictures about Extremes: The Films of John Frankenheimer*. In 1967, however, *Grand Prix* was applauded alongside other spectacle films and considered proof that the epic genre had not "croaked its last." Stephen Farber, writing in *Film Quarterly*, would therefore contrast *Doctor Zhivago* (1965) with its "3½ hours of pretty snowscapes and moony sentimentalities set to the twitter of the balalaika" against the "unusual, even daring appeal" of *The Bible, Khartoum, Hawaii, The Sand Pebbles* (all 1966), and *Grand Prix*. His point was that even in the age of television and at a moment in which the spectacular film seemed to be losing "imagination," a filmmaker such as Frankenheimer still successfully managed to exploit the spectacular possibilities of film. "The screen," writes he, "may be 40 feet wide, the scenery lush, the sound loud enough to blast you from your seat, but the vision of the spectacle film-maker has been bleared by the 21-inch screen in the livingroom. Nothing in *The Sound of Music* (1965) or *Doctor Zhivago* really fills those big, empty spaces" (Farber, "Search" 12).

A return to this question of pictorial grandeur might facilitate another interpretation of Frankenheimer's film, one that allows us to consider his work within a broader cultural and artistic context than scholars have, to date, allowed. The history we must draw upon—not as tangential as it might at first appear—is that of the Grand Prix de Rome, that artistic competition dating back to the seventeenth century that was long known as simply the "Grand Prix" and that was radically altered by André Malraux after the revolutionary events of 1968. There is an equivalence between Frankenheimer's *Grand Prix* and the Grand Prix de Rome that extends well beyond the obvious overlap in their respective titles. *Grand Prix* was a spectacular cinematic event on the eve of the "actual" Prix's demise, and this indicates the extent to which film had claimed the traditional role and function of the *beaux arts*, particularly that of academic painting. Hence, while Frankenheimer's film might very well document the 1960s in terms of the popularity of car racing or the proliferation of cinéma vérité or even the passions and interests of the filmmaker himself, it might also illustrate the extent to which Hollywood film had taken the style and structure of the French academy for its own.[1]

This is not a case of literal transference. Clearly, there was never a moment in which one discipline slid into another, or one nation passed a baton to another, or that a change in artistic hierarchies was formalized. Indeed, it might even appear odd to be arguing for the ascendancy of American film at the very moment that we see the breakdown of the traditional studio system, an emerging international art cinema, and the proclivity of the twenty-one-inch television screen. With the emergence of narrative film, at the opening of the twentieth century, film began to reconfigure the hierarchy of the arts, and it was precisely at this moment that the Grand Prix de Rome admitted women to its competition, was embroiled in some well-publicized disputes, and consequently began to lose some of its original prestige.[2]

By 1966, film had its own institutions and awards and the popularity and importance of these certainly eclipsed painting. Particularly with a film like *Grand Prix*, which was shot in Europe and nominated for an Academy Award, we have an example of the ways in which American film adopted the practice and purpose of the original Grand Prix de Rome. In both the case of the Grand Prix and that of Hollywood films, such as—for several reasons—*Grand Prix*, there was a valuation of institutional and technical proficiency. In both cases the recipients could only be young artists (predominantly men); and in both cases what was at stake was the custody of a global artistic culture. Therefore, two small detours are in order, to explain the origin and purpose of the French Académie and the first Grand Prix, and to briefly recount the history of the Academy of Motion Picture Arts and Sciences so that we may more clearly understand John Frankenheimer's relation to it.

The Académie

Le Grand Prix de Rome was part of the Académie Royale de Peintre et du Sculpture, and so it was also part of the reforms that shaped French artistic life in the mid-seventeenth century. This was not only a time when the bourgeois demanded privileges and when populations were in rebellion. It was also the point at which artists in France broke away from the older and more traditional corporation of the "*maistres jurés peintre et sculpteurs*" (certified masters of painting and sculpture, a body formed in 1391 but reaching further back) to found a union (the Académie) for the purpose of defending the rights of artists. On February 1, 1648, the painter Charles Le Brun—then twenty-nine—held the Académie's first public class; by 1663 he was the director of the Académie, and in 1666 the Prix de Rome—Rome suggesting that France was precipitating its own Renaissance of art—was established (see Grunchec *Grand Prix de Peinture*).

What did these changes introduce? First, they saw the reorganization of artistic pedagogy. The traditional focus on practical study was joined to the theoretical study of anatomy, perspective, life drawing, and modeling (Thullier 63). Second, they saw the centralization of artistic practice. Not only did the various independent *ateliers* follow the curriculum of the Académie, but through its monopoly on life drawing, for example, Louis XIV and his minister Jean-Baptiste Colbert controlled the imagery produced by French artists (Boime 282). Third, the Académie encouraged the participation of people from diverse backgrounds: amateurs, artists, and above all students were solicited in the hope that they would ensure the future glory of the French arts. It was this paradoxical emphasis upon democratic participation in the arts that saw the establishment of public scholarships and that enabled men from poorer backgrounds to join the Académie's ranks (see Thullier 74–75). Fourth, the Académie introduced a ranking of artistic subject matter, so that historical painting superseded that of still life, landscape, and genre. This meant, initially, that subjects such as "The King Granting Peace to Europe" (1671) and "Louis XIV Crossing the Rhine" (1673) were the designated subjects of the Grand Prix (Boime 283). Later, it saw the joining of political dominance and power with high art: as Albert Boime explains in his article "The Prix de Rome: Images of Authority and Threshold of Official Success," the adjectives *haut*, *grand*, and *élevé* describe both history painting and its depicted subjects (283).

The Académie was abolished in 1793, and three years later its art instruction was reconstituted under a newly formed Institut. After the revolution of 1848, the Institut was renamed the École des Beaux-Arts (in 1863) and granted independence from the French government. Throughout this period, even while regulations changed, the École maintained international prestige and artistic dominance. This meant that even if artists did not attend the École (and Géricault is a famous example of one who didn't), it was impossible to avoid its influence (see, more generally, Grunchec *Grand Prix de Peinture*).

The Grand Prix de Rome

The Grand Prix de Rome, an annual competition organized by the École, was long considered the crown of all institutional achievements. Strict rules governed its undertaking: in order to enter the competition, an artist had to win first prize in one of the secondary contests known as the *concours d'émulation* or *petit concours*. Open only to single men who were French and under the age of thirty (this last provision was added in 1813), it was tightly policed. In painting, just ten artists successfully made it to the final round. They were sequestered into rooms in the Château de Compiègne for seventy-two days, where they were given twelve hours to execute a sketch upon a given theme and then expected to use this sketch as basis for a 113.7 × 146.5 cm canvas. At the end of the competition, the canvases were publicly exhibited alongside the preparatory sketches (a variance between the two was forbidden) and the Académie assembled to vote. The press and public were also in attendance. The Grand Prix was not only important for the young male participants but considered a highlight of the Parisian social season throughout the nineteenth century (see Grunchec *Grand Prix de Rome* 26–27).

The prize gave the winners five years of residence in the French Academy in Rome (see Grunchec, *Grand Prix de Rome* 27; and *Grand Prix de Peinture* 105–10; on the joining of academic practice with royal interest see Boime 283). The aim of this sojourn was to replicate the treasures of the city. In its strictest form, the winner saw a formal list of what exercises had to be achieved each year. More generally, however, the point was for the painters to copy famous Italian painting, for the sculptors to model statues after the antique, and for architects to execute plans of all the palaces and edifices in Rome. This would then be returned to France to become the property of the French government. As Boime explains, this residency was essentially an exercise in "the extraction of aesthetic wealth." He states:

> The first Prix de Rome nominees were valued not so much for their originality as for their ability to replicate existing objects. Louis XIV and Colbert wanted multiple editions of all the treasures in Rome, and their demand survived as a fundamental element of the Prix de Rome

tradition. Ever after, pensioners at Rome were required to execute as part of their annual obligations, or envois, a careful copy of a recognized masterpiece, which became the property of the state. . . . The French Academy at Rome, the home-away-from-home for the Prix de Rome winners, served as a kind of colonial headquarters for the extraction of aesthetic wealth. (Boime 283)

Tales of Transference: The American Academy

The American Academy of Motion Picture Arts and Sciences was established in 1927 at the instigation of Louis B. Mayer. Conceived as an organization whose members would be drawn from across the cinema's industrial practices, it promoted itself early on as a type of modern-day artistic Académie, with actors, directors, writers, producers, and technicians together constituting its makeup. Membership in the Academy was based upon involvement in the industry and was available at the outset (as it still is today) by invitation only. While membership has greatly expanded—from an initial thirty-six members there are now more than six thousand—so too has the breadth of its industrial practices. Film Editors, Music, Sound, and Visual Effects are all branches that, by the time of Frankenheimer's involvement in film, were included in its constitution. The most visible (and certainly the most famous) function of the Academy is its annual awards. In order to receive an award, one must first be nominated by members in an anonymous vote; in the 1960s, roughly five contestants were chosen for each category and each branch then voted a finalist to win the category. Begun in 1929, these awards were successively and successfully expanded to include more categories and to engage bigger and wider audiences. By the time Frankenheimer's *Birdman of Alcatraz* was nominated for an Academy Award in 1961 (his first film to be so nominated), the Awards were watched on live television by a global audience and had become, if not in title then at least in function, the Grand Prix of twentieth-century culture.

When Boime describes the Grand Prix de Rome as "the first Academy Award, except that it is difficult to imagine a nineteenth-century Marlon Brando refusing to accept it," he is therefore attempting to translate, to a contemporary audience, some of the aura that the prize traditionally represented (Boime 281). The parallels that can be drawn between the traditional Grand Prix and the American filmmaking industry by the time *Grand Prix* was made in the mid-1960s can, however, be readily recounted. On the most obvious level, there is the fact that an art form was organized into a nationally centralized industry that was democratic in its acceptance of outsiders. Hence, just as people from the provinces and towns were historically accepted into the French Academy in Paris, so too was Frankenheimer, a New York boy, able to make his way into the Hollywood film industry even though he had trained elsewhere in television. Moreover, those who could win the Grand Prix were—like Frankenheimer, nominated for successive Academy awards—largely young men who had demonstrated aesthetic worth in the build-up to the final competition. While in France this meant that an artist was eligible for the prize only if he had won an initiating award, for Frankenheimer it meant that he could be granted nomination precisely because he was a familiar director who had already enjoyed critical success. The two prizes were also similar in being awarded annually by a nationally appointed Academy, the results determined in both cases by an anonymous vote with the international public and press avidly following the outcome. There is also overlap in the fact that changing institutional practices ensured film's capacity to maintain its importance as a cultural industry, as well as the fact that democratic participation in the industry (through the agency of a film studio) gave patronage to young men who, like Frankenheimer, showed particular talent and were eager to learn. Moreover, stylistic change could only gradually be traced through an examination of successive prize winners, since it was not *avant garde* challenge that was condoned in the awards but the capacity to engage contemporary concerns within a fixed and established format (the narrative feature film, generally running to 120 minutes in the 1960s and following an aspect ratio of 1.85:1).[3] That it was drama rather than comedy that generally won the "grand prix" of the American Academy is also telling: like the distinction between history painting and landscape painting in the Grand Prix de Rome, there was a hierarchy of preferred form.[4]

That *Grand Prix* was nominated for Best Picture in the Academy Awards in 1966 is important, because Frankenheimer's work was therefore one of the (roughly) five films competing for the "grand prix." That it won Best Film Editing, Best Sound, and Best Sound Effects but was not in the running for the more prestigious Best Director and Best Picture awards (which were won by Fred Zinnemann and his *Man for All Seasons* [1966]) is also significant since, on a basic level, we can note that a film about contemporary car racing in Europe was secondary to a film about Henry VIII and his dealings with Sir Thomas More. Here the traditional distinction between landscape and history plays itself out, since the film that won was a dramatic feature about monarchy, the other a picture largely focused upon foreign landscapes. Although Frankenheimer included amorous subplots in an effort to broaden his film's appeal, most commentators saw the various relationships between Pete Aaron (James Garner) and Pat Stoddard (Jessica Walker), Jean-Pierre Sarti (Yves Montand) and Louise Frederickson (Eva Marie Saint), and Nino Barlini (Antonio Sábato) and Lisa (Françoise Hardy) as little more than an insertion of stereotype into the otherwise realistic landscape of Formula One racing (see Farber "Spectacle"; and Armstrong 72–73).

Even the fact that *Grand Prix* was a Metro-Goldwyn-Mayer superproduction costing over ten million dollars is relevant to the parallels being drawn between the history of French academic painting and the Hollywood film industry. Just as the younger painters were sequestered in their studios and had three months to produce a painting from an initial sketch, so too did Frankenheimer's 1,250,000 feet of uncut 70 mm film have to be edited down in a three-month period in the studio in Culver City so that it could be released to the public by December the same year and compete for the 1966 awards (Pratley, *Films of Frankenheimer* 65). Moreover, we have the promotion of the film as a reserved-seat feature, with the implication that it was part of an august institution that (even in the absence of royal subject matter) only admitted products that were *haut, grand,* or *élevé.*

Frankenheimer would endorse the fact that he was a director of quality films. Describing himself as a filmmaker who tried to get ideas across in "the most artistic way we know," he distinguished himself from others who were merely (what he called) "company directors" or "traffic cops." As he explained, he took his work seriously, sought to realize his own vision within the limitations of the commercial film market, and (with producer Edward Lewis) initiated projects that were driven by his desire to put a specific story onscreen. For example, *Grand Prix* as well as *The Fixer* (1968), *The Gypsy Moths, Seven Days in May* (1968), *The Manchurian Candidate* (1962), and *Seconds* were all works inspired by this pair and not by the studios (see Pratley, *Cinema* 76–77 and Frankenheimer's comments in the preface). While some critics would nevertheless compare *Grand Prix* unfavorably to Claude Lelouch's *A Man and a Woman* (a film also featuring racing scenes and made on a budget of only $150,000, and which won the Palme d'Or in 1966), others would argue that *Grand Prix* was an artistic achievement precisely because it managed to create art from within the conceptual and practical constraints of Hollywood. Citing Erwin Panofsky, Stephen Farber therefore applauded *Grand Prix*'s capacity to create "art from machinery and from business." Again, the fact that a work had to be produced within given restraints is relevant, since it was precisely this focus upon a uniform art industry, within the constraints of which young talents had to exercise themselves, that traditionally ensured entry to the Grand Prix de Rome.[5]

Sending Stuff Home

Evidently, while the question of ownership changes as we move from the monarchical demands of Louis XI and the Grand Prix de Rome in seventeenth-century France to MGM's funding a Hollywood feature film in 1966, there remains a shared (and colonial) effort to extract cultural wealth as realistically as possible for domestic audiences. There is also a shared seriality: just as artists sent multiple editions of treasures back to France, so too did Frankenheimer replicate not just one Grand Prix but a series of Formula One race experiences. The aim of both processes was to provide something that was unavailable at home, and to offer it in splendid abundance in such a way as to highlight not only the glories of the culture from which one had taken one's spoils but also the institution that was underwriting the process. Indeed, the fact that *Grand Prix* enabled audiences to see a color film of European Formula One races that had actually run during the year was unique, since television had yet to broadcast the live event in color (Germany would be the first to do this, beginning the following year). The verity of what audiences were seeing was reinforced through the film's onscreen credits, in which the organizations and clubs behind the Monaco, Dutch, Belgium, and United States Grand Prix were listed in reiteration of the fact that the audience had indeed enjoyed spectacular artifacts that had been pieced together anew. Moreover, the "Watkins Glen Grand Prix Corporation" concludes this credit as "The United States Grand Prix." Here, the Grand Prix has not only been literally brought home through film, but has been newly named and nationalized.

The fact that *Grand Prix* was extremely long is also significant. Running at 179 minutes, it gave audiences a guide through the sites and sights of the season's most famous locations (the Circuit de Monaco, Clermont-Ferrand in France, Spa Francorchamps in Belgium, Circuit Zandvoort in the Netherlands, Brands Hatch in England, Watkins Glen Grand Prix in America, and Monza in Italy). While automobile racing in itself was not new to American audiences—it had, after all, formed part of American sporting life since 1895, when Herman H. Kohlsaat (the publisher of the *Chicago Times-Herald*) had first sponsored a race (see Betts 253)—this vicarious attendance at otherwise distant and inaccessible circuits was novel for viewers. As Frankenheimer explained, the film was a kind of "miniscule examination of an entire season of racing" (qtd. in Pratley, *Films* 65).

As I have already suggested, *Grand Prix* provided less a touristic view of exotic locales than an all-embracing sense of participating in the events themselves. Hence, in the crowd shots, where faces either fill the screen *en bloc* or are captured anonymously alone, there is the possibility for the viewer to invest in the fiction of physical presence. We are able to scan, stare, and visually isolate the public; we allow the camera to function as our material substitute. By contrast, in the shots of the races, the viewer is afforded a sensory panorama entirely denied those really watching the Grand Prix from the sidelines. As Garner comments in the film, "Spectators can't really see very much of the race." However, film viewers are able to see, and always ideally. We are brought in close to the drivers and vehicles; offered close-ups of engines, meters, even spark plugs; in general provided with a deluge of visual detail that verifies our privilege. No longer on the sidelines and held at bay, we are offered an otherwise impossibly intimate view of the cars. We are also sometimes even inside a car, driving through the adventure. As the trailer for the film triumphantly announces, film viewers are "at the wheel, flat out, at 185 miles an hour."

At the same time that there is this encroachment upon (and into) the Formula One cars, there is an enormous variation of views offered of the race. Remote-control cameras mounted on cars, shots taken from helicopters, and 1000 mm lenses provide a visual variety entirely denied real paying spectators of the race. It was therefore only the filmgoer who was omnipresent, who could boast to have seen the event from a range of angles, distances, and perspectives. Seeing the movie was better than being there.

At the wheel, flat out. Race sequences shot from inside the vehicles in *Grand Prix* (Cherokee Productions, 1966).
Digital frame enlargement.

That the cars featured in *Grand Prix* were either the Formula One cars used in the races themselves or Formula Three cars "dressed up" to look like the new three-liter Formula One vehicles is significant, since the film viewer's position as privileged spectator is never challenged by the status of the film as a narrative fiction. Even the fact that the actors were all trained to drive plays into the fiction, since the shots cut into the real racing sequences therefore featured the actors (with one exception) driving "on the race course itself," in their respective racing cars. "We sent all our drivers to driving school," said Frankenheimer. "James Garner was a great athlete and he came out of it a very, very good driver. Yves Montand came out of it very well, as did Antonio Sábato. The only one who didn't was Brian Bedford, who couldn't drive at all, and we had to double him all the time. But the other guys were really driving their own cars and they did very well" (qtd. in Emery 258–59). And just as the cars and drivers were "real," so, too, were the car crashes, since Milton Rice designed a special hydrogen cannon for Frankenheimer that propelled cars like projectiles through the air.

The views afforded of the European car itself—particularly those of the Ferrari, being assembled inside their factory—were also significant in that they again offered filmgoers a peek into a space that was otherwise off-limits to the spectators of the races. What was on show in these scenes was therefore not a stage set but a complex automobile industry devoted to fine craftsmanship now, for the first time, recorded for public viewing (on Ferrari opening up "his factory, cars, everything" for the film, see Pratley, *Films* 65).

Grand Prix was Frankenheimer's first color film. The decision to film in color was related to this effort to make *Grand Prix* visually accessible to audiences: Frankenheimer stated that he used color film precisely because he wanted people to be able to "tell the cars apart, the red one from the green one" (in *Films*

66). In other words, Frankenheimer wanted the Italian red car (the Ferrari) to be differentiated from the British racing green of BRM (British Racing Motors), Lotus, Cooper, and Vanwall. Without the guide of dialogue, and perhaps even ignorant of specific car makes or companies, viewers were thus able to interpret the racing sequences when vehicles passed each other on the track.

While *Grand Prix* was scored by Maurice Jarre, it was the use of sound effects and sound by Gordon Daniel and the MGM sound department that brought the film its respective Academy Awards. Again, this returns us to the limitations of watching the Grand Prix live as compared to the variety of perspectives afforded the film viewer. When the engines roar we have an indication of how it might sound to physically stand on a sideline. This is a loud, aggressive, and impatient sound, drowning out reflection. During the races, however, this is not all that we hear. There is, for example, the sound of a single and simple heartbeat pumping at the film's opening just before the Monte Carlo Grand Prix begins; later, there is the superimposition of personal dialogue over the close-up of each driver's face as they race. In this way, we enter the driver's physiological and emotional world: we are inside the car, we hear cars passing at a distance but then we come in close and hear intimate and reflective thoughts that are never (and can never be) articulated to a live audience.

Even the personal narratives recounted in *Grand Prix* were based on actual people and events. Therefore, the film did not so much switch between separable modes or models (from truth to fiction, document to narrative, and so on), but instead went on recounting detail. As Frankenheimer explained:

> I wanted to try and show what racing was really like and every single incident in the film is based on truth. In some reviews, critics said that the story was not as good as the racing sequences. I think that is false criticism. While the racing sequences were done well, the story *was* good and if you look at what has happened in racing since that film was made you will see how true and tragic it was. Lorenzo Bandini was killed at exactly the same place that our accident happened in Monte Carlo. And Bandini, who was a Ferrari driver, helped me stage the accident. Jackie Stewart won the Dutch Grand Prix this year with a broken arm in plaster. Our man won the Dutch Grand Prix with a bad leg. Every incident in the film is based on something that really happened in racing. (qtd. in Pratley, *Films* 64)

Going on to explain how the actors incarnated known drivers, Frankenheimer stated:

> I don't particularly want to say who the actual people were, but I think it's no secret that the American driver played by James Garner was based on Phil Hill. The English driver was certainly based on Stirling Moss. The Yves Montand character was a composite of three drivers—Fangio,

Wolfgang von Tripps and Jean Behra, the French driver. Eva Marie Saints's character was based on an actual woman named Louise King who was married to Peter Collins, a Ferrari driver who was killed. She later became involved with Mike Hawthorne, Peter Collins' best friend, the world champion and also a Ferrari driver, and he was killed in a road accident. I can go through each character in that film and tell you who they were in real life, which I don't think you can do in many films.[6] (64)

Relevant to this focus on truth is the fact that Garner races and wins in a car that was built by a newly emergent Japanese team headed by Toshirô Mifune. Again, we have "real" racing events recorded since the wealthy industrialist Soichiro Honda, having entered Formula One racing only in 1964, achieved his first win in 1965 with the American driver Richie Ginther. Between the Frankenheimer film and the original Prix de Rome, there is also a related presumption of skill: just as participants in the Grand Prix de Rome needed to be technically competent, so did Frankenheimer and his team, both in conception and in execution of the film: in *Grand Prix* we have Phil Hill (who was the only American-born Formula One driver to have won the World Drivers Championship) used as an advisor to the project, as a character in the film (Tim Randolf), and as a model for the central character played by James Garner.

Splitting Screens

One aspect of *Grand Prix* that has not yet been mentioned is the split screen, that multiplication of the image into so many perfect and repetitive rectangles, all contained within the one grand Cinerama frame. On one hand, this could be considered a mere show of bravura, a kind of purely visual flourish that would allow Frankenheimer's film to be incorporated in that ever-growing category, the cinema of attractions (see Gunning 63–70). Indeed, by replacing narrative sequence with simultaneity in the traditional triptych form, or by splitting the picture into six, twelve, or even sixty-four frames, *Grand Prix* demonstrates the remarkable technical capabilities of the medium. We are pulled out of narrative into spectacle, out of a competitive race into the pleasure of visual display alone.

These moments in which narrative is at a standstill are not, however, only about the clever implosion of the screen. They also point to Frankenheimer's conscious mining of an alternative, avant-garde practice, and thus speak to the way in which he accommodated artistic change. As Frankenheimer would explain, his use of the split screen was drawn from Francis Thompson and his film *To Be Alive!* (1964), Charles Eames's film for IBM, and the World Series on television (see Pratley, *Films* 64). The first, a documentary film about children growing into adults, was screened at the 1964 New York World's Fair and was projected onto three separate eighteen-foot screens that showed material simultaneously. The Eames films—particularly *The Information Machine,* which was screened in the IBM Pavilion at the Brussels World's Fair in 1958—instead used multiple images on only one screen, computers abstracted through close-ups, and opened with the argument that it was artists who saw the development of information technology since they "were seldom bored with anything . . . [and] could speculate and could predict." Finally, from television Frankenheimer learned how to juxtapose the voice of a pre-recorded interview with the tension of live competitive play.

As Frankenheimer's choice of examples indicates, films appeared at World's Fairs where they articulated a global humanism that saw the filmmaker propagated as a spokesperson—if not a leader—in the visual arts. His filmic work also drew upon the changed aesthetic of the television and so was capable of responding to and learning from an emerging media that was itself based upon the idea of simultaneity. What might also be suggested here is that Frankenheimer's split screens adapted and incorporated Pop Art into their embrace. Andy Warhol's 1962 *Marilyn Diptych, Twenty-five Colored Marilyns,* and *One Hundred Cans,* as well as his 1963 *Double Elvis, Triple Elvis, Jackie III,* and—significantly—*Orange Car Crash Fourteen Times,* illustrate how even *Grand Prix*'s subject matter might be understood within the context of an emergent pop culture. This was a culture that fixated upon the star, the car, and the role that reproduction and repetition played in the creation and emptying out of cultural meaning.

We seem far from the Grand Prix de Rome and its celebration of the carbon copy in this turn to American Pop art. Indeed, just as the Grand Prix de Rome was based on the idea that a copy could replace or at least stand in for an original work of art, Frankenheimer seems instead to be indicating that we might lose sight of originary objects or events. His fracturing of the frame seems to be less about the car or the car race than a celebration of film's capacity to visually

The split screen, incorporating Pop Art, in *Grand Prix*.
Digital frame enlargement.

reproduce itself. Even at the level of narrative, *Grand Prix* highlighted the importance of reproduction. For example, Mifune forces Garner to watch himself drive onscreen as part of his training. Rather than performing practice runs or going through tactical plans, Garner is made to sit and see. He had to watch himself on film; it was only through the recorded image that he could return to an event and learn, finally, to win.

Garner goes on to beat Scott Stoddard (Bedford) to the finish line at Monza. As the loudspeaker announces, the Japanese cars driven by an American "have challenged and conquered the might of European Formula One teams in spite of all the years of experience and development behind them. But it's a sad end." We conclude, therefore, with an echo of Jean-Pierre Sarti's (Montand) death. Garner is alone as he walks slowly to the finish line. We see the cracks in the pavement and the debris that litters the empty stadium. The championship is over and this is a moment of self-reflective closure.

However, this vision of an empty stadium marks another, different type of victory. For it is film that has made the car race so artistic and so beautiful. Unlike Renaissance Rome, which the original Grand Prix sought to document, we join Garner in modern Italy. Entirely denied its artistic history, it has no artifacts on display: there is only the decay of the track and the littered reminder of consumptive greed. Even the race that has been run will be watched only once it has been refashioned as a visible object by film. Indeed, it is film's splitting of the screen, its poetically overlapping images, its abstraction of mechanical function, and its ability to bring grandeur to quotidian detail that make a space like Monza an aesthetic treat. As Garner pays witness to the desolation of the track, we therefore realize that film alone made the Grand Prix so visually grand and technically spectacular.

Izo Yamura (Toshirô Mifune) forces Pete Aron (James Garner) to watch himself onscreen.

Digital frame enlargement.

An enormous shift has thus occurred. Where I could earlier trace the transferences from one Academy to another, I now have to speak of separable practices. With painting, artists were asked to copy works of art and to then send these home. With film, meaning was instead created *a posteriori*. Frankenheimer consequently returned to America and to the film studio in order to make *Grand Prix*. In other words, he was not a custodian of history but was instead responding to contemporary culture and events. And while these might certainly be ugly, repetitive, and/or destructive, they could also be retroactively shaped by film into a different, aesthetically pleasing object.

NOTES

1. Within the context of cinéma vérité, for example, a discussion of a film such as *Eddie* (1960) could be related to *Grand Prix* (see Breitrose 36–40 and, on *Eddie*, 37–38).
2. See, for general reference, Woldu and Queuniet about the elimination of Maurice Ravel in the Prix de Rome in 1905; and Fauser, about the efforts that women made to enter and win the Prix de Rome at the turn of the twentieth century. What is also interesting about the early period in film is the function the car plays in comedic chase films.
3. Precise information on exact lengths is hard to establish. The Academy defines a feature film as a film whose length is (as a minimum) 40 minutes. See also *http://www.infinitypointo.com/60/imdb-film-length-project*, which states that the average length of a feature film in the 1960s was 127 minutes. See Bordwell et al., esp. chap. 1 ("An Excessively Obvious Cinema"), for a discussion of how Hollywood cinema was bound by established and enduring rules.
4. Note that the Grand Prix de Rome in History Landscape was created in 1816 (some twenty years after the first Grand Prix) and was abolished in 1863.
5. See Farber 16–17, where he criticizes John Simon's characterization of *Grand Prix* as a "cloying bit of craft" as opposed to the imagination and artistry of *A Man and a Woman*. See also his citation of Panofsky (17), which cites a phrase from "Style and Medium in the Motion Pictures": "Movies, he [Panofsky] says, unlike any of the other arts, organize material things and persons, not a neutral medium, into a composition that receives its style, and may even become fantastic or pretervoluntarily symbolic, not so much by an interpretation in the artists' mind as by the actual manipulation of physical objects and recording machinery."
6. Note that even dialogue had some of its basis in "fact." Pratley therefore cites Frankenheimer describing a visit to John Houseman in the following way: "I was in California and I was miserable, I hated it. I drove down to the beach and went to John's house, which was always pleasant to visit because there were always people there you wanted to meet, the food was always great, and his wife is a marvelous woman. I looked around that beautiful day on the ocean and said 'God, John, you're lucky to live here' and he said, 'Luck, dear boy, has nothing to do with it,' which is a line I used a great deal in Grand Prix: 'Luck has nothing to do with it.'" Pratley, *Cinema* 78.

Families

Crashing In

Birdman of Alcatraz

TOM CONLEY

"The First Epistle of the Green Lover" [*La Première Epistre de l'amant vert*], composed and written in Burgundy in 1505 and first printed in 1512, is a fitting epigraph to a study of John Frankenheimer's *Birdman of Alcatraz* (1962).[1] In that famous poem, Jean Lemaire de Belges, historian and poet at the court of Margaret of Austria, sought to alleviate the melancholy of his patron princess, Margaret of Austria, by "personifying" himself as the parrot that the queen had lost in the summer of 1504 when her attendants inadvertently left the caged bird in a room in the company of a pet mastiff. When they returned to discover that the dog had made a meal of the parrot, they soon witnessed the queen sink into grief. Lemaire took upon himself the task of pulling her out of the dumps by rewriting the sad turn of events from the bird's point of view (much as Robert Montgomery effects with his subjective camera in *The Lady in the Lake* [1947]), but with a novel twist: he had the parrot become so disconsolate in the absence of the queen that it committed suicide by thrusting itself into the dog's jaws. The elegiac verse, said to raise Margaret's spirits, soon became so renowned that Lemaire wrote a second epistle in which the "green lover" told of his visit to Hades and of his resurrection from the lower depths into the Elysian Fields.

Lemaire's poem shares affinities with *Birdman of Alcatraz* not only because the author "becomes parrot" through wit and invention but also for the reason that the filmic "verse" is written from a standpoint (or perch) of someone "in the cage." Robert Stroud (Burt Lancaster), the character whose long penitentiary life the film chronicles, is shown behind bars, in cages of different sizes, in which this angry man slowly finds a way to wisdom. A reassessment of this film of almost fifty years ago—a feature manufactured in the context of a plethora of "prison films" of the postwar era—reaps uncommon reward. It is not because *Birdman* is a heartwarming tale of a spiritual itinerary in which cruelty and ire give way to the radiance of inner calm. Rather, *Birdman* inverts (much as had Lemaire for his listeners) a viewer's expectations about the nature of incarceration. It reconsiders the nature of closure and confinement by telling of what is done with it by such men as those for whom it is a condition of life. Except for the opening and closing shots the entire film takes place in the cage. The effect is so pervasive that the viewer wonders if Frankenheimer's feature reflects on a broader relation that cinema keeps with incarceration. Its apparatus is one that aims to locate and hold the viewer in its grip. The impression is salient because the film never purveys the (specious) idea that redemption comes to inmates who allow the prison to "correct" them. The viewer quickly realizes that Frankenheimer conveys the debilitating effects of confinement through cinematic form. Today the film can be "read" through some of the most luminous and ostensibly difficult, or even mystical, pages of Michel Foucault's *Discipline and Punish* (*Surveillir et punir*, 1975), an epochal work about the history and experiential architecture (what Foucault calls "the form of the content") of the penitentiary that Frankenheimer anticipates and even, in his own way, explicates.

Lemaire's poem brings forward the situation that prevails in *Birdman*. The point of the self—the "I" represented in the account (written originally by Thomas Gaddis, then adapted for the screen by Frankenheimer)—is split. Stroud the hero is both *I* and *he*, at once a first-person and a third, through whose eyes the world is seen from inside a cage, yet whose field of view, thanks to the camera, comes from without. Lemaire's *l'amant vert* or "green lover" laments from across a tomb in which he has consigned himself, while in *Birdman* we see Stroud living out a life of no future from within a cell, a space from which his impressions are relayed through the explicit voice (often in voiceover) of the biographer who introduces, frames, intervenes, and caps the story.

From Credits to Story

The issue of point of view and alteration of convention becomes apparent in the framing of the story from the end of the credits to the beginning of the narrative. The first shot that moves from the credits to the geography of the film establishes a double view, a view taken both from the inside and the outside of an implied cage. The front-credit ends with an extreme close-up of a pair of hands coddling a chick (which the title helps to identify, so obscured is the bird in the dark surrounding), freezing into an abstraction of riddled lines in black and white. As the bar-like fingers grow large, a slow zoom into the image reveals the island of Alcatraz (which the title has also served to indicate) seen across the choppy waters of San Francisco Bay. The credit quickly fades out and the skyline comes forward. The effect is engineered to momentarily confuse the extreme close-up of the hands that hold the bird with the prison in an extreme long shot. The home and hearth of the chick become the scenographic view of the island-citadel that extends in front of a landscape where, far in the background,

Mount Tamalpais is visible to the north. A first shot of the island is briefly shown before the director's credit line dissolves into the image. Disposed between the edge of the shoreline and the choppy waters, between the unyielding, "molar," or telluric quality of the "rock" on land and the moving, fluid, atmospheric, or "molecular" feel of the waves that agitate the craft from which the shot is taken, Frankenheimer's name melds into the stony ridge before the site is viewed integrally once again, albeit for an instant.[2]

No sooner is Alcatraz seen than the panorama dissolves into a long shot of the hillside of San Francisco that leads down to the Embarcadero. The fore- and middleground are occupied by a parking lot from whose two empty spaces a man, dressed in a dark overcoat, walks toward the camera. A low wire fence surrounds another enclosed area, and then yet another further in the background. A warehouse or garage stands between the parking lots and the hillside on which two soaring apartment buildings are under construction.

So far, the film emerges into view through vaguely bar-like forms between the fingers shaping the nest. The image seems to go "into" an open space that holds the prison-fortress on the island. The rhetoric of the credits and opening shots makes clear that *one prison dissolves into another*, and that the film itself is part of the matrix of incarceration. A containing wall, a penitentiary, and a city: an oneiric *inside* of the fondling hands gives way to a classically topographic image *outside*, that morphs into another of a recognizable urban space, clearly shot on location, that seems to belong to the tradition of the many locative sequences—taken in known urban spaces, in daylight—common to film noir.[3] The transition articulates the spatial and historical paradoxes that will drive much of the film.

A voice-off fills the space of the dissolve from the island to the city. It first emanates as if from nowhere and through a loudspeaker, leaving the impression that it is announcing what the film will be showing: "You will see all the manmade and natural beauties [ominous music fills the background] in the most spectacular bay in the world. You will pass beneath the famous Golden Gate Bridge." The camera tracks along smoothly in accord with the description of the harbor tour before stopping to reveal the origin of the voice, a seated man, faintly visible in the background, who speaks into a microphone at the entrance to "Pier 43½."

A sense of emptiness prevails. Before reaching its term, the pano-track follows the man who passes in front of a diesel locomotive that moves forward from the left. The voice-off continues its description of the Golden Gate, "considered by most authorities to be one of the most striking structures [yet in the image-field, at the same instant, the locomotive is just that] ever created by man" (the "man," now in medium view and definitely recognizable as actor Edmond O'Brien, is safely beyond the rails on which the locomotive is moving). The shot accelerates along its career as O'Brien goes by a moored ship while the voice-off drones, "From the Bay, you will be thrilled by the magnificent view of

A long tracking (and establishing) shot on location records Tom Gaddis (Edmond O'Brien) approaching the Embarcadero from which he will gaze upon Alcatraz, in *Birdman of Alcatraz* (United Artists, 1962).
Digital frame enlargement.

the San Francisco skyline." Having walked ahead, O'Brien is now shown from behind, gazing at two signs on which are displayed "View Alcatraz." The voice (now *in*) continues to describe everything the film will refuse to show: "Your cruise ship, the Harbor King, will circle Alcatraz, a maximum security prison containing the most dangerous criminals in America." As the seated speaker puts emphasis on "America," O'Brien stops as if to face offscreen and to call that key word into question.

The twenty-eight-second shot, a miniature tour de force, cuts to an extreme close-up of O'Brien in profile, frozen for an instant, much in the manner of a mug shot, looking to the right. The character is suddenly identified with criminals by virtue of the voice enumerating names of former inmates. The island "has been the home of some of the most notorious figures, such as Al Capone, Baby Face Nelson [as "Face" is uttered O'Brien's face begins to turn away] and Machine Gun Kelly." The camera follows him as he walks ahead and passes four pay-for-view telescopes aimed at Alcatraz. The panoramic view moves by the telescopes—underscoring that their point of view as touristic objects almost doubles that of the camera, which finally sets the island in the center of its field (now at a longer distance from the water than in the first shot) and also before O'Brien's gaze. The binocular telescopes become implicit allegories of the penitentiary gaze, with the exception that, unlike a panopticon, they are outside the prison—but nonetheless inside the film.

The motion of the two shots that lead to this point implies that the medium that will tell the story is one that confines and that with its "objective" view it seeks to control those who are drawn into its field. At this point, when it invites the spectator *not* to see what the hawker is selling, the film reflects—and coyly reflects upon—its own power, a power that the shot, as it continues, further emphasizes: another voice, at once *off* and *in*—it cannot be found on the screen because the speaker has turned away from the camera—locates the viewer when stating its own geographical "truth": "That's the Island of Alcatraz." A short pause intervenes before O'Brien continues in a tone that recalls the roles that had cast him as a seedy hero who moves from one side of the law to the other: Hank Fallon, the double agent for whom gangster Cody Jarrett (James Cagney) had fallen "like a kid brother" in *White Heat* (1949), or Jim Reardon, the insurance investigator who weeds his way into the underworld of *The Killers* (1946). He also recalls Frank Bigelow, the vacationing insurance agent, a would-have-been bigamist, who was ultimately the tragic hero of *D.O.A.* (1950). At this point it is impossible to know if the speaker is within or outside of a milieu of evil-doers. The voice interrupts the viewer's memory of O'Brien's former roles: "There's a man leaving there after seventeen years of imprisonment. His name is Robert Stroud." A pause gives way to the beginning of the narrative told in the same voice in and off: "He spent the greater part of his life behind bars—including forty-three years in solitary confinement. He's never used a telephone or driven an automobile. The last time he broke bread with another human being was in 1916, the year that Kaiser Wilhelm ordered the sinking of the *Lusitania* in World War I."[4] Another pause: suddenly the man, his left hand on the sea wall, turns directly toward the camera, his face shown in the style of a frontal mug shot. In lip-synch he avows, almost with a scowl, "My name is Tom Gaddis. I wrote a book about this man."

Of nearly a minute's length, the shot serves as the threshold to the story, a flashback introduced by a straight cut laying stress on its currency here and now. A complement to the first pano-track of the landscape and the industrial topography of the harbor, the shot moves effortlessly from what is far to what is near. In the midst of what seems to be an invisible style of editing the camera nonetheless unsettles us. We are situated outside of one penitentiary but by implication are confined within another.

Leavenworth or Lyons

The greater part of the narrative takes place within the hero's cell in the federal penitentiary at Fort Leavenworth, Kansas, and it is there that the prisoner happens upon the sparrow that changes his life. Much of the footage that tells of his metamorphosis underscores the exiguous space of the cell and the courtyard where he finds occasional solace, atmosphere, and, finally, biological life. A swirl of breeze and wind bequeaths to him, like manna, the bird that he will nurture. The cell, seen from inside and out (thanks to the bond he develops with his guard [Neville Brand]), seems to expand and become something of an infinite intimacy. Now and again some shots, frequently linked in dissolves, depict Stroud doing his ablutions or attending to everyday life. Others show how he builds cages and avian paraphernalia for his birds. The storyline begins to recede when the close-ups become a narrative that moves from a script of self-edification to a reflection on the nature of meditation. The hero's physiognomy is isolated in an abstract décor of lines and grainy surfaces, the result being—here the virtue of the film—that we tend to see him reflecting on the nature of isolation. Here and elsewhere *Birdman* veers away from the topical prison film that deals with the ways inmates seek to escape (as in *The Big House* [1930], *I Am a Fugitive from a Chain Gang* [1932], *Each Dawn I Die* [1939], or *Brute Force* [1947]) or to foment riot (as in *Big House USA* [1955]).

When the Leavenworth sequences are taken independently of their narrative, they bear uncommon resemblance to the close-ups of Fontaine, the prisoner of the Montluc fortress in Lyons that Robert Bresson had shot in *Un Condamné à mort s'est échappé* (*A Man Escaped* [1956]). Much of that feature is given to the hero's face as it looks and listens to the ambient sounds about him—the squeak of a guard's leather shoe, the metallic crunch of a latch bolt locking a door, the thong-thong-thong of a key that a German strokes against the iron balusters of a stairwell, the rickety squeak of a bicycle that a sentry rides in making his rounds. Although Fontaine plots a way to escape, he often seems captured in thought about the very nature of sensation.

The parallel does not end there. Much of Bresson's film tells of the hero's inventions of everyday life. He obtains a pencil and paper, objects vital for survival, by dangling a string to a trio of men who make their daily promenades in the courtyard below his cell. He then explains (in first-person voiceover, in contrast to the third-person voiceover in which Gaddis/O'Brien locates what is happening to Stroud) how he fashioned a knife and chisel from a soup spoon; how he undid the wire coils of a bedstead to weave with stolen fabric a tensile cord; how he shaped a piece of an iron window jamb into a hook he then attached to the cord to enable him to cross from one wall to another. The film documents the tactical *bricolage* in which Fontaine (François Leterrier) was engaged in the continuum of isolation. And so does Frankenheimer's film, when Stroud invents a bird's nest from a woolen sock he refolds into a cup-like vessel, or when he constructs the first of many cages from strips of wood he cuts from boxes, the ends of which he chars to fit in the grooves of the struts.[5] It takes pains to illustrate how he uses heat and cold to cut and fashion the bottom of a soda-pop bottle into a dish where the bird can perch and dip its beak to drink water. Where Bresson's hero uses creative invention to move *out* of the prison in Lyons, Frankenheimer's finds ways to burrow further into its confines: and so much that his world eventually transmogrifies into a labyrinth of cages (in a series of remarkable dissolves) where he gets lost. The birds that proliferate

In a series of dissolves, cages, like the birds they contain, begin to proliferate. Prisons multiply within prisons.
Digital frame enlargement.

(before they die of a virus and then, thanks to his art of observation and empirical method, new generations are born again) become visual and auditory signs of a space that opens inwardly and that results from the hero's art of meditation and practical thinking. Stroud's story is ultimately that of burgeoning empathy gained through his relation with the birds and then, philosophically, through the project of prison reform growing from what he learns through his affection for his sparrows and canaries.

The two films diverge when two different intercessors reorder the imbroglio of creative meditation. Bresson's masterpiece takes a radical turn when a young man, Jost (Charles Le Clainche), is thrown into Fontaine's cell. He disrupts the hero's plans as well as the autonomy of his meditation. Fontaine is compelled to probe him to see if he is a stool pigeon or if, youth that he is, he has mental and physical gumption enough to escape with him. Much of the latter part of the film is devoted to the *doubt* the intercessor inspires and the bonding that results from their laconic exchanges. The gaze Fontaine casts upon Jost is analytical. What he sees does not initially yield much; time, however, allows him to witness the emergence of a collaborative and kindred spirit. By marked contrast, Stroud's intercessors are so obviously born of Hollywood that (perhaps by hindsight in 2009) they seem to call the scenario into question. During his stay in Leavenworth, two figures enter into Stroud's life. The first, his mother (Thelma Ritter), has remained with him since he committed the crimes that brought him to where he is. Implied is that he remains so attached to her that the oedipal tie might have been partial cause of his criminal past, this especially implied in a sequence in the mess hall in which he behaves much like James Cagney's Cody Jarrett in *White Heat*, who goes crazy when, by word of mouth passed from one inmate to the next, he learns of his mother's death. Where Jarrett rose up and both embraced and slugged whoever was in his way, Stroud, having been told that he cannot see his mother, struggles with a guard and inserts a knife into the man's belly. Everywhere her photographic image holds sway over the space it adorns. The picture accompanies the hero from one cell to the next until he reaches a higher stage of sexual (and meditative) awareness when, by way of the ornithological passion they share, a second woman (Stella Johnson)—his future spouse—enters his life. The mother, threatened by the younger woman's hold upon her son's empathies, begs him to abandon her. In a final solution to his oedipal condition, he steps upon and crushes the photograph much as he has been squashing insects under his feet in order to nurture his avian surrogate children. His accession to autonomy is complete, we soon learn, when he leaves both Leavenworth and the woman who had moved from Indiana to Kansas to live in his proximity.

Where the Freudian stakes are patent in this sequence of the film, so also are those of the history of cinema on which much of *Birdman* is built. The good-and-bad mother, the figure who nourished and coddled Stroud but who refused to let him fly out of her nest—to the contrary of the sparrow (named "Runty") he encourages to leave the oedipal cell that had given life to the birds—enters the feature as an icon. When we see the name Thelma Ritter onscreen, memories of the cinema (*All About Eve* [1950], *The Mating Season* [1951], *Pickup on South Street* [1953], *Rear Window* [1954], *Daddy Long Legs* [1955], *Pillow Talk* [1959], *The Misfits* [1961], etc.) for which she had been famous come forward. Her characters are seen again in the riddled face whose eyelids get baggy, whose cheeks become furrowed with wrinkles, and whose lips shrivel and pucker over the longer passage of time (1916–1962) that the film relates in two hours. Somewhat like Gloria Swanson's in *Sunset Blvd.* (1950), in the recollection it inspires of times past, Ritter's face locates an itinerary: from a realm of action, in the silent cinema flourishing at the time when the narrative flashback begins (yet before Ritter's career), to a postwar era of suspicion. Ritter's aging face cues the spectator to observe how Stroud weathers his years and how, too, his sensory faculties belong to an earlier age of cinema.

A Korean Conflict

The Freudian narrative locates the film in a history that includes both cinema and a confluence of events in which the dynamics of family romance are in play. In Bresson's *Condamné*, a man escapes the horrors of a history that his autobiography recalls. With regard to that film, the memory of deportation and of the murder of European Jewry and political opponents to Germany's National

Socialism might have been a fact that its public preferred to forget (as Marcel Ophuls would later make clear in The Sorrow and the Pity [Le Chagrin et la pitié, 1969]). At a moment synchronous with Night and Fog (Nuit et brouillard, 1955), Bresson makes visual reference to the Hôtel Terminus where Gestapo agents inform Fontaine that he will soon be executed. Fontaine escapes what throughout the film, in offscreen cries of men tortured and gunshots of firing squads, is taken to be an unearthly world. At the end he and his young friend descend the containing wall and escape into the steamy realm of an uncertain salvation. Correlatively, Birdman stresses the history of a recent war that an American public would have preferred not to remember. It alludes to the Korean conflict that preceded the cold war and, in the American-Soviet divide, to a general sense of immobility and isolation.

The final major sequence of Frankenheimer's feature takes place in Alcatraz. It begins where Stroud embarks on the boat passage that carries him (and, confined in a separate area, the children of the guards) across the water of San Francisco Bay as if it were the River Styx: yet insofar as the first shots had already located Alcatraz in a real world at the shore of a growing and prosperous city, upon initial viewing it is difficult to know what narrative or polemical angle to expect after the setting of this voyage. Will the film advocate penal reform? Will it emphasize how a regime of isolation and monotony crushes the victims of the penal system? At its end, will the film have somehow drawn a history of prison films through its depiction of the present moment?

Two structural elements in the Alcatraz portion of the film respond to these questions forthrightly. The first runs through the film and, in accord with the oedipal scenario, draws attention to the cliché, "enemy brothers." Stroud has a nemesis in his commanding warden, Harvey Shoemaker (Karl Malden), who follows—or, better, accompanies—him from one prison to the next. He is Stroud's *other*, his Robinson (as Bardamu might have it in Voyage au bout de la nuit), who looks at the inside from without just as Stroud looks at the world from within. Shoemaker watches the man whom he had at first despised become the honest, visionary, and guru-like figure that he is in the final shots. The words of contempt that the two men spat in each other's faces early in their lives give way to heated intellectual (one might call it virtually amicable) dialogue about the nature of imprisonment and its effect upon those undergoing its depredations. After being denied the right to continue the research he had been undertaking at Leavenworth, now in the desolating conditions of Alcatraz, Stroud hits upon the idea of writing a book about incarceration. It uncannily foreshadows Foucault's conclusions in Discipline and Punish, published thirteen years later.

In a courtyard at Alcatraz, then, like the place where Stroud found his first bird at Leavenworth, an idea and a project are born. While conferring with a prison chaplain and warming up to a game of handball—the game of games, the "perfect game," the most fabulous of all sports, requiring ambidexterity and strategy as no other, and a game born of prisons—Stroud's light bulb goes on.

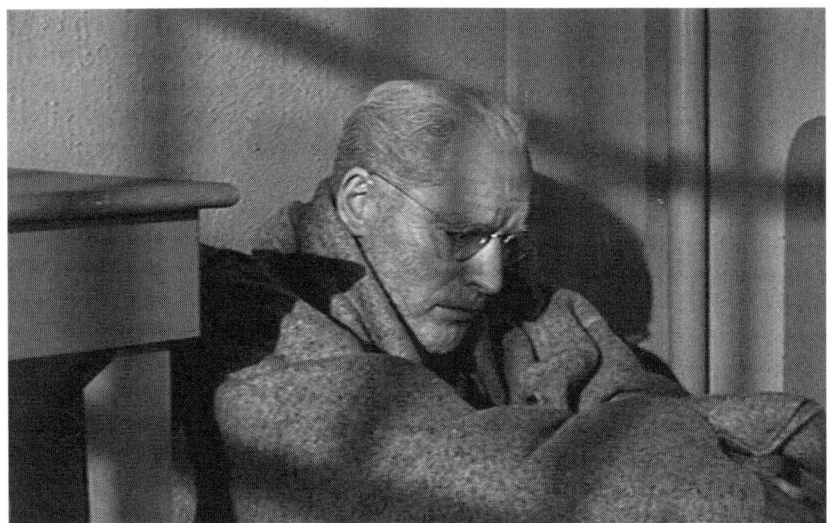

Robert Stroud (Burt Lancaster) meditates in the confines of Alcatraz, his vision partially obscured by the shadows cast by the bars of his cell.

Digital frame enlargement.

He decides to write not about himself but about the criminality of incarceration and the nefarious effects of its purported regimes of "correction" and so-called "rehabilitation." So true to the Hollywood mold that it calls the tradition of prisoner-warden interactions into question by way of mirroring, Stroud's ensuing debate with Shoemaker remains unresolved. The warden, having striven bureaucratically throughout his entire career to enable a small degree of rehabilitation, is upstaged when Stroud offers a polished manuscript that argues for more radically humane solutions.

Resolution is deferred (Hollywood *oblige*) when the second structural element intervenes. In the midst of the two men's debate over penal reform, a prison riot is fomented by some of Stroud's fellow prisoners trying to crash out of the citadel. The ringleader obtains two guns that enable the men to open their cells and lead a charge. The event initially resembles Don Siegel's *Riot in Cell Block 11* (1954) but soon recalls the Korean conflict of the preceding decade: Stroud's fraternal nemesis Shoemaker calls upon the army to quell the uprising that has turned the inside of Alcatraz into a battleground of bent iron and rubble; soldiers lay the citadel to siege, blasting it with tear gas, machine-gun fire, and bazooka-launched armor-piercing cannon. The inside is so trashed that the viewer wonders if the implied aim was to destroy the prison in a flurry of gunfire. The sequence enacts violence on what Stroud had called into question through meditation and writing. That he is shown quiescent, ensconced in his cell while his fellow mates are gassed and gunned, indicates where the filmmaker's sympathies are found. Stroud prefers an inner rehabilitation, gained by experience and access to knowledge, which the film takes to be its example.

Crashing In

In the midst of the riot Stroud "crashes in." In the tradition of the prison movies out of which *Birdman* emerges, inmates usually harbor the hope of finding freedom. In *High Sierra* (1941), a past model of the genre, the tragic hero (Humphrey Bogart) finds himself "pardoned" from the Mossmoor Prison in Indiana thanks to an unnamed underground that summons him to pull a heist at Palm Springs in exchange for his release. Everything goes awry. He is enmeshed in an orphic webbing of fatality that leads him up the eastern slope of Mount Whitney where, when "turning back," like a modern-day Orpheus, he is shot from behind. Dropped to the foot of the mountain, his body is mourned by his modern-day Eurydice (Ida Lupino), among a group of bystanders that bears resemblance to a choir in a Sophoclean tragedy. Blinded by what she had witnessed (and thus becoming something of a female Oedipus), she asks a member of the group gathered around the scene, "What does it mean, to crash out?" To which "Healy" (Jerome Cowan), a tough journalist in a trench coat, responds, "You mean, sister, you don't know what it is to crash out? Why it means . . . to be free." The orphic hero has fallen victim to his destiny but has ultimately "crashed out" of an imbroglio so infernal that all the human condition seems to be a universal prison.

By marked contrast, Frankenheimer's Stroud crashes *into* a world of the same order. He finds solace in self-containment that comes with accession to knowledge. At the film's end a motorboat brings the hero to the pier where the harbor cruises had been announced at the beginning. He lands and finds Gaddis, his biographer (or hagiographer) who (for the duration of the film) has been awaiting the pleasure of meeting him before he is transferred to a penitentiary in Missouri. No matter where Stroud goes, this sequence makes clear, the wizened man is one with himself. He is free to meditate much in the way that Michel Foucault, in the wake of prison riots in the early 1970s, wrote of inmates who rose up against "an entire state of physical misery that is over a century old: against cold, suffocation and overcrowding, against decrepit walls, hunger, physical maltreatment. But they were also revolts against model prisons, tranquillizers, isolation, the medical or educational services" (30). Protest against loathsome "rehabilitation" to which prisoners are subjected might have been the topic of the book that Stroud never published and that Foucault completed in his stead. In "crashing in," in acceding to a state of meditation inside of his cage, Stroud shows how the "soul" is "an effect and a nascent instrument of a political anatomy." Frankenheimer's film offers a way of thinking about how this "soul" is the "prison of the body" (34). Finally, recalling what poet Jean Lemaire's green lover intuited in his cage and what drove him to crash into the jaws of the mastiff that swallowed him, Frankenheimer's film prompts reflection on the cages in which we are ordered to live. Seeing it now, and seeing it in view of the many blogs recounting the nature of life in the squalid and overcrowded prisons of our time, inspires a politics bolder than what *Birdman of Alcatraz* might have initially sought.

NOTES

1. The first printed copy (following the manuscript of 1505) is found in Jean Lemaire de Belges, *Les Illustrations de Gaule et singularitez de Troye . . . avec les deux epistres de l'amant vert* (Paris, 1512) [Harvard Houghton Library Typ 515.12.55]. For a readily available transcription in modern typography, see Gray 25–35.
2. The distinction of "molar" and "molecular" qualities of atmosphere is drawn from Deleuze 111–13. The director's name is in fact "volatile" and protean, where those of the characters become numbers permanently stenciled on the clothing they wear.
3. Edward Dimendberg carefully studies how the "strolls of characters" in urban places tend to condense the "metropolis into a spatial fragment" (119). The person walking, at once the "user" and the "spectator" of the city, see immanently, in contrast to the Icarian "bird's eye" view—never seen in Frankenheimer's film—that suggests omniscience. At its outset *Birdman* works through and out of this feature of the noir tradition.
4. The voice is slightly incorrect. The *Lusitania* was sunk on May 7, 1915, and not on orders from the kaiser.
5. *Bricolage* is not taken lightly. The regretted Claude Lévi-Strauss launched the concept in the first chapter of *La Pensée sauvage*, a work synchronous with *Birdman*. For Lévi-Strauss, *bricolage* is as much a mental as a physical process, which indeed both Bresson's and Frankenheimer's films make clear.

Walking the Line
with the *Fille Fatale*

LINDA RUTH WILLIAMS

Made some years after Frankenheimer's early golden period of 1962–1966, the underrated 1970 film *I Walk the Line* does not announce itself as a work of great significance. Based on *An Exile*, Madison Jones's 1967 southern gothic novel, *I Walk the Line* is at first glance a desultory story of the Tennessee backwoods focused on the midlife crisis of Sheriff Henry Tawes (Gregory Peck). Yet underneath the slight narrative, its subject matter is quietly scandalous, a sex-crime yarn laced with noirish suggestions of taboo pleasures, playing out some of the issues and anxieties that John Boorman's far more successful *Deliverance* was to revisit two years later. Despite its sparse aesthetic, *I Walk the Line* is saturated in sex, from the deputy's open surveying of a porn magazine at the station to the repeated (and rejected) bedroom opportunities Tawes's wife creates, to the visiting federal officer's suggestion that what the town needs is a hotel "with hot sheets." And then there is Alma McCain (Tuesday Weld), the teenage girl/woman from a bootlegger's family who lures the married sheriff into her bed, and whose wrong-side-of-the-tracks activities seem to extend to incest.

This chapter discusses sex, women, and family in Frankenheimer's film, and looks at what is for me its most difficult issue, the erotic portrayal of its young female lead, a portrayal *I Walk the Line* neither evades nor exploits. Weld's nubile *femme fatale* character can be contextualized through later teen seducers, making *I Walk the Line* an important text in the prehistory of sub-genres that were to become central to 1980s and 1990s U.S. cinema: the erotic thriller and erotic melodrama. Whilst more celebrated or notorious 1970s texts such as *Play Misty for Me* (1971), *Looking for Mr. Goodbar* (1977), and *Eyes of Laura Mars* (1978) have been clearly acknowledged as prototypes of these later genres focused on dangerous pleasures (see Williams *Erotic*), *I Walk the Line* is rarely discussed in this context, even though its heady—if also curiously underplayed—cocktail of sex, law, and family crisis establishes it as highly prescient. Yet the story is so slight that Pauline Kael called it an "anti-audience film" (*New Yorker*, December

5, 1970):[1] Tawes becomes enamored of Alma after deciding not to charge her and her brother for a driving misdemeanor. Alma's father (Ralph Meeker) encourages the affair in order to ensure that Tawes protects the McCain clan's illicit whiskey operation: Alma is both reward and collateral exchanged in an unspoken agreement between lawman and criminal. When the sheriff is pressed to locate and arrest the elusive bootleggers, he asks Alma to elope with him, but—through violence—she demonstrates that she was only ever keeping him sweet for her family's sake. Tawes is left despairing, with a ruined marriage, a broken family, and a lost reputation as a lawman.

This story is also told in parallel musical form. The film gets its title from the iconic Johnny Cash song after which the 2005 biopic of the man in black (James Mangold's *Walk the Line*) was also named, although Frankenheimer used Cash as collaborator rather than figure of tribute. Vocalized and instrumental versions of eight Cash songs, newly penned or specially re-recorded, sporadically punctuate and comment on the action. Cash had contributed to a number of movie sound tracks prior to *I Walk the Line*, and was at this point developing something of an acting career (Miller 200–201). Frankenheimer even remarked that the "picture was definitely directed around the songs" (Pratley, *Films* 105), making this an interesting case in the ongoing interrelationship of popular music and New Hollywood. Voiced by Cash's deep baritone, this musical narrative reinforces the sense that this is Peck's film; Frankenheimer saw Cash as the orator of Tawes's conscience (Pratley, *Films* 106). Peck certainly (and characteristically) thought of the film as his, too, writing to Frankenheimer after principal photography was completed, "A comment is that while you have directed a smashing picture, you have not yet devoted the same tender care to the editing. . . . Now, you can tell me to go to hell if you want to, and wrap the picture up as it is. We'll still be friends. But we can't be friends unless I can speak freely and give you my honest opinion" (Peck to Frankenheimer). This starry combination of Frankenheimer, Peck, and Cash may make *I Walk the Line* irresistibly a male story. However, I read it here as a women's film.

Failed Males and Female Troubles

In the arc of Frankenheimer's career, it is easy to read this film as the beginning of a fallow period, and it is usually passed over in favor of *Birdman of Alcatraz* (1962), *The Manchurian Candidate* (1962), and *Seven Days in May* (1964). When shooting started in Tennessee, a year or so on after the June 5, 1968, death of his friend Bobby Kennedy,[2] Frankenheimer had already distanced himself from Hollywood and set up home in Paris, and was questioning his place in cinema per se. When it was released, critics called *I Walk the Line* pallid and centerless; Pauline Kael wrote that it "is half over while you're still wondering when it's going to start, and finally it's over but never did get started." Another reviewer judged that "no Frankenheimer film was ever tedious, until *I Walk the Line*, which is singularly uncompelling from the moment, very early on, when you see the way things are going" (*Financial Times*). Some of this might be attributable to its meandering, languid narrative. *Sight and Sound*'s Richard Coombs saw *I Walk the Line* as indicative of Frankenheimer stepping down from a "readily identifiable, pyrotechnical style" to something "more self-effacing, static and muted." Kael accuses Frankenheimer of loitering over every shot "trying to squeeze art into it."

With film-historical hindsight, this uncompelling loitering was perhaps what would become *most* compelling, most valued, about U.S. films around this time. Thomas Elsaesser discusses the antiheroism of the neo-heroes in the early 1970s, imbued as they seemed to be with "an almost physical sense of inconsequential action, of pointlessness and uselessness . . . which speak of a radical skepticism about American virtues of ambition, vision, drive" ("Pathos" 282). *I Walk the Line* is steeped in this critical ennui. For Elsaesser, whilst road movies of the period are driven by their genre, their heroes are driven by very little, combining "the unmotivated hero and the motif of the journey" (280). *I Walk the Line* is not a road movie, but Tawes and Alma's relationship is framed by cars, so it's worth briefly considering this framing idea of being "driven." Tawes spends a lot of time in his police car, and confrontations involving vehicles instigate and conclude this pessimistic narrative, but there is no romance or purpose to it. Without direction, as it were, he travels up and down the same road, from nowhere to nowhere else. Despite being a character in the grip of sexual passion, Tawes is more reactive than active. Even when describing his childhood home, now sunken to make room for a dam (another *Deliverance* connection), he can only passively relate himself to cataclysmic change: "You see the lake over there?" he says to Alma. "That was our place." "You mean they took it from you?" she asks, and he replies, "They took *us* from *it*." He fantasizes about whisking Alma away to Canada or California, yet just drives around in circles. Frankenheimer designated this an authorial theme: "Your life cannot change—you are what you are" (Pratley, *Films* 104). So while his lust (perhaps love) pushes the narrative, it doesn't drive it too hard. If this is loosely a crime yarn prefiguring earlier and later films focusing on a duped cop and a *femme fatale*, there is little urgency here.

From the point of view of the men involved—in the production, and fictionally—*I Walk the Line* is then a film beset with failure, though not perhaps the kind of glorious heroic failure for which films of the late 1960s and early 1970s are celebrated. There are surely two kinds of failed males at large in the cinema of this period: those romanticized for their antiheroic psychic or social incompletion addressed by Elsaesser and others, and those whose flaws are rather more mundane and less epoch-defining. The despair of *Five Easy Pieces* (1970), *Two-Lane Blacktop* (1971), or *Thieves Like Us* (1974), the impotent heroes celebrated in Robert Kolker's *A Cinema of Loneliness*, the incoherent texts and damaged psyches of Robin Wood's *Hollywood from Vietnam to Reagan*, all exemplify the first kind of failure, and have come to speak for their moment. Sheriff Tawes can't get no satisfaction either, but he's unlikely to be reclaimed as a historical cultural icon or symptom. Indeed, his frustration is bound to a wider constellation of dissatisfaction: *I Walk the Line* was a box office failure; it was a film that Frankenheimer initially regretted agreeing to direct; it *didn't* feature his preferred choice, Gene Hackman, in the lead role (Columbia hired Peck over Frankenheimer's head);[3] and it is a film about a man who himself fails to secure the girl who's seduced him, in the process allowing his family to fall apart. Tawes even fails to "arrive" in death: Frankenheimer shot a suicide ending, but it was roundly rejected by preview audiences (Pratley, *Films* 104). Cash and Frankenheimer wanted to name the film after the Cash song "Face of Despair," but Columbia wouldn't let them do that, either (105). Peck's performance was poorly reviewed, and even Peck himself thanked providence that "people remember us for our best work.... No-one comes up and says 'I hated you in *I Walk the Line*'" (Haney 358). Frankenheimer respected Peck for the image change required in performing this flawed character. Casting the unalloyed hero of *Gentleman's Agreement* (1947), *The Guns of Navarone* (1961), and, perhaps most famously, *To Kill a Mockingbird* (1962) (Peck's Atticus Finch ranked first in the American Film Institute's 2003 list of cinematic heroes) was an interesting risk, but the courage of it was all but lost on contemporary reviewers, who saw him as miscast and at odds with the film's sparse, hopeless aesthetic. Though to some extent the unmanned-man is Frankenheimer's stock in trade, this tinge of disappointment both within and without the story might account for why the film has been neglected.

From a woman's point of view, however, *I Walk the Line* emerges as a more successful, if troubling, text. What good reviews it got stood upon the women's story, which emerges around the edges of Tawes's central malaise, and upon the performances of the female stars: Estelle Parsons as Tawes's spurned wife, Ellen, as well as Weld. Cineastes' tastes at the moment of the film's release focused on Tawes's existential-sexual crisis, but the relationship of these women to the family and to Tawes throws up far more interesting questions. I say "women" here, but one of the key issues this film poses, perhaps despite itself, is that of the uneasy boundary between girlhood and womanhood. The anxiety around sexualized girlhood in Frankenheimer's film and the male desire it provokes make the politics of young female flesh as central to *I Walk the Line*, and to its cultural moment, as its primary story of flawed masculinity and sacrifice.

The first significant narrative event is Tawes's meeting with the bra-less Alma, and from this moment her nubile sexuality is established as the prime bait and commodity in the trap that ensnares the sheriff. The question not just of sexuality but of minority is central to her interrogation about a truck she claims she has crashed, concealing her kid brother's crime (criminalized and criminalizing children are at the fore from the start, as they are in the novel).[4] Tawes asserts that he saw a *boy* driving, but his half-joking question, "You're sure not a boy, are you?" requires an answer that reinforces both gender and youth: not boy *but girl*. Alma's age is uncertain, although the film characterizes her as

First view of the *fille fatale* (Tuesday Weld as Alma) in *I Walk the Line* (Columbia, 1970): "And you're sure not a boy now, are you?"
Digital frame enlargement.

particularly young in conjunction with her confirmed and suspected sexual partners, with the imperious Tawes (played by a graying fifty-three-year-old Peck) and with her own father Carl McCain (the forty-nine-year-old Meeker). Since Weld was herself twenty-six when filming started, and spring/autumn liaisons between younger women and older men are not uncommon in Hollywood, this may seem unremarkable. Indeed, *I Walk the Line* is ambiguous about where it locates Alma across the child-adult boundary. As Kristen Hatch makes clear in her useful essay on the history of cinematic images of sexualized adolescent girls, uneasy representations of sexualized "girls" have not always regarded age of consent as a compellingly definitive demarcation. Indeed, the editors of the volume in which Hatch's essay appears take "girlhood" as a wide brief, meaning anything from tweenie to teen to "coming of age" girl-woman to young female adult (Gateward and Pomerance 14–15). Hatch discusses the controversial 1956 film *Baby Doll* in terms of images of child abuse even though its erotically infantilized girl-woman protagonist (Carroll Baker, twenty-five when the film was released) is nineteen and married.[5] *I Walk the Line* is more vague than *Baby Doll* about Alma's age, although contemporary reception material consistently shows that she was read as a teenager; she was never referred to as a woman, always a girl—or worse. One contemporary reviewer called Alma a "young, nubile dolly-dish" (*Daily Mirror*); another an "infantile little tramp" (*Financial Times*); a third a "wily nymphet" (*Daily Mail*). Terms such as "nymph" (or its diminutive), previously rehearsed in reviews of Stanley Kubrick's 1962 film *Lolita*, suggest the extreme youth of the girl while evading the charge of child abuse via a mythological gesture.[6]

So what does the teen girl mean here, as a being positioned between father and lover, criminal family and transgressing lawman? After the truck crash, Alma returns to her all-male family and is questioned about whether her interrogation gave the sheriff the scent of moonshine. Yet the dialogue soon confuses scent with Alma herself, as if she reeked of the illicit industry of her kin (bootlegging is read by the federal agent as an almost inherited condition: fathers teach sons, who teach their own sons, in a tradition protected by women). Sensual apprehension of the lone female in their midst generates some resonant dialogue that circulates around that most earthy and yet ephemeral of senses, scent: "How do you know he smelled you most?" asks McCain of Alma's encounter with Tawes; "How do you know he didn't smell the whiskey most?"—to which her elder brother interjects, "She's wearing violets not whisky." The exchange is jaw-droppingly revelatory, suggesting a family of males sniffing out signs of guilt, crime, and sex emanating even from the bodies of their own close kinswomen. The scene also smacks uneasily of incest, with brother and father looking intently at Alma as they conjecture imaginatively about how much Tawes must have wanted to touch her, in the process revealing how much they want to touch her—or have already. Further, and in a way that is not true of Jones's novel, Frankenheimer's film infantilizes Alma in the company of her father, piling taboo on taboo. Later into the narrative, Alma's father crouches by her bed promising her new dresses. She squeals with delight like a little girl, but the sense that she is being paid both for taking care of the suspicious Tawes and for taking care of twisted McCain hangs heavy in the air. Yet unlike the noirishly sultry seductress of Jones's novel, *I Walk the Line*'s Alma is more ambiguous, presenting first as an amoral backwoods girl rather than an immoral noir *femme* (though she does provoke the film's most starkly nourish—and urban—sequence, when Tawes has to scour the nighttime lonely streets, searching lost cars in the hopeless quest for a missing incriminating letter, while his deputy watches silhouetted in a lone lit window above, and agitated dogs bark into the darkness). Perhaps speaking directly to early 1970s audiences, Weld's Alma appears more free-spirited than her novelistic counterpart, who seems to have walked into Jones's 1967 novel out of a 1940s B-noir. The fey naïveté of Weld's Alma attracts Tawes; the novel's older-seeming Alma tortures him.[7] The novel is also told entirely from Tawes's point of view, whereas the film does give us some privileged views of Alma with her family, not least when they take spontaneous pleasure in a drive-in movie (George Marshall's 1969 Jerry Lewis vehicle *Hook, Line and Sinker*).[8]

Frankenheimer's Alma seems then to be both more autonomously sexual and younger than her counterpart in the source material. As I argue in an article looking at revenging teens in neo-noir since the 1990s ("Woman Scorned"), the sexualized adolescent girl has been a strong motif in recent cinema. The rise of teen genres has seen various creative teen-inflected spins on established forms, and neo-noir is no exception, with noir's *femme fatale* being downsized into a *fille fatale* (a term also deployed by Hatch). Frankenheimer's Alma looks forward to this *fille fatale*; Jones's Alma looks backward to a more adult *femme*. Of course, dangerously sexualized girl-women are not new in Hollywood (Weld herself had starred as a murderously deranged *fille fatale* cheerleader in the 1968 film *Pretty Poison*), though perhaps there have been more of them since the 1980s: Steven

Woodward argues that "the Lolita figure is to this day the dominant image of the feminine form of aggressor. In her, beauty is not the image of spiritual goodness but a mask over corruption" (313). The dominant trend in recent neo-*noir* hybrids has been to figure the girl/woman as a psycho-pubescent, dangerous to the men she ensnares and making up for the lack of whatever power full womanhood might denote through (usually) irrational violence. With only a few exceptions, box office excitement is generated by demonizing this *fille fatale*. Given the pervasive suspicion of teens in wider culture (ephebiphobia, or fear of youth, a variation on paedophobia, or fear of children), it is not surprising that adolescent girls would be the particular focus of distrust, with young female sexuality presented as perilous or deranged. One reviewer of *I Walk the Line* made youth explicitly the index of deception: Alma's role is of "a dazzling child of nature whose innocence of expression is only equaled by her duplicity of mind" (*Daily Telegraph*). Of course, cinema is full of scheming or untrustworthy young women, but sexual entrapment by the underaged is a specific trope. Teen-noirs such as Katt Shea Ruben's *Poison Ivy* (1992) or David Slade's *Hard Candy* (2005) present Lolita figures as lures for men, goaded into (the potentially criminal activity of) responding to them sexually. In Alan Shapiro's *The Crush* (1993), Alicia Silverstone never becomes the male protagonist's full sexual partner (exonerating him therefore from acted-out paedophilia), yet she is sexualized enough to try, and thwarted desire drives her revenge. *Hard Candy* dramatizes a fourteen-year-old girl's action against paedophiles in a way that is confidently politically engaged, whilst Matthew Bright's *Freeway* (1996) seems to deliver a strong blow for girls abused by older men. However, these films still flirt with—and (being exploitation films) exploit—widespread images of sexualized adolescent girls' bodies, before those girls get their revenge.

Weld's Alma prefigures these teen *femmes* in a number of ways, though her political context is rather different. In their confused and haphazard worldview, the more recent films reflect anxieties about girls' complicity and ability to consent, and are clearly aware of the "girl-power" emphases of third-wave feminism. Some, such as the coming-of-age films that Sarah Hentges discusses, are overtly teen-focused. A version of *I Walk the Line* reworked from Alma's point of view would be an intriguing film indeed. Generally speaking, the recent *fille fatale* films take one of two positions, either lining up with adult-framed backlash texts to demonize the *fille fatale* (both the aforementioned *Poison Ivy* and Ian Corson's *Malicious* [1995] as teen formations of *Fatal Attraction* [1987]) or using her as a vehicle for propounding a mainstream form of exploitation-flavored liberation (*Freeway*; *Hard Candy*). Timothy Shary briefly reads films depicting adult-teen pairings as being "adamantly ambiguous in placing 'blame' on both characters for their illicit desires" (213). Although Alma might look something like her generic descendants, she functions rather differently in the politics of Frankenheimer's film. While the age difference between the pair is constantly foregrounded, Henry's transgression is presented as infidelity rather than paedophilia. This may be because, as Hatch shows, there was a radical shift in perceptions of the morality of such relationships from the mid-1970s onward. American society in general and Hollywood in particular have "become steadily less restrictive regarding sexuality since the 1960s," but "we have become increasingly enlightened regarding the problem of child sexual abuse since that period, when child victims of incest and molestation were regarded as sex delinquents" (164). Before the mid-1970s, courts and media "downplayed the adult's role in the molestation of children, attributing such acts to feeblemindedness or impotence on the part of the adult" (170–71). Afterward, a widespread cultural urge to re-designate children as innocent and the more thorough criminalization of sexualizing children on film in 1977 shifted the terms through which young female sexuality would be proscribed and prescribed. *I Walk the Line* precedes this shift. It also legally exonerates Tawes through the revelation that Alma has a husband in prison, deeming her notionally "legal."

However, like a number of other U.S. states, Tennessee doesn't have a single age of consent, and existing laws are ambiguous. For instance, it is, and was then, legal for minors younger than sixteen to be given a license to marry in special circumstances.[9] Let's not forget that Baby Doll was also married. Alma may then be any teen age, and the film's anxiety about crossing the line is underpinned by the fact that her first "date" with him takes place in Tawes's courtroom,[10] while their second is accompanied by Cash singing "On This Side of the Law," a song written for the movie that asks in its chorus: "On this side of the law, On that side of the law, Who is right? Who is wrong? Who is for and who is against the law?"

"Flesh and Blood Needs Flesh and Blood": Women/Class/Family

Alma's *fille fatale* neo-noir daughters are more starkly drawn by their genres than she is in this film; perhaps it is a strength of Weld's performance, or of the complexity of Frankenheimer's film, that her motivations and pleasures are more ambiguous. Her manipulativeness makes it hard to tell how far she is herself the manipulated daughter of a felon family. Frankenheimer may be known for his male studies and flawed heroes, but it is women who deliver the stand-out performances of *I Walk the Line*, to the extent that Peck seems to function primarily as witness to the more positive performances of the women laying claim to him. Reviewers consequently praised Weld and Parsons at the expense of Peck (see *Financial Times*, *The Times*, the *Daily Telegraph*, *The Observer* and the *Sunday Times*). This may be because he speaks little, while both Alma and Ellen copiously verbalize to seduce or secure Tawes's affections. Although reviewers focused on Weld's physique, her cheerful, uneducated chit-chat is also a lure. Tawes succumbs, and as this threatens his previous respectable sense of self (from which he has become, in the title of the novel, an exile), so it also threatens his family. If Alma talks to ensnare him, Ellen talks to keep hold of him, working hard at doing all the emotional leg work involved in redrawing the map of their shifting marriage. Frankenheimer stages their heartbreaking encounters in ambivalent domestic locations, particularly architectural openings, primed to reinforce Tawes's lack of commitment—doorways, verandas, and two encounters on the stairs, where she is either definitively up or down, but he hovers in the process of moving away, in between.[11] Ellen's incessant chattering keeps the boat of their family precariously afloat. Her talk is pitched against the abyss of his silence, particularly in bed. It also does double service in providing the audience with a relationship backstory: Ellen originally seduced Tawes; perhaps he never loved her; she feels him to be her intellectual superior. We know from her Oscar-winning performance in *Bonnie and Clyde* (1967) that Estelle Parsons can deliver a knockout combination of the shrill and the small-minded, but here hysteria is softened by desperation and devotion. With apron and hair pins, Parsons convincingly essays a woman uninterested in liberation, who turns to *Reader's Digest* for her psycho-sexual insights into men's need to "seek out a girl."

The generic form that was to develop in backlash-era erotic melodramas and thrillers would position a figure like Alma as family-threatening because sexualized and single. For Susan Faludi, the typical backlash morality tale as it was to unfold in the 1980s featured a good mother winning and an independent woman getting punished ("the backlash thesis: women were unhappy because they were too free; their liberation had denied them marriage and motherhood" [141]). Destruction of the family would become a common motif in the grown-up erotic thriller and its teeny spawn (a twist on the problematic absent families of *noir*). Films like Adrian Lyne's *Fatal Attraction* or Andrew Stevens's *Scorned* (1994) set a precedent for teen-marketed fare that featured an attractive young Lolita

Alienation and domestic imprisonment: the spurned Ellen (Estelle Parsons) after Tawes (Gregory Peck) has retreated from her.

Digital frame enlargement.

figure entering a respectable middle-class home with a mission to seduce and then destroy not just the (straying) male but the nuclear domestic unit itself. Alma's threat to Ellen's domain might make *I Walk the Line* the *Fatal Attraction* for the American renaissance generation, moved wholesale from city to country and backward from the mid-1980s to the late 1960s. Yet however *fatale* she might seem in duping Tawes, Alma kills no one (although she does spear him with a meat-hook in the movie's denouement). And while Tawes's bourgeois family is threatened (like that of Michael Douglas's Dan in *Fatal Attraction*), Alma's underclass clan thrives. Indeed, she acts not out of lust, it seems, but out of loyalty, shoring up the interests of her family with every seductive maneuver. The women's fight over Tawes might then be seen as a fight for two different kinds of family rather than a backlash-inflected fight to destroy the family on the one hand or shore it up on the other. Alma departs from the film hugging her younger brother on the back of the family flat-bed, having defended her men against the man she duped, once he is no longer useful. Alma's mantra is, "You got your people and I got mine." This remains uneasily sexualized: as Cash sings in accompaniment to Tawes's last desperate car chase, "Flesh and blood needs flesh and blood." Sexual bodies need each other, and blood relatives need their own. The intimacy of sex and kin is too close for comfort, feeding into a stereotype of backwoods interbreeding.

So while *I Walk the Line* is certainly steeped in sex, this cannot be disentangled from its vision of class and belonging. Recent teen noir stories have also been strongly inflected by social difference, with disempowered young women such as Vanessa in *Freeway* or Ivy in *Poison Ivy* using their nubile sexuality to avenge the poor lot that life has dealt them, or more privileged girls such as Kathryn in Roger Kumble's *Cruel Intentions* (1999) using sex to shore up their social power. Kelly and Suzy in John McNaughton's *Wild Things* (1998) are differently inflected as rich and poor teen *fatales*. Frankenheimer also adopts distinct visual paradigms for the two sides involved in *I Walk the Line* as a class-focused sexual morality tale. Tawes's family, respectably embedded in the core of their community, are homely and always seen securely surrounded by the paraphernalia of domesticity. A comfy veranda shields them from the intense Tennessee climate, and Tawes's aging father laments less fortunate folks who fail to "hold onto something as ordinary as shade." The disempowered have to labor in the heat: Alma's menfolk seem most at home in the fiery industrial atmosphere of their still, hidden in an underworld basement beneath the floorboards, where they are seen, partially clad, stoking and slaving, sweating and feeding the furnace. A lurid cinematic aesthetic has long infused movies that marry heat with sex and crime, especially associated with southern states. However, if *I Walk the Line* looks as parched as such desert-noirs as John Dahl's *Kill Me Again* (1989) or *Red Rock West* (1993)—all dusty scrubland and peeling paint—for the most part there is a coolness about its Panavision view. Certainly—the sweaty inferno of the still notwithstanding—it doesn't touch the tropicality of other overheated southern erotic thrillers such as *Body Heat* (1981) or *The Hot Spot* (1990). But even without a moral center, *I Walk the Line* visually loads the dice of sin against the McCains in metaphorically presenting their illicit activity as hell, and as *hot*—sexually as well as thermally.

I Walk the Line plays out this sexual melodrama through an aesthetic agenda that is then both rich and austere, and that also positions this disenfranchised rural South as America's underclass. Yet the McCains are the only people in the film who seem to work particularly hard. Presented as itinerant—Alma enters and leaves the film in a truck—they arrive, then set up and stoke their still, then leave. They are mobile. Henry's world is different. Wide Cinemascope landscapes in bleached-out colors, accompanied by pristine silence for most of the sound track (when Cash isn't singing), contribute to its enervated stillness, giving the narrative a lack of urgency and underpinning the sense that in this obscure corner of the South little happens. Frankenheimer has said that he wanted the film to look like an Andrew Wyeth painting as *The Gypsy Moths* had (Pratley, *Films* 105). Thomas Elsaesser calls such a cinematic space "the kind of scenery precisely nowhere and everywhere in America, and therefore furnishing an important element of abstraction without being itself the least bit abstract" (290). As the film opens, and then again as it closes, David Walsh's camera lingers on assorted homely faces found by Frankenheimer in the Tennessee shoot, from plain to grotesque. For Armstrong, this establishes the landscape of the film as also one of failure, a stranded wasteland (Armstrong 147–48). The technique of using local extras and letting their down-home folksy looks "speak" for the location they inhabit was to be emulated two years later and rather more famously in *Deliverance*, shot in Georgia and South Carolina. In that film, southern faces signify inbreeding and threat to city folk, the hostile manifestation of what Carol Clover has called "urbanoia." Frankenheimer's

The neo-noir trap begins to bite: Sheriff Tawes framed by federal officer Bascomb (Lonny Chapman) and scheming deputy Hunnicutt (Charles Durning).
Digital frame enlargement.

Tennessee faces suggest lives lived in ascetic hardship—patient, God-fearing, *white*—and are so central to the film's view of people as both lost and trapped that they bookend the movie, providing the establishing shots over which the credits roll as well as the film's meandering concluding thoughts, and recall Walker Evans's sharecropper documentary photographs of the 1930s. However, the McCains aren't trapped—yet. More than the bourgeois Taweses, it is the poor white folks, disenfranchised by economics and geographical isolation, who are walking a precarious line, and Frankenheimer places them in a landscape of scrubland, breaker's yards, and aestheticized human detritus. As Alma's father says, without their illicit whiskey still "we might as well be niggers." Without young women to pass around, this might also be true. Alma's willingness to lend her body to the lawman, the glowing sign of his transgression, enables her family to evade a more precarious social state.

NOTES

1. All citations of press materials are from the British Film Institute collection of newsprint reviews. These were cataloged before it was the consistent practice to include the name of the reviewer and the page on which the review appeared, so I have usually included name of publication only. Reviews of *I Walk the Line* without page number include those in the *Daily Telegraph* (Patrick Gibbs, April 30, 1971), the *Financial Times* (David Robinson, April 30, 1971), *The Observer* (George Melly, February 5, 1971), and the *Sunday Times* (Dilys Powell, February 5, 1971); reviews with neither author name nor page number include those from the *Daily Mail* (April 28, 1971), *The Guardian* (April 29, 1971), the *Daily Mirror* (April 30, 1971), and *The Times* (April 30, 1971).
2. Armstrong cites filming as starting in the fall of 1969 (29); Pratley writes that in January 1970 Frankenheimer first "became involved in" *I Walk the Line* (*Films* 99). It was released in the United States on November 18, 1970.
3. Frankenheimer has said that casting Peck "killed the movie . . . having him play a Tennessee sheriff just shot credulity all to hell" (Champlin 121).
4. Early on in the novel, Tawes gives evidence at a court case focused on boys engaged in a pornography distribution ring, their labors paid for by a trip to a prostitute (Jones 24–25).
5. "At nineteen, Baby Doll is hardly too young to be married, particularly by the standards of 1950s American society. Nonetheless, in commentary on the film, she was consistently referred to as Archie's 'child bride,' connoting the moral decay of the old South" (Hatch 169).
6. The term "nymphet" itself had been popularized in Vladimir Nabokov's 1955 novel *Lolita* to designate sexually alluring girls between nine and fourteen: "their 'true nature' is not human, but nymphic (that is demoniac); and these chosen creatures I propose to designate as 'nymphets'" (16).
7. Frankenheimer discusses the changes made between novel and screenplay in an interview with Pratley: "The wife was an impossible character in the book, constantly nagging at him, and I thought that made it much too easy for him, that's just so clichéd—the husband leaves the nagging wife and goes with the young, pretty girl. . . . The girl was more of a bitch too, really turning on him in the end" (*Films* 104).

8. They watch the movie from the back of their flat-bed. The Tawes family also watch this film, with serious solemnity, from their closed-in car in a different part of the audience.
9. See *http://criminal.findlaw.com/marriage/marriage-basics/state-age-of-consent-laws.html*. See also "Tennessee Age of Consent," archived at *http://blog.laborlawtalk.com/2006/11/09/tennessee-age-of-consent/*: "An individual must be at least 18 years old to legally consent to sex with an adult, under Tennessee law. However, people as young as 13 years old may legally consent to sex with a partner who is less than 4 years older."
10. Here, as in other ways, the film is chaster than the book, where Tawes and Alma engage in sex on a bed in a prison cell.
11. Alma, too, has a powerful encounter with Henry as he sits on some stairs, but being one of the film's visual set-pieces—a rendezvous in a crumbling house, with the stairs he waits on artfully precarious—aesthetics overwhelm emotional resonance.

Live TV, Filmed Theater, and the New Hollywood

John Frankenheimer's *The Iceman Cometh*

JAMES MORRISON

In 1973, John Frankenheimer made a film version of Eugene O'Neill's *The Iceman Cometh*. This play about the denizens of a seedy tavern on New York's Lower East Side in 1912 transpires over two days during which the regulars receive a visit from the mysterious yet folksy and charismatic Hickey, a salesman who visits once a year to carouse with the habitués and relate colorful tales of his travels. On this visit, though, Hickey discloses that he has come to offer salvation to the patrons—to free them from their "pipe dreams," as he puts it—a revelation that triggers dramatic recriminations and, ultimately, Hickey's confession that he has murdered his wife. Over four hours in length, with little in the way of conventional redemption to offer, the play failed resoundingly on its first Broadway run in 1946, but was restaged a decade later with some success. By the time Frankenheimer filmed it, it was encrusted with the status of a "classic."

An Equivocal Pedigree

Frankenheimer's version was the first entry in the American Film Theatre (AFT) series, a sequence of fourteen films released between 1973 and 1975, all adapted from plays and shown to subscribers only in runs limited to four screenings per film—two evenings and two matinees—in theaters across the United States and Canada. The American Film Theatre was originated by Ely Landau, a producer whose best-known previous venture was *The Play of the Week*—a television series of classic and contemporary dramas that ran from 1959 to 1961 on New York's Channel 13 and in syndication, and that included a 1960 performance of *The Iceman Cometh* directed by Sidney Lumet and starring Jason Robards Jr. as Hickey, in a reprise of his off-Broadway performance in the 1956 revival (the role had been originated by James Barton). The telecast reached a large popular audience and contributed greatly to the play's ultimate, if unlikely, enshrinement in the

American canon. It was a key reference point in discussion of Frankenheimer's film version over a decade later, especially regarding comparisons between Robards's performance as Hickey and that of Lee Marvin, who plays the role in the film. All these contexts conditioned the reception of Frankenheimer's film, which was typically damned with faint praise, celebrated for the qualities of its ensemble acting but ultimately dismissed as merely a "filmed play" (Kael, *For Keeps* 353). Yet, in part because of the same heritage that guaranteed its marginalization, Frankenheimer's *The Iceman Cometh* is ripe for rediscovery as a definitive film of the New Hollywood.

Although nearly every reference to AFT in film criticism slights the series either for its commercial failure (Roberts 30) or for its artistic shortcomings as "canned theater" (Mast 50), it remains a pioneering experiment in independent distribution, virtually without precedent, and it provided models for subsequent efforts like John Cassavetes's self-distribution of *A Woman under the Influence* in 1974. In its own advertising, AFT emphasizes the "unique" quality of its offerings, an aura secured by their limited exhibition: "If you don't see them" at one of the four scheduled screenings, warned the ad that ran in *New York* on September 24, 1973, "you'll have missed the chance" (27). Certainly this campaign has about it more than a whiff of the middlebrow "prestige" picture, and its "roadshow" pomp—subscribers purchased reserved seats for the screenings—may have seemed in days of the New Hollywood like a throwback to the waning of the studio system in the sixties with its "special events" mindset, though it also paved the way for a half-hearted revival of "roadshow" exhibition for films like *The Deer Hunter* and *Days of Heaven* (both 1978), when the New Hollywood was already starting to seem like a thing of the past amenable to desperation tactics of its own. In practice, AFT broached the divide between art-cinema and commercial distribution practices, a rift dominant since World War II, as the five hundred theaters in which AFT booked its films nationally included urban art houses as well as suburban or "neighborhood" theaters and even some mall venues at the dawn of what would later be called the Cineplex.

But for its persisting ties to a theatrical heritage, AFT might have been seen from the start as a key offshoot of the New Hollywood rather than a divergent and hopelessly diluted strain. After all, the New Hollywood successively introduced influences of the art film into the mainstream, itself eroding that barrier between the two and effectively cultivating a belated lineage of cinematic modernism in American movies. The plays adapted by AFT ranged across classics of modernism (Brecht, Ionesco, Genet, and O'Neill), if not avant-gardism or postmodernism (Pinter, Albee, and others). They trafficked in styles and attitudes that were concurrently finding new berth in American movies of the day, which bristled with bouts of pop existentialism—from *The Graduate* (1967) or *Five Easy Pieces* (1970) to *Taxi Driver* (1976)—and made exploratory forays into the imagery of the surreal—from Robert Altman's *Images* (1972) to David Lynch's *Eraserhead* (1977). While some of the directors tied to AFT projects had worked previously either exclusively or almost entirely in theater—such as Peter Hall (*The Homecoming*, 1973) or Tom O'Horgan (*Rhinoceros*, 1974)—most were filmmakers with distinguished careers in cinema, including several whose work helped to lay groundwork for the emergence of the New Hollywood such as Tony Richardson (*A Delicate Balance*, 1973), Lindsay Anderson (*In Celebration*, 1975), Joseph Losey (*Galileo*, 1975), and Frankenheimer himself. AFT's ad campaign specifically addressed the attribution of "filmed theater": the films, the above-cited ad proclaims, are "not simply taken from the stage but transformed to the screen with the intimacy and power only film possesses." Such avowals were of little use, as the final verdict on the series was for the most part that its products were unworkable hybrids, "neither play nor film" (Crist 57).

It would run sharply against the grain of the era's self-conceptions, yet one could write a viable counter-history of the New Hollywood around key stage adaptations, from *Who's Afraid of Virginia Woolf?* (1966) to *The Killing of Sister George* (1968), *The Boys in the Band* (1970), *Little Murders* (1971), *Cabaret* (1972), or *Lenny* (1974). Yet if, as Susan Sontag suggests, the evolution of cinema largely involves its successive "emancipation" (134) from its theatrical heritage, the New Hollywood routinely congratulated itself for having finally shrugged off those origins once and for all. Indeed, writing about Steven Spielberg in 1975, Pauline Kael cites an unnamed "older" director as follows: "[Spielberg] must never have seen a play; he's the first one of us who doesn't think in terms of the proscenium arch. With him, there's nothing but the camera lens" ("Notes" 136). Key players in the New Hollywood, like Spielberg or Altman, may have worked in television before turning to film, but few came from the theater, which became during this brief renaissance more than ever cinema's "other," rife with a "tradition-of-quality" that fell quickly into disrepute in this neo-New Wave. Yet, as Sontag also notes, this kind of opposition may itself derive from a kind of philistine fallacy, locating the essence of either art in their points of contrast and mistaking the crossbred, "impure" nature of both theater and film.

"Televisual" Film

Frankenheimer's *The Iceman Cometh* adds the further complication of mixing stylings of "live television" with elements of theater and film, a combination virtually designed to challenge an aesthetic of pop modernism predicated on conceptions of "pure cinema." Indeed, that AFT films had only delimited exhibition suggests something of a return to the model of live TV, in which—even though shows were often taped and typically re-ran—a single performance of a given program cast about itself an aura of irretrievability, reflected in the AFT cautions that if you didn't see their films on the few occasions when they were shown, you would have missed them. Oddly enough, Frankenheimer's status as a pioneer of live TV in the fifties, a key dimension of his auteurist profile, was rarely invoked in reviews of this, the film in the director's oeuvre to which it is most relevant (though it is worth noting that the limitations of its run meant the film was rarely reviewed at all outside a handful of national magazines and newspapers). AFT was quite serious in its insistence on the cinematic bases of its products. According to Ralph Woolsey, cinematographer on *The Iceman Cometh*, the producers demanded widescreen shooting using hard mattes—creating an aspect ratio of 1.85:1 within a standard 1.37:1 frame, and precluding mis-framing in theatrical screenings—rather than shooting full frame to facilitate later television exhibitions. Woolsey declares, "It was a movie, really," *not* composed for "the damned television frame" ("AFI Seminar" 168).

Yet to miss the intertextual resonances and stylistic affinities with live TV is to exaggerate the film's theatrical heritage. Indeed, Frankenheimer's film exists in a complex relation to Lumet's 1960 television production, while Frankenheimer himself noted how much the experience of making the film owed to his days in live TV (Armstrong 64). In production, Frankenheimer returned to techniques of television, shooting as much as possible in chronological order on a tight schedule. Though he ruled out the use of closed-circuit monitors that often accompany multiple cameras, he shot with two cameras simultaneously in many scenes, according to Woolsey ("AFI Seminar" 167), and three in the banquet scene, according to Frankenheimer himself (Frankenheimer, "Filming Iceman" 37). While most filmmakers of the time would have been "dismayed" ("AFI Seminar" 169) by the whole idea of the project—a four-hour script with a single setting—Frankenheimer was not, as Woolsey attests, precisely because of his former work in television, and no doubt his recollection of Lumet's successful rendering.

According to many historians of live television, it was principally a writer's or performer's medium, with the director functioning mainly as a stage manager or performance coach and the camera serving chiefly as a transmitter or, very secondarily, a recorder. In one recent account of the emergence of televisual style, John Thornton Caldwell attributes a kind of zero-degree style to live television drama, including Frankenheimer in the category of "actor's director" who "could not have cared less about the grade of fog filter used on the set" (77). Going back to the actual programs after countless such debunkings of "the ideology of liveness myth" (Caldwell 27), one is astonished to rediscover their technical acumen and stylistic flair—to note, indeed, how much of Frankenheimer's cinematic style was forged in these precincts. Indeed, as Stephen Bowie remarks in a perceptive overview of Frankenheimer's career, "As the live TV director who took the medium in an explicitly cinematic direction, Frankenheimer was actually the least typical" (Bowie). His compositions-in-depth and two-shots with each character positioned in a different plane of space appear as early as "The Comedian" (1957), and although these have a functional purpose—to minimize switching among cameras—they achieve expressive effects from the start. As the camera weaves between the two characters (played by Mickey Rooney and Edmond O'Brien), they waver tensely between closeness and depth within the frame, their kinetic alternations in space working out visually the shifting power relations between them. In "The Days of Wine and Roses" (1958), the social-problem piece about alcoholism that remains Frankenheimer's best-known television production, careful moldings of light create discomfiting noirish effects from the first scene, in which a drunken man emerges from a town hall meeting and enters an alleyway, disappearing offscreen but casting a flaring, grotesque shadow onscreen as he gulps from a bottle. Later, Frankenheimer uses deep focus, within the admitted limits of the medium, to evoke the intractable powers of demon rum, placing a bottle in the extreme foreground, exaggerating its scale, while tormented characters languish in the background of the image—a trope that recurs in *The Iceman Cometh*.

As striking as the technical quality of Frankenheimer's work in television is its range, perhaps most apparent in his 1959 adaptation of Henry James's *The Turn of the Screw*, starring Ingrid Bergman. Adapting James's florid ghost story—including effects that uncannily prefigure Jack Clayton's 1961 film version, *The Innocents*—Frankenheimer continues to develop a style based in long takes with deep focus, but also experiments within the composition, using superimpositions and long, slow dissolves while filling the frame with eerily reflective paneled mirrors and meshed draperies through which the camera often peers, all recalling the stylistic excess of Max Ophuls and Josef von Sternberg, while creating qualities of density and abstraction within the image and laying the groundwork for some of the effects of *The Iceman Cometh*. Though countering typical characterizations of early TV's minimalism (it is worth noting that the teleplay was the first to be broadcast in color on the NBC network), the production is also a remarkable exercise in narrative and psychological concision. Contrary to the claims of the debunkers of the "ideology of liveness myth," TV drama in the 1950s did not tend to use its "liveness" as a selling point. In the programs, their status as live broadcasts is rarely mentioned, registering mainly at the level of style in their remarkable compression and intensity. The same qualities infuse *The Iceman Cometh*—certainly at the level of performance, where the decision to shoot chronologically with simultaneous cameras, though not directly visible onscreen, yields remarkable returns. Although it may seem strange to speak of "compression" in a film of four hours, Frankenheimer's own account chronicles his effort to reduce the play's running time only to discover that any cuts diminished the intensity that was dependent on exacting repetitions in the text (Frankenheimer, "Filming Iceman" 36–37).

Considering the relation between film and theater, Sontag remarks that "cinematic virtue does not reside in the fluidity of the positioning of the camera nor in the mere frequency of the change of shot. It consists in the arrangement of screen images" (141–42). The distinction underlying this claim is between the "logical" space of the stage and the "alogical" or discontinuous space of cinema. Like Sontag's examples of "films considered objectionably theatrical" (142)—namely, Hitchcock's *Rope* (1948) and Dreyer's *Gertrud* (1964)—Frankenheimer's seemingly "theatrical" construction of space within a single setting in *The Iceman Cometh*—really also, of course, televisual—presents a highly complex treatment of cinematic space, his use of lighting, framing, camera movement, and editing continually displacing "real" space with a sort of virtual space that gives new meaning to O'Neill's text.

Dynamic Stasis

One of the key effects of the film is its sense of bodies stranded in space, always in relation to one another, yet strangely isolated within the same frame. In his stage directions, O'Neill places unusual emphasis on bodily configurations as the play opens. In the beginning, most of the characters are frozen in drunken slumber at their tables in Harry Hope's saloon, and O'Neill painstakingly observes minutiae of their positions: "Hunched forward, both elbows on the table . . . Chin on chest, hands folded in his lap . . . Head sideways . . . arms dangling to the floor . . . head drooping jerkily toward one shoulder . . . His head is thrown back, his big mouth open" (9–10). These pronounced notations of physicality are especially notable in a play of so little action; in describing characters' movement, by contrast, O'Neill is straightforward and direct, eschewing detail: "Larry rises from his chair to look at Hope and nods to Rocky" (11). It is only in repose that the playwright can see his characters for what they are—perhaps only in repose that they can be what they are. For all its seeming disapproval of passivity, the play reserves its harshest condemnation for action, as embodied in the person of Hickey. A traveling salesman who serves as a principle of movement amid the bar's conditions of stagnation, Hickey introduces a dynamic momentum into the static space of the tavern, weaving among the inert patrons as he delivers his manic promises of redemptive disillusionment. Yet his offer of liberating the denizens from the grip of their illusions is ultimately revealed as the most destructive "pipe dream" of all, and Hickey himself exposed as that stalest of American clichés, the confidence man who has bought into his own shell game.

Visually, Frankenheimer's adaptation frames O'Neill's play as a veritable essay on the dialectics of stasis and dynamism—the very opposition that has defined the relation between theater and cinema since Erwin Panofsky remarked on the "stasis" of stage space and the "dynamization of space" (71) in film. In fact, Frankenheimer deletes from his version much of the already delimited movement that O'Neill prescribes in the stage directions. For instance, in the film, Larry (Robert Ryan) does not "rise" as called for in the passage cited above, but remains rooted to his seat for most of the action. What motion there is of figures within the frame—except for the case of Hickey (Lee Marvin)—is typically stylized, spasmodic, and abbreviated, suggesting again and again a momentary release from stasis that quickly lapses back into dormancy. Though setting the stillness of the others into disquieting relief, even Hickey's

Frankenheimer's depth of field captures a "dynamic stasis" in *The Iceman Cometh* (Cinévision Ltée., 1973).
Digital frame enlargement.

movement bears a quality of weariness from the start, especially by contrast to Robards's famous rendition, comparatively fleet and rapid-fire in its knowing oratorical bombast.

For long stretches, the camera's movement, too, is severely delimited within individual shots—by contrast with most of Frankenheimer's work, including his television dramas, marked as they are by a very mobile camera. In these sequences, aside from a brief pan or track or a slow zoom—each technique made doubly expressive by contrast with the immobility surrounding it—the camera remains static, capturing the muted action from what often seem like peripheral or sideward perspectives because of the density and mass of each image in deep focus with bodies and faces receding from foreground to background. Although he is mounting a visual essay on immobility, Frankenheimer has by no means reverted to the frontal compositions of traditional "filmed theater," with the screen figured as a variant of a stage proscenium, and characters arrayed as if facing an imaginary audience. In relation to the camera, placement of figures in the frame is often oblique, and while there is little movement within the image, movement from shot to shot is sharp and precise, cutting on hard graphic lines across much space. Indeed, if the depth of field is often complemented by a stringently held long take, more often the film lurches forward by patterns of editing that could be called rapid, even clipped, at least in their relation to the dialogue. Combining these techniques, Frankenheimer discovers just what the material calls for—a dynamic means of observing stasis.

The use of deep focus and long takes reflects the influence of Orson Welles that Frankenheimer often acknowledged, but the manner of Frankenheimer's integration of editing places his style in *The Iceman Cometh* closer to that of William Wyler. In films like *The Little Foxes* (1941) or *The Heiress* (1949), both stage adaptations, Wyler uses the long take with depth of field to suggest initially a cinematic equivalent of theatrical space, but introduces forceful editing patterns and insinuating camera movements to underline the constantly shifting witness-point from which the action is viewed, by contrast to the fixed viewing position of the theatrical spectator. As in Wyler, so in Frankenheimer these purposeful variations in perspective and shot scale most powerfully convey the director's interpretation of the material. In keeping with attitudes of the New Hollywood and themes of his own work, Frankenheimer's reading of *The Iceman Cometh* is a revisionist one. Standard interpretations of the play understand it as saying, in the words of Robert Brustein, "that man cannot live without illusions" (340); Frankenheimer's version coheres with much of the director's own work in its contention that, on the contrary, people *must* live without illusion, because illusions are ultimately impossible to sustain.

The dramatic cadences of O'Neill's late plays are incessant. One character provokes, another takes umbrage, the first yields, the other forgives—and the pattern repeats itself, over and over. To this rhythm *The Iceman Cometh* adds the metrics of self-laceration. With bibulous derision or sodden rage, the characters constantly lash out at one another, but their most direct scorn is reserved for themselves. Ritually repenting their convulsive attacks on their fellow sufferers, they can never forgive their own failings. Harry Hope's bar may be, as Larry declares, the "Palace of Pipe Dreams," but it is also the vault of lost illusions, and nobody there needs a messiah-in-reverse like Hickey to bring the news of nihilism. It is not the sad reprobates, coming face to face with misery in every swig of hooch, who need to be convinced that life has no meaning; it's the bourgeoisie—busily engaged in the oblivious futilities and caught up in the happy delusions of progress that all the bar's patrons, including the former revolutionaries, have left behind—and the bourgeoisie make no appearance in *The Iceman Cometh*.

Frankenheimer's delicately nuanced patterns of framing, editing, and camera movement repeatedly emphasize the characters' knowledge of their own condition, not their ignorance or denial of it. In an early sequence, Parritt (Jeff Bridges), the son of Larry's former colleague in the anarchist movement, comes to the saloon after having betrayed his mother (a character based on Emma Goldman) to authorities; as Larry tells him about the bar's habitués, a slow pan across the room shows each of them in succession, ending on a close-up of Harry Hope himself (Fredric March). As often in the film's moving shots, the camera's movement has an ambling, gentle, uncertain quality. At times, as it surveys the room, it slows and tilts, as if unsure of its own destination—as it roves past a banister, it pauses as if it might mount the stairs. Though its movement is loosely synchronized with Larry's narration, the staging in depth places characters in variable planes, so it is not always clear who within the frame is being discussed. The camera evinces a quality of reticence. Never seeming to avert its gaze, it refrains from probing; even the zoom-ins to tight close-ups are slow and delicate, gentle as caresses (and Woolsey remarks that this device, a direct legacy from television, is used in a muted manner due to a special lens [an Angénieux 20–120] that avoids "a zoomy look" ["AFI Seminar" 169]). Frankenheimer seems to be searching for a way to observe suffering without violating it, and in this sequence the camera, even as it ends the shot with a view of the sleeping Harry, gives the impression of moving past rather than fixing on its object, of gazing rather than staring.

As the camera brushes past McGloin (Clifton James), a former cop, we hear Larry relate the man's graft-riddled history: "[He] got too greedy and when the usual reform investigation came he was caught red-handed and thrown off the force." Instead of reacting with hostility to this contemptuous characterization, McGloin—listening in a mild doze—gives a wry, fond smile, saluting the bracing honesty of Larry's account. Though McGloin fantasizes about his return to the force, even he, the most deluded of the bunch, is granted an air of self-awareness in Frankenheimer's rendering in moments such as this.

For the rest, nearly every character in the play delivers a monologue of captious self-criticism, tortured even when lightheartedly inflected, and all are crueler by far to themselves than to the others, or than the others are to them. Just as the rhythms of the play alternate between attack and withdrawal, mollification, and pardon, so they move between wrenching self-contempt and make-shift delusion. While typical stagings emphasize the ultimate pathos of the characters' pipe dreams, Frankenheimer keeps these rhythms constantly in play, suggesting simultaneously the fragility of these delusions and the painful self-awareness that stokes them. His interpretation is infused at nearly every level by the basic yet rare perception that O'Neill's characters know exactly how miserable they are. Even at their most raucous, they are never deluded about that.

How the characters respond to Hickey's appearance in Frankenheimer's film is a key gauge of the overall treatment, especially by contrast to Lumet's handling of the scene in his television version. Lumet's production is most attuned to the garrulousness and humorous self-dramatization of the characters—he might as well be directing Sean O'Casey as Eugene O'Neill—and he keeps the spirit of the play as buoyant as possible for much of the action, as an ironic counterpoint to the work's ultimately tragic undertones. Robards's Hickey is a quintessential huckster, bluff and vivacious—kin to Harold Hill in *The Music Man* (a Broadway hit the year after the revival of *The Iceman Cometh*). His entrance is heralded by a brief, extreme close-up, a cut-in that is one of the few moments when Lumet departs from the appearance of "liveness" in the production. This tight shot of Hickey's face springs up abruptly, followed by a quick reversion to the master shot of the whole set, with Hickey/Robards romping boisterously at the back of the room, far from the camera. Even as Robards's Hickey portends the sinister tidings he brings, he retains his energetic charm, and when he reveals his murder in the final monologue, the patrons are understandably thunderstruck. Given the force and extent of this dramatic turn, their final pledge to testify to Hickey's insanity to save him from execution plays as collective self-deception, the last sad lie of a gallery of heedless rogues.

This revelation is far less sharp in Frankenheimer's film because Marvin's Hickey, unlike Robards's, is unmistakably malevolent from the start. It is clearly to foster this reading that Frankenheimer cast Marvin, with his star-text as the heavy, rather than Robards (who by some reports never recovered from being passed over).[1] Visually, Frankenheimer precisely reverses Lumet's rendering in order to underline Hickey's diabolical demeanor from the start. While Lumet's cut-in of the initial close-up emphasizes how Hickey's sudden arrival jolts the atmosphere of the bar—the long shot that follows showing Hickey's convivial interactions with the group—Frankenheimer begins with a long shot that moves in sharply and inexorably to a high-angle close-up. Hickey enters in the depth of the frame, without fanfare, with the implication that he might be just another one of the regulars. But the camera's traversal of the room's space as it moves

Lee Marvin's Hickey is unmistakably malevolent from the start.
Digital frame enlargement.

toward him is incisive and resolute, contrasting with the gentle, shambling camera movements that come before, and the high-angle with which the shot culminates is held in a crisp, withering tableau as Hickey finishes his grotesque jig, showing his expression as at once a pained grimace and a malign leer. The only obvious stylistic flourish in the film up to that point, this shot lays bare Hickey's mania as soon as he appears. In Frankenheimer's version, when Harry says as Hickey is finally being hauled off, "Every one of us saw he was nutty the minute he showed up here," he's not laying the groundwork for another pipe dream but stating the obvious, which the audience too has seen just as clearly from the start. Through reaction shots to Hickey's manic-depressive vaudeville, Frankenheimer further enhances his sense of the other characters' keen awareness, by contrast to Hickey's general obliviousness.

Despite prompting from the producers in the name of "transforming" the work to the cinema, Frankenheimer refused to "open up" the play in the ordinary sense of cinematic adaptation of theatrical works. As Frankenheimer declared, "You can't impose that kind of reality [e.g., exterior location shooting] on O'Neill—you'll ruin the play" (Champlin 135). At the same time, the film "opens up" the space of the setting in a distinctively cinematic way, and Frankenheimer rejects a traditionally naturalistic aesthetic. *The Iceman Cometh* "claims to be a very realistic play," according to Frankenheimer, but "it is not at all" (Frankenheimer, "Filming Iceman" 37). Rather, in the director's words, it is "romantic," "idealized," "symbolic." On the face of it, Frankenheimer's approach seems concrete and "realistic," but he employs cinema's "alogical" vocabulary to reintroduce elements of abstraction into the visual image for thematic purposes. For example, throughout the film, he works with a formalist's precision with the distinction between offscreen and onscreen space, specifically cinematic in comparison to parallel oppositions in theater and television. In live television, a character momentarily off-camera remains actually and virtually present within the dramatic space, while in theater, a character is either onstage or off. In cinema, a far less literal dialectic obtains—figures offscreen, even if still dramatically "present," may no longer be there at all once we cut away from them—and Frankenheimer exploits this difference to create a prevailing oneiric dimension in the space of the saloon. Late in the work, after a banquet celebrating Harry's birthday, for example, the action recommences the following morning, as the bar is being reopened for the day. A long take begins the sequence, from a vantage point the camera has not occupied before, observing an employee (Moses Gunn) sprinkling sawdust on the floor. Following him, the camera picks up Parritt, apparently sleeping at one of the tables. Beyond him, in the depth of the visual field, we see Rocky (Tom Pedi), the bartender, dispensing one of his corrosive monologues, concerning the events of the night before. In the play, it is clear he is addressing Larry; in the film, Larry is offscreen, and we do not see him until the monologue is complete, when the camera pans slightly to reveal him just offscreen right. Though most characters are onstage for the majority of the action, only a few are onscreen at any given time; Frankenheimer, however, constantly overlaps space from one shot to the next and places figures in the background of the frame beyond foreground action in nearly every shot. Thus, he constantly emphasizes the characters' fate of being stranded between absence and presence—an effect that heightens the sense of their being at once ubiquitous and evanescent, interrelated yet isolated from one another. The overriding implication is that any one of them could disappear at any moment.

Frankenheimer's Hybrid Art

Absorbing energies of both the theatrical and the televisual, the images of *The Iceman Cometh* remain distinctly cinematic. One sense in which this is clearly the case involves the predominant use of a split-diopter, a lens filter that enables differential focus within the image to provide an extremely close field of vision in one segment while simultaneously yielding maximum depth throughout the rest of the same image (Pratley, *Films* 141). This device is used to suggest ironic or psychological relations among characters within the frame, as for instance in the sequence described above. After a cut to an angle on Larry as Rocky continues talking to him, Parritt remains in the extreme foreground, now framed against Larry and Rocky on either side of his apparently sleeping body in the extreme background. Though Parritt appears unconscious, as the shot is held,

Frankenheimer's compositions suggest both the separateness and the relatedness of the characters.

Digital frame enlargement.

we see increasing signs of bodily affect that pronounce his awareness of what is going on behind him, furthering Frankenheimer's vision of a tormented self-consciousness rather than a comatose indifference. Varying scales, angles, and lenses, Frankenheimer finds an astonishing number of vantage points on the same space, and—departing markedly from televisual practice—often builds scenes without master shots, repeating only a few angles over the course of such sequences as Hickey's opening dialogue with the patrons. By the end of the film, it seems there is no angle from which the space has not been seen, often looking markedly different with a mere shift of perspective or light. Frankenheimer "opens up" the play only in the sense that he finds so many ways of looking at the trapped, tragic people who populate the film.

The traditional interpretation of O'Neill, that his plays concern the follies of self-deception, robs most productions of the richest, if bleakest, implications of the playwright's work. In *The Iceman Cometh*, for instance, Hickey believes he is teaching his fellows to face the unyielding truth of their lives, and a version like Lumet's takes this conviction on faith. In Frankenheimer's version, however, Hickey is portrayed ironically as the least self-conscious character, in contrast to the rest, who alternate between benumbed delusion and unforgiving self-exposure. Privileging the latter, Frankenheimer's approach excavates deeper meanings from O'Neill's text. Frankenheimer denies the comfort that Lumet gives by implying that if only the characters could understand themselves, they could rouse themselves from their stupor. In his version, Frankenheimer makes clear that they have achieved self-reflection, and yet it has provided no ground for positive action. This is a bitter conclusion indeed, but one with firm bases in O'Neill's text, in elements often slighted in production, including stage directions that emphasize characters' inwardness, such as this gloss on one of Larry's most pointed speeches, where he is said to speak "with increasing bitter intensity, more as if he were fighting with himself than with Hickey" (O'Neill 168). By contrast with Lumet's single-minded satire, Frankenheimer's approach also enables an attitude of lenience and forgiveness toward the characters that echoes O'Neill's own attitudes, as when he writes of the need to show "the atmosphere of [the bar], the humor and friendship and human warmth and deep inner contentment of the bottom" (Bogard and Bryer 257). Though revisionist, Frankenheimer's version of *The Iceman Cometh* brings it closer to the truths of O'Neill's art, perhaps, than any other version on film or video.

In its revisionist ardor, Frankenheimer's film squares readily with the terms and traditions of the New Hollywood, yet its hybrid nature—poised among traditions of film, theater, and television—troubles its easy acceptance within that canon. Devoutly modernist in sensibility, its demystifying impulses—coming at a time when great projects of demystification seemed newly afoot in the existentialist or surrealist vein, and brandished as signs of cultural virtue—exceed those of nearly any film of the era, which cannot boast the substantiality of *Iceman*'s Nietszchean rage or the scope of its Schopenhauerean sympathies.

Rooted as it may be in theater, the film commands a range of formal inventiveness that could be invisible only to the most inveterate "purist"—or, indeed, to just about everyone. With performances among the greatest of any work of the seventies, the film gains some of its distinction, as so many films of the period did, through the complex juxtaposition of "old" Hollywood (March, Ryan, Marvin) with "new" (Bridges). The reception of O'Neill's play is checkered enough, one would have thought, to have ushered a film version of it into any canon-on-the-make that defines itself *against* tradition; yet clearly, if not for its basis in "classic" theater, Frankenheimer's film would be counted as a classic of its own day. So evidently is this the case that arguing for its promotion in such terms feels a little false, especially as it seems to place off limits the film's most irrefutable claim—its greatness.

NOTE

1. Though Marvin's performance was roundly criticized on the film's initial release, Frankenheimer was extremely pleased with it. As he wrote in a letter to Pamela Marvin, the actor's widow, "I believe *The Iceman Cometh* to be one of my best films, and a great deal of that is due to Lee."

Ashes, Ashes

Structuring Emptiness in *All Fall Down*

MURRAY POMERANCE

To begin with the most salient feature of John Frankenheimer's third film, *All Fall Down* (1962), this James Leo Herlihy story of a dysfunctional family in contemporary middle America, written for the screen by William Inge, centers largely on a slick young man who goes by the improbable name of Berry-berry. As played out by Warren Beatty—who was twenty-four years old when he shot this picture (and already a compadre of the screenwriter, from their work on *Splendor in the Grass* [1961])—Berry-berry's attitude (and this film was made at a time when in the eyes of grown-up America everything of a young person's being and experience could be summed up as his "attitude") is something of a cross between the unpredictability of Elvis Presley, the purposiveness of Bud Stamper in *Splendor*, the struggling impetuousness of James Dean (he is "the latest cinemale to step into the late Jimmy Dean's blue jeans," opined *Time*), and a kind of strung-out desperation, as audiences had seen with Richard Widmark in Jules Dassin's *Night and the City* (1950) and with Vic Morrow in Richard Brooks's *The Blackboard Jungle* (1955). Berry-berry takes a shine to girls, at least up to a point, whereupon in a self-indulgent wreck of oedipal frustration he goes violent and gets himself incarcerated. ("Be certain that you capitalize fully on Warren Beatty when setting up your local campaign for 'All Fall Down,'" crooned the pressbook, offering the suggestion that theater managers might "Conduct a 'Look Alike' contest through a local disc jockey. Prizes can be tickets for those who most closely resemble Beatty.") Berry-berry seems to have no particular sense of a future, which is to say, no plans, no hopes, no dreams of anything beyond the entrapments of the present, a present in which he is constantly being addressed or questioned or marveled at or spoken about, as seems always to be the case with paragons. Everyone in his family dotes on Berry-berry, each in a different way. I want to say more about Berry-berry, and particularly about the irreducible name he bears (with such placid equanimity).

An Impression of Himself

It is not by accident that in the paragraph above I repeat the name Berry-berry so many times, indeed that I perhaps give the impression of working hard to achieve that repetition. I wish to bring it about that if as you are reading these passages there seems to be a voice actually speaking the words in your head, you are hearing the name Berry-berry again and again, precisely as one does when watching this film. A slight discomfort at this repetition is one of the overwhelming sensations that comes with watching *All Fall Down*, far more impressive in its way than seeing Berry-berry onscreen brooding, gazing, cajoling, or protesting, even though he is, in the flesh, the "very hot" Warren Beatty (Frankenheimer, *Conversation* 64); even though, like Edward Albee's *American Dream* (created the year before), it is entirely true that he "ought to be in the movies" (133). Everybody who meets him on camera seems to have a formal, polite, and direct if not hostile and vengeful relation with Berry-berry: so that his name is invoked often when people speak; everyone has something to say about him. If the boy had a more conventional name and people kept uttering it over and over, we might stop hearing it as a discrete referential sign and begin to concentrate instead on the person the name was attached to. In this case, however, we don't stop hearing the name as a sonority, a pure indicator. We don't quite manage to penetrate through the shield of the sound of "Berry-berry" to find Berry-berry himself, whoever or whatever he might turn out to be. It might be said that Berry-berry is continually in flight from the body and persona that are named Berry-berry, that are indicated or remembered when people sing his name—that he is only and always the impression of himself.

As Berry-berry himself never strikes one either visually or characterologically in the way that the name itself does—red, fruity, playful, joyous, ebullient, musical, and rather callow—the sound secreted within it, and freed on every pronunciation, has an essence all its own, independent of the Berry-berry we get to meet as a situated man. In the sound there is something juvenile: repetition, the invocation of the edible, the musical doubling that is also a compulsion. Homonymously hinting at crippling deprivation and disease, even the weaknesses implicit in malnutrition or vitamin deficiency, it immediately calls up nothing other than the protection of the mother against such debility, the mother doting and cooing, the mother watching, the mother always present. One might say that Berry-berry's mother is always upon Berry-berry's shoulder (a "noisy old parrot," *Time* called her). Further, "Berry-berry" might have been invented because of its sound, as a playful moniker, and so it calls up the primitive, the anthropomorphic, the untutored. If untutored, in modern America, then yet again disabled. And is Berry-berry not wholly wounded, given that in his muscularity and ripeness he has difficulty socializing, expressing himself, restraining his impulses with women, having and saying a self? Is not Berry-berry a boy who has difficulties? Might he not be, in the eyes of others, certainly the eyes of his parents, even now in young adulthood, still and always a child? And might it not signify that in addressing him or pointing to him, those who speak Berry-berry's name refrain from contracting it in affection or as an example of social proximity, as other names might be contracted, such as that of his young brother Clinton? It is—Berry-berry—always a name fully articulated, in the way that one works hard to pronounce every syllable of a word that is foreign, and at the same time a name ringing like a bell, perhaps a school bell. There is a spasm of embarrassment that passes through us, therefore, when we hear people speak of Berry-berry, particularly when we hear people overlay the acoustic signal "Berry-berry" upon the introspective, tranquil, feline figure that Warren Beatty so glowingly presents.

(And what is most salient in the sounding of "Berry-berry" is not that boy, not that figuration, but the person calling the name, who most frequently in this film is . . . Clint. It is Clint saying "Berry-berry" that "Berry-berry" invokes, and the curious Berry-berry that Beatty performs is an outering of Clint's imagination and desire. To Clint we will return.)

The sound of Berry-berry's name also invokes, and repetitively, a queer hint of mispronunciation, as though what people mean to say in calling up the thought of him is actually not berries (and more berries) but "very very." Here comes Very-very now. And we must wonder, very very what? Very very good looking, to be sure. Very very unsuccessful. Very very promising. In fact, promising to be very very resplendent. And yet, because the character is nothing but promise, not resplendent at all. Not good, either. Not safe. A boy with a huge smile and a hang-dog look, because authority is always getting him down and always will. Very very lovable, perhaps; certainly a person who very very much needs to be loved. Something is electric, very very electric, in Berry-berry, to the degree that he is so stunningly and immediately attractive, and at the same time deeply fearsome. (Once again: all this in Clint's mind.) And something is electric in the charge with which people speak his name. Every enunciation of it is macrologia, a doubling that is unnecessary except for emphasis and sheer multiplication, thus a magnification—a constant emphasis that must be articulated again and again. To hear him spoken of, or spoken to, is to feel that he is being doubly summoned, or summoned and then summoned again, summoned out of desire not impatience, yet desire that cannot or must not find its end.

The very sound of Berry-berry's name spoken again and again in *All Fall Down* may provide sufficient motive for some viewers to be irritated and dismayed. Bosley Crowther was sharply disappointed, for example, noting that the "persistent assumption that everybody, including the cretin's kid brother, who is played with bright-eyed and almost breathless rapture by handsome young Brandon De Wilde, and an old-maid friend of the cretin's mother, played desperately by Eva Marie Saint, would be so blindly devoted to this persistently noxious young brute provokes a reasonable spectator to give up finally in disgust. They all must be crazy in this picture."

His mother Annabel (Angela Lansbury) calls him Berry-berry in two distinct tones, that of the soothing, embracing spirit of protection and nourishment and that of the demanding harridan who issues directives, makes plans, keeps score of one's tiniest failures and successes. Echo O'Brien (Saint), the svelte daughter of Annabel's close friend in Toledo, visiting the household on a kind of reprieve, or tour of punishment—it is never really clear which—pronounces "Berry-berry" with the hesitation of the girl whose passion has immediately been kindled for the person beneath the name. The father, Ralph Willart (Karl Malden), an owner of some real estate and self-made success, that is to say, a man who expects his son to log achievements as briskly as he has done, has a gruff, even resentful tone when he speaks of Berry-berry, or when he refers to his son as "that big rhinoceros." And narrating this tale, telling us of Berry-berry the apple of his eye, Berry-berry the brother who is the center of his world, Clint's is a sweet angelic haunting voice, a voice for whom anyone who could be named Berry-berry is a natural force, a voice in which the musicality of Berry-berry's name sounds out in every utterance and belies all practical intents.

Clint (Brandon De Wilde) is the object of my focus here, as he is the object of Frankenheimer's focus in this film. One could say that *All Fall Down* is built to make transparent and vibrant for us a single transformative moment in this boy's life. But to approach Clint, one must hear his resonant young male voice saying the name of Berry-berry over and over and over, because that, principally, is what Clint does, that is his life. "Yes, Berry-berry. No, Berry-berry." Dreams of Berry-berry, plans for Berry-berry, concern for Berry-berry, measuring of himself against the ineffable Berry-berry. Against the Berry-berry who is an orchard of a personality, a flamboyant excess of color and form, whenever Clint invokes him in that hiatus full of confusion and desire that boys occupy before they are men, or which boys did occupy in the America of the 1960s, when it was still possible to yearn achingly for glory.

A Cup of Coffee

In order to grasp the form that Frankenheimer has built in this film, it is hardly necessary to rehearse the dialogue of eventfulness, since little happens in the story beyond a young man discovering that his admired older brother, who has impregnated an impressionable girl, does not have the courage to stay with her but runs out on being offered the news, whereupon she drives herself off a cliff. Considerable screen time is taken up establishing the characters: Clint as a virginal naïf with big eyes for the big world; Echo O'Brien as the nymphomaniac tease who comes to visit and immediately collars this boy, the only available meat on the market. In his innocence he takes her teases for love poems, and commits to her body and soul. Annabel dotes on an absent older son, who is in Florida ostensibly starting up a business (but actually in jail, for maiming a bar girl); he is the center of this mother's universe, and she spends her life planning and directing his nonexistent future. In this role, and her subsequent work for Frankenheimer in *The Manchurian Candidate*, Angela Lansbury creates what may be the greatest portrait of desperately repressed femininity in postwar American cinema, and more than earns John Russell Taylor's estimate that she is "the best thing the British Labour movement has yet produced" (144). Indeed, a scene was curtailed in which, first seeing him after his long absence from home, Annabel kisses Berry-berry in a way that the Production Code personnel found "a good deal more than merely motherly or possessive" (Vizzard); it had been scripted this way—

> As Annabel enters, the men fall silent. Annabel looks beautiful now as she draws closer to Berry-berry. Ralph and Clinton stand like grooms. There is a deep seriousness in Berry-berry's demeanor, as Annabel approaches him and stands before him. Then suddenly *she moves into his arms—and they kiss*. When the kiss is ended Annabel begins immediately to cry.

—and Frankenheimer had noted to himself, his focus on Lansbury and her immense power, "Photograph the hell out of her." Beleaguered Ralph, genius that he is, and lashed for life to Annabel and her fixations, does everything in his power to avoid every situation into which he is thrust in this family, except and until the tragedy that explodes the situation. And Berry-berry, shining but hollow—"almost insultingly good-looking in a typical American way . . . no talents at all, except what you see," like the "American Dream" (Albee 137)—twists and turns through the tragedy that his callousness or carelessness set in motion, eager to break away from Ralph and Annabel while at the same time guarding the adulation that Clint cannot shade in his wondering, trustful eyes. Berry-berry confesses to Clint at one point that he doesn't like life very much and the kid, hungry to please him, urgently itching to be Berry-berry in every respect, affects an appropriately heavy tone and says that he agrees: not because he wants to be liked by this object of his love, but because he wants to be the object of his love. It is through loving Berry-berry that Clint is learning to love himself.

When finally Berry-berry comes home to Cleveland, and ambles into the great gothic house whose shapeless interior is a kind of analogue of Annabel's emptied womb—"If *anybody* could afford a house," Karal Ann Marling asks, "and all houses were pretty much the same, what distinguished the occupants of one little box from their next-door neighbors?" (253)—there is evident, almost instantaneously, a repulsion between the boy and his parents, between the effervescently groping present and its past. He musters politeness, even good humor, but as soon as he possibly can be he is on the run to a nearby orchard, "genuinely romantic," where he keeps a room (J. Thomas 7). "I'll be back. I'll be back real soon." But Ralph, never the fool, can see the cord splitting. Repetition as surrender: "He's just going out for a while. He'll be back." And soon afterward, as Clint finds Berry-berry in his hideaway and cajoles him to come back to the house, just for a cup of coffee, repetition as prayer: "Just sit and have a cup of coffee, just a cup of coffee." The scene of Berry-berry parading into his parents' kitchen—into the kitchen, that is to say, that was once his as much as anyone else's but in which nothing is cooked now, in any sense of the word, for him—is a tour de force. Annabel must almost be manhandled by Ralph to sit quietly at the table rather than leaping up to fuss at Berry-berry's appearance in the doorway (because when he is in her sights a trigger is pulled: she is filled with a spirit that propels her in every direction at once, with fear and urgency).

Soon, from upstairs, Echo makes an appearance. As she is introduced to the elusive, celebrated Berry-berry, here in the same room in which Clint has been edging his brother back into the family, one can feel the aura being delicately, even surgically, stripped from the youth. Clint, who until now, in moment after stirring moment, has been "her guy," as she's put it, is suddenly only the houseboy, although of this status change no one gives the slightest indication, least of all Echo, who has effected it with her sophisticated vocal tone, and Clint himself, now firmly nailed to his cross. One night while Clint lies in bed, his skin as smooth as fruit, Berry-berry makes a confidence: "You saw her first. I wouldn't touch her without your permission"—this an absolute afterthought, of course, since Berry-berry is nothing but impulses and satisfactions and has indubitably already touched her, and touched her again. We are reminded of the girl in Florida, her scarred face, the dingy jail cell (where, purely for fun, and because he had come to have great affection for him, Frankenheimer arranged to have Beatty locked up alone for several hours after shooting [Frankenheimer, *Conversation* 65]), just as Clint is reminded of Ralph's barbecue party, where he walked over to serve Echo some meat and looked up and saw that already she had gone off with Berry-berry into the bushes of love.

The world of childhood is invoked and reinvoked throughout the film: Annabel's excessive and hysterical maternity; Ralph's optimism about a future long lost; Echo's nervousness with the Willart family, quite as though she hasn't got her feet on the ground yet. Clint is clearly still a child, and Berry-berry is his fantasy creature quite as much as his living brother, a fetish and talisman of hope and perfection that the boy clings to in anxious desperation. "Too naïve for credibility," nayed Crowther; and "DeWilde is a prig," voted John Thomas rather insensitively (7), failing to grasp that for Clint, Berry-berry is the spirit of hope and truth, the animal configuration of form and presence that a kid must possess and hold close, so that through contagion its magical powers can rub off. Notwithstanding Kael's carping query, "Does anybody really grow up the way this boy grows up?" (31), how else is a boy to lose his boyhood? The American Dream again.

Frankenheimer's own copy of the July 23, 1961, script showed the extent and magnitude of Clint's self-isolating hunger for someone or something to contact, coupled with his overwhelming innocence. "Slowly camera pulls back revealing Clinton crouched on the upper landing near the head of the stairs. He is clad only in his pajama-top, writing furiously and smoking a cigarette":

> Dear Ralph and Annabel, I suppose this will come as a shock but I have just killed myself and am now lying in the bathtub. I suggest you get a doctor or a policeman to force the bathroom lock, which was never much good anyway, and pull the plug and all my blood will go down the drain. I am sure the policeman will rinse out the tub for you if you request ...

"We need more," Frankenheimer penciled in, but he got less, since it was necessary to acquiesce to a March 31 demand of Geoffrey Shurlock's: "We ask that Clinton be wearing his full pajamas."

More than a general and rather vague portrait of the human condition under capitalism—a window through which the critical eye can see the systematic disenfranchisement of womanhood; extension of, and identification through, maternity; rampant unemployment; disaffection and disenfranchisement of youth; generational discontinuities produced through rapid social change; replacement of social power by sexual hunger—*All Fall Down* points very specifically to the failures and inadequacies of the American project after the 1950s have faded, this at a time when renewal is being purveyed as a force that will reshape culture. "Now people no longer have any opinions; they have refrigerators" (qtd. in Marling 267). A vision of Camelot reborn suffused the media of the early 1960s and influenced the consciousness of the middle class, while the military-industrial complex continued its monstrous vegetable growth and social equalities remained a fantasy. "The national spirit," writes Marling, "was all shook up even as the body politic reposed inert before the picture tube, waiting to be zapped by secret signals from networkland" (187). In this film, a lengthy opening sequence culminates on location on the Overseas Highway, U.S. 1, that leads northward from the Florida Keys: as far as the eye can see in every direction (the aperture is stopped down to f64 with the result that the images have an exceptional crispness and depth in the dazzling sunshine), and excepting the smooth, white, empty—and thus entirely promising—open road elevated on pylons above the dark vast sea, the screen shows nothing but the dark plane of the water and receding space kissed by a clear horizon. Cinematographer Lionel Lindon shot much of this scene from a helicopter (*All Fall Down* Pressbook). In such a space, all things really do seem possible (or equally hopeless), every direction leads to one paradise or another (or nowhere). This is the zone from which America would launch its spacecraft to explore the stars. And Clint, adolescent epitome of the generation that would inherit America under the leadership of John F. Kennedy (Berry-berry, for all his emotional childishness, can look down at him, because he came of age in the days of Eisenhower and Nixon), lives and breathes on the exciting cusp of anticipation, always watching for the knightly figure of the brother to materialize: on this open road, in the space between their shining eyes, within the sere precincts of the overdomesticated home. Having bussed down to Florida to find Berry-berry, he is dismayed to have to bail him out of jail. They jaunt off on a hike down the road—toward infinity—but Berry-berry gets picked up by a disaffected married woman (Constance Ford) who wants him "to crew her yacht." When will Berry-berry come home again, put his feet inside the door? One senses with Clint that his every gesture, every breath, are produced in the delirium of imagining that, invisible, Berry-berry is there to watch, approve, and guide him. The *Monthly Film Bulletin* praised "Frankenheimer's skill in enlisting sympathy on Clinton's side" (74).

But back to that cup of coffee Clint is so eager for Berry-berry to share in the Willart kitchen, primarily because most (younger) readers of this essay may understand by "coffee" only the mass-produced carriage-trade logo-saturated product that is available in identical shops the world over in a seemingly unlimited number of decorative varieties. "A cup of coffee" in the middle-class kitchen of the late 1950s and early 1960s was something else altogether, and so Clint's invitation has a very particular specificity and meaning. To enjoy "a cup of coffee" in the kitchen meant committing oneself to a social—but at the same time private and domesticating—encounter. It meant sitting down, probably at a table covered with a cloth of some kind. It meant china cups and a percolator, with the aroma of coffee filling the room, and perhaps some confection as an accompaniment—a coffee cake, some macaroons: certainly not something that sprang out of the air but something that had been made locally, very locally, within the same four walls. Thus, it meant recognizing that the event as whole—if not the preparation of the coffee or accoutrements themselves—was broadly encompassed by the responsibility of mom, since, as Alan Mintz and Susan Kellogg note, "The fifties ideal of a marital partnership was based on the assumption of a wife's role as hostess and consort" (187); mom, that is to say a "frustrated, repressed, disturbed, martyred, never satisfied, unhappy woman" (Friedan, qtd. in Ehrenreich and English 205). Coming home for "a cup of coffee" meant agreeing to enter her emotional and conceptual territory, which implied subjecting oneself to a certain kind of conversation about civilized and civilizing matters involving frustration, repression, and martyrdom even for a male child. It meant living in "that strange area of nostalgic Americana," as Pauline Kael suggested, "where the familiar is the Freudian grotesque" (31). A "cup of coffee" was reserved for an adult moment, a moment in which futures would be invoked, futures and plans, plans and relationships, relationships and proper behavior, proper behavior and the dangers of regressing to childhood. A "cup of coffee" meant a corrective conversation, an edifying conversation, a moment of formal socialization all smoothed over by the quality of the materials produced and the high taste that was presumed and invoked.

Coffee has yet another meaning. As Wolfgang Schivelbusch points out, while there is a connection between daze (the condition produced by the consumption of alcohol) and mystification, and more generally between the use of liquors and group feeling, the coffeehouse has throughout its history been dedicated to the support and preservation of the individual identity: "In coffeehouses the *I* is central" (177). Further, suggests Schivelbusch, coffee produced and came to symbolize a "drinker's good sense and business efficiency" as contrasted with "the alcohol drinker's inebriation, incompetence, and laziness" (19), and had been understood since the late seventeenth century as a beverage that "awakened a drowning humanity from its alcoholic stupor to middle-class common sense and industry" (34). Coffee was a "beverage of sobriety" and a "means of curbing the sexual urges" (37), not to say a soft technology for producing a "rationalistic, middle-class, forward-looking body" (39). Schivelbusch goes so far as to assert that coffee is "*the* symbolic drink of the bourgeois order" (85). And what order, rationality, and awakening are pointed to in this film but those of the workaday life with its assuring guarantee of progress to a height? This is the order that might free from the chains of her anxiety a troubled mother of the late war years, a woman who has not yet had the opportunity to benefit from the "warm and comforting language" Dr. Benjamin Spock would offer only later, by the time she is pregnant with Clint, but who with her first-born was subjected instead to childcare manuals and pervasive cultural influences that forcefully expressed "anxiety and fear about children's health, safety, and happiness" (Mintz and Kellogg 188), fear, in short, that Berry-berry might very very easily succumb, being as he was a war baby, who could not benefit from the relaxed and more lavish childrearing practices that would soon come into vogue. Also imbricated in the rational order that coffee perfumed would have been Ralph's plans to make it big some day—he is a mathematical genius, but what is that?—to climb out of his basement and stand tall in his own house.

Berry-berry knows, therefore, that a "cup of coffee" in the Willart kitchen is a pretext for a grilling, an endless list of stinging questions that progressively reveal one as what John Russell Taylor calls "the fine young cannibal son" (144). The coffee itself will be delicious, but the acculturations Berry-berry will have to imbibe along with it are poisonous, yet he does not want to refuse the charming Clint, who is all swept off by dreams of wonderment, improvement, and fraternal happiness. He does not want to ward off the innocence of Clint, because he has lost his own, and Clint is his only connection with the person Berry-berry can never be again.

Clay

Because he comes in for coffee, Berry-berry encounters Echo: not according to a naturalistic logic of "realism," since she is in the house and the two of them can meet in many ways if this moment does not occur; but in the truth of the diegesis, since this is precisely how, and when, it happens. Echo, who has been playing with Clint in a way that Berry-berry can immediately see (but of which Clint himself is innocently blind). Meeting Echo, he must have her—what else does he know but the grasping touch? All of the tragedy of this awkward arrangement of faces and styles emanates from this sacred cup of coffee, whereas Clint believes only in the happy formality, the delicious aroma, the warm comfort, the promise of a conviviality that has long since disappeared.

It is worth noting that with the sole exception of Clint, there is not a character in *All Fall Down* who has not rather spectacularly fallen down—from dignity, from renown (even from the higher mathematics), from success, from the everyday to that vulgar zone in which debility and distress meet happenstance. (It was also true, as Frankenheimer commented in the 1990s, that "MGM dumped the movie" itself; they had enormous theaters booked for Minnelli's *The Four Horsemen of the Apocalypse* [1962], which died on base, and "they put our little movie in those big houses" [Frankenheimer 65].) Consider the degradations: at the beginning of the film, Clint disembarks from a Greyhound bus in the Keys (all the way down from Cleveland) and meets the proprietor of a down-in-the-dumps hotel who, descending a steep staircase to hear what Clint wants, informs him that his brother is (down) in the lock-up. Clint shifts to a local saloon where some girls who have fallen out of respect are entertaining the scant few customers by pole dancing. Their madam (Madame Spivy) is a rough, lower type, as is Hedy (Evans Evans), one of the dancers who has been victimized—that is, beaten down—by Berry-berry. In the jail is a pair of guards whose moral standards have fallen, since they are willing to pocket Clint's hard-earned cash as a bribe—"bail money"—for freeing Berry-berry. Walking along the Seven Mile Bridge, Berry-berry hitches a ride with a pair of girls out for a quick pick-up and some lower-class fun; Clint is offered as bait to one of them. Then, at a diner, Berry-berry sells himself as labor to the married woman looking for pleasure. The same will happen later in Cleveland with a schoolteacher (Barbara Baxley) out one evening for thrills beneath her station. As to the Willart family and their fragile guest: Ralph is a purported genius who has descended to trundling real estate for a living; Annabel has been degraded by her own unshaped anxieties and fears; Echo is reduced to picking up teenage virgins and convincing them she loves them—it is almost painful to watch Clint's credulous surrender to her charms; and Berry-berry himself is little more than a hanger-on and bully with big dreams and a big view of himself. The falls of this film put dreams and hopes in conflict with contingencies, the essential formula—especially when the tension happens in the family—of melodrama.

As a melodrama, *All Fall Down* neatly reflects the shape and constructive principles outlined by Thomas Elsaesser: "The persistence of the melodrama might indicate the ways in which popular culture has not only taken note of social crises and the fact that the losers are not always those who deserve it the most, but has also resolutely refused to understand social change in other than private contexts and emotional terms" (47). Here, there are two social crises witnessed by our protagonist-narrator Clint, the broader and more historical fragmentation of this family (as a model for bourgeois families of the early 1960s in general), with the parents split apart into separate privacies and the children a provocation for continual panic and alarm; and the more isolated and localized crisis of Echo's pregnancy, Berry-berry's implication in it, and the resolution that brings about her death and Berry-berry's alienation. As to deserving fate, none of the protagonists in the Willart family has committed any act against his or her own humanity beyond what can be attributed to the compulsive limits of a discreet (and neurotic) personality. It is difficult, then, to think of Berry-berry or Echo as guilty of abuse or seduction. And it is true enough that the broader social fabric of widespread sexual repression coupled with widespread addiction to interpersonal allure, the context in which Berry-berry's narcissism takes root and flowers, is barely hinted at in this motion picture, all of the linkage between pain, suffering, and degradation being set between individual psychopathologies and individual emotional cataclysms. It is not strictly true of Frankenheimer as a filmmaker, however, that he relies on a "formal language (of lighting, staging décor, acting, close-up, montage and camera movement)" to fill in or compensate for "the expressiveness, range of inflection and tonality, rhythmic emphasis and tension normally present in the spoken word" (Elsaesser 51), because he has cast his film carefully in terms of the musicality of the actors' voices as made manifest through their utterance of the script. Malden's rich and cajoling baritone, Lansbury's shrill alto held always in check so as to hone the sharpness of its edge, the contrasting soothing coo of Saint's voice, and the pervading, brooding silences produced by Beatty, an enigma buried inside a marble exterior, work together to produce a chamber ensemble that speeds forward through various emotional registers, always evidencing a fundamental lack of fit, as one might find also in the chamber music of the modernists, Berg, Ravel, Hindemith. As Elsaesser notes of the domestic melodrama in general, so, and markedly, of *All Fall Down*: "The tellingly impotent gesture, the social gaffe, the hysterical outburst replaces any more directly liberating or self-annihilating action, and the cathartic violence of a shoot-out or a chase becomes an inner violence, often one which the characters turn against themselves" (56).

The final thrust of this film, which is also its conceptual center and its true beginning, is the disillusionment of Clint. Clint is our object, or at least our principal shape, the reason for the light, this having been evident even to insiders: "The concentration of the film was on the wrong person," said Karl Malden more than forty years later. "It was on Warren Beatty. It should have been on the little boy.... He is the *only* one in the picture that *changes*" (D. Bell 62). He has been crouching in the teeming rain outside the window that gives into the basement where Berry-berry and Echo are confronting one another and she is revealing her pregnancy and his responsibility. As Berry-berry runs out, abandoning her—indeed, leaving the house altogether and retreating to his secret aerie at the orchard, that space in which he exists as the person we never truly meet—and as, drenched to the skin, Clint runs up to Echo's bedroom to see her packing and ultimately driving away from the house—"Will you be back?" "Oh *yes*! *I'll be back!*"—it dawns on the boy that the idol of his life, the older brother whose name has come out of his mouth like a birdsong all through this film, the

Berry-berry whom one can hardly anticipate too fervently or gaze at with too sharp a sense of longing, is only damaged goods, only, as the *Hollywood Reporter* put it, "clay from the waist down" (Powers "All"). Yet, what a curious peroration! We are all, it need hardly be said, clay. But "clay from the waist down"—an attempt, certainly, to deprecate Berry-berry as nothing but false, nothing but artificial, and an attempt that in its profoundest depths fails because clay is the most we can ever hope to be. The deeper meaning here might be, this boy has become fully himself only below the Mason-Dixon line, in his sex, in his southerliness (which is why he must linger in Florida and is so hesitant to come back north). Clint has not become clay at all yet. Clint is still conceptual, still utterly oneiric, still a believer in the power of sunsets.

In a freeze upon the boy's realization, Frankenheimer makes plain what all the fragments of the film have been swirling around: why he has detailed a picture of this family, a family in which virtually everyone, everyone but only one, has fallen; why the voices have chanted "Berry-berry" so insistently. If Clint's hero is only the shell of a hero, not a charismatic figure but a cipher, still *that is what heroes are*. And the Willart home, a symbol of middle-class complacency and sanctimony, is only the shell of a home, an "Echo chamber"—this one is a chamber of horrors, to be sure—a Yeatsian "rag and bone shop of the heart" wherein we may hear one another's warmest riddles. America, so full of promise, is just such a place, and we broadcast our hopes there. Now in a silent thunder, Clint must go to the orchard himself, must enter the shack that will soon enough be dust, climb the worn stairs, to confront the man who would not be a man. "You told me you didn't like life, and I said I agreed with you, just to go along. But I *do* like life, Berry-berry." Indeed, Clint has finally spoken the truth, and to himself. "I *do* like life," actually, and for what it is, and now the sound of that offputting name—a name that one must not pronounce—no longer has a shamanic ring in Brandon De Wilde's tranquil, but always carefully shaped, voice. It is elemental syllables, bubbling bricks of the edifice we build together—"nervously loquacious," wrote Kenneth Burke, "at the edge of an abyss." Berry-berry is finally seen, finally encountered as an emptiness surrounded by a membrane that will collapse: not godly but tender, not bigger than life but life itself.

Clint had arrived at the orchard while Berry-berry was outside somewhere, and had lain in wait for him with a loaded gun. Now he shows his weapon. "I intended to kill you." As he walks away it is evident in the relaxation of De Wilde's lithe body not that Clint's resolve has dissipated, nor that his sense of honor is lost, but that Berry-berry no longer strikes him as a focus of purpose. He was a fetish that has lost its flavor, and this is the maturing disillusionment. As the boy descends the stairs and walks out among the fruit trees under the morning sky, we see from the clarity of his gaze—his eyes are screwed down a little in focus as they have never been before—that Clint, too, has fallen, and can now live his life. He has fallen from childhood's pinnacle of innocence and wonder to a view of the world as a real place, and of Berry-berry as only a person, like

From left, Karl Malden, Angela Lansbury, Brandon De Wilde, William Inge, John Frankenheimer, Warren Beatty, and Eva Marie Saint at a read-through for *All Fall Down*.
Courtesy of the Academy of Motion Picture Arts and Sciences.

himself, who could not manage to sustain around himself the glimmering aura of promise but had finally needed—and wondrously failed—to come through.

Clint walks away from the barn, from his brother, and from his previous self, with uniform steps and in utter silence, the silence of silent cinema, in fact, while the wind blows gently among the blossoms. He does not sing—and yet we know that he must be imagining to himself—those words that come up from the long-buried trench of our shared forgotten past:

Ring-a-Ring-O'Roses,
A pocket fulla posies,
Ashes, ashes,
We all fall down.

Secrets

An American in Paris

John Frankenheimer's *Impossible Object*

JERRY MOSHER

> I love the movie. Maybe because it's like your sick child or something. It's really the most personal movie I've ever made.
>
> John Frankenheimer, 1975 (Gross 46)

In 1970 John Frankenheimer and his wife, actress Evans Evans, moved into a flat on the Île St. Louis in Paris while he edited *The Horsemen* (1971). The couple had been married in France in 1963 while Frankenheimer shot *The Train* (1964), and they spent considerable time there during the production of *Grand Prix* (1966). This time, however, they did not plan an immediate return to the United States, deciding instead to rent out their Malibu beach house. The couple began taking French lessons for two hours a day with a coach from the Comédie Française, and Frankenheimer studied cooking at Le Cordon Bleu. "Little by little we both realized that we loved it there and we fitted in very well," Frankenheimer recalled (Pratley, *Films* 135). After completing the editing project, he spent five months working with Michel Guérard at the chef's celebrated Pot au Feu restaurant in nearby Asnières (Bryson 42). The director had given up competitive race car driving after several friends died on the Formula One circuit, but in France he continued to "drive out in the country and obey the speed limit" (Pratley 123). And Frankenheimer was particularly pleased when, after enduring several years of critical drubbing in the United States, he was fêted at the Cinémathèque Française with a retrospective in April 1971.

"We were going to the Old World to find a new rhythm for our lives, with a true conviction that we had left behind our old relics forever," wrote American expatriate F. Scott Fitzgerald in 1924 (Fitzgerald 17). A half-century later, John and Evans were not inclined to dive into fountains or dance on tabletops, but like Scott and Zelda and many Americans in their wake, the Frankenheimers were seeking a new life in a country they perceived to be more culturally and politically sophisticated than their own. And, like many expatriates, they were also running away from something. After achieving commercial and critical success with a string of paranoid thrillers and action films in the mid-1960s, Frankenheimer had stumbled professionally as he sought new challenges within a disintegrating Hollywood studio system undergoing major reorganization. His World War II comedy *The Extraordinary Seaman* (1969) was so awkward and unfunny that MGM shelved the film for more than a year before dumping it into theaters with little promotion; a *Los Angeles Times* critic called it "the most total fiasco since the Edsel" (K. Thomas). *The Fixer* (1968), a heavy-handed adaptation of the Bernard Malamud novel, generated mixed reviews and lackluster box office, despite an Academy Award nomination for star Alan Bates. Two fine dramas set in rural America, *The Gypsy Moths* (1969) and *I Walk the Line* (1970), were sabotaged by studio politics and paltry distribution. And *The Horsemen*, conceived as a three-hour epic about the ancient game of buzkashi, had been downsized by Columbia Pictures to two hours while Frankenheimer was still shooting on location in Afghanistan. "Aside from *The Fixer* it's been a disappointing period," the director said in 1971. "I badly need *The Horsemen* to be a success" (Pratley 115). It wasn't.

Compounding Frankenheimer's troubles was the devastating assassination of his friend Senator Robert F. Kennedy, who was staying with the Frankenheimers during the California primary election in June 1968. The director drove the Democratic presidential candidate to a victory celebration at the Ambassador Hotel in Los Angeles, and was nearby when the senator was shot. Frankenheimer went into a deep depression. "We are in terrible trouble in this country," he said in December 1969. "There's been a terrible void since [Kennedy] was killed" (Pratley 95). So after editing *The Horsemen* in Paris in late 1970, Frankenheimer decided to stay on. "I was going through a phase in my life when I thought I wanted to live permanently in Europe," the director said. "I had been deeply affected by the death of Bobby Kennedy. Evans and I loved France, we thought we wanted to stay there, and I wanted to see if I could work within their system" (Pratley 127).

The result was *Impossible Object* (1973), an unabashed work of art cinema that reflected the director's personal obsessions and newfound creative interests during his nearly three-year expatriation in France. British author Nicholas Mosley's source novel, published in 1969, was a kaleidoscopic view of an adulterous affair, consisting of eight interconnected stories from multiple perspectives, each introduced with a hallucinatory prose poem that contemplated subjects such as God, Nietzsche, love, and war. Frankenheimer's film smoothed out some of the wrinkles in Mosley's screenplay (which had been intended for director Joseph Losey), but its multiple flashbacks and flash forwards, fantasy sequences, and meditations on the paradoxes of living and loving remained true to the novel's experimental style and metatextual concerns. Obvious influences were European art films like Losey's mordant *Accident* (1967, adapted by

Evans Evans and Alan Bates in *Impossible Object* (Euro International Film, 1973). Courtesy, PhotoFest New York.

Harold Pinter from Mosley's 1965 novel) and Federico Fellini's autobiographical *8½* (1963), both of which portrayed conflicted artists and intellectuals involved in adulterous affairs. The sexual frankness of Bernardo Bertolucci's *Last Tango in Paris* (released in Paris in December 1972) would make *Impossible Object* look tame in comparison, but European production allowed Frankenheimer to depict sexuality more explicitly than he ever had in Hollywood, even after the demise of the Production Code in 1968. (Images from a fantasy sequence featuring topless women at a Felliniesque pool party would appear in the January 1973 issue of *Playboy* magazine.) *Impossible Object*'s art-cinema credentials were bolstered by the participation of art-house stars Alan Bates and Dominique Sanda, as well as such veterans of French cinema as cinematographer Claude Renoir (who had shot *The Horsemen*) and composer Michel Legrand. Several scenes involving French characters were shot in French with English subtitles, an opportunity that Hollywood producers never afforded the director when he made *The Train* and *Grand Prix*.

Frankenheimer continually worried about his film's narrative coherence, but art cinema's inherent self-reflexivity and ambiguity proved liberating, allowing him to examine his infidelities and self-doubts, as well as the social pressures that discouraged their admission, without the need to defend or condemn them. "I don't think it was an indulgence," the director said. "I was trying to find a whole other way to tell a story—either successfully or not. It was not a conventional use of time, place and events. I found it interesting to experiment this way" (Pratley 130). Indeed, *Impossible Object* represents the furthest the director ever strayed from the strictures of classical storytelling. After discovering that European film producers could be even more capricious than their American counterparts, Frankenheimer would soon be back in the United States, directing a faithful screen adaptation of Eugene O'Neill's *The Iceman Cometh* (1973). "We are Americans, and this is where we belong," the director told *Daily Variety* (Beaupre). He would then return to directing action pictures and political thrillers for the final three decades of his career. Frankenheimer's brief embrace of European art cinema in *Impossible Object* thus provides a unique opportunity to examine the director working without the familiar tools of goal-oriented characters, cause-effect logic, and narrative closure.

Impossible Object, unfortunately, has been nearly impossible to see, largely due to the bankruptcy of its production company before the film was even completed. After a rushed première out of competition at the 1973 Cannes Film Festival, the film received only limited exhibition in Western Europe. Attempts to secure a U.S. distributor proved futile; negotiations were poorly handled and were not helped by the director's diminished bankability[1] The film's only official video release (a truncated, pan-and-scan version distributed in England), was retitled *Story of a Love Story*—perhaps to exploit the popularity of Erich Segal's best-selling book and hit movie *Love Story* (1970)—which only further obscured the film's artistic merits and literary pedigree.

By Frankenheimer's own admission, *Impossible Object* is a flawed and occasionally confusing film (Pratley 133), and at times it makes one feel that critic Andrew Sarris's condemnation of the director's "strained seriousness" is deserved. Yet it also contains exhilarating moments of intimacy, joy, and despair, capturing the tumultuous emotions and irrational actions churned up by an illicit affair, when common sense and decorum are overwhelmed by a giddy intensity of feeling. "The impossible object is to lead the life that you visualize for yourself and to be able to compensate for that," Frankenheimer said (Blume). In the wake of career failures, marital problems, and political turmoil, the familiar structures and institutions at home no longer offered the director much comfort or support. Frankenheimer's voluntary exile into French culture and art cinema might have appeared dilettantish, but it was not an act of nihilism or ennui. Rather, it was motivated by his earnest, hopeful, and conventionally American search for new ways to make sense of an increasingly nonsensical world.

The Improbable Project

Impossible Object depicts the midlife crisis of Harry (Bates), a British writer living in southern France with his American wife, Elizabeth (Evans Evans), and their three sons. Harry meets Nathalie (Sanda) in a Paris museum and they begin a passionate affair; her husband, a French television producer (Michel Auclair), hires thugs to intimidate the couple in a futile attempt to break up the romance. Harry separates from his wife to work in Paris and continue the affair; he and Nathalie travel to northern Africa (with their spouses' apparent approval) and have a child together, but the baby is killed in a boating accident. Devastated, Harry and Nathalie return to their spouses, but years later they meet again in Rome, and—perhaps—resume their affair. Harry's fantasies are laced throughout the narrative and include an extended sexual sojourn with Hippolyta, his "dream woman" (Lea Massari).

In his novel and screenplay, Mosley was not so much interested in the characters and their actions, but rather in the ways the characters *perceive* their actions and the actions of others. The work grew out of the author's own experience of adultery in his mid-forties. "I was both a man involved in a love affair, and I also felt myself watching myself," Mosley said. "I used to think, what the hell am I doing? One becomes hopelessly involved in things, but one can watch oneself—and this is not hopelessness" (Flannagan, "Way" 97). In Mosley's fiction, identity is fragmented between "the self that acts and the self that observes itself acting," and it is the latter self that recognizes patterns within the fragments and makes them whole (Flannagan, "Nicholas" 68). The novel's final prose poem states, in essence, Mosley's aims: "I wanted to write you something impossible, like a staircase climbing a spiral to come out where it started or a cube with a vertical line at the back overlapping a horizontal one in front. These cannot exist in three dimensions but can be drawn in two; by cutting out one dimension a fourth is created. The object is that life is impossible; one cuts out fabrication and creates reality. A mirror is held to the back of the head and one's hand has to move the opposite way from what was intended" (Mosley, *Impossible* 218).

Critics generally praised the novel's conceptual audacity but found its execution strained and its drama elusive. "This is black art and difficult fiction—as difficult to read as to review," began John Leonard's review in the *New York Times*. "This is a novelist's novel, tricky, brilliant and irritating." Saul Maloff, writing for the same paper, noted that Mosley's writing demonstrates "a kind of showy virtuosity that induces, at most, a grudging admiration," but "without some notion of causation. . . . *Impossible Object*, quite literally, begins dissolving before one's eyes." In England, after *Impossible Object* made the short list for the first Booker Prize in 1969, the chair of the judging committee reported, "In some ways and places everyone thought it strained, miscalculated, even absurdly pretentious; but three at least of the stories were separately effective, and everyone found too that the author's method could produce resonances so strange and fine that the novel was not to be set aside" (Mosley, *Efforts* 209–10). Frankenheimer's ambitious, flawed, but occasionally virtuosic film adaptation would be received in similar fashion.

It might seem strange that a novel roundly criticized for its lack of "dramatic validation" and "the felt absence of dramatic center" (Maloff) would be optioned for a movie, but several reviewers noted Pinter and Losey's successful adaptation of *Accident* and suggested that *Impossible Object* was suitably Pinteresque to warrant similar treatment. "As with Pinter, so with Mosley: style is everything—a way of seeing around corners and at sharply-tilted angles," wrote Moloff. "Like Pinter, Mosley is most effective—which is to say first-rate—when he is most menacing, deadly." Leonard noted the novel's "obsessive images" and compared its search for meaning in abstraction to Alain Resnais's *Last Year at Marienbad* (1961). And at the end of the novel Mosley himself coyly acknowledged cinema's impact on storytelling and the imagination: "I have given you an unhappy end like those of your favorite films—the girl shot over and over in snow like a rabbit, the car drowning in a few inches of water" (Mosley, *Impossible* 218).

Impossible Object was optioned by Jud Kinberg, who had produced screen adaptations of critically respected British novels such as John Fowles's *The Collector* (William Wyler, 1965) and *The Magus* (Guy Green, 1968). Executive producer Robert Bradford (husband of best-selling British author Barbara Taylor Bradford) put up the majority of the $1.6 million budget for the film's Paris-based production company, Franco London Film. After Joseph Losey decided not to direct Mosley's screenplay, Kinberg enlisted Frankenheimer, who had been looking for a film to direct while in Paris. Dirk Bogarde and Catherine Deneuve, who had been slated for the lead roles, were replaced by Bates and Sanda, and the setting was changed from England to France.

Mosley's self-reflexive romantic drama was an unlikely project for Frankenheimer, but the director saw in *Impossible Object* a chance to return to his roots in psychological family melodrama (such as *The Young Stranger* [1957] and *All Fall Down* [1962]) while approaching the form in a new, more experimental way. Frankenheimer admired Pinter and Losey's screen adaptation of *Accident* and was eager to tackle an even more complex and interior rendering of infidelity. Mosley's tale of a writer in the throes of an extramarital affair appealed to Frankenheimer, whose retreat to Paris with his wife was partially motivated by the need to save their marriage. The director, known as a ladies' man in Hollywood circles, had had a rather public affair in 1968 with twenty-one-year-old Mitzi Trumbo, daughter of screenwriter Dalton Trumbo, during the production of *The Fixer* in Hungary. *Los Angeles Times* gossip columnist Joyce Haber alluded to the affair in a 1971 profile of Frankenheimer, noting that the screenwriter for *The Fixer* and *The Horsemen* "no longer speaks to John, for reasons that involve a female relative. 'I don't blame him,' says Frankenheimer wistfully" (Haber).[2] Frankenheimer's intentions to confront his marital infidelities in *Impossible Object* were made clear when he cast his wife in the role of the writer's shrewish, cuckolded spouse. "It would be nonsense to say it isn't autobiographical," the director said on the set in October 1972. "It's a story of a man who can give love, but who can't take it. It's easier to give, but to be vulnerable enough to receive . . ." (Blume).

Frankenheimer had recently seen Alan Bates on stage playing the title role in Simon Gray's *Butley*, in which an English professor breaks up with his wife and male lover on the same day. "The leading character in [*Impossible Object*] is very close to Alan personally—so is Butley, and in this picture Alan gives the same kind of performance as he gave in that play," Frankenheimer told Bates biographer Donald Spoto. "In *Impossible Object*, you have to feel sorry for the character, you have to like him—women in the audience have to like him. I need an actor with every nuance: comedy, pathos, the chaos of everyday life and no self-pity

Alan Bates and Dominique Sanda on the French one-sheet poster for *Impossible Object*.
Collection Jerry Mosher.

whatever. I saw all these things in Butley, and when I found the script for *Impossible Object*, I realized only Bates could play it" (Spoto 135). Indeed, Bates shoulders the burden of making the film cohere through its multiple jumps forward and backward in time, and his charming, nimble performance continually lifts the picture out of its existential doldrums.

Bates, like Frankenheimer, took a personal interest in *Impossible Object*. The actor, who had numerous long-term homosexual relationships but remained secretive about his sexual orientation throughout his life, in 1970 married Victoria Ward, who gave birth to their twin sons that year. Within two years after the wedding, Spoto notes, "relatives and friends started to notice that the marriage endured only because he wanted desperately to maintain the image of a respectable middle-class family life and because he felt an obligation to her" (Spoto 132). On the set of *Impossible Object*, Bates said that he "liked the way Mosley looks at this man and his three relationships—wife, mistress, fantasy mistress. It's witty and honest. . . . I don't want to get heavy about it, but the character puts himself in this situation, wondering whether it's really worth it and whether it's possible. And of course from the title, it's impossible." Bates's co-star Dominique Sanda knowingly summed up his predicament: "Alan's right for the part because he's always two in one" (Blume).

In fact, principal photography for *Impossible Object* was delayed until Sanda gave birth to her son, fathered by French actor and notorious ladies' man Christian Marquand—who was married to actress Tina Aumont. Frankenheimer shot footage of a pregnant and naked Sanda, which was used in *Impossible Object* when her character Nathalie, Harry's mistress, is pregnant with his child. Promiscuity among film professionals on location is hardly unusual, but as filming of *Impossible Object* officially commenced, the blurring of reality and illusion so integral to Mosley's novel was already being enacted by the principals in Frankenheimer's production beyond anyone's wildest expectations.

Story of a Love Story

Before agreeing to direct *Impossible Object*, Frankenheimer had met with Mosley in London to discuss his concerns about the screenplay's elusiveness. Pacing back and forth in his hotel room, the director wanted to understand, Mosley recalled, "why I had written it in different pieces and from different angles that seemed almost but not quite to fit together; and what were the flashes here and there—real events, or in people's minds? So I embarked on my party-piece about impossible objects—it is life itself that does not seem quite to fit together; but in so far as you can look down on the ways in which you seem to be in pieces, then perhaps you are not" (Mosley, *Efforts* 241). The fundamental issue underlying the romantic triangles in *Accident* and *Impossible Object*, Mosley told Frankenheimer, is the fact that people are always acting in order to behave in a social manner and play the roles they are expected to play—as clever writers or imperious

Oxford dons, faithful husbands or doting wives, and so on. "We are trying to impress people or charm people or get something out of them or put something over on them. This is what I call acting, and that is what people write scripts and plays about, about this sort of thing happening," Mosley said (Flannagan 91). It is only in times of intensity or crisis, in Mosley's view, that people stop watching themselves—and it is these moments of non-acting that constitute a certain "reality," and reveal what people truly want. Intrigued, Frankenheimer continued to ask questions and pace around the room "like a caged tiger and baring his teeth," then ordered breakfast and decided he would direct the picture (Mosley, *Efforts* 242).

Frankenheimer asked Mosley and his wife to stay in Paris during production in the summer of 1972, and began revising the script with assistance from Kinberg and others. The director's intrigue gave way to apprehension. In script conferences, Frankenheimer and Kinberg started demanding answers from Mosley: "Is this or that really happening or is it in the mind? What is the reasoning here, what is the motivation? Then suddenly—How will this be understood by an audience in some small town in the American midwest?" Mosley remained adamant that the "flashes" throughout the script were the glue that held it together, serving as "memories, premonitions, and resonances." In Mosley's view, "it need not be differentiated too clearly what is inside or outside the mind: an audience needs to become involved, not to be made to understand." Unsatisfied, Frankenheimer and Kinberg finally insisted, "Look here, Nicholas, when all is said and done, what we have here is just a good straightforward love story!" Mosley countered, "But what we have not got here is just a good straightforward love story!" (Mosley, *Efforts* 243). Soon thereafter, the author was told his services were no longer required, and he and his wife left Paris.

Mosley, who considered removing his name from the credits, would eventually need a lawyer to get permission to view the film in Paris before its release. Afterward, he was predictably disappointed, but offered grudging admiration. "The skeleton of my script was there: but not the style, the knowingness, the irony of acting/not acting, whatever resonances might have made sense of all this," he recalled. "Actors acted as if they were either joking or sincere: but the point had been the passionate struggle to find, or create, what sincerity or non-sincerity might be. . . . But I felt John Frankenheimer had been brave in trying to stick even to the skeleton of the script, and I was sad that I had not myself been able to stay to give the bones more flesh" (Mosley, *Efforts* 246–47). Mosley had also been disappointed with Losey's adaptations of *Accident* and his original screenplay for *The Assassination of Trotsky* (1972), and was forced to acknowledge that his concept of "acting/not acting" was better realized in his fiction: "Actors couldn't act this. Directors couldn't direct it. Even though Losey, Frankenheimer, and the actors such as Alan Bates all said—This is so interesting! Yes, we can't wait to get on the set and try to do this. None of them could" (Flannagan 91).

In spite of the writer's complaints, Frankenheimer's revised script preserved many of Mosley's flashes and imagined sequences. For example, after a teenage girl is electrocuted at a birthday party for Harry's son, it is revealed that Harry is actually telling this story to Nathalie in a Paris cafe—and that it is only a story. "People like an unhappy ending," Harry says. "It makes them feel good." But Nathalie doesn't like it: "God, Harry, I never know what's true and what isn't with you." The audience is often left wondering as well, as Harry continually revels in his ability to be a God-like creator of stories and a duplicitous adulterer. In the cafe he tells Nathalie that she, too, is a poet, "but you don't know it," thus propagating Mosley's idea that social interaction is dependent on fabrication and role-playing. "You'll see what I mean some day," Harry says, and the scene ends ominously with a two-second flash forward to the capsizing of their boat in Morocco, which will drown their baby. In the Moroccan sequence at the end of the film, Nathalie does in fact write poetry, and she says in voiceover, "It sometimes frightened me how he would say something that was not true, and it would become true."

Mosley's handling of the drowning, and his insistence on providing multiple endings, created the most nagging narrative problem for Frankenheimer. The baby's death occurs because Harry is not much interested in looking after it, and Nathalie does not want to be like Harry's wife, isolating herself at home to take care of children—so they bring the baby with them on the boat. The drowning constitutes the unhappy ending of the novel's eighth and final story, but in the subsequent prose poem Mosley calls attention to the artifice of endings: "There is also a happy end, though this is less explicit. But you always read books more for form than content" (Mosley, *Impossible* 218). Indeed, the child that appears with Nathalie and her older daughter Danielle in the novel's second and fifth stories, which actually occur later in time, could very well be the same baby. In his original screenplay Mosley refused to resolve the question of whether or not the baby dies; in the final scene, Harry encounters Nathalie in Rome, and they discuss a "happy ending" as her husband is seen in the background playing with a two-year-old child, which could be Harry's (Mosley, *Efforts* 206–07). In Mosley's view, "so long as the chance of seeing it like this is just there, it will not matter if an audience will or will not accept it" (Mosley, *Efforts* 209).

Frankenheimer, however, believed that the drowning of a baby would be so powerful an audience would not accept that it might only be a story. "The death of the baby is absolutely essential to make the film work," he told Pratley in 1975. "There was no way we could *not* kill the baby" (Pratley 130). His elegant solution managed to be more straightforward while preserving Mosley's multiple endings. Harry and Nathalie thus meet in Rome after being apart for several years, and her husband is seen playing with their daughter Danielle—there is no smaller child. Harry says he is writing their story, and Nathalie asks if it has a happy ending. When Harry tells her she doesn't like happy endings, Nathalie quickly retorts, "It was you that made it unhappy." The film then cuts to the final Moroccan sequence, the only part of the film narrated by Nathalie, a slow-building, straightforward, twenty-minute narrative culminating in the baby's drowning and the parents' desperate search for it along the shore. Back in Rome, Harry asks, "Did you think that was the end?" Nathalie says yes. "Well, it isn't," Harry replies, and the film ends with the possibility that they will resume their love affair.

The final Moroccan sequence—especially the capsizing of the boat among large waves—is beautifully shot and edited, but the dramatic climax Frankenheimer hoped to achieve is undermined by the film's preceding eighty minutes of lies, evasions, fantasy sequences, and nonlinearity. *Impossible Object*'s continual blurring of reality and fantasy wears down the viewer's emotional investment and identification. The film's drama was further undercut by the obvious lack of chemistry between any of the principal actors: Sanda's performance is often distant and wooden (Frankenheimer admitted that her "otherworldly quality" might have been a problem [Pratley 131]); Evans Evans is given little to do but scold Bates like a clucking hen; and Michel Auclair as the cuckolded husband is a humorless, avaricious television producer (his profession is clearly one of Frankenheimer's autobiographical touches). Only Bates manages to charm as Mosley's stand-in.

Self-reflexivity and lack of affect are commonly employed in art cinema to create emotional distance, producing a critical viewing framework consistent with the principles of Bertolt Brecht's *V-Effekt*.[3] Mosley certainly endorsed such an approach in his stated goal to depict "the self that acts and the self that observes itself acting." Frankenheimer, however, seemed to want it both ways: to remain true to Mosley's metatextual novel while still delivering the emotional power of a Hollywood melodrama. As eager as he was to experiment with new cinematic forms, interviews during and after the production suggest that his heart wasn't quite in it. After a screening at the 1975 Stratford International Film Festival in Canada, when audience members voiced concerns about the film's narrative obscurity and unbelievability, Frankenheimer practically apologized as he backpedaled from the film's art cinema trappings, stating that "the picture would be better if we removed some of the flashes, to show it more as a straightforward story. But it is too late now" (Pratley 128).

The backpedaling had, in fact, begun before the production was even completed. In the summer of 1972, the promotion of *Impossible Object* as a simple love story was in full swing. A full-page advertisement announcing the start of shooting in the July 13 issue of the *Hollywood Reporter* carried the tagline, "The high adventure of love . . . A passionate chase through the tangled byways of the heart" (15). Three months later, a *Los Angeles Times* interview with the director on set in Paris, titled "A Love Story That Doesn't Die," began by highlighting the fact that Frankenheimer's new picture did not take place in a jail cell or "grease pits"—it was a love story. "I'm beginning to find more what I want to do—subjects that explore the relationship between men and women," Frankenheimer said. The reporter noted that scenes filtered through the protagonist's imagination "give Frankenheimer a chance to show his great virtuosity, but he is proceeding with restraint: 'I in no way want to confuse audiences. That's showing contempt. Our function is to tell a story, as David Lean says'" (Blume).

One cannot be certain whether Frankenheimer here was attempting to assuage the fears of wary American distributors or simply speaking his mind. The director would later claim that he had enjoyed working with Mosley, who "writes for an audience far above the average movie-goer. I never thought or intended this to be a movie for a broad audience—rather it was a question of making the script work for those who were attracted to it." At the 1975 Stratford screening, however, Frankenheimer praised Losey and Pinter's riveting adaptation of *Accident* and wistfully noted that, with Mosley adapting his own novel, "our production lacked one element that *Accident* had, and that was Harold Pinter" (Pratley 127–29). Whatever the case, one thing is certain: even after Frankenheimer's script revisions, *Impossible Object* would never be confused with a David Lean film; its narrative is too ambiguous and excessively complex.

Frankenheimer's declaration of respect for his audiences, and his evocation of Lean—as opposed to more obvious influences like Fellini, Antonioni, Losey, or Resnais—reveal his American pragmatism as well as his unfamiliarity with the promotion and reception of art cinema. In this market, he was out of his element. By 1972, one would not find a Fellini or Antonioni straining to explain their films to reporters or expressing concern about audience comprehension. The European auteur director was expected to remain as aloof and enigmatic as his films, and it was the audience's job to do the interpreting. Frankenheimer, on the other hand, viewed himself as a working professional, not an auteur.[4] He would always struggle—in his own mind, anyway—to be taken seriously as more than just a director of action pictures. His eagerness to explain the significance of his films was conditioned by more than a decade of toiling in live television and the Hollywood studio system, where he continually used stylistic virtuosity to transcend the limitations of genre formulas. With *Impossible Object* most of those limitations had been removed, leaving Frankenheimer with little to rebel against; consequently, the director felt the need to create some straw men of his own. But as a voluntary exile in France, Frankenheimer, unlike the blacklisted Losey, never needed to embrace European art cinema as an oppositional mode of production. For Losey it was a matter of reinvention and survival; for Frankenheimer it was an intriguing experiment. Frankenheimer would not attempt another art cinema project, and he would soon return to Hollywood and genre filmmaking. After the experience of directing *Impossible Object*, Frankenheimer might have regarded art cinema in the same way poet Robert Frost regarded free verse—it was like playing tennis without a net.

Of Time and Place

With its radically nonlinear depiction of a failing marriage and adulterous affair, *Impossible Object* is an exemplary cultural artifact of its time: a brief span in the late 1960s and early 1970s when the decline of classical Hollywood cinema and the rise of New Wave filmmaking encouraged formal experimentation in commercial cinema, and the decline of the institution of marriage and the rise of the sexual revolution encouraged experimentation in intimate human relationships. By the 1980s, this period of artistic and social upheaval had been eclipsed by global blockbuster films, "family values," and the specter of AIDS. Frankenheimer, speaking in 1975, thought the global economic recession at that time had already made the film's social concerns commercially irrelevant: "I feel it has a very special time. I find the film has dated in many ways because of the subject matter. . . . how do you *sell* this movie now? I don't know. I certainly knew how to sell it then" (Pratley 131).

Viewed several decades later, *Impossible Object*'s formal audacity and questioning of the social construct still merit admiration, but at times—especially when Harry is exclaiming that he feels "like God"—it seems like just another elaborate artifice concocted by privileged white European males to obfuscate and justify their philandering. Harry's many references to God are characteristic of the self-reflexive artist; "like Gods at play," Robert Stam notes, "reflexive artists see themselves as unbound by life as it is perceived (Reality), by stories as they have been told (Genre), or by a nebulous probability (Verisimilitude)" (Stam 129). Harry's wife and children, unfortunately, are still bound by reality, genre, and verisimilitude, and their suffering is evident. Harry's whimsical attempt to orchestrate a children's game in the cellar, for example, goes tragically awry. Adam, Harry's oldest son (Sean Bury), fears his father is using the game to seduce his girlfriend, Cleo (Isabelle Giraud-Carrier), in the cellar's shadows; his worst fears are realized after his younger brother (Marc Dightam) removes a dangling light bulb (to prevent Adam from turning it on and seeing Harry and Cleo hiding in the dark) and Cleo is electrocuted, forcing Harry to give the girl mouth-to-mouth resuscitation. Encountering this scene, Harry's wife exclaims, "Why, why do you do it?" before leaving to call a doctor. When Adam, trembling, inquires whether Cleo is dead, Harry does not reply; instead, there is a quick flash forward to the capsizing of the boat in Morocco. Harry's imaginative leaps in time and space and his blurring of reality and fantasy enable him to dodge the painful ramifications of his actions, but Frankenheimer's camera captures the agony residing on Adam's stricken face.

Reviewing Mosley's novel in 1969, critic John Leonard observed that "the deracinated European intellectual, in search of sensual reintegration and a meaningful commitment, trapped in abstractions and artifice, flirts with fascism. Sex-acts become mutual woundings." In philandering there is the risk of losing it all, of making no contact with anyone, "but the risk itself is ritualized, made abstract, becomes another game of terror like the hide-and-seek the narrator plays with his children." Ultimately, Leonard notes, the intellectual turns against "the art forms that have failed to make sense of the game. . . . Mockery is the last remaining lifestyle" (Leonard). Mosley, Pinter, and Losey excelled at this game and made careers out of it, but for Frankenheimer it was all too abstract and decadent.

If *Impossible Object* had found an audience, Frankenheimer might have been able to make more films in the 1970s about the intimate relationships between men and women. One can imagine him being comfortable directing the type of urbane, middle-class adultery drama that actor George Segal popularized in the early 1970s, such as *Loving* (1970), *Blume in Love* (1973), or *A Touch of Class* (1973). But Frankenheimer was not a writer-director and had little facility with comedy, which limited his options. He continued to be a director for hire, saddled with action pictures and political thrillers made from second-hand scripts. "[It's] really a struggle to get pictures made and to get the right material," he said in 1989. "What you don't want to do is just continually get material with fingerprints all over it. You've got to get yourself in a position where material is being submitted to you before it's being submitted to anybody else" (Easton). The original script for *Impossible Object* had some of Joseph Losey's fingerprints on it, but the film nevertheless represents a period of creative expansion when Frankenheimer was still searching earnestly for new cinematic forms of expression. In *Impossible Object* there remains an air of hope and grace that is lacking in many of the desultory genre outings the director made in the 1980s. Reflecting on his nearly three-year expatriation in France, Frankenheimer noted that "it was a beautiful time in Paris, and it was responsible for *Impossible Object*, which I do think was an important step in my career" (Pratley 135). While not a wholly successful example of art cinema, *Impossible Object* is worthy of distribution and further study, if only for Alan Bates's charismatic performance and the film's unique place in the director's oeuvre.

NOTES

1. Frankenheimer has continually claimed that executive producer Robert Bradford loved *Impossible Object* and consequently botched the sale of the film's U.S. rights by asking for too much money, which contributed to the bankruptcy of Franco London Film. Bradford refuted these accusations in January 1974, claiming that the bankruptcy of Franco London Film had nothing to do with *Impossible Object*, but was the result of a previous tax claim by the French government. European rights to the film had already been purchased by producer Alexander Salkind, who was unable to secure a U.S. distributor. Responding to Frankenheimer's wishes to reedit the film, Bradford said that Frankenheimer was merely a salaried director with "no proprietary position in the negative." Frankenheimer "brought the film in on time but was well over the $1.6 million budget," and Bradford's only complaint was the director's decision to order only forty-one minutes of musical score for the film. Bradford was "amused, if puzzled" by Frankenheimer's claim that he kept the production operating in Morocco by financing it with personal credit cards (Landry).

2. Comedian Steve Martin, who was dating Mitzi Trumbo in Los Angeles when she left for Budapest to join her father on the set, confirmed the affair and Frankenheimer's continuing proclivities in his 2007 autobiography: "Mitzi sent me a gentle and direct Dear John letter. She had been swept away by the director John Frankenheimer, who, twenty years later, tried and failed to seduce my then wife, the actress Victoria Tennant, whom he was directing in a movie [*The Holcroft Covenant*, 1985]" (Martin 96–97).
3. *Verfremdungseffekt*, or *V-Effekt*, a term coined by German playwright Bertolt Brecht in the 1930s, is a theatrical and cinematic device that discourages the audience's passive acceptance of an illusory world created by the actors. By disengaging the audience's emotional identification with the characters, this distancing device, or "alienation effect," encourages a critical spectatorship that intellectually engages with the work's social and political ideology.
4. Asked in 1979 if he considered himself an auteur, Frankenheimer replied, "I'm responsible for everything because it's my choice. But I certainly don't think I'm an auteur. No. I'm not a writer, I'm not a cameraman, I'm not an art director, I'm not the fellow who makes each splice in the film" (Applebaum).

Shot from the Sky

The Gypsy Moths and the End of Something

DENNIS BINGHAM

One of the problems for historians of most arts is the "transitional figure." Neither traditionalist nor rebel, neither one who resists a new aesthetic nor one who innovates it, the transitional artist is likely to be overthrown with the old stalwarts when revolution comes. Such is the case of John Frankenheimer, who at the close of the sixties and the dawn of the New Hollywood was not yet forty years old. However, the end of his string, which he ran out swiftly and elaborately, coincided with the demise of if not the studio system then certainly Old Hollywood. Just about every American film from the years 1969 and 1970 has about it the feeling of the End of Something, either in terms of the film movement from which it emerges or the culture of which it is an expression. Political assassinations, race riots, protracted and brutal war, upheaval in the universities: an era, a way of life, was ending and what was unclear, in Hollywood as well as elsewhere, was what would take its place.

Like most American films released in the second half of 1969, Frankenheimer's *The Gypsy Moths* appeared in the giant shadow of Dennis Hopper and Peter Fonda's *Easy Rider*, which was part exploitation biker movie, part art film, all youth audience phenomenon. *Easy Rider*'s tagline was "A man went looking for America. And couldn't find it anywhere." No one seems to know where to find America that year. As Americans grope for an end to the American-exceptionalist debacle in Vietnam, the titular gang of *The Wild Bunch* creates senseless carnage in Sam Peckinpah's limits-pushing western. Wyatt and Billy, the hip western wanderers of *Easy Rider*, find murderous hippie-hating yahoos at the end of their trail. *Butch Cassidy and the Sundance Kid* inserts the cool, contemporary personae of Paul Newman and Robert Redford into an end-of-the-frontier western flavored with anachronistic Burt Bacharach–Hal David tunes, while the stars crack one-liners like a washed-up vaudeville team on their final tour. The two westerns are metaphorical: the nineteenth century collides with the twentieth. *Easy Rider* plays its druggy heroes for melodrama; the youthful rebels are too mythically honest and genuine to exist in the corrupt real world of America. D. W. Griffith would have understood. All these films end in the masochistic deaths of the protagonists; all are what Molly Haskell categorizes as buddy movies, with women on the sidelines, providing short-term sex partners for the men but nothing else.

In such a climate *The Gypsy Moths* is as transitional a film as one can find. In this artful adaptation of a "cult novel" written and self-published in 1955 by James Drought, a trio of parachute-jumpers travels the Midwest performing skydiving shows at small-town airfields. The men spend a Fourth of July weekend preparing to put on a show in a Kansas town where the youngest of the three happens to have family. In both film and novel, the stunt jumpers are finely differentiated; there is the enigmatic "old pro" of the group, Mike Rettig (Burt Lancaster), the excitable, pragmatic business manager Joe Browdy (Gene Hackman), and Malcolm Webson (Scott Wilson), "the kid," now in his early twenties. The town where the three stop is home to Elizabeth and John Brandon (Deborah Kerr and William Windom), Malcolm's aunt and uncle. The couple's failure, years before, to adopt Malcolm, who was orphaned when he was ten by a car crash that killed both his parents, opened a rift in the Brandons' marriage that has not healed.

This description may make the narrative sound like a 1950s family melodrama made ten years too late. A plot about gaudily masculine men who stir up a repressive small town might sound as if it belongs in *Picnic* (1955) or *Some Came Running* (1958). By the time of *The Gypsy Moths*, Frankenheimer had developed a repertoire built on family melodrama (*All Fall Down* [1962]), cold war intrigue (*The Manchurian Candidate* [1962], *Seven Days in May* [1964]), and adventures of male protagonists in extreme situations of which they strive to make the best (*Birdman of Alcatraz* [1962], *The Train* [1964]) or of which they test the limits (*Grand Prix*, *Seconds* [both 1966]). Frankenheimer's style culminates in *The Gypsy Moths*, which is brash and demure, clean and dense, obvious and elliptical.

Frankenheimer drops us into the Kansas living room of the Brandons quite as if we have parachuted and it is up to us to figure out how to react. The director said that while he preferred to begin the story as the novel did, with the three men driving into the small town, he felt compelled, by what Oliver Stone once called "movie reasons," to open with the stunt divers in the thick of action. So the film starts off with the struggle between narrative and spectacle. Within that tension looms the question, Where is life to be found? Is it in the seemingly moribund small town, or in the pointless wandering of the lone wolf? At a time when many young people were rejecting small-town values, Frankenheimer's film faces the small town as an intractable American reality, not easily left behind even if one manages to escape it. With the exception of its go-go club, the little town shown in the film (actually Frankenheimer used locations near Wichita) might not look like a place that could have still existed in the late 1960s, an impression that is distinctly false. In the feature-length audio commentary Frankenheimer recorded for the 2002 DVD, which was released two months after his death, the director says that having recently returned to that part of the country he found "that in thirty years it hasn't changed very much."

Frankenheimer avoids easy targets. In Drought's novel, John Brandon is a college professor (thus, easily characterized as a superior-sounding mediocrity). In the film, that John's occupation is not specified eludes the broad swipes at caricatured authority types with which the cinema of these years was fairly rife. Frankenheimer allows a sense that Brandon is a failure as a man to emerge out of Mrs. Brandon's point of view, rather than to be stamped in the man's characterization. For another example of the filmmaker's intervention, in the novel (which is narrated, in the manner of Fitzgerald or Salinger, by its young male protagonist) there had been a previous episode just before the plot begins, in which Rettig waited until he was terrifyingly close to the ground to pull his ripcord. This incident, which occurred in Keokuk, Iowa, takes the form of a flashback inserted midway through the tale and printed in italics, in the style of Faulkner in *The Sound and the Fury*. In the movie it provides the pre-credits prologue, but when Malcolm throws up the incident to Rettig, the name of the town with which the older man finds himself confronted is "Appleton" (Wisconsin). Why would the director of *The Manchurian Candidate* choose for his burg of contention Senator Joseph McCarthy's hometown? Some questions answer themselves.

Thus is Frankenheimer just as capable of being self-allusive as the most reflexive *nouvelle vague* director. In more character development not supplied in the novel, Browdy says in post-coital conversation with the sympathetic (though unnamed) waitress (Sheree North) he picks up at the town's go-go club, "One of these days, I'm gonna cut out. Gonna go out to Hollywood. Gonna get me a job as one of them stuntmen. They make good dough. I know that for a fact." The inside joke is hard to miss. Delivered with unshakable quiet conviction as only Gene Hackman can. On a film in which he is surrounded by stuntmen, Hackman, like Frankenheimer and the film's producer, Edward Lewis, would know "for a fact" that stuntmen "make good dough." In fact, maybe Browdy will go to Hollywood and double for Gene Hackman on a film called *The Gypsy Moths*, much as Larry Parks is shown in *Jolson Sings Again* (1949) playing Larry Parks auditioning to play Al Jolson (Larry Parks) in *The Jolson Story* (1946). Too bad that American critics were less apt than their French counterparts to recognize and appreciate the particularly American self-referentialities he constructed.

Unexamined Lives

The crisis of masculinity and desire for human connection that the men bring with them—and their inability to express it in ways other than self-destruction—are expressive of America at the end of the 1960s. Frankenheimer's direction provides formal contradictions that are central to the film. The cinematography takes off from the color-coded costumes of the parachutists—red for Rettig, white for Browdy, and yellow for Malcolm—which literally set the tone for a film with a bright, primary-colored palette. Contrasting with the film's visual design is its pacing. Shot mostly on location, with a few studio interiors in Hollywood, the film takes its pace from the natural rural settings and the small-town culture. The family melodrama (a genre practically extinct by the late 1960s) collides with the story of the three men, especially Rettig, who (like so many other characters played by Lancaster) brings internal conflict with him. The film manages to be more of a heterosexual romance than its source novel, more of a buddy story, and ultimately more a male-oriented tale of a loner. With Lancaster and Kerr—famously paired as illicit lovers in *From Here to Eternity* (1953)—the only stars billed above the title, the film probably looked like a throwback. The film not only deals with generational conflict, however, but portrays the moral bankruptcy and despair of the older generation, which it expresses much more in the anomic style of a 1960s European art film than in the 1950s American cultural style of *Picnic* (1955), *Rebel without a Cause* (1955), or J. D. Salinger's novel *The Catcher in the Rye* (1951).

As if these were not enough fences for one film to straddle, Frankenheimer called it one of the best examples of the type of film he likes to make: "character-based action movies." His choice of words can be taken two ways; one in the obvious context of an action film—in this case a movie about stunt sky divers. The film's three aerial sequences compose nearly a fourth of the running time—a pre-opening-credits prologue; the parachute-jumping show for which the men have come to town and the film's major set-piece; and Malcolm's climactic solo act near the end. These were filmed by Carl Boenisch, a documentary photographer and parachutist who jumped with other sky divers over 1,300 times in order to get all the footage Frankenheimer needed. However, this is an action film in a subtler way, too: characters here express themselves in action rather than in words or emotions, and they struggle to do that.

Drought's book could be called a youth novel, told from the point of view of a young man who learns from the travails of his older partners. Drought, who had been an air force paratrooper, seems influenced in his first novel by *The Catcher in the Rye*. Malcolm could be Holden Caulfield a few years later. Having questioned life and having found it worthless, the young protagonist has now run off to join a circus of sorts. Malcolm worries about each jump. Browdy, on the other hand, views what they do as "a business." He doesn't perform the most dangerous stunts because, as he says, "I recognize my limitations—secret of my success in life." Malcolm and Browdy either look for or are sure they have found ways not to die, while Rettig, it turns out, looks for ways and reasons to live: not finding any, he opts not to.

The secretive Rettig is a familiar postwar type, the intruder, The Man We Don't Know, the superficial figure who masks an unseen world, a man who is himself an infiltration of something alien into the vaguely unsettled world of "normality." By the 1960s, this type could be revealed to be heroic, like the initially mysterious Virgil Tibbs of *In the Heat of the Night* (1967) whose rectitude and authoritative air turn the tables on the Mississippi racists who accost him at their train depot in the middle of the night. By 1969, then, this closed-mouthed character type was overused though versatile. One wonders if Frankenheimer presented his film in a Godardian postmodern spirit, with characters and situations so unoriginal and familiar that they needed no introduction and could no longer be played straight, except to critique the ideologies they represented. A queer theorist might say that Rettig brings a queer feeling to Bridgeville, Kansas. Although duly heterosexual, Rettig is so taciturn and laconic that he brings these usually heteronormative, masculine signifiers all the way through to the Other side, so to speak—into passivity, submission even unto death—even while the female characters in the film often take the initiative and play the roles of men in patriarchy. Compared to the women, the men in this film lead unexamined lives.

Rettig/Lancaster does not bring any sort of outside threat to the oddly named "Bridgeville" (a bridge takes you from one place to another; it is not a destination in itself), with its off-putting "welcome" sign, "If you lived here, you'd be home now." What he brings them is death, in the starkest, most abstract form. He even makes a black, Jackson Pollockesque blot on the ground when he dies. Colin Wilson, in a 1966 essay on James Drought (1931–1983), writes that "Rettig wants to fall farther than anybody has ever succeeded in doing. He overdoes it, and he kills himself" (6). But Rettig's death is no accident, as Malcolm, who narrates the novel, realizes. "Rettig had faced death; he had gone to meet it; he was devoted to it. Now what was left? Nothing. Rettig didn't exist anymore, not even in my mind, except as a pile of brokenness and that wasn't Rettig. . . . Death is not the test of a man. A man's life is the only test he'll ever have. Facing death is like signing my name over and over to a letter I put off writing because I'm afraid to say anything" (97, 99).

In the film, Burt Lancaster plays a man with a twisted kind of serenity. Like God, he can know "the day and the hour" of his death. Thus death-obsessed, the movie's Rettig looks for reasons not to die, and failing to find any, especially after Elizabeth rejects his nonsensical offer to take her away with him (To go where? To live how?), he makes his choice.

Dumped

While Hollywood at the end of the 1960s was nearly bankrupt and panic-stricken at the realization that its primary audience was now mostly male and overwhelmingly young, *The Gypsy Moths*, not unlike other films in the marketplace, was itself taken up with issues of age and gender. "Rettig was thirty-five," narrates the novel's Malcolm, "the old pro among the three of us" (6). A thirty-five-year-old was, of course, a senior citizen to the ever-younger audiences that Hollywood now realized was its market; in *Wild in the*

Streets, American-International Pictures' 1968 hit, a rock star "organizes to give fourteen-year-olds the vote, becomes president of the United States, and sentences the over-thirty to detention camps where they are force-fed LSD" (Perlstein 279). Furthermore, 1969 ended the period—which begins almost with the movies themselves—when stars were supposed to be ageless. A fifty-five-year-old Cary Grant could run tirelessly through Hitchcock's obstacle course in *North by Northwest* (1959); seven years later Grant decided that he would retire rather than visibly age onscreen. In *The Gypsy Moths*, Burt Lancaster, as tightly wrapped at fifty-five as his character's parachute pack, played Drought's and Frankenheimer's "old pro" and found himself up against the likes of newly hired MGM president James Aubrey.

"The older stars are going to have to play older roles if they want to work with us," Aubrey told a *Time* interviewer in early 1970. "We can't make a picture with Burt Lancaster and Deborah Kerr groping with each other any more. That's obscene. It's like watching a couple of grandparents pawing each other" ("Hollywood"). Aubrey had become known as "the Smiling Cobra" during his tenure as head of programming at CBS in the early 1960s, when he put low-brow fare like *The Beverly Hillbillies* on the air to the disgust of CBS president William Paley. Deborah Kerr, who was forty-seven, would seem perfectly well cast as the middle-aged housewife Elizabeth Brandon. When Aubrey pegged "older stars" to "older roles," however, he really meant that older people shouldn't be shown onscreen making love. The words of Aubrey, who himself was fifty-one in 1970, seem to evince a horror of aging. Men and women his own age look to him like "a couple of grandparents"; why would any fiftyish patron go to the movies and pay to watch what he can see at home—in the mirror? Perhaps Aubrey was not speaking of or for himself. People his age were scarcely going to the movies at all. Identifying with youth in fact became standard business in Hollywood in the wake of *Easy Rider*. Middle-aged actresses in particular were supposed either to play grandmothers or to disappear.

Deborah Kerr got the message. In an extraordinary letter written to *Time* from her home in Klosters, Switzerland, and sounding a bit like Mrs. Anna Leonowens in *The King and I*, she began with a lesson:

> *The American College Dictionary* (since the accent is on youth) defines obscene as: "offensive to modesty and decency," which is how Mr. James Aubrey characterizes the love scenes between Burt Lancaster and myself . . . in an obvious reference to *The Gypsy Moths*, an MGM film that predates his assumption of supreme power in Culver City.
>
> It seems to me, however, that age is not a prime factor in determining what is offensive to modesty and decency. A film about young people can be equally obscene as one about middle-aged people in love, the aesthetic sense of the director and the artists involved providing the all-important, decisive element.

> I realize, of course, that to argue aesthetics with Mr. Aubrey would be quite futile, as the producer of *The Beverly Hillbillies* is apparently a stranger to "the science which deduces from nature and taste the rules and principles of art" (*American College Dictionary* again). It would be like arguing honor with a mule. Or a cobra. (Kerr)

However elegantly Kerr framed her indignation, she was whistling past the graveyard. Hollywood was swiftly erasing both "older stars" and "older roles." All these figures, without whom the postwar period in films would have been unimaginably different, suddenly seemed the very opposite of the buzzword heard most frequently in 1970, "relevant."

Kerr's sardonic letter can be taken as an indication of the hard feelings over the way *The Gypsy Moths* was handled. Virginia Wright Wexman explains that

> the once great and powerful Metro-Goldwyn-Mayer was sold to financier Kirk Kerkorian, who wanted the studio's logo to put on his Las Vegas hotel. . . . This corporate instability led to many inefficiencies, not the least of which was a revolving-door system for top executives. Each new regime was, quite literally, inclined to ignore the films made under the auspices of the last group in its quest to make its own mark. Thus many worthy productions got dumped or shelved. (288–89)

Wexman could have been thinking about *The Gypsy Moths*, which "never really, really got released," Frankenheimer says in his commentary. In a sentence apparently expurgated the director says, "_____ hated this movie. Because to him it was not the exploitation-picture type of thing that he wanted to make." It is hard to imagine why Warner Home Video would censor Frankenheimer's retelling of old industry war stories, blanking out the name of James Aubrey, who died in 1994. Betty Comden and Adolph Green, recounting a much earlier chapter in MGM history, described the moment they realized that musicals were on the way out. They looked at newspaper listings for *It's Always Fair Weather* (1955) and found that whereas their previous films by the Freed unit at MGM had always played at "The Music Hall," as they put it, this one was running at drive-ins (*Musicals*). How low can you get? *The Gypsy Moths* got *both* treatments: the Music Hall *and* the drive-ins. The movie, in the first year of the MPAA Ratings System, also had the distinction of bearing both an M (the ancestor of PG, which was later divided to make PG-13) for its premiere engagement on August 28 at Radio City Music Hall, a family-friendly venue for which the film's two scenes of partial nudity were trimmed; and an R for its "wide" release three months later.

The first-run showings of *The Gypsy Moths* in many cities—Indianapolis, for example—took place at a chain of drive-ins. The film opened on November 26, the day before Thanksgiving, second only to Independence Day as the most American of holidays. Drive-ins from the 1950s to the 1970s constituted roughly a fourth of all exhibitions in the United States. They were considered second- or third-rate ways to see and exhibit a movie, however. Films opening at drive-ins were not reviewed by newspapers in most cities; publicity was virtually nil. So when Frankenheimer refers to the movie as "not really having been seen," this is what he means. But imagining the sight of Frankenheimer's stunt jumpers and high-flying cameramen in vivid reds and yellows against his clear blue Kansas sky seen on the screen against a crisp, dark Indiana night in late autumn does have a poetic charm to it. Midwestern popcorn munchers watching the spectacle after a turkey dinner from a heated Ford Country Squire perhaps didn't differ much from the film's midwestern farmers diverted by sky-jumpers on a Fourth of July weekend. For Frankenheimer, nonetheless, MGM's verdict on the movie was clear: "They dumped it."

Lancaster: Breaking Out

While Deborah Kerr encountered a fate common in all eras to American film actresses over forty, Lancaster's and Gene Hackman's appearances in the film encapsulate and highlight Frankenheimer's "rightful place," as Stephen Bowie puts it, "as the key transitional figure" between the late classicism of the 1950s and the New Hollywood of the 1970s. Hackman, who occupied as much screen time as Lancaster and Kerr, was the representative of the New Hollywood; this was his first film following *Bonnie and Clyde* (1967), as Frankenheimer proudly states in his commentary. Browdy would seem to be the type of part Burt Lancaster usually portrayed. Although Lancaster played varied roles in his long career, he often enjoyed the most success as likable, dominating extroverts in such films as *The Hallelujah Trail* (1965), *The Professionals* (1966), and *Elmer Gantry* (1960), the last having won him an Oscar.

Frankenheimer and Lancaster, in their fifth and final movie together, seem game to play with the surface and depth of a star persona the audience thinks it knows; the actor is cast against type. In 1981, Vincent Canby cited a pattern of Lancaster's, one of the first stars in the post-studio era to sustain his own production company and maintain control over his career, to "play off one film against another, one 'pop' film against another film reeking of class." Canby named the comedy western *The Scalphunters* (1968) with its "free-wheeling, resourceful frontiersman" as presenting "a Burt Lancaster we could trust. We had known him a long time" ("Of Time" D13). *The Gypsy Moths*, however, is unlike many Lancaster films in which the star appears to grapple mightily with the desire to "act" outside his accustomed range. All of the Lancaster-Frankenheimer films more or less combine the "pop" and "class" modes; with this director, the actor melds the confidence, physical grace, and larger-than-life presence of the "star" Lancaster with the lived-in complexity that Lancaster often aimed for and sometimes missed in his "serious films," such as *Come Back, Little Sheba* (1952), *The Rainmaker* (1956), and *Judgment at Nuremberg* (1961). Lancaster's presence was so intense and vivid that he could set off his own physical bulk against the silence and solitude of an isolated character like Rettig.

Taking advantage of the "new freedom of the screen" ushered in by the replacement of the Production Code by the Ratings System in November 1968, Frankenheimer abruptly cuts from topless scenes at a go-go club the men visit their first night in town to the sight of Mike and Elizabeth brazenly having sex in the small-town matron's living room while her husband broods upstairs. This is actually a less sensational (and less visually striking) reprise of the illicit love scene between Lancaster and Kerr on the beach in *From Here to Eternity*, a shot that became one of the iconic images of the 1950s. Their love scene here holds subtleties nonetheless. Both characters use their lovemaking to send messages. Elizabeth experiences the visit of the airfield daredevils over a Fourth of July weekend in a carnivalesque spirit, viewing it as a chance to suspend the order of things and protest her repression.

In an earlier scene only referred to in the novel but enacted in the film, the reticent Rettig tags along with Elizabeth to her women's club meeting, where he demonstrates in cinema-friendly images the details of how a parachute is packed and opened. After the ladies have left and Rettig reassembles his gear, Elizabeth suddenly asks, "You have contempt for us, don't you?" Rettig doesn't deny the charge, so when she follows up, "Why are we contemptible to you?" he replies, "You care?" After picking up Elizabeth's ambiguous reaction shot, Frankenheimer cuts away. Rettig, the glamorous loner from out of town, is the blank screen onto which Elizabeth Brandon projects her own contempt—for herself, her husband, her small town, and her ordered, dull life. Elizabeth searches—but not very far—for a way to live. As a woman being supported comfortably by her husband, she knows that her choices, such as they might be, were made long before, and now they are limited, indeed. She is the only character who tries to read Rettig at all, and she misreads him. He sees her as a fellow lost soul, but rather than hoping for another way to live, as she thinks, he looks around desperately for a reason not to die. Rettig keeps all his desperation within him, which makes him a modern character in a recognizably melodramatic framework. His unspoken desperation makes him the archetype of the American male who keeps to himself. The film undercuts this archetype, however, by suggesting a layer of vulnerability and hurt. Drought's novel is a fifties misunderstood-youth-rite-of-passage story, but a film made almost fifteen years later becomes overlaid with a patina of sixties alienation. A Hollywood film whose star kills himself, and twenty minutes before the end of the film yet, probably could never have been made in the fifties. This is a movie from post-*Psycho* Hollywood, made after the rules as to what to expect from an American film had been considerably loosened.

The attitude toward the small-town Kansas milieu is somehow respectful, but the town is also rather unpopulated, with Mrs. Brandon the only character who represents the stagnancy and deathliness of the place. A running gag shows

Disturbance at the women's club. "Why are we contemptible to you?" Elizabeth (Deborah Kerr) asks as soon as the others have left. *The Gypsy Moths* (John Frankenheimer Productions, 1969).
Digital frame enlargement.

the high school band leader (played by Thom Conway, an aging former vaudevillian who was Burt Lancaster's dialogue coach) gradually coaxing a performance "with feeling" out of his players. On their big day, the city's Fourth of July parade, the conductor leads his band around the corner toward the town square—only to find it deserted. Everyone is at the airfield to watch Malcolm's duel with death in the "memorial jump," undertaken to pay for Rettig's funeral (no pun intended). So much for tradition and civic pride in Bridgeville.

In a sense, Frankenheimer is harking back to impulses much older than cinema—the thrill of challenging death, the reassurance that death cannot always win. In the film, Browdy, at the microphone, announces Rettig's "cape jump" to the crowd, as Frankenheimer starts with a shot of even-countenanced Lancaster in medium close-up, flapping the cape stunt's black batwings as the camera pulls back. "He'll be traveling in excess of 200 miles per hour. The fastest we've gone up to now is about a hundred so you can see the difference. Another thing: Unless he holds his arms absolutely correctly, the wind can break them right off. Also, attached to each foot will be this smoke flare so he'll leave a trail through the sky that you'll be able to follow. That is, unless the flare malfunctions and burns his legs, which it has a nasty habit of doing. Hey, let's hear it for Mike!"

Even as the crowd forms, Browdy explains to an ambulance driver, who is slow to comprehend that he isn't just standing by on the off chance he'll be needed, that he is part of the act. Browdy delights in the showmanship of playing up the danger involved as much as they can. However, after the stunning montage sequence that cross-cuts from Rettig in the sky to the crowd on the ground—to Browdy, to Malcolm, and back to Rettig himself—as they all know that he's passed the point of no return and can no longer open the chute in time, Rettig crashes into the ground, and an all-too-convenient rain comes down from nowhere. Browdy shoos away the crowd that has gathered to see the body. "Get away, you morbid creeps," he shouts. "Get out of here!"

This is another echo of fifties Hollywood, as Frankenheimer recalls the morbid crowds of Billy Wilder's *Ace in the Hole* (1951) and Robert Wise's *I Want to Live!* (1958). But he doesn't really indulge in disgust for a thrill-happy public. What we see here is more a sense of chaos that can suddenly break out in life. The same goes for the overflow crowd that spills onto the airway the next day to see Malcolm's follow-up cape stunt. As we do, they need to see a satisfying conclusion, after all. We all need to know how it ends, to have closure. Even the sign showing that the owner of the field has hiked his price from Sunday's one dollar to Monday's two just seems in keeping with good old American capitalism. If only—Frankenheimer would say—Jim Aubrey had worked so hard to draw crowds. But would anyone come to see Burt Lancaster go splat? The world will never know. Even though Browdy's shouts to the crowd in the bedlam following Rettig's death may seem hypocritical, they are shown simply as all part of a complex person. He cared about Rettig. He crosses himself over the black smudge that is all that's left of Rettig, Catholic that he is (even though his religion has not stopped him from bedding down with strippers, a mortal sin). The carnival music plays on diegetically, until someone (audibly and offscreen) thinks to take the needle arm off the record. The music, too, provides irony in counterpoint. The overall sense is that life sometimes can never adjust fast enough to tragedy. Time has a nasty habit of going on, regardless. Meanwhile, Malcolm, young and passionate, pulls the cord and opens Rettig's chute, which is as much a useless heap on the ground as Rettig now is—a demonstration that Rettig never even attempted to open it. Why?

Ambiguity Itself

The film gives a sense that the moment when Rettig "goes into the ground," a moment I feel is among the most stunning and shocking in all of 1960s cinema, is for its director the end of the movie. Frankenheimer said that the film builds up "to this air show, which you feel is going to be the crowning event, and then it turns out that it isn't." Frankenheimer appears to find in it a climax he can't top. Indeed, not only is the air show the climax to which the narrative, by convention, is building, but Rettig's death heads off audience expectations. The narrative, enacting the day of the air show, proceeds along three tracks. After the morning showers let up, the men in their beat-up '59 Dodge, which pulls the covered trailer full of parachutes and other gear, are shown arriving at the airfield. They stop the car and begin to set up. Browdy meets the young pilot, shows him what to do, gives him a suitcase phonograph and records, and tells him to round up some kids in order to help out. Frankenheimer shows the logistics of how such a show comes off, in other words. Cut to the Brandons' living room, where Annie (Bonnie Bedelia), a young college student who rooms with them, presents herself to leave for the show. All in one shot, as John asks, "You certain you won't come along?" Elizabeth remains behind on the sofa. Having rebuffed Mike's offer, she is not going to witness his "crowning moment."

With Elizabeth literally *left* behind, the film cuts to Rettig at the airfield, in the foreground on the *right*, as if matching her position. Meanwhile, Browdy in deep focus issues his orders to four young boys; his voice is all we hear. In a montage of thirteen shots in all, Browdy talks while Rettig, expressionless, looks. He sees the stands begin to fill with spectators. Back to Rettig, as a slow zoom begins to move in on him. His head turns slightly, as does the camera from his point of view; he sees people stroll in from their cars. Zoom in closer; another head/camera turn, more aimless this time, toward the crowd. Closer in to him; faster, a moving point-of-view shot, even more aimless than before. Return to Rettig, back to the camera movement, as we are in the point of view of a man whose eyes are shifting, whose mind is wandering. Back to him; as we come closer, his own point of view becomes more erratic: a rapid zoom to a windsock. Back to Rettig, still closer. Now a shot of the loudspeaker. Finally, we hold on the shot of Rettig looking off, while Browdy and the children have completed their entire action, which is an instruction of how to help the divers recollect their chutes when they are back on the ground. The real story,

Rettig (Burt Lancaster) stares off while life goes on all around him. Even reputed film theorist Lev Kuleshov couldn't have made meaning from this deep-focus shot, intercut with erratic point-of-view shots. *The Gypsy Moths* (John Frankenheimer Productions, 1969).

Digital frame enlargement.

however, is Lancaster, and it plays as a series of French New Wave–style jump cuts of him, broken up by a succession of shots that in effect stare off into space. Not until the shot of Lancaster has reached its final composition do we really register how hooded in shadow his eyes have been the entire time. Add this to the sound track and background action, to which Rettig is oblivious, and the eyeline matches to nothing in particular, and we get a montage sequence that is ambiguity itself.

A more conventional film would create psychological realism by a simple sequence of Rettig looking and seeing that Elizabeth isn't there, and showing his reaction. But this is nowhere near that simple. By the time the three men are out on the field, ready to start the show, with the sunlight fully on them, we finally see Annie and John arrive in the stands, through a telephoto shot. A return two-shot of Malcolm and Rettig shows them putting on their packs. Malcolm mutters indistinctly what sounds like "I see Anne." A straight-on close-up of John is followed by a medium close-up of Rettig, shown partly from the side, not facing straight ahead. Not only does this render Rettig's state of mind ambiguous, but it objectifies him, an impression that is immediately intensified by a cut to the waitress Browdy has picked up, shown with a girlfriend, who asks her, "Which one is he?" "The one in white" (Browdy), she says, deliciously motioning with the ice cream bar she's eating. "I like the one in red better," replies the friend, about Rettig. "Yeah. So did I," says the waitress. "But what the hell, the way things worked out, I got no complaints."

Moving toward the New Hollywood

Stephen Bowie uses this dialogue as evidence of the film's sympathy for women. But if that were the case, this probably would not be the waitress's last appearance in the film. Nor would she go unnamed. The dialogue between the two women, however, is another of the film's reflexive discourses. Of course, a woman (who is literally in an audience) would be assumed to prefer Burt Lancaster, the world-famous movie star and handsome romantic lead, over Gene Hackman, the character actor with ordinary looks. Thus is foreshadowed the changing-of-the-guard that is about to take place in the industry, as the coming decades find Lancaster receding into character-actor ranks, while Hackman becomes a New Hollywood star. Moreover, the exchange reaffirms our sympathy for Rettig, as it makes clear that he could have "had" the pickup, instead of returning to romance the older woman played by Kerr. But again we see the rite of passage to the frankly misogynist New Hollywood of the early 1970s where Hackman's characters pick up unnamed younger women (as in *The French Connection* [1971], where his boorish Popeye Doyle has an offscreen tryst with a college girl, for no narrative purpose except to affirm his heterosexuality), while the concept of glamorized leading actresses like Kerr playing complex, realistic leading parts becomes relegated mainly to Hollywood's past.

In the novel, Malcolm comes to realize why Rettig has ended his own life. In rejecting sky-jumping, he is embracing life. In its resolution the film rejects a certain kind of life-affirming certainty that still came easily in the 1950s; but to male filmmakers exercising the "new freedom of the screen," even a conclusion in which young man and woman go off together feels like knee-jerk romanticism appropriate for the Old Hollywood of automatic happy endings. In this rejection, Frankenheimer makes a gesture that anticipates the New Hollywood, all right. It typifies the worst of it, and renders the film otherwise confused. Bowie finds that "the most sympathetic characters . . . are women." This is true if one sees women stuck with no options as "sympathetic," women who remain frozen in place, left behind by men who are, of course, free to move on. Surely, the John Frankenheimer who works as beautifully with a trio of actresses as divergent from each other as Kerr, North, and young Bonnie Bedelia doesn't mean to leave his female characters as if the film doesn't care what happens to them—and the North and Bedelia characters are left, as Hackman and Wilson leave them, with scarcely a word. Even a poster to the film's Internet Movie Database message board laments that Malcolm and Annie "should have hooked up. It was obvious they liked each other. They looked cute together. But at the end, he leaves first to get on a train for 'I don't know where.' . . . At least he could have given her his ripcord to remember him by."

In the novel, Malcolm and Annie meet up at the very end and go off together, to her parents' farm out in the country. In the reality of the early 1950s a young woman who has slept with a man under the roof of her benefactors may feel ashamed to go back, or may have realized that she is too much a part of the loveless couple's hypocrisy to go on living with them. A young man who has chosen life over periodic face-offs with death may prefer being with her to being alone. On the other hand, while Rettig has allowed Elizabeth to see his neediness, she rejects it. She tells her husband in the film's penultimate scene that Rettig asked her to come away with him and that the thought "terrified me." In choosing to keep on accepting her narrow lot in life, to recognize her limitations, she resembles Browdy. Annie, on the other hand, visibly falls in love with Malcolm when she sees how deeply Rettig's death has affected him. Frankenheimer's camera holds on her until she cuts off Malcolm in mid-sentence and kisses him. The film fades out. The next day, Annie stands by Browdy at the airfield; her reaction as Malcolm makes his jump is what we're led to care about most. Drought's narrator/Malcolm may have taken Annie against her will. A chapter ends as follows: "When I came to Annie's door I opened it quickly and stepped in. She was asleep; she didn't wake up for a few minutes. For a few minutes she didn't even know I was there" (108). The next day, moreover, there is no one but Browdy (and most of the town) to see Malcolm jump. Annie, who disappears from the house, doesn't come, and neither do the Brandons. In the film, however, all of them go to the "memorial jump." Even Drought's ending, Holden Caulfield–like, seems to be apologizing for its corniness. The word "phony" appears on the third-to-final paragraph, describing the Fourth of July fireworks that go off in the night sky as the couple walks to the station. Frankenheimer keeps the fireworks—by this point he seems loath to dispense with any striking visual touch—but scuttles the reconciliation.

As if persuaded by the alienation of his fictional Rettig, Frankenheimer cannot bring himself to believe in even the tentative connection with which Drought ends his book. Therefore, *The Gypsy Moths*, straightforward but ambiguous, realistic but glamorous, conventional but challenging, is caught with a conclusion that lacks conviction and resolution. It's an empty ending, which might have been the best an honest artist could make.

Frankenheimer and the Science Fiction/Horror Film

CHRISTINE CORNEA

John Frankenheimer's death in 2002 prompted a broad reevaluation of this director's body of work in a flurry of tributes and critical accounts remembering his films and his impact upon the industry (see Combs; Holmes). But rather than reconstructing a coherent picture of his work across the films he directed, these accounts tended to concentrate on the biographical detail of his life. Consequently, discussion of his work was often considered in terms of cycles that corresponded to particular phases in his personal life. Reports focused upon the break with his early film success in the 1960s following the assassination of his close friend, Robert Kennedy, in 1968. His sporadic output, flirtation with a variety of new Hollywood genres, and readiness to work within a commercial mainstream in the 1970s and 1980s was usually read alongside his struggle with depression and alcoholism. Here we are presented with the picture of the tortured artist, whose personal and professional life was very much bound up with the turbulence of a post-1968 political, social, and cultural scene. Commentary continues with Frankenheimer emerging from "the darkness,"[1] mirrored in a return to form in the mid-1990s cycle of "quality" made-for-television movies (*Against the Wall* [HBO, 1994], *The Burning Season* [HBO, 1994], *Andersonville* [Turner Pictures, 1996]), and mini-series (*George Wallace* [Turner Network Television, 1997]). Until, finally, the prospect of a cinematic rebirth, with the critical and commercial success of *Ronin* (1998), was cruelly cut short when complications following a back operation brought about Frankenheimer's untimely death in the middle of pre-production planning for the film *Exorcist: The Beginning* (released under the direction of Renny Harlin in 2004).

In contrast to the interpretive framework outlined above, I am bringing together three films that cut across the formative phases identified in recent criticism. *Seconds* (1966) was produced when Frankenheimer was at the peak of his early success in the film industry; *Prophecy* (1979) surfaces in the middle of his "dark days"; and *The Island of Dr. Moreau* (1996) was made during what

Richard Combs refers to as Frankenheimer's "reformation" period (Combs 51). Against the grain of the personalized accounts of Frankenheimer's work, these films are assembled according to their generic status. Broadly concerned with the disturbing impact of science and technology upon society and upon individual human subjects, these films can be categorized under the hybrid heading of science fiction/horror.

Keen to distinguish science fiction from the horror genre, Vivian Sobchack claims that where the science fiction film "is concerned with social chaos, the disruption of social order," the horror film "deals with moral chaos, the disruption of natural order" (30). Even as Sobchack acknowledges that the lines between these two genres are not always easy to draw—referring to the difficulties involved in defining the Monster or Creature film cycle of the 1950s, for example—she proposes a distinction based upon their varying modes of address. Here Sobchack stresses that where science fiction films tend to be dispassionate and analytical, the horror film works to evoke fear (39–43). Focusing specifically on the 1950s cycle and covering some of the same examples that Sobchack identifies as generically contentious, Patrick Lucanio also sets about distinguishing between science fiction and horror film genres. Concentrating less on overarching themes and more on narrative structure, Lucanio argues that science fiction can be distinguished by its particular emphasis on plot to the detriment of character development, whereas the horror film emphasizes character over plot and is more concerned with the nature of the human psyche (1–20). However, in contrast to Sobchack and Lucanio, J. P. Telotte is less inclined to forge such strict divisions. Taking the impact of science and technology upon the human subject as his central focus, Telotte recognizes a hybrid film form that "straddles the horror and science fiction genres" (72). According to Telotte, science fiction/horror can be traced back to earlier novel-to-film adaptations like *Frankenstein* (James Whale [1931]) and *Island of Lost Souls* (Erle C. Kenton [1932]). Films like these, Telotte contends, explore "a fundamental impulse in our society," that is "the desire to render the body a manipulable and subject thing, ultimately little more than the raw material upon which the scientific spirit might exercise its will to artifice and stamp its scarry imprimatur" (75). The body has long served as a naturalizing metaphor for society, its institutions, and social arrangements (see, for example, Shilling, Turner). However, in these films this reassuring metaphor is literally deconstructed, presenting us with a fearful picture in which the body in question is manifestly reconfigured to serve the dangerous and unchecked whims of the technocrat. In this way the science fiction/horror film can offer up a forceful critique of a society in which our very sense of humanness and selfhood are threatened.

While questions of proper classification are rife within film genre studies, the debates outlined above do provide a useful starting point in a reading of *Seconds*, *Prophecy*, and *The Island of Dr. Moreau*. For here, I would argue, are three films that appear to draw upon elements associated with the thematic and formal concerns of both the science fiction and horror film. For instance, although each of these films extrapolates upon topical areas of scientific development and social organization, each is also focused upon the personal journey of a central male character. In these films, science and technology work not for the betterment of humankind but in the service of exploitative private enterprise. Even as the male protagonist comes to represent a point of emotional and moral resistance, each film paints a bleak picture as he is ultimately overwhelmed by the forces stacked against him. There is most certainly an oedipal drama at the heart of these films, as each male protagonist faces off against a lone father figure. But as the films progress it becomes apparent that the paternal figure is merely the ineffectual representative of an indifferent and amoral power structure. In this, the films are most concerned with patriarchal power, with masculinity and the survival or otherwise of the human male subject. In Frankenheimer's clashing together of these two genres, the three films therefore display an odd mix of the "cool" detachment that Sobchack recognizes as a feature of science fiction, and the affective mode associated with the horror film.

It is my contention that this hybrid film genre offered Frankenheimer a suitable vehicle with which to pursue his ongoing interrogation of institutional power. Indeed, having closely followed the startling examination of cold war politics in *The Manchurian Candidate* (1962) and *Seven Days in May* (1964), *Seconds* is commonly understood as the final film in Frankenheimer's "paranoia trilogy" (see, for example, Ecksel; Conolly; and, in this volume, Sterritt). But, as Stephen Bowie puts it: "*Seconds* extends the assumption of homicidal political conspiracies in *The Manchurian Candidate* and *Seven Days in May* to the private sector" ("John Frankenheimer"). In this, *Seconds* can also be seen as an interesting precursor to the more prominent cycle of science fiction/horror films that emerged in the late 1970s–1980s, with the likes of *Demon Seed* (Donald Cammell, 1977), *Alien* (Ridley Scott, 1979), and *The Terminator* (James Cameron, 1984). Turning a critical eye on the dehumanizing power of the corporation was to become the province of this later cycle of films, in which the human protagonists struggle to retain their selfhood as the cold logic of the corporate machine asserts its control. Like the earlier films that Telotte identifies, this struggle is played out upon bodies that are violently probed, penetrated, lacerated, and technologically reconstituted. Of course it was this period that really saw the erosion of old-style government control and the emergence of the capitalist corporation as the dominant institution for much of the western world. However, the 1960s witnessed the stirrings of this power shift. The Chicago School's opposition to Keynesian economic policies was gathering momentum during the 1960s, and a warning shot was fired over the bows of John F. Kennedy's administration with the publication of Milton Friedman's *Capitalism and Freedom* in 1962. It was the later Republican administrations of the 1970s and 1980s that came to embrace Friedman's monetarist policies, cutting back on government regulation of the private sector to allow for "the organization of the bulk of economic activity through private enterprise operating in a free market" (*Capitalism* 4). At the same time, the 1960s also saw the beginnings of a consumer protection movement, launched by Ralph Nader's scathing indictment of the American automobile industry. For Nader, writing in the mid-1960s, the "great problem facing contemporary life is how to control the power of economic interests which ignore the harmful effects of their applied science and technology" (*Unsafe* ix). While Friedman may have promoted his ideas as providing the necessary conditions for individual freedom, Nader saw the "moral imperatives" of a free and just society as threatened by the "conformity and rigidity of corporate bureaucracies" (356). Against the utopian vision of Friedman's unfettered free market, Nader was calling for ordinary citizens to question the power of the large corporations and for stronger government interventions in defense of the nation's citizen-consumers.

Science Fiction/Horror and the Body: *Seconds*

Seconds can be read as being set against this 1960s backdrop, at a time when anxieties surrounding the shift from a "producer-ethic to a consumer-ethic" (Agnew 376) became particularly evident, and when the future of American democracy and individual freedom within an already established consumer society were hotly and publicly debated. Speculating upon the rising power of corporate capitalism and the effects of the consumer society upon traditional social structures, *Seconds* provided the audience with a nightmare vision in which the illusion of individual freedom sold to the unsuspecting individual is maintained by a murderous business corporation.

The film's protagonist is an affluent, middle-aged banking executive, Arthur Hamilton (John Randolph). The opening scenes reveal Hamilton's privileged but mundane existence, following his daily commute from the city and exposing the orderly seclusion of his domestic life with his wife in Scarsdale. The antithesis of a typical Hollywood leading man, Randolph's pudgy physique and pared down performance paints the portrait of a rather dull and ordinary person. Hamilton's dissatisfaction and alienation are most obviously illustrated in the unsettling editing and framing techniques employed in an early bedroom scene in which his wife initiates intimate contact with him until, registering his lack of response, she eventually pulls away. Beginning with a slightly distorted, wide angle, long shot, the couple is squeezed into the far right of the frame. An abrupt edit accompanying his wife's advances is followed by a quick montage of angled, close-up shots as she kisses him. When she pulls away, the close-up remains vehemently fixed on Arthur Hamilton and his blank face fills the screen. Keen to escape the monotony of his existence, Hamilton is lured to a meeting with a clandestine business company that, for the princely sum of $30,000, promises him a new life. Waiting nervously, he is offered a beverage, and immediately descends into a drug-induced world in which he attacks and rapes a young woman. In this exaggerated echo of the earlier bedroom scene, the visual flamboyance of the film is developed even further. Here a surreal and claustrophobic environment is created by the Escher-like, geometric distortions of the set design, the use of fish-eye lens and forced perspective, as well as angled framing and abrupt editing from mid- or long shot to extreme close-up. Hamilton later learns that "The Company" staged the whole event and has filmed his attack on the girl as "insurance," to make sure that, with no way back to his previous reality, he signs up for the life-changing process.

Like *The Manchurian Candidate*, *Seconds* moved away from the standard practices of classical Hollywood, drawing upon visual and narrative devices associated with European art cinema and the existential themes of the French New Wave as well as revealing affinities with countercultural aesthetic sensibilities. While this kind of formal intervention was to become a common marker of the auteurist cinema that emerged in the New Hollywood of the late 1960s to mid-1970s (see Schatz 14–15), Frankenheimer was criticized by some for his experimental approach to filmmaking. For instance, Andrew Sarris did not place Frankenheimer among his "pantheon" of fully fledged auteurs back in 1968. Instead he was marked out as "talented" but "pretentious" and listed under the heading of "strained seriousness" (189). Although Sarris recognized a "modern form of social consciousness" in Frankenheimer's earlier films, he was not fond of the "synthetic technique" and "stylistic eclecticism" that he saw in some of the director's political thrillers (193–94).

Even as the visual stylistics adopted in *Seconds* are justified as an expressionistic portrayal of Hamilton's inner turmoil, this does not discount the element of social critique at the heart of the film. Once he has signed up for the life-changing process with the mysterious "Company," a sequence of scenes details Hamilton's psychological coaching and physical transformation through the plastic surgery to which he is subjected. As his bandages are unraveled it becomes apparent that not only has Arthur Hamilton been "reborn" as Tony Wilson, but John Randolph has been replaced by matinée idol Rock Hudson. At one level, this absurd metamorphosis also spoke to a growing, middle-class obsession with cosmetic surgery in the 1960s. Fueled by consumer culture and an increasing emphasis upon self-improvement, the facelift boomed in the 1960s and 1970s. Elizabeth Haiken's study of this period in plastic surgery details how it fed into a wider doctrine that "encouraged Americans to find private, personal solutions to social problems" (15). In this context, the language of psychology was co-opted in the selling of cosmetic surgery, the idea being that changing or improving outer appearance offered a route to inner happiness and psychological well-being.

Where plastic surgery had been sold to women primarily as a way to increase sexual attractiveness, the marketing toward male customers emphasized economic imperatives. For instance, youth and vigor were touted as vital attributes in a competitive labor market and the male facelift was peddled as a way to increase the chances of success in the world of work. This attempted masculinization of cosmetic surgery sought to counteract gendered taboos, but anxieties surrounding these procedures and their cultural meaning still circulated. In part, this is attested to by the depiction in *Seconds* of a man who is transformed into a veritable Adonis and subsequently provided with a carefree and hedonistic lifestyle. Hamilton is not seeking to climb the career ladder or to attain economic success; on the contrary, he wants to jettison these aspects of his old life. The aggressive extremes of masculine desire used in the "marketing" of this literal lifestyle product to The Company's male clients suggest the level of threat that consumer society presented to traditional notions of masculinity.

As is made clear at the beginning of the film, Hamilton's search for a more meaningful life is bound up with his evident loss of a properly masculine libido. His new identity as Wilson apparently realized, he takes up residence in a fashionable Malibu beach house. When he begins an affair with the beautiful Norma (Salome Jens), the playboy lifestyle seems complete. Yet persistent problems surface with his adjustment to the new body, and his nightmare really begins when Norma is revealed as a mere employee of The Company. Realizing his new life has not really changed him, he returns to The Company in the hope of trying again with yet another manufactured identity.

The twist in the tale is that if Hamilton/Wilson wants to undergo a further procedure, The Company's economic imperatives require that he deliver up another prospective client. Refusing to subject anyone else to this experience, he is approached by the "old man," The Company's founding father (Will Geer). At this point, the old man confesses that his original intention to provide a valuable service has been perverted by commercial obligation. The Company has grown to such an extent that it is now run by a "board of directors on a profit-sharing basis," the old man tells him, and it looks set to expand exponentially. In his examination of the corporation as represented across a range of recent science fiction and science fiction/horror films, Kirby Farrell comments: "Corporate structures dilute responsibility and mask some of our ugliest motives, while increasing our capacity to inflict harm" (104). The old man may well have confessed his sin, but, equally, the corporate structure that he describes allows him to evade responsibility. While Hamilton's salvation may be signaled in his refusal to abide by The Company's demands, once he has been sucked into this all-consuming world he will simply be served up as a fresh corpse in the "rebirth" of another client. In extracting the client from the social sphere of his old life without raising too many questions, The Company uses a replacement corpse to stage his apparent death. The full force of this corporate horror is brought to the fore in the final scenes, as Hamilton/Wilson is once more wheeled into the operating theater where his grisly execution by cranial drill is carried out. Just before the drill penetrates his skull, the camera turns to focus directly into the deathly glare of the surgical light in the operating room.

In general, *Seconds* was not well received upon release. Although the mobile camera and experimental lens work (expertly executed by James Wong Howe), along with Ted Haworth's surreal sets, revealed Frankenheimer's art-film ambitions, the film was given a hostile reception when it launched at Cannes. According to Gerald Pratley, French and European critics denounced the film as "cruel and inhuman" (*Films* 56). British and American critics hardly responded more positively: one described *Seconds* as "flat" and lacking in imagination (Rev., *Monthly Film Bulletin*); another in *Sight and Sound* judged it "uncharacteristic of Frankenheimer" (D. Wilson 46); while James Powers in the *Hollywood Reporter* saw *Seconds* less as an art film than a "top-drawer exploitation item" (3) (see also Rev., *Daily Cinema*; Farber "Reviews"). It seems that Frankenheimer's discernible move from the more respected political thriller genre confused some critics and devalued this film as an authored work.

Nevertheless, over the years *Seconds* accrued a cult following and a grudging respect from critics. In fact, a 1984 piece in *Film and Filming* cited *Seconds* as the director's boldest accomplishment to date, and declared that "the apprehension that technology was overwhelming the individual" was the most notable theme in Frankenheimer's films ("John Frankenheimer" 16–18). I would say that the critical revaluation of the science fiction/horror genre had much to do with later, more favorable assessments of this film. For instance, while the science fiction or science fiction/horror films of the 1950s had long been considered trivial, by the early 1980s academics like Peter Biskind began to understand how the genre's lowly status may have provided a convenient cover for serious political comment. Biskind traced what he saw as covert political/ideological undercurrents in these 1950s films made in the shadow of the Red Scare, the anticommunist witch-hunts carried out by Joseph McCarthy, and the constraints brought about by the House Un-American Activities Committee (102–59). Although the 1960s context allowed for a more knowing and complex cold war critique in Frankenheimer's provocative political thrillers, like the earlier science fiction or science fiction/horror films of the 1950s, the narrative simplicity and apparently "flat" characterizations of *Seconds* belied the film's metaphorical complexity, which might partly explain earlier reception of the film. In retrospect, it is easier to understand the cultural significance of *Seconds* as a science fiction/horror film, and to read the shocking depiction of a now corporate technoculture worked out over the male body.

Ecology and Science Fiction/Horror: *Prophecy*

It was not really until the late 1970s and early 1980s that the science fiction/horror film reemerged to become a respected mainstream form. In fact, the next science fiction/horror film directed by Frankenheimer was released the same year as *Alien*. Like *Alien*, *Prophecy* had palpable links with the 1950s cycle of science fiction/horror films, only now it was clearly greedy capitalism and corporate culture rather than cold war politics that came under the critical spotlight. A heartless disregard for human life was sutured to a corporate ethos in both these films, but where the protagonists in *Alien* were set adrift in space and inhabited a distant, future world, *Prophecy* was more direct in its approach, presenting viewers with a frightening picture of the here and now.

The opening credits of *Prophecy* set up the urgent nature of the film, featuring a group of men with their dogs, struggling through a forest at night. As if taking up where *Seconds* left off, the torches that the men carry shine directly into the camera lens and strike out across the screen, giving the audience glimpses of the surrounding vegetation of the forest. In the aural foreground is the stark sound of the wind and panting animals, which abruptly gives way to discordant music when the dogs appear to pick up a scent and the men race behind in hot pursuit. The lead hound hurls itself over a cliff edge for some unexplained reason and the dismayed men follow it down into a gully. Screams are heard and this opening sequence closes as the camera zooms in on the helmet lamp-light of an obviously terrified man.

Prophecy's protagonist Robert Verne (Robert Foxworth) is a medical doctor with a passionate interest in social and environmental issues. Leaving his work with the poor African American community in the squalor of the city slums of Washington, D.C., he heads off to the rural climes of Maine on a mission for the Environmental Protection Agency. Accompanied by his wife, Maggie (Talia Shire), who the audience learns is pregnant, the doctor finds himself in the middle of a dispute between a local Indian tribe and a paper mill, well meaning but apparently unable to understand what he is dealing with in this strange environment.

Requesting an inspection of the paper mill to check for possible contaminants, Verne is given a guided tour by the owner, Bethel Isely (Richard Dysart). This visit is handled in quasi-documentary fashion, with Isely detailing the various parts of the manufacturing process against the backdrop of a working mill. The use of a dry, documentary approach is not entirely unusual in science fiction; for example, a number of the 1950s films opened with documentary-styled sequences. However, it is more unusual to find this kind of approach so blatantly adopted this far into a science fiction or science fiction/horror film's main narrative. The impression is that this was intended to serve an overt educational purpose and to signal a serious intent on the part of the filmmakers. The film's engagement with the environmental issues of the day was therefore writ large in the way that this sequence sets up a comprehensive and realistic background for the horrific events that follow.

Studies surrounding the harm caused by industrial waste and the increased use of pesticides in the 1960s gave rise to various ecology and environmental movements toward the end of that decade, and the Environmental Protection Agency was set up in the United States in 1970. Although Isely protests that the mill is not harmful to the environment (stating that the area surrounding the mill is "more stable today than when God himself made it"), an audience familiar with the context may well have doubted this character's claims. This is particularly the case given the film's reference to Maine, which Ralph Nader famously called "corporate country" in the 1974 publication of *The Paper Plantation: Ralph Nader's Study Group Report on the Pulp and Paper Industry in Maine* (Osborn ix). Verne's tests finally prove that the local river has been contaminated with mercury, and further references to the film's realistic foundations are slipped in when he explains the effects of mercury poisoning with reference to the Minamata disaster in Japan. The population of the city of Minamata began showing signs of deformity and disease in the 1950s, and the Chisso Corporation's local chemical factory was suspected of contaminating the water supply. But it was not until 1969 that the corporation was forced into court, at which point this news story received fairly widespread international coverage in the press.

After this extended set-up, the second half of the film finds our intrepid doctor, along with Maggie, local tribespeople led by Hawks (Armand Assante) and Ramona (Victoria Racimo), and later Isely, trapped in the forest with a gigantic and deformed female bear hot on their heels. When Maggie spots two deformed bear cubs caught up in a netting trap, Verne rescues the one surviving infant, arguing that the animal is "evidence." It is this action that brings the wrath of the mother bear down upon the group and initiates the ensuing chase through the forest. Aware of Verne's ambivalence about starting a family, Maggie has kept her pregnancy a secret. But knowing that her own offspring may be affected because she has eaten fish from the local river, she finally tells Verne that she is going to have a baby. This revelatory moment marks a distinct shift from the wider social concerns and "cooler" mode of address as a feature of science fiction, to the more personalized moral concerns and affective address of horror. At the same time as it reminds viewers of Maggie's particular perspective on these events, it forces Verne to engage with their impact on a personal and domestic level. In this sense, Verne and viewer are drawn into a feminine realm, which is sharply delineated as horrific in the terms of this film.

In her reading of both *Alien* and the later science fiction *Blade Runner* (Ridley Scott, 1982), Mary Ann Doane suggested that these films responded to the advent since the 1960s of technologies of reproduction, such as birth control, artificial insemination, in vitro fertilization, surrogate mothering, and so forth (169). Also, in an application of Julia Kristeva's work on abjectivity and the representation of the feminine, Barbara Creed explored the ways in which horror films deal in various forms of monstrous femininity, often associated with the mothering and reproductive functions of the female (7). For instance, in *Alien* Creed read the horrific presence of the parthenogenetic mother, the mother who can reproduce without the intervention of the male. In her reading of a further film example, *The Brood* (David Cronenberg, 1979), Creed examined the female character Nola's parthenogenetic birthing of deformed and gruesome children.

Maggie, Ramona, and Verne (*left to right:* Talia Shire, Victoria Racimo, Robert Foxworth) work to keep the deformed bear cub alive in *Prophecy* (Paramount Pictures, 1979).
Digital frame enlargement.

Exhibiting the kind of schlock body horror that made Cronenberg famous, the narrative of this film explained that Nola's "children" are the literal manifestations of her inner rage and anger. Although the mothers figured in *Prophecy* are not properly parthenogenetic, Creed's ideas illuminate the codes and conventions drawn upon in the film and the particular prevalence of the mother figure and birthing in similar films circulating at the same time. So, even as a film like *Prophecy* might seem to be about the hazardous forces of commercial and technological production, it is just as much concerned with the generative capacities of reproduction. Taking Doane's and Creed's observations into account, I would contend that the science fiction/horror film is most concerned with unsettling traditional boundaries between nature and technological culture, between reproduction and production, between feminine and masculine realms. In this, science fiction/horror often foregrounds its own generic melding, which is made all too clear in *Prophecy*'s rather abrupt shift from one generic mode into another. As I have commented elsewhere, "The clashing of genres here allows for comment upon the kind of world views that each has to offer" (see Cornea 7). The horror of Maggie's pregnancy is augmented and illuminated in Verne's attempts to offer a scientific and rational explanation for the unholy mess that the mill has unleashed upon the surrounding natural environment.

The obvious connections made between Maggie and monstrosity also suggest that the mother bear enacts Maggie's hidden rage. In the absence of any effective action by Verne, Isely's eventual slaughter by the bear can be understood as Maggie's revenge upon the man whose irresponsible behavior in allowing the use of mercury at his mill has threatened her unborn child. Additionally, the gendering of the monster has broader implications in being another among many popular cases at the time of the feminization of a colonized subject. As

Frantz Fanon's early work taught us, the colonized subject is frequently situated within sexualized discourses; functioning as Other for the colonizer, the colonized subject is often feminized. Likewise, oppressed or marginalized by a dominant white culture, it is easy to see how the African American city dwellers featured at the beginning of the film and the Indian tribespeople of the forest take up a place on the feminine side of a gendered opposition in this science fiction/horror film. So, the actions of the bear can more broadly be read as the revenge of the feminized subject against an abusive white patriarchal society.

Science Fiction/Horror and the In-Corporated Body: *The Island of Dr. Moreau*

Frankenheimer's association with this genre might well have ended with *Prophecy*. However, when Richard Stanley was fired as director on the remake of H. G. Wells's *The Island of Dr. Moreau* (published in 1896), the producers, New Line Cinema, asked Frankenheimer to take over the film. Presuming that the main plot of Wells's novel is well known, I confine myself to the briefest synopsis of the original narrative. An upper-class gentleman called Edward Prendick is the lone survivor of a shipwreck. Rescued by a passing ship, Prendick is transported to a South Pacific island populated by strange beast-folk. The inhabitants of the island are ruled over by a cold and calculating physiologist called Dr. Moreau, who is assisted in his scientific pursuits by the drunken medical doctor, Montgomery. Eventually, Prendick learns that Moreau is conducting cruel experiments in vivisection and the inhabitants are actually animals that the physiologist is attempting to turn into human beings. The fragile order of law that Moreau imposes on his half-animal/half-human subjects breaks down and, following the murders of Moreau and Montgomery, Prendick finally escapes the island to return to England. Of course, this most recent film adaptation of Wells's novel was not the first: previous adaptations include Erle C. Kenton's previously mentioned *Island of Lost Souls* (1932) and Don Taylor's *The Island of Dr. Moreau* (1977). Nevertheless, there are some notable contemporary twists applied to the 1996 version that Frankenheimer directed. Wells's more or less overt critique of vivisection is, for instance, updated in the portrayal of Dr. Moreau (Marlon Brando) as a geneticist, who splices human DNA with animal tissue in an attempt to create a civilized race of beast-people. Although the critical directness notable in both *Seconds* and *Prophecy* has all but disappeared in this later film, these changes do place *The Island of Dr. Moreau* within a contemporary milieu and suggest a certain level of social comment.

In its updated image of science and technology, the film resonated with high-profile scientific events of this period. For instance, genetic engineering of one sort or another was a hot topic in the 1990s, and the successful cloning of "Dolly" the sheep in July 1996 (officially announced in 1997) reignited ethical debates surrounding the biological sciences. Furthermore, a line can be traced between the anti-vivisectionist sentiments of Wells's time and the expanded concerns of later animal rights or animal liberation movements. Various academic and populist publications worked to bring the aims of animal rights movements to public attention in the 1990s (see, for examples, Rachels; Francione; Singer). Also, the activities of organizations aimed at protecting animals from the abuses of science were widely reported in the press throughout the 1980s and 1990s, moving the issue of animal rights from the fringes into the mainstream.

In addition, the film's introduction of the United Nations envoy, Douglas (David Thewlis), who takes over from Prendick in the original novel, surely engages with the contentious status of the UN at this time. The post–World War II image of the UN as a peace-loving organization was severely challenged with the advent of the Gulf War of 1990–91 when, in response to the occupation of Kuwait by Iraqi forces acting under the orders of President Saddam Hussein, the UN-authorized war saw a coalition of military forces storm the region and drive Iraqi forces back across the border. While the UN condemned the Iraqi invasion as a direct violation of Kuwaiti territorial rites and set itself in opposition to Iraq's history of human rites abuses, as many have commented, UN intervention was also motivated due to the region's importance as a supplier of oil for the Western world (see, for example, Austvik). Protection of the delicate balance between the area's major oil-producing states therefore was of prime importance for commercial reasons: to keep the price of oil stable and, for the United States, to protect the interests of its major oil-producing ally, Saudi Arabia. Following the Gulf War, reports emerged of strange disorders suffered by veterans and of birth defects thought to be connected to the veterans' exposure to chemicals or radiation during the war. Accusations that the UN had failed to control coalition forces (the U.S. forces in particular), as well as the UN's inevitable association with what became known as Gulf War Syndrome, undermined

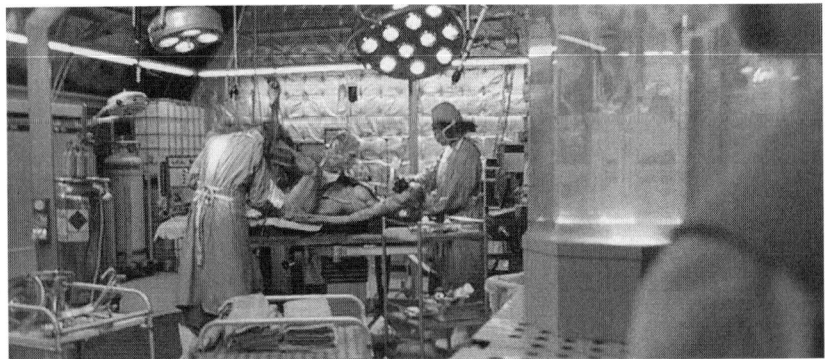

What Douglas sees as he discovers the horrific procedures behind Moreau's biological research in *The Island of Dr. Moreau* (New Line Cinema, 1996).

Digital frame enlargement.

its progressive remit to promote world peace and protect human rights. Clearly, it is possible to read Douglas's contact with Moreau and his hybrid creations as an ironic commentary on the UN's contemporary role in the world.

From the outset, Douglas makes clear that he is on an important peace mission, but his efforts to contact UN authorities are thwarted: first when he is imprisoned in the main house on the island, and second when he discovers that the radio transmitter has been disabled. Falling back on the corporate law by which he claims to be bound, Montgomery (Val Kilmer) tells Douglas that the people who fund the project on the island are afraid of being sued. This is the excuse he uses to imprison Douglas in the house, to apparently ensure Douglas's safety and avoid expensive litigation. Of course, this is not the real reason for the imprisonment. Although it is made clear that Montgomery enjoys asserting his authority over Douglas, the incarceration also avoids the possibility that Douglas might learn the dreadful secrets behind the biological research. Douglas's position is further compromised by his attraction toward the alluring Aissa (Fairuza Balk), described as Moreau's daughter. Having broken out of the house, he is halted by the sight of Aissa dancing on the veranda. The growing romance between the girl and Douglas is repeatedly challenged: first when Douglas learns she is a genetically altered wild cat, and then when the serum that keeps her human is destroyed after Moreau's death. Douglas is forced to witness her regression, and shows palpable fear when she develops threatening and protruding canines.

Like Nora in *Seconds* and Maggie in *Prophecy*, Aissa leads our protagonist into an uncertain world where the usual rules of civilized behavior do not apply. However, unlike Nora, who is simply in league with The Company, or Maggie, whose monstrosity is displaced onto the bear, Aissa is an "exotic" character in whom female and monster are one. On the one hand, this threat as "power in

Moreau (Marlon Brando) introduces Aissa (Fairuza Balk) and his most immediate family of beast-people in *The Island of Dr. Moreau* (New Line Cinema, 1996). Digital frame enlargement.

difference" can be read in Douglas's reaction to Aissa's regression (see Hollinger 306). However, what is also interesting here is that the audience learns Moreau has extracted Douglas's DNA with the intention of using it to halt Aissa's regression. So, it would seem that Moreau's corporate-funded scientific work actually threatens to erode a gendered difference between these two characters. Perhaps the fear in Douglas's reaction has more to do with the realization that they might be the same and the threat to a white male-defined hegemony now has less to do with a gendered or racialized difference than the erosion of difference in a world defined by consumerism and corporations.

Wells's Moreau was one of the original mad scientists, a figure that was repeatedly taken up in the science fiction or science fiction/horror film genre. But where earlier film versions had depicted him—in line with the novel—as cold and cruel, this new Moreau is more accurately described as a misguided buffoon. In fact, British reviewers leapt on Brando's performance of this character, describing his somewhat absurd portrayal as "camp" (Brown 41) and "hilarious" (Newman 38).[2] Unlike the old man in *Seconds* or Isely in *Prophecy*, Moreau is portrayed as a perversion of the father figure from the outset. While he attempts to present himself as benevolent and loving in his rule over the beast-people, he finds it necessary to inflict pain upon them in order to control their animal urges. Eventually, the beast-people come to realize that his actions are not those of a benevolent father and they rise up against their controlling overlord, murdering Moreau and destroying everything he stands for. As a figure that is vital to the accession to power of the properly masculine subject, the failure of the father as corporate figurehead is crucial in these three films. In his examination of how the body has served as a central metaphor for society and, conversely, how the body has been socially disciplined and understood, Bryan S. Turner has argued: "Capitalism, far from requiring patriarchal domination, actually undermines patriarchal power by transforming the nature of the household unit. Insofar as patriarchal power survives, it is largely a defensive ideological reaction against socio-economic changes which erode male dominance in both the public and private spheres" (143). The repeated failure of the father figure in all these films to maintain authority, to accept responsibility, to uphold a properly coherent, stable, and civilized masculinity is therefore signaled by the female figures' potency and the male protagonists' descent into chaos and horror.

Even before *Moreau* was released, reports about personality clashes and problems in production abounded. The studio cancelled the planned preview for the press, and, as expected, critical response was overwhelmingly scathing. Nevertheless, I would say that it remains an important film in reading across Frankenheimer's body of work. Reflecting on the fact that Wells's novel was a significant forerunner to what was later known as the science fiction or science fiction/horror genre, we can see that this particular film adaptation makes it easier to draw a retrospective generic boundary around the three films discussed here. Reading back, there is the sense in which this 1996 adaptation drew together elements found earlier in *Seconds* and *Prophecy*. The misguided aspirations of Dr. Moreau can be likened to those of The Company's founding father in *Seconds*, and to Isely's actions in *Prophecy*. Also, the scenes of genetic and surgical alterations secretly carried out on the animals brought to Moreau's island evoke memory of similar procedures in the former films. In themselves these elements are appropriate to the science fiction/horror film as a genre, but that is not to discount the presence of certain authorial markers or trademarks that can be traced across the three films. For example, the particular use of specialized lighting (the surgical lamp in *Seconds* and *Moreau*, the torch lights in *Prophecy*, and so forth), which is pointed directly into the camera lens to momentarily white out the film image, is repeated in all three films. Also, elements of the absurd can be found in all these films, signaled through bizarre events/images and the use of performance.

In assessing how Frankenheimer, as an authorial figure, negotiated with the re-genrefication of a New Hollywood, it is perhaps not surprising that on occasion he turned to the science fiction/horror film. While his overt use of art-film devices decreased after *Seconds*, this hybrid genre did offer Frankenheimer the opportunity to deploy the kinds of visual and dramatic devices that critics like Sarris found so distasteful in his political thrillers. Also, while *Seconds*, *Prophecy*, and *Moreau* can be distinguished from the political thrillers or prison films that Frankenheimer is more often associated with, the themes of entrapment, paranoia, and conspiracy certainly cross generic borders and are very much present in all three science fiction/horror films. Moreover, it is possible to see in all these films a kind of social conscience at work, particularly as pertaining to topical areas of scientific development at the time of each film's release and to the rise of consumer capitalism and corporate power.

NOTES

1. Gary Sinise used these words in his tribute (59).
2. Newman's review did acknowledge possible links here to satirical aspects of the original novel as a possible justification for the clumsy comedy in the film. However, inferring a lack of directorial control, Newman ends by saying that too "many cooks have spoiled yet again one of the world's most filmable books" (38).

The Fixer

A Jew Who Could Be Any Man, Any Time, Anywhere

R. BARTON PALMER

An adaptation of Bernard Malamud's popular 1966 novel of the same name, *The Fixer* (1968) may be understood as part of an important sub-group of Frankenheimer's projects that also includes *Birdman of Alcatraz* (1962), *Against the Wall* (1994), and *Andersonville* (1996). Or so, at least, suggests Stephen B. Armstrong, who in his frankly auteurist account of the director's career, argues for an elemental connection these films share because their main characters find themselves prisoners of one kind or another. As Armstrong sees it, the typical Frankenheimer film traces protagonists who are "trapped in situations which cause mental and physical anguish," but the worlds depicted in the four prison films offer no real possibility for those characters to "extricate themselves from these traps." Instead, Frankenheimer's prisoners "completely lack the ability to change their conditions," and such pessimistic resolutions are said to contrast strongly with the director's other works, in which the confrontation with difficulties both internal and external is instead negotiated with "varying degrees of success." There is much to recommend Armstrong's view of the particular form of *agon* at the heart of the typical Frankenheimer film and of the ways that the prison films deviate somewhat from the pattern. In the case of *The Fixer*, however, his reading of the ending is perhaps too literal.

No Exit?

A Jew living in Russia in the first decade of the twentieth century, Yakov Bok (Alan Bates) certainly faces something of a Sartrean dead end: he has been imprisoned indefinitely for a crime he did not commit, awaiting a trial that, he hopes, will set him free. The police use every form of torture at their disposal to make him confess in order to strengthen the case of the prosecution, whose broader context is a supposed Jewish conspiracy, but Bok will not give in. Stubborn just like his main character, Frankenheimer steadfastly refuses to even hint at Bok's eventual deliverance. The film ends instead with the long-awaited trial just beginning as Bok, in a kind of flash forward voiceover after the echoing sound of the judge's gavel, offers a powerful proclamation of self as his plea: "The name is Yakov Bok. A Jew. An innocent man. Also your brother." If his liberation from an unjust incarceration remains in doubt, Bok, who had hitherto fled to cultural anonymity and emotional isolation, now embraces a humanism that brings him closer even to those who have persecuted him. This change of heart is arguably the outward sign of a change of condition, an escape from a hitherto imprisoning *mentalité* of radical individualism that had seemed to promise liberation (from Jewishness, from more than perfunctory communal connections to others, including the *goyim*), but had paradoxically resulted only in Bok's arrest and incarceration. An intimation of this shift surfaces in an earlier scene where Bok avers, so that a jailer hears and agrees, that Jesus' Jewishness makes them all brothers.

Malamud's novel, to be sure, also ends on a somewhat optimistic note, but of a rather different kind. His Bok is still in custody, imagining his trial rather than entering into its initial phase. In the theater of his own mind, he is given the opportunity to indict the czar (a sick and pathetically inarticulate man, his "phallus meager"), who, so Bok thinks, has encouraged the virulent antisemitism that has victimized him and his fellow Jews. Contemplating what statement to make to the court, Bok considers his conversion from self-centered indifference to a deeply felt commitment to political change:

> One thing I've learned, he thought, there's no such thing as an unpolitical man, especially a Jew. You can't be one without the other, that's clear enough. You can't sit still and see yourself destroyed. . . . Long live the revolution! Long live liberty! (Malamud, *Fixer* 334, 335)

In the novel, Bok thus comes to share the Enlightenment vision of a society transformed by the acknowledgment of natural rights, expressed, most famously perhaps, by Thomas Paine: "A Nation has at all times an inherent indefeasible right to abolish any form of Government it finds inconvenient, and establish such as accords with its interest, disposition, and happiness" (Paine 92). Bok prefers to embrace these politics in the form he encountered in his reading of Baruch Spinoza (who is, like him, a problematic Jew, expelled from the Amsterdam community for heresy and forced to adopt a Christian first name). "What is it that Spinoza says?" he asks himself in the novel. "If the state acts in ways that are abhorrent to human nature it's the lesser evil to destroy it" (Malamud 335). Frankenheimer's Bok, we might say, comes to a more complex understanding of modern universalism: his vision of community in which all are in some sense brothers coexists uneasily with the undeniable fact that some, being Jews, share a different, more exclusive bond.

Both novel and film demonstrate that this aspect of his identity is ineradicable; Bok's attempts to assimilate to Russian society at large only bring his

Jewishness to the fore, as his individuality is subsumed in a vicious ethnic stereotype from which deliverance seems problematic at best. Early in the film, Bok asks a fellow Jew with whom he has sheltered during a pogrom: "What is a Jew to do?" The answer: "Become a Zionist." But then neither novel nor film, treating characters firmly rooted in a Russia convulsed by nationalist passions and ideological conflict, struggles to resolve or even explore this aspect of the "Jewish question." In both versions of the story, Bok is a figure of resistance rather than revolt, a man whose ethnic nationalism is embryonic at best, subsumed by abstract Spinozan imperatives and possibilities. Frankenheimer's Bok is characterized in particular by his steadfast sense of self, by his persistent defiance of (or, perhaps better, indifference to) an evil system, even if he cannot hope for or participate in its eventual overthrow.

The Law Is Written in Your Heart

The Fixer offers an only slightly altered account of the 1913 Menachem Mendel Beilis case, which in the wake of the Dreyfus affair in France (Dreyfus was released from Devil's Island in 1906 and restored at that time to his previous military rank) turned a harsh light on the failure of the Russian government to control violent outbreaks of antisemitism. Beilis was accused, on very thin circumstantial evidence, not of treason (like Dreyfus) but of a more elemental violation of communal bonds, of "blood libel" in the murder of a Christian boy, allegedly killed so that his flesh could be used to make Passover matzos. As the case unfolded, it became clear (as both Malamud and Frankenheimer emphasize) that the government used the incident to inflame hatred and fear of the Jews in order to divert popular attention from widespread dissatisfactions that might otherwise have fueled anger at the czar and his increasingly ineffective rule. In both novel and film, the Black Hundreds, a counter-revolutionary and ultra-nationalist party that received the blessing of the Orthodox church and firmly supported the Romanovs, instigate pogroms against the terrified Jewish minority. Frankenheimer tells us that their slogan is "Save Russia from the Jews," and the intent of the Black Hundreds in the Beilis case, as in its fictionalization, was to make the position of the country's Jews untenable.

And yet early twentieth-century Russia is by no means Nazi Germany. Here an ideologically neutral version of the law still prevails, at least in theory, and Jews have not lost their civil rights. In a vindication of sorts of the country's creaky bureaucracy, Beilis was eventually put on trial and acquitted. In a scene closely imitated from the novel, Frankenheimer's film offers ironic proof that the system "works." Bok is at one point threatened with summary execution by a prison official, but this is averted when a court official intervenes, saying that the prisoner has already been transferred to his jurisdiction and so cannot be harmed. Found innocent of the flimsy charges, Beilis emigrated to Palestine and, soon afterward, to the United States, where he died in 1934, but not before publishing a sensational account of his troubles: *The Story of My Sufferings* in 1926. In order to sharpen his novel's critique of antisemitism and strengthen his argument that in post-Holocaust America Jews who are eager to assimilate cannot afford indifference to politics, Malamud does not allow his fictional protagonist to go free. This is where novel and film most significantly depart from the facts of the case; they emphasize the obstinacy of Bok's resistance and the popular protests it fostered, not his eventual victory.

It is fitting, then, that the film opens with an act of refusal whose full meaning emerges only gradually and whose reversal the plot traces in agonizing detail. Without any establishing shots or commentary to indicate time and place, the camera shows hands as they repair a straight razor, which this "fixer," who is in his early thirties, then uses, along with scissors, to remove his thick beard and ear curls. In some haste, he throws some meager belongings into a horse cart and drives off. The wagon soon loses a wheel, but he persists, cutting the horse loose from his traces and riding off bareback. Eventually this man (as yet unnamed) comes to a large city, where a political rally is taking place overseen by mounted, sword-wielding soldiers, who then ride through the streets killing unfortunate passersby and destroying shops. The city, we learn, is Kiev, and the time is the early twentieth century. The central square is convulsed with a parade of men carrying banners and beating drums, cheered on by eager bystanders. What is first a demonstration soon becomes a pogrom, as the marchers (belonging, we later learn, to the Black Hundreds) and their accompanying mounted Cossacks pour aggressively through the gate that leads to the ghetto, beating and killing the Jews they come upon.

The camera locates the country man on these streets and shows him taking shelter in a shop, where he hides with another refugee, a bearded itinerant tailor (David Opatoshu), to whom he reveals that he too is Jew, Yakov Bok. He confesses to the tailor that he never felt deeply about his ethnicity. To shed that ethnicity, then, is to seek out a life in the wider world, not to surrender a meaningful connection. This is why Bok had fled the communal isolation of his rural *shtetl*, with its limited opportunities, for the greater cosmopolitanism of Kiev. The city, he hopes, will afford him the anonymity to lead the isolated existence that is his chosen way of life now that his wife has left him and he has no other family. This information is communicated very briefly and allusively in a subjective flashback as Frankenheimer deemphasizes the particularity of Bok's experience and character. The pogrom, of course, provides Bok with yet another reason to abandon his Jewishness, one that Frankenheimer presents as more compelling than his family troubles.

For Bok, shaving the beard that is the outward sign of Jewishness is not the denial of traditional spirituality. It is instead a practical act that inaugurates a complex process of self-emancipation. Bok's actions are meant to be understood in some sense as paradigmatic, illustrative as they are of the startling change in status (including assimilation and secularization) that characterized the

Jewish experience throughout much of nineteenth- and early twentieth-century Europe, if not to the same degree in Russia, where (although there were notable exceptions) Jews were not accepted into the larger society (see Nathans). The movement from Jewish particularity to Gentile generality also suits Bok as an admirer of Spinoza; it recalls, in fact, that philosopher's experience as well as his deep interest in ethical speculation. But the natural consequence of Bok's actions is a renunciation of the Law. First arriving in Kiev, Bok seems hesitant to stake out an identity as "anybody," persuaded perhaps by the ravening Cossacks and their murderous companions that he needs to shelter within the community that he has in some sense abjured. So he takes up residence in the ghetto with his erstwhile companion the tailor, and it is only an eminently practical consideration that brings on further change. Bok can find no work among his co-religionists, and when told by his friend that he does not look Jewish, he determines to pass as just another Russian in order to survive.

Despite the regulations confining Jews to the ghetto (where they still need the official residence permit that Bok lacks), he goes into the Russian sections of the city hoping to find employment there. But because he has no connections, work in his trade as a fixer willing to repair anything proves difficult, and his situation begins to seem desperate. A chance act of kindness then provides an unexpected opportunity. Despite his initial reluctance, Bok comes to the aid of a man who, he sees, is wearing the lapel button of the Black Hundreds and has passed out drunk on the frozen street. When the man's well-dressed daughter Zinaida (Elizabeth Hartman) comes on the scene, it is surprisingly revealed that the man is no derelict, but a well-off factory owner named Lebedev (Hugh Griffith). The next day, Lebedev hires Bok as an overseer out of gratitude and gives him a place to live. Not longer afterward Zinaida, who finds Bok attractive, attempts to seduce him. He hesitates before agreeing to sleep with the woman (he is as lonely as she is), but cannot complete the act when he realizes she is menstruating. Hurriedly gathering up his clothes after spying some bloody underclothes, Bok flees in a kind of primal terror.

It is this refusal that sets into motion a chain of ultimately tragic events. His hasty departure from the bedroom is no considered, moral act, but a reflex, and it seems nothing less than the outward sign of Bok's flesh deep inability to ignore completely the Law he was born into, one of whose strictures forbids intercourse with an "unclean" woman. Worried earlier when stripping that his circumcised penis would reveal his identity he covers himself with a towel, but ironically discovers soon afterward that the Gentile culture into which he has sought to blend disgusts him with its own surprises. In each case, elementary difference reveals itself. If Bok is going to live and work among "the people," he should be able to sleep with their women, which is more or less what he mumbles while talking himself into Zinaida's bed. But it is not to be. Without thinking, Bok seems to understand her lack of shame as a sign that, like the *goyim* more generally, Zinaida fails to make the distinction that lies at the heart

An abortive romantic encounter between Yakov Bok (Alan Bates) and Zinaida Lebedev (Elizabeth Hartman) leads ultimately to his arrest and imprisonment, in *The Fixer* (MGM, 1968).
Digital frame enlargement.

of Judaism as a way of life, between those things divinely marked as proper for human use and those that are not. The Law, it seems, is written in his heart, and he simply cannot bear to touch her. In no way nonplussed at her erstwhile lover's dismay, Zinaida finds his finickiness about the menstrual blood inexplicable, underlining the unbridgeable gulf between the two cultures.

Clearly, Bok cannot escape his identity simply by quitting the *shtetl* and, his appearance strategically altered, attempting to pass as *goy*. His ineradicable Jewishness, which is more than a matter of facial hair, good looks, or place of residence, will give him away. His Jewishness, in fact, shows itself unwilled to him, and this seems a certain sign that it will make itself manifest to others as well. If the prison toward which the plot delivers him promises no deliverance, neither does the self that has been his since birth. In a sense, then, the prison simply concretizes Bok's failure at self-transformation, showing that he will be treated as a Jew however much he wants to be seen by others as what he is not. When first sheltering with the tailor, he declares himself neither religious nor political. The impossibility of this self-definition becomes clear when his companion then reasonably inquires: "Do you describe a horse by saying what it doesn't do?" A horse is a horse is a horse, and it cannot will itself into some other form of being. The Enlightenment project of self-fashioning based on a universal form of human nature is shown to be inadequate to the deep force of communal connections, which are at least in part defined by blood and thus do constitute for Bok an undeniable *Gemeinschaft* whose nature will soon be revealed to him, for ill but also for good.

Bok finds himself suffering as the Jew he is (rather than as an individual to be held responsible only for what an individual does, a person to be guided by, and judged according to, Spinoza's strictures about conduct). Bok, in fact, comes to suffer *the* diasporic Jewish fate itself. He is arrested for the "blood accusation" that speaks to an archetypal form of antisemitic calumny: the charge of a taboo-breaking uncleanness, which rhymes ironically with Bok's perception of Zinaida's menses as forbidden abjectness. At first, however, he is falsely accused of a crime that any man, Jew or Gentile, could have committed. Zinaida, who is eager to take revenge for being rejected, cries rape, but the charge is quickly dismissed once the investigating magistrate, Bibikov (Dirk Bogarde), realizes that the woman was in fact the would-be seducer and is simply bitter at having been scorned. The light that the investigation shines on Bok, however, reveals his Jewishness, which he confesses to the sympathetic and worldly Bibikov, who finds it insignificant. Bok, he comments, may have violated the law by leaving the Pale of Settlement, but this is what many others have done as well.

Such is the nature of the second charge, however, that Bibikov cannot dismiss it, even though its absurdity is also manifest to him. Asked by an old Hassid if he can shelter one night in his room, Bok agrees, and the man, as if fated to reveal his host's secret, leaves behind a fragment of Passover matzo. A Christian boy turns up murdered in the neighborhood that same night (the likely victim, it later appears, of parental violence), but the body seems strangely drained of blood. Suspicion falls immediately on Bok, and he is accused by the virulently antisemitic public prosecutor Grubeshov (Ian Holm) with having conspired with the wandering Hassid to kill the boy in order to make the ritually required bread from his flesh. In this way, the supposed cannibalistic strictures of the Jewish faith would be upheld. The bit of matzo found in his room is all the proof that Grubeshov needs to be convinced of Bok's guilt.

More evidence, however, is necessary if the case is to be taken to court and successfully prosecuted. Mistreated, then tortured, Bok refuses to confess. After Bok has spent some time in jail, Bibikov, the westernized Russian who believes in toleration, turns up dead, hanging from the rafters, more likely murdered than a suicide. Though Bok at one point contemplates suicide himself, he is strengthened by his realization that the particular murder charge that has been wrongly leveled against him as an individual means that he has come, in fact, to represent the Jews. He thus cannot accede in his own destruction, for to do so would ally him with the persecutors even as his death would offer proof of Jewish cowardice, even guilt. His assertion of innocence takes on a different meaning. The ineradicable identity that, in his desire to escape it, actually overtakes him becomes both the cause of his troubles and the source of the strength he needs in order to extricate himself from them through a kind of Gandhian perseverance. Bok's moment of *éclaircissement* involves a central paradox. Meaningful individuality (becoming somebody rather than anybody) is delivered to him through the embrace of shared ethnicity, but this does not mean he has to abandon his Enlightenment ideals. For he now feels that he is innocent both as a Jew (for the charge of cannibalism has no basis in reality) and as an individual (he did not commit the murder). Failing to get a confession, and responding to

Bok is arrested for murder by the authorities after the discovery of a telltale matzo in his room.

Digital frame enlargement.

the growing public outrage over the case, Grubeshov agrees to bring the matter before a magistrate, and the uncertainty of the outcome is spectacularly dramatized by Frankenheimer, who provides a potent image of early twentieth-century Jewish cultural politics. Bok arrives at the court and proceeds alone through a huge crowd of cheering (and jeering) bystanders, some who want him released (including rabbis holding up Torahs for him to see) and others, including members of the Black Hundreds, who are obviously eager for his blood.

A Cinema in Extremis

In its search for emotional appeal and transcendent meaning, art, especially that of the popular kind, customarily avoids unvarnished reality. In the American commercial cinema, everydayness usually appears so stylized as to proclaim itself an italicized form of the extraordinary (cf. *Marty* [1955], *The Best Years of Our Lives* [1946], even the "shockingly realistic" *Kids* [1995]). So we might say that all Hollywood films, one way or another, are about "extremes." "I love pictures about extremes," Frankenheimer once admitted, in a moment of uncharacteristic self-reflection. "I seem to deal in extremes" (qtd. in Armstrong 6). Being in prison, by anyone's definition, would constitute an extreme state, so *The Fixer* obviously fits into this general category.

It is unarguable that Frankenheimer's filmmaking characteristically places characters in extraordinary situations that test their investment in self, their commitment to living as who they are, their daring if often failed attempts at realizing some vision despite obviously disastrous consequences, and, perhaps not least of all, their ability to endure tremendous suffering and somehow survive as individuals. Frankenheimer's engagement with such moralism (the plots of his films generally turn on decisions freighted with ethical consequences) is not always optimistic. If his vision of experience is routinely humanistic in the broadest sense, it is based on a kind of Lutheran refusal, especially in those projects (of which, as we will see, *The Fixer* is certainly one) that can be readily identified as personal. Here we stand, Frankenheimer's characters say, and we cannot do otherwise; in this, Yakov Bok is typical. The refusals of these characters, elevating or even heroic, usually turn out to be unhappy, at least in the conventional Hollywood sense. Frankenheimer's characters survive arduous trials that threaten to dissolve or counterfeit identity, but this survival often paradoxically requires the willed dissolution of self or some equivalent fatal sacrifice. Consider, for example, the shooting of the hostages at the end of *The Train* (1964) after the Resistance fighter Labiche (Burt Lancaster) refuses to let a shipment of French artworks be routed through to Nazi Germany. Labiche is successful in preventing the theft of a national heritage, but at the cost of the lives of innocents who, never consulted, could not agree to the sacrifice they would be called upon to make.

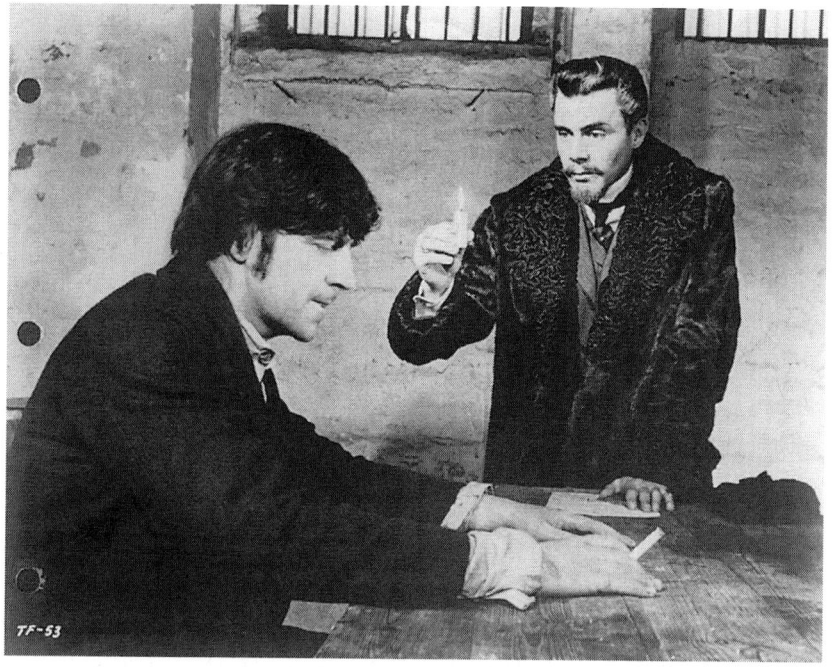

Interrogated by the public prosecutor Bibikov (Dirk Bogarde), Bok is found innocent of the rape charges leveled by Zinaida, but Bibikov, who is later found dead, cannot help him in the murder case.
Digital frame enlargement.

Refusal always figures centrally in Frankenheimer's more interesting productions, but as a motif it often goes against conventional narrative expectations. And these productions are as a result often his least acclaimed, such is the gap between the artistic value of his portrayals of the human condition and the judgments rendered by the box office and critics. This is certainly the case in *The Fixer*, which was met with viewer indifference and poisonous reviews. Consider the similar case of *The Gypsy Moths* (1969), which likewise did poor business and was shunned by the critics. The extremeness of that film is exemplified by the fate of its main character, skydiver Rettig (Burt Lancaster), who, apparently disheartened by the refusal of Elizabeth (Deborah Kerr) to make a new life with him, commits suicide by refusing to open his parachute during a group performance. He plummets to his death as the other members of his team watch in horror. The next day, his colleague Malcolm (Scott Wilson), making the same dive in Rettig's place, also feels a pull toward self-annihilation. At the last moment, however, he does yank the ripcord and lands safely. In the process Malcolm loses his thrill-seeking fascination for skydiving, discovering that he is no longer compelled to follow a "profession" that involves the constant testing of the will to live. Writing in the *New York Times*, Vincent Canby interpreted Frankenheimer's intentions accurately, remarking that the film was marked by a "deliberate, humorless piety," a phrase that precisely captures the unconventional seriousness that pervades *The Gypsy Moths*. The film, which Canby hated, tellingly made the reviewer nostalgic for classic Hollywood action films ("low-budget" and dominated by "pecking order" male action). Such films do not question, but validate traditional notions of masculinity through ritualistic trials of strength and expressions of courage.

Though engaged in a profession that depends on the constant exercise of these very qualities, the characters in *The Gypsy Moths* are more driven in the end by the ethical sensibility that is *pietas* in the classic sense: a respect for those social forms (work, sexual intimacy, comradeship) in which dignity, and hence a reason for living, might be discovered. Even when it depends on an unusual anatomizing that deconstructs conventional notions of the heroic, Frankenheimer's moralism has proved less than attractive to one of America's more sophisticated critics. Canby found himself yearning instead for predictable dramatizations of righteous violence, and that judgment speaks volumes about the national indisposition to appreciate an art dedicated to exploring the central question of how (or indeed whether) to live, which is what Frankenheimer's characters, finding themselves *in extremis*, must always struggle somehow to answer. In this struggle, Yakov Bok's fascination with Spinoza appears as paradigmatic for Frankenheimer's filmmaking as a whole, and it is revealing that he, like Rettig and Malcolm and others among the director's characters, is tempted by suicide.

The refusal that defines the collective responses of Frankenheimer's characters assumes its most complex form in *The Manchurian Candidate* (1962), a film that met with more critical approval than *The Gypsy Moths* because, among other reasons, it was carefully structured by the intersecting experiences of two protagonists, one who is more or less conventionally masculine and heroic, Major Bennett Marco (Frank Sinatra), and another who is in essence an antihero, perhaps even something of a villain, if only *malgré lui*, Sergeant Raymond Shaw (Laurence Harvey). Because of this double, even contradictory structure, the film may be summarized in terms that suggest the most conventional of character arcs and emotion-arousing reversals, as each must respond to a brainwashing, received as a prisoner of war in Korea, that threatens, in different but related ways, to control him. Such a summary, however, underestimates the extremeness of the plot. In a radical and unexpected twist, the brainwashed Shaw transforms himself from an ersatz to a genuine hero by preventing a military coup in which he has unwittingly played a major role. But to save his country he must murder his own mother and stepfather. He thus wills himself into becoming the worst kind of pariah, paradoxically carrying out the kind of self-destructive act that his communist brainwashers had intended him to perform, yet, because chance and his own strength of mind permit, doing so to achieve the opposite of their intentions. If, having shot down his parents, he finds it necessary to turn the rifle on himself and blow out his brains as well, the viewer is asked to understand this extreme finale as not only heroic, but life-affirming.

But this final sequence, driven by a suspense that is founded on those false assumptions, is preceded by a moving scene in which Frankenheimer allows us to see how Shaw is now prodded by the increasing horror of the infamy that, robot-like, he has coolly perpetrated upon command. Weeping confusedly, sensing the hitherto unfathomed horror of all he has done, Shaw begins to come to himself (as the clichéd phrase has it) in a phone call to Marco. The irony, of course, is that such a return, because it requires the commission of what in some sense is just as evil as what he has done, can hardly be salvific. In his own view, these final murders, the only ones he intends to commit, are self-damning. Arguably, these deaths must be paid for by the forfeit of his life, so completely do they violate the most deeply rooted of all taboos. And yet these killings also hold out the possibility of redemption because, in their punishment of the guilty and their partial remediation of the damage caused by their depredations, they restore the moral order Shaw has violated. In a turn of cosmic irony, this act both affirms and denies the transformation effected by his communist handlers. Shaw becomes the effective assassin they trained him to be, but, Samson-like, destroys both the elaborately conceived plans he was meant to serve and also those close to him who were intending to benefit from his dehumanization.

All the bewildered killer can utter, before finally putting the muzzle under his chin and pulling the trigger, is a desperate, inchoate plea: "Oh, God, Ben." In this moment of pained, transcendent communion, Shaw, we might say, speaks for many of Frankenheimer's protagonists, who seem compelled to follow to their peril, but also glory, the extreme logic of self-asserting refusal. It is Marco who correctly interprets and passes the final judgment on Shaw's actions, imagining the kind of conventionally unconventional citation that the man should have received were his deed one that could be publicly acknowledged.

Like *The Manchurian Candidate*, *The Fixer* also concludes with an endorsement of the heroism inherent in a Lutheran "no" ("I cannot do otherwise") that is simultaneously an affirmation of some greater truth, an assertion of self in the face of condemnation both within and without. It does not matter, as Malamud and Frankenheimer both realized, whether Bok is vindicated or exonerated by the court; what is important is that he presents himself before that court with that solidity of self he has come at last to possess, even if, like Raymond Shaw, it is *in extremis*, an affirmation of identity that may well be followed by his destruction.

More of What I Feel about Life

A traditional auteurist account of *The Fixer* and its place within the director's body of work, following the path laid out by Armstrong, is arguably compromised by a number of flaws, none, perhaps, more serious than the tendency (which I have here exemplified) to unify and thus "make sense" of a career by interpreting the films that constitute it as expressions of a limited set of themes. These films would be the textual reflexes of that supposedly essential quality of the gifted artist, a set of obsessions that demand continuing expression. Collectively, they enable a career to be conceived as a set of self-revealing messages, providing in composite a consistent impression of personality. This messaging distinguishes the auteur from his less valued and more numerous colleagues, the mere metteurs-en-scène, who simply translate to the screen the ideas of others and for whom, therefore, the prized category of the "personal" film does not exist. But because they must be formulated at a fairly abstract level in order to be properly inclusive, such themes, as guides to reading, often impose dubious kinds of unity on substantially disparate projects, producing blindness as well as insight. They provide an illusory sense of wholeness or consistency that minimizes the effects on a directorial career of inevitable professional vagaries: the elusive, limited, and limiting opportunities to make films; the chanciness of unpredictable, often disabling changes within the industry, within popular taste, and within critical fashion; and most crucially the ebb and flow of the creative impulse itself, the alternating flickering or bright burning of inspiration, that most indispensable and over-mythologized of neoromantic inner states.

In its traditional form, the auteurist insistence on an inevitably reductionist classification of different projects by theme, in other words, offers synchrony as an approach to the anatomizing of a directorial oeuvre, lending it a Saussurean orderliness that no diachronic analysis, which must be occupied with the messy improvidences of the moment, can provide. The critical pursuit of thematic classification, in the manner of a Leavisite reading, transforms the textual multiplicities of a career into a set of ideas that can be readily analyzed and evaluated, simplifying the task of understanding what a director has accomplished. And, as a protocol for the reading of an individual film, the search for theme poses a similar risk: that the linear unfolding which is textual semiosis is reduced to its supposed intended product, the message or (more tellingly) point that becomes crystallized after the always dispersing flow of images and sounds has run its course.

Despite the inevitable inaccuracies attendant in generalizing, I do not disavow what I have written above about Frankenheimer as a director fascinated by the self-defining possibilities of the obdurate refusal and the centrality of that refusal to *The Fixer*. In its vaguely existentialist emphasis on the decisive act, such an approach to his films responds deeply both to the vagaries of his biography (his own refusal, for example, to continue living in America and working within the Hollywood industry, at least in a traditional fashion) and the temper of his times, the sense in which, as Colin Wilson puts it in his influential paean to tortured individuality, *The Outsider*, the thinking man of the postwar era like Frankenheimer could not "live in the comfortable world of the bourgeois, accepting what he sees and touches as reality. . . . What he sees is *essentially* chaos." The outsider refuses to accept as order what he feels deep within is not. He cannot escape his haunting "sense of strangeness, of unreality" and must strike out on his own, like Yakov Bok and the protagonists of many (if not all) of Frankenheimer's film, in order to explore alternative possibilities, however fruitless the search may turn out to be (Wilson 15).

The understanding provided by an auteurist critical glance will move beyond distorting generalities and other forms of conceptual neatness only if it is enriched by a deep archaeology of context. And context must be more than the other, ostensibly similar films that the director has "signed"; ideally it must also include a rich trove of all the significant facts that production history reveals, facts that point more toward the particularity of the individual project. The critic, in short, must attend to the textual *parole* as well as to the directorial *langue*. Such contextualizing, of course, inevitably reveals the various ways in which authorship itself and thus meaning are more often dispersed than concentrated, with the director shown to be speaking for himself but also for others, thus problematizing the notion of a unifying theme with its supposed origin in self. If this project in some sense challenges the neo-romantic notion of textual production as "expression," somewhat paradoxically it can also confirm one of the judgments of traditional auteurism, namely the persistence of true artists in the pursuit of speaking themselves.

And this is true for Frankenheimer's filmmaking in general, and most especially so in the case of *The Fixer*. As the director recalled some years later, it was in looking over Malamud's book while it was still in page proofs that he discovered how the novel expressed "more of what I feel about life" than any other property he had previously considered. It was through re-voicing Malamud that he discovered how he could best express his own views on struggle and identity (and in the process comment on a Jewishness he shared with novelist and main character). This movement of artistic consciousness, flowing outward even as it turns inward, interestingly mimics the spiritual journey of Yakov Bok. As we have seen, Bok discovers that it is *through* being (mis)identified as the "eternal Jew" that he comes at last to be himself. He is able finally to speak himself through a string of significant abstractions that apply equally to the group that he has come to feel (has in fact been forced by circumstances to feel) that he represents. Like his co-religionists, he is innocent (of an ethnic calumny containing no truth), even as he acknowledges being both a Jew and also the brother of all others, including the *goyim*.

Jewishness as Metaphor

Perhaps the most important fact of the film's production history is that Frankenheimer was given the novel's proofs to read because he was known by the novelist's agents to be already working on a Malamud project (with scriptwriter Paul Sylbert), hoping to make a film version of an earlier novel, *The Assistant*, published in 1957. Interestingly, as Frankenheimer reports, this script was already well advanced when the proofs for *The Fixer* arrived; the other project was quickly abandoned, and Frankenheimer, eager that the best possible screen version be confected from a source for which he felt such enthusiasm, hired noted screenwriter Dalton Trumbo, with whom he worked closely (including going back to the facts of the Beilis case) in order to produce the script (Pratley, *Films* 79–81).[1] As Frankenheimer and company were working on the script, *The Fixer* became a literary sensation. Selling many thousands of copies and gaining for him considerable acclaim, winning both a National Book Award and a Pulitzer Prize, the novel, in fact, made Malamud's literary career, whose viability, at the time of its release, was certainly in question. As did critics at the time, who were not informed about the film's production history, it would be easy enough to misunderstand Frankenheimer's screen version of the novel in conventional terms. How surprising would it be, after all, that one of the most critically acclaimed best sellers of the decade was made into a Hollywood film, following an industry pattern well established at that point for several decades? But this is not the case. What is important in this screen adaptation is not the connection between filmmakers and written source, but the prior intellectual connection that had developed between the novelist and the director.

What first drew Frankenheimer's attention and interest was Malamud's approach to depicting the human condition, expressed consistently and poignantly (to invoke the language of auteurism) in two novels that are superficially quite distinct in terms of subject matter. *The Assistant* is an exploration of Lower East Side immigrant culture that paradoxically uses as a central structure and touchstone the life of Saint Francis of Assisi, with whom the novel's main character, the aptly named Frank, is obsessed. In this novel, imprisonment is also a central theme, here taking shape sociologically, as the entrapment of the immigrant Jews by their economic marginalization and alienation from mainstream American culture. For Malamud, however, in Robert Alter's famous phrase, "Jewishness is metaphor," a structure grounded in real experience that speaks (in the Spinozan sense) a more general truth. Here Alter speaks of *The Assistant*, but his analysis of its philosophical themes applies equally, perhaps even more forcefully, to *The Fixer*:

> Imprisonment, like the condition of being a Jew with which it is elsewhere identified, is seen here as a general image for the moral life with all its imponderable obstacles to spontaneous self-fulfillment: it is living in concern for the state of one's soul, which means knowing with an awful lucidity how circumscribed the will is in its ability to effect significant change, how recalcitrant and cowardly it can be. . . . The prison, like the *schlemiel* who is usually its chief inmate, is Malamud's way of suggesting that to be fully a man is to accept the most painful limitations. . . . Malamud sees in the collective Jewish experience of the past a model not

only of suffering and confinement, but also of a very limited yet precious possibility of triumph in defeat, freedom in imprisonment. (34–35)

Alter echoes the view that Malamud himself expressed of Jewish writers in the diaspora, who, assimilating but also resisting the mainstream cultures in which they find themselves strangers in some sense, are pressured toward "intertwining theirs with others," which results in the "historical conversion of the Jews to a kind of universal man." And so, "every man is a Jew though he may not know it," a recognition that "should ally human beings to one another" (Malamud, "Jewishness" 137). Or, as Frankenheimer put it, commenting on what he acknowledged as the main theme of *The Fixer*, "Although Bok was a Jew, he could be any man, any time, anywhere" (Pratley, *Films* 80). This paradoxical universalism, so tellingly expressed in the film's final line, was the essence of the fiction from the beginning, the story of a Jew that was not, in the final analysis, simply a Jewish story. Rather it was a story in which the particularity of Jewishness is both affirmed and denied—and yet this particularity was not the starting point for the novelist. Like Frankenheimer searching for sources through which he could express his views on life,[2] Malamud too, as he put it, had long "determined to do a novel using political or social experience as the basis of my fiction" (qtd. in P. Davis 239). He rejected a number of possibilities, which tellingly also dealt with prisoners: the cases of Caryl Chessman, Sacco and Vanzetti, and Alfred Dreyfus. Malamud finally decided that the embattled French officer was a "dullish man, and though he endured well he did not suffer well" (qtd. in Davis 240).

Malamud finally settled on the Beilis case because it was "hard to believe, but it is the truth" and also because it possessed "the quality of the humiliation and mistreatment of the Jews under the Nazis" (qtd. in Davis 241). The novel, Malamud avers, was intended as a fictionalization—indirect to be sure—of the Holocaust. And yet if the case could be recounted as an analogy for the racialism that ultimately results in the Final Solution, Yakov Bok finally triumphs, if only in the theater of his own mind, over the forces that would crush him in order to oppress the people with whom he has hitherto been only superficially connected. He is pointedly not a victim, and that label, so Robert Novick argues, was "actively shunned" by most American Jews in the 1950s and 1960s, who "regarded the victimhood symbolized by the Holocaust as a feature of the Old World that they, likewise, were putting behind them. . . . Among the useless and outworn characteristics to be sloughed off was the common negative stereotype of the whining, complaining, of the self-pitying Jew—the stigmata of the Jew as victim" (Novick 121–22).

Such an approach to representing (or, perhaps better, evoking) the Holocaust has met in the last two decades with increasing criticism. Ezra Cappell, for example, complains that Malamud's "always assimilated, paper-thin Jews are unable to shoulder the awesome historical weight they are forced to bear"

(Cappell 39). Even though noted critic Granville Hicks advocated the reading of *The Fixer* as Holocaust fiction in which the novelist's intent is for "one man to stand for six million," Cappell, among others, has argued that the book reveals Malamud's "inability to create an effective Holocaust story" because he has "severed ethnicity from religion" in a misguided attempt to universalize the destruction of European Jewry under the Nazis (qtd. in Davis 257). This approach to writing (and reading) the Holocaust during the middle 1960s was widely acclaimed, as the widespread enthusiasm for Anne Frank's universalism makes clear. *The Fixer* in fact takes much the same approach to providing a moral understanding of the century's most significant event for the world's Jews as Edward Lewis Wallant's *The Pawnbroker* (1961; film version by Sidney Lumet released in 1964), in which a Holocaust survivor's work as a pawnbroker in postwar Harlem forces him to acknowledge that the Jewish experience of the Holocaust is more importantly universal than particular, a collective injustice similar to others, like the structural poverty and racism then endemic in the American inner city.

But while Bosley Crowther praised *The Pawnbroker*'s moral vision, Renata Adler railed against *The Fixer*'s universalism, remarking that such a drama requires a "note of particularity to have meaning or to register at all" and ignoring completely the way in which Frankenheimer, following Malamud, dramatizes in Bok a certain quality of the modern Jewish *mentalité*. Moreover, she does not read *The Fixer* as in any sense a Holocaust film (though it was its indirect evocation of that event that in large part made for the novel's success), and in this judgment she has been followed by film historians, as Frankenheimer's film does not appear on notable lists of Holocaust films.

The most significant failure of criticism, however, has been to ignore how the screen version of *The Fixer*—using Malamud's text as a structure through which the director might voice his own views—treats with subtlety and understanding important questions posed by the fact of ethnic identity, particularly Jewish identity, in a post-Enlightenment world. Bok comes to understand himself as both a Jew *and* the brother to every man; his story is thus emphatically not, as *Variety* proclaimed, simply "a ponderous diatribe against injustice" (qtd. in Armstrong 185). He is both an individual, with the enduring claim to be treated as himself in a modern court of law, and, willy-nilly, the representative of a *Gemeinschaft* that determines, for both his ill and good, who he "is." To put this another way, Bok refuses to allow himself to be subsumed by a lie that vilifies an entire people, even as he embraces the import of that lie (he comes to accept that he is a Jew like any other). He is both assimilated and set apart, special and ordinary, undefined by history even as he embodies a particular form of history, a character in the mold of Frankenheimer's most interesting protagonists, whose refusals are also always affirmations that define who they have come to be.

NOTES

1. Frankenheimer and Trumbo consulted Maurice Samuel's well-researched account of the Beilis case, coincidentally published the same year as *The Fixer*.
2. Consider, for example, the director's remarks about Richard Condon's *The Manchurian Candidate*, a novel that, Frankenheimer confesses, "had great social and political significance for me at the time," or what he says about James Drought's *The Gypsy Moths*, which "fitted in well with what I was trying to say at the time, the matter of choice" (qtd. in Pratley, *Films* 39, 88).

Jonah

BILL KROHN

One characteristic of directors trained in television is their extraordinary stamina. John Frankenheimer pays tribute to that underrated virtue in *The French Connection II* (1975), where Gene Hackman's pursuit on foot of Fernando Rey making his getaway by boat is far more engaging than William Friedkin's famed *French Connection* car chase (1971). Out of shape after his detox, dodging through Marseille crowds with his eye on the boat that he isn't even sure contains his quarry, almost too exhausted by the end to clamber over a low barrier when he finally sees an opening onto the water, Hackman squeezes off two shots as Rey emerges onto the deck, sure that his Droopy-like adversary has been left far behind. Bang bang!—Rey, startled, tumbles back and the film is over. Frankenheimer's career was like that chase.

Continuities

We know how it began: a director he was seconding on a live episode of *Danger* saw himself on camera, cried "Save me!" and threw up on his assistant director, who proceeded to finish the show. Promoted to director, the assistant soon found himself doing prestige dramas and, when the Young Turks of the cathode tube hit the pavement in the late 1950s, arty movies. That *Danger* episode was about an escape from a German prison camp, which set one of the topical templates for the subsequent career. Frankenheimer's next big break came when he was hired to replace the director of *Birdman of Alcatraz* (1962) and saved the film. Prison was now locked in as a Frankenheimer "obsession," although like many directorial obsessions, it was acquired by accident.

The offscreen substitution must have also lodged in his subconscious, because it's the basis for the commie plot in *The Manchurian Candidate* (1962), a film he selected to make when he was riding high: the red-baiting Democratic candidate for vice president is supposed to replace his running mate at the top of the ticket when the man is slain by a hypnotized drone during his victory speech to the TV cameras. Senator Jordan's observation of the red-baiter, that "if John Iselin were a paid Soviet agent, he could not do more harm to this country than he's doing now," is a classic liberal line,[1] and Frankenheimer was nothing if not a classic 1960s liberal (Jacobson and González 45). When Frank Sinatra called his friend President John F. Kennedy on behalf of worried UA executives to get his okay before proceeding with the film, JFK, a rabid cold warrior who kept trying to have Castro assassinated (Hersh 268–93), said it was one of his favorite books, along with the James Bond series.

Then JFK was assassinated, and after Frankenheimer devoted himself body and soul to Robert Kennedy's 1968 primary campaign for president, which at one time was supposed to end with a victory dinner at Frankenheimer's home in Malibu, Bobby was assassinated, too, by a real-life hypnotic drone, with a second gunman administering the killing shot (see Melanson; O'Sullivan). Kennedy had asked Frankenheimer to stand with him on the platform when he made his victory speech, but he demurred, thinking it would look bad for the candidate to have a movie director next to him. "The man standing next to him was shot, too," he told Charles Champlin. "If I'd been with him, that would've been me." But in a way, it was as if it had been.

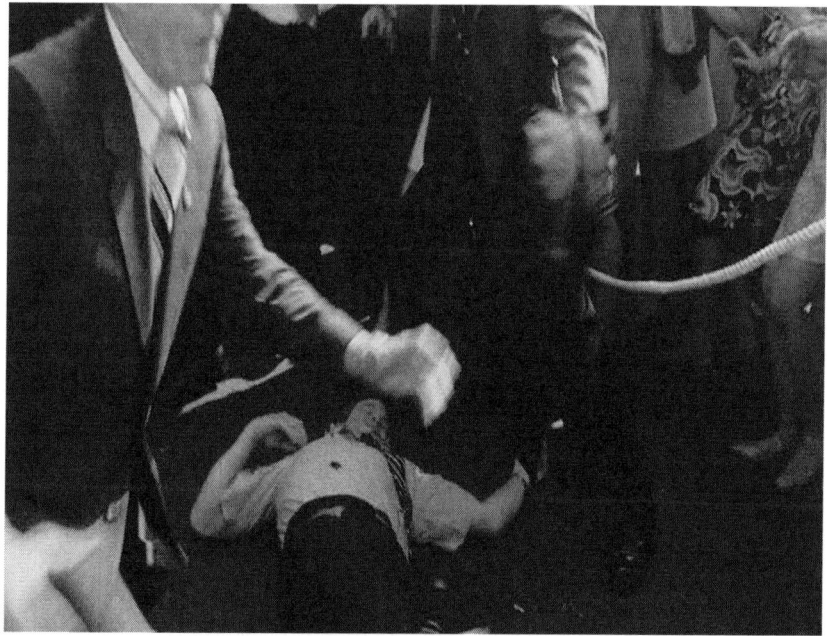

When Wallace (Gary Sinise) in *George Wallace* (Turner Network Television, 1997) is shot while campaigning for president, the scene recalls images of Robert Kennedy after he was assassinated in Los Angeles.

Digital frame enlargement.

"My world was over as I knew it," Frankenheimer later said of Bobby's assassination (Thurber and King). He fell into depression and drink, and his career went south, with occasional oases of commercial success. His films also changed, keeping abreast of the times. The early Frankenheimers are made up of Orson Welles shots reconfigured into contrast-y black-and-white images that would stand out on the small screen and certainly stand out on a big one. One habit he never kicked was deep-focus shots of big heads looming in the foreground while homunculi in sharp focus listen in the background.

But even before the second Kennedy assassination his style had undergone modifications: a car nut like Kenneth Grahame's Mr. Toad, Frankenheimer had discovered auto racing and broadened his directorial palette to include multiple images with *Grand Prix* (1966). After the assassination, he studiously blended into the Hollywood New Wave, so that he had the distinction of figuring prominently in two Manny Farber *fatwas* against two completely different schools of cinematic hotshots: "Hard Sell Cinema," about the New York School of the 1950s and 1960s (Polito 477–86), and "The New Breed of Filmmakers: A Multiplication of Myths" (716–21), where other, bigger targets included Francis Ford Coppola and Martin Scorsese.

Frankenheimer achieved success with *French Connection II* and again with *Black Sunday* (1977). The film is more of a comic book than the novel, where the Mossad agent who would be played by Robert Shaw compares himself to Hitler for using torture to obtain information about the plan. In the film version, this agent has no self-doubts, and nothing in Frankenheimer's history suggests that he would ever have used this character to raise any. In fact, the bomb-laden dirigible targeting the Super Bowl is a blue-screen descendent of the Soviet sneak attack, scheduled for Christmas Eve, that is portrayed with stock footage in "Forbidden Area," Frankenheimer's first drama for *Playhouse 90*, aired in 1956.

The debut episode of that distinguished live-television series, "Forbidden Area" is no *Judgment at Nuremberg* (1961). "Pick a time, like when free men are worshiping the Prince of Peace, then strike!" intones the offscreen voice of the series's producer, Martin Manulis. The scene where the Soviet agent (Tab Hunter) is interrogated about baseball by his invisible handlers follows an uncanny opening sequence (scripted by Rod Serling) where a discussion of baseball in a Chicago bar becomes increasingly sinister until we realize that the bar, manned by a creepy bartender who seems to have more than baseball on his mind, is somewhere near Moscow and the seemingly banal conversation about sports statistics is part of a final exam for saboteurs. The stunning opening of this forgotten broadcast may even have given Frankenheimer the clue for how to film the sequence in *The Manchurian Candidate* that goes back and forth between a boring lecture on hydrangeas happening somewhere outside New Orleans and a blood-curdling demonstration of brainwashing happening somewhere inside communist China—a scenography that is implied in only the vaguest terms by Richard Condon's novel.

The Manchurian Candidate, for all its supposed paradoxes, puts onscreen the paranoid fantasy that underwrote the Vietnam War, but like the best moments in "Forbidden Area," it "hallucinates" the ideology of cold war liberalism in the same way that Sergei Eisenstein's The General Line (1929) "hallucinates" Stalinism, to use Jean Narboni's formula for that film's double-edged quality (20).[2] Frankenheimer would continue to mirror the ideology of liberalism by crawling inside its paranoias until the very last phase of his career, when paranoia and its consequences became the subject of his most lucid film, Path to War (2002), but the hallucinatory quality of the early black-and-white thrillers would be replaced by realism, with the megacephalic signature shots continuing to lurk around the edges of the mise-en-scène. Like Jaws (1975), Black Sunday appears to be happening in the real world. And on September 11, 2001, it did.[3]

Reluctant Prophet

Interviewed on the set of The Island of Dr. Moreau (1996), Frankenheimer identified the stylistic unity of his work in the 1990s as follows: "The look of this film is very similar to the look of my last four movies—a very fluent style with lots of moving shots and depth-of-focus shots. It's a very realistic look." Counting backward takes us to Year of the Gun (1991), a feature film that is rarely talked about in conjunction with the director's triumphant return to television except as the last of the series of genre efforts whose dismal box-office performance made it necessary. But Frankenheimer is right: Year of the Gun did contribute to the evolution of the dynamic, in-your-face camera style used in Against the Wall (1994), a style powered by the invention of the Steadicam, which had an obvious appeal for a director who once wrapped a camera cable around a fountain on the set of a live TV drama until the camera could barely move.

What's more, Year of the Gun is also thematically related to the series of films kicked off by Against the Wall because it is about revolution. Set in Italy in 1978, this adaptation of a best seller by a journalist for Newsweek recounts fictional events surrounding the kidnapping of Italy's former prime minister Aldo Moro by the Red Brigades, a clandestine revolutionary organization that was making headlines throughout the 1970s.

A Malibu liberal with close ties to the Kennedy family, Frankenheimer seems an unlikely filmmaker to be interested in revolution. But the 100 days he spent working for Bobby Kennedy had been a revolutionary experience within the fluid confines of the electoral process, not only because RFK was leading an insurgency against the candidate decreed by his own party, but because that one-of-a-kind campaign, happening at a once-in-a-lifetime moment, channeled the energies of diverse groups looking for an alternative to politics as usual.

The coalition that came together around the Kennedy campaign in the spring of 1968 included civil rights activists and Black Panthers, Cesar Chavez's Farm Workers' Union and Democratic machine politicians, blue-collar workers and Wall Street protesters, all drawn together by the Kennedy legacy and the mantra "Peace in Vietnam": just about everyone was there but the outraged supporters of the donnish Eugene McCarthy, who had been the first Democratic candidate against the war. RFK himself was a changed man after his brother's death: the enforcer with the brass knuckles emerging reluctantly from the shadows, quoting Aeschylus and Camus in his last speeches and daring death while generating an outpouring of popular fervor unlike anything America had seen since the end of World War II had brought on the chilly consensus of the cold war.

That had been Frankenheimer's revolution—one of many that briefly took shape in the sixties, only to be co-opted or blown away—and he spent the rest of his life trying to figure out what had gone wrong. In *Year of the Gun*, Andrew McCarthy plays David Rayborne, a disillusioned sixties radical who gave up on politics after being implicated in a fatal explosion in a bomb factory. He's in Italy to finish a novel about the Red Brigades that unfortunately outlines a plan to kidnap Aldo Moro (Aldo Mengolini), the politician who was forging an alliance between the center-left Christian Democrats and the Italian Communist Party, and the revolutionaries take this MacGuffin very seriously when the manuscript falls into their hands. In one grimly comic scene, when they stake out Moro's apartment, they find Rayborne in the bushes doing the same thing.

Emerging intact from the ensuing bloodshed to peddle a best seller on a TV talk show,[4] Rayborne sees his prophecy come true—Moro's kidnapping is reenacted by Frankenheimer as an anticlimax to his thriller plot. Moro ends up dead like Robert Kennedy, and it is Frankenheimer's sense of having been an accidental prophet, or perhaps catalyst, for both Kennedy assassinations that gives weight to the portrayal in *Year of the Gun* of the relationship between a fictitious thriller in the tradition of *The Manchurian Candidate* and a real-life terrorist act.[5] The fact that Moro's death at his captors' hands had long been a subject for conspiratorial speculations in Italy—his "historical compromise" scared the United States as much as it did the revolutionaries would only have made the parallels more interesting to Frankenheimer when he tackled the subject in 1991.

Misconstruing the film's highly personal reflections as standard-issue rant about the complicity of the media in political violence, critics praised Frankenheimer's depiction of a country in the grip of a revolutionary struggle but found Andrew McCarthy and Sharon Stone out of place in any story with pretenses to realism. (Is that why the two of them hide in a movie theater displaying Italian *Star Wars* posters when they're escaping from the Red Brigade goons?) For his next film Frankenheimer would focus on realistically portraying the Attica prison uprising and relegate his stars, Samuel Jackson and Kyle MacLachlan, to supporting roles.

Revolution and Utopia

The Attica prison uprising was the subject of a radical documentary made at the time by Cinda Firestone, and the politics of *Against the Wall* are not that different from Firestone's, even if the dramaturgy is traditional, interweaving parallel stories of characters played by a white and a black star with the depiction of events at the New York state prison. The thesis, which was confirmed by a hearing and a lawsuit after the event, is that the order by then New York governor Nelson Rockefeller and his commissioner of prisons, Russell Oswald (Phillip Bosco), to take the prison back by force caused the deaths of twenty-nine inmates and nine prison guards who were being held hostage, all mowed down by the guns of the local police. Frankenheimer presents the uprising as a revolution, part of the larger revolution that was brewing in America in the late sixties—the head guard (Frederic Forrest) says this to the new guard (MacLachlan) who is our surrogate, and an upstate New York cop announces that retaking the prison will be payback for the hippies and black revolutionaries who are causing him sleepless nights, just before he joyously slaughters everyone in sight.

Most of the leaders of the uprising saw themselves as revolutionaries with limited, reasonable aims—reform of Rockefeller's prisons and amnesty for the takeover of Attica—and their ally in the film is Commissioner Oswald. This well-meaning man insists on negotiating, even though the warden, whose callousness and brutality has caused the uprising, wants to retake the prison immediately before the situation gets out of hand. Oswald is supported by Rockefeller (shown only as a beaming headshot) for four days, and obtains twenty-eight concessions demanded by the convicts, but when negotiations break down over the issue of amnesty and a personal visit from "Rocky"—and when the commissioner himself is almost taken hostage—he and his boss order the fatal onslaught.

By leaving open the tactical question—was immediately retaking the prison a better option than negotiating, then attacking?—Frankenheimer shows that the contradictory behavior of Rockefeller and Oswald was the worst option of all. Rockefeller was the most prominent example in the 1960s of that now-extinct species, a liberal Republican, and he still harbored presidential ambitions for which he was ready to sacrifice the lives of the working-class guards and the black convicts to avoid looking soft to the electorate. The film not only sides with the limited revolutionary aims of the prisoners; it uses a revolutionary situation to shine a critical light on the liberal alternative. That is exactly what happened in the United States in the late sixties and early seventies, which left us scathing satires like Phil Ochs's "Love Me, I'm a Liberal" as a reminder of how having the idea of revolution on the table once blew open the airless enclosure of our national politics.

Frankenheimer always planned to do a film about Bobby Kennedy, but the Kennedy family, more risk-averse than its male scions, entrusted the job to its court painter, David Wolper. Perhaps in compensation, Frankenheimer's next film for HBO, *The Burning Season* (1994), told the story of another revolutionary stopped by a bullet, Chico Mendes, who built a union of Brazilian rubber-tree tappers to block the deforestation of the Amazon and was assassinated by one of the big ranchers whose plans for expansion he was opposing.

At one point, Mendes is flown to the United States by a filmmaker who wants to portray him as the leader of a green revolution, to which he mildly objects that he wants to save the trees for the rubber tappers, not for a bunch of tree humpers in Beverly Hills. This facile self-flagellation is of a piece with the film's insistence on giving equal time to the viewpoint of the fascist ranchers—which is to say that the whole project is handicapped by the script Frankenheimer inherited from executive producer David (*Chariots of Fire*) Puttnam, particularly when it keeps shoving an old woman with what is known in Hollywood as "a great face" in the forefront of every scene showing Mendes's unionists. Perhaps that is also why Raul Julia's ironic, passionless Chico Mendes is more like Eugene McCarthy than he is like Robert Kennedy.

Frankenheimer bounced back artistically with *Andersonville* (1996), produced by the southern mogul Ted Turner. The story of the hideous prisoner-of-war camp for Union soldiers in Andersonville, Georgia, had been something of an ideological football in the 1950s. Novelist MacKinlay Kantor, who also wrote Curtis LeMay's memoirs, won a Pulitzer Prize for his 1956 best seller about the prison that implicitly evoked memories of the Shoah in support of America's postwar alliance with Germany against the threat of communism, with much time devoted to exonerating innocent farmers living on the outskirts of the compound (see Smithpeter chaps. 1–3 passim). Saul Levitt's 1959 Broadway play *The Andersonville Trial* (filmed for PBS in 1970, at the height of War of Vietnamese Liberation) was a revisionist take on the story that portrayed the sadistic commandant, Henry Wirz, as a tragic scapegoat.

The script that Turner commissioned from veteran TV writer David Rintels for his follow-up to the hit TNT miniseries *Gettysburg* went back to prisoners' diaries for its source and focused on doings inside the prison. Echoing the view that Andersonville had been the American Auschwitz, Frankenheimer told Charles Champlin that he hesitated to take on the massive project because "I was becoming the *mavin* of prison movies" (201). But he found a dramatic thread in Rintels's script that links *Andersonville* with *Against the Wall* as a film that uses its prison setting for reflections on revolution: the armed revolt of prisoners that brought an end to the reign of the Raiders, a group of blue-shirt Kapos in league with their jailers who had been living high by preying on their fellow prisoners.

Once the Raiders have been disarmed in a fierce battle, Commandant Wirz (straightforwardly portrayed as a loon) allows them to be tried for murder and thievery in hopes that the concession will help him maintain order. During the trial in the prison yard, which is the dramatic centerpiece of a four-hour epic of starvation, disease, and cruelty, the debate turns on the legality of hanging prisoners who have committed crimes against their own, given that Federal Army law has no force in the prison setting—an ambiguous situation recalling the short-lived revolutionary community led by a Black Muslim (Samuel L. Jackson) that springs up in the yard at Attica. These scenes of "the other Andersonville Trial" set forth an ideal of justice where Revolution is reconciled with Law, like the public tribunals set up after the Cuban Revolution to curb popular reprisals and punish wealthy landowners, state officials, police, soldiers, straw bosses, and hired thugs for crimes committed during the Batista era. The prison-yard court is a dramatic situation for representing the utopian ideal of any revolution that aims at founding a new society after the shooting is over.

The Island of Dr. Moreau

The history of the film that marked Frankenheimer's return to features after *Andersonville* is murky, and that may be why it is the most interesting of his unofficial quartet of films about revolution. The young South African-born writer-director Richard Stanley was replaced in mid-production at the behest of the film's star, Val Kilmer, and Frankenheimer brought along the screenwriter of *Against the Wall*, Ron Hutchinson, who had already done a rewrite for him on *The Burning Season*. (Legend has it that Stanley stuck around, disguised as a dog-boy extra, and watched the film being finished—IMDB lists him as the uncredited actor who played the "Melting Bulldog Boy.") When the film subsequently tanked, everyone but the special effects artists scattered, casting blame in all directions and making it impossible to assign responsibility for specific details, but my guess would be that *The Island of Dr. Moreau* is a Richard Stanley film largely shot or re-shot by Frankenheimer and patched up by Hutchinson with a voiceover to cover gaps created by Kilmer, whose erratic behavior had been a problem for all concerned.

In his allegory of Darwinism (originally published in 1896), H. G. Wells predicted not only gene splicing, which substitutes for vivisection in this version of the story, but that other modern invention, the concentration camp, ruled over by a Mengele type who is operating on his experimental subjects without anesthesia in his House of Pain. In Stanley's rewrite, that horror becomes an obstetric hospital, and Moreau becomes another in the gallery of villains Marlon Brando played at the end of his career. The anti-imperialist actor makes Moreau a caricature of the White Man's Burden, who is wearing sunglasses and covered with what looks like SP-200 sunscreen when first we see him: a sweet, dotty, benevolent dictator who wants the beast-men to call him "Father." Unlike Wells's Moreau, he is not the amoral embodiment of the blind evolutionary process, but a believer in the perfectibility of Man who forbids his subjects to eat meat, keeping them under control with injections of hormones and endorphins, boring sermons from the Speaker of the Law (Ron Pearlman), and electrical implants that he uses to zap them when they disobey, permitting him to grandly forgive transgressors after a showy public trial instead of killing them.

Dr. Moreau (Marlon Brando) in *The Island of Dr. Moreau* (New Line Cinema, 1996) is a whited sepulchre: Western imperialism wearing the grotesque mask of enlightened benevolence.
Digital frame enlargement.

Moreau's cagy reactions when it begins to dawn on him that Hyena (Daniel Rigney) and his henchmen have not come to his private compound in the middle of the night on a friendly visit (Hyena has torn out his implant . . .) set the comic tone for a series of violent scenes—beginning with Moreau being eaten alive by his creations—that portray a revolution where Murphy's Law rules. When Hyena gets his hands on a machine gun, he handles it with all the aplomb of Pedro Armendariz's general delightedly trying out his first Gatling gun in *The Wild Bunch* (1969). (An uncredited Walon Green, the screenwriter of *The Wild Bunch*, was one of Richard Stanley's co-writers.) "Burn it!" shrieks Hyena, setting fire to the dock and ship that are the island's only link to the world. (He is echoing "Let it burn!" shouted by the nihilistic leader of the uprising [Clarence Williams III] in *Against the Wall*.) Rather than fall into the hands of Azazello (Temuera Morrison), her "father's" dogman major-domo, who has started to regress in a particularly unpleasant way, the panther girl Aissa (Fairuza Balk) imitates Mae Marsh's stoic virgin Flora escaping from Gus the black rapist in *The Birth of a Nation* (1915). Moreau is Kurtz in clown face (*Apocalypse Now* writer Michael Herr was another uncredited collaborator on Stanley's script), so that Montgomery (Kilmer's character) doing his impression of Moreau is a travesty of a travesty, and so on.

The flurry of film references, which is probably the work of film school graduate Richard Stanley (except for the self-quotation from *Against the Wall*), reduces the dyad of Third World insurgency and enlightened imperialism (which is still official U.S. policy in 2010, under the deluded rubric of "nation building") to a carnivalesque riot of clichés; but that dyad was Frankenheimer's, too. After playing thoughtful variations on it in three films for television where the Law is the utopian horizon of Revolution, he films it masterfully as an impossible contradiction at the end of *Moreau*, where the Law is a ghastly joke: "A series of propositions they called the Law battled in their minds with the deep-seated, ever rebellious cravings of their animal natures," says Wells's narrator. "This Law they were ever repeating, I found—and ever breaking."

The ending of the film feels like something Frankenheimer devised with Hutchinson to go out on a positive note: the Speaker, a dogboy, and the tiny sloth-man watch the epitome of European civilization, Douglas (David Thewlis), sailing away on a makeshift raft, after the Speaker has refused his offer to help them stop their regression to bestiality: "No more scientists," the Speaker says, which puts the emphasis on the old wheeze about the dangers of tampering with nature, but after I saw Frankenheimer's rough cut someone added a pessimistic epilogue from H. G. Wells.[6] A lawyer who was on a peace-keeping mission for the UN when a plane crash stranded him on Moreau's island, Douglas fears his fellow men when he returns to civilization, recognizing in them the same unstable mixture of reason and instinct he has seen in the beast men. I assume that Frankenheimer added or at least OK'd the epilogue and the documentary montage of violent images accompanying it, which echoes the first images of *Against the Wall*, where peace demonstrations alternate with violent repression (the assassinations of Martin Luther King and RFK, the massacre at Kent State) to frame a historical context for what happened at Attica.

George Wallace and *Path to War*

In between his last two films for television, Frankenheimer made two more features, both thrillers, the genre that had kept him working during the years of his alcohol-fueled breakdown. Critics spoke of a return to form in *Ronin* (1998), and that's just what's wrong with it: the scenes of the heist being planned are textbook examples of what Manny Farber meant by "Hard Sell Cinema," tailored to the tube and wildly overstated on the big screen. Because Frankenheimer is still trying to make legible on an eight-inch screen the antagonism that sixth-billed Sean Bean feels toward Robert De Niro the instant he joins the group, Bean indulges in expressions of loathing and impotent fury so outrageous every time he gets his close-up that one wonders why he isn't drummed out of the group on the spot. Then at the end, Mr. Toad takes over and finally gets to stage a car chase better than the one in *French Connection*.

But *Ronin* made money and *Reindeer Games* (2000) cratered, shot down by the same critics who had adored the efficient mechanics of Mr. Toad's last wild ride (the last unless we count the car-chase coda in *Ambush* [2001], made appropriately enough as a commercial for BMX). Knowing that *Reindeer Games*, one of Frankenheimer's most personal films (with a superb, understated performance by Ben Affleck), was recut by the studio and trashed by the critics, one can understand why he kept going back to the freedom of television, as he did after first experiencing the slings and arrows of feature filmmaking while doing *The Young Stranger* (1957).[7] On that occasion he proceeded to make television history by directing forty-two episodes of *Playhouse 90*, an experience to which he harked back in his last two television films.

Although *George Wallace* originated again with TNT, it strikingly recalls Frankenheimer's 1957 *Playhouse 90* episode "The Death of Manolete" in one respect: that docudrama was scripted by bullfighting expert Barnaby Conrad, who had written a book with the same title, and a young TV writer, Paul Monash; four decades later Monash teamed with Marshall Frady, the author of *Wallace*, to write *George Wallace*. Frankenheimer said he was surprised when he read the script, which drastically rewrites the story of one of the worst villains in the civil rights wars of the 1950s and 1960s, and he would say the same thing about the script HBO sent him for *Path to War* (2002) after Barry Levinson dropped out of the project, which portrays Lyndon Johnson and his advisors as more conflicted about the escalation of America's war against North Vietnam than they admitted publicly at the time they were pursuing their ruinous policy.[8]

While stopping short of exonerating Wallace and LBJ, Frankenheimer portrays them with sympathetic understanding, which is particularly justified in the case of Wallace by the transformation he underwent after being crippled in the attempted assassination by the mysterious Arthur Bremer. During the period after Wallace had been born again and reconciled with Alabama's black community, who helped elect him to his fourth term as governor, he invited the paroled Bremer to the governor's mansion so he could forgive him, but Bremer demurred. The potent melodrama of the scene where Wallace (Gary Sinise) spontaneously goes into Martin Luther King's old church on a rainy night and asks the black congregation for forgiveness has been exaggerated in the film, but it also really happened.

The real agenda of these last two docudramas is political, however, because Wallace, like Johnson, was a liberal Democrat at the start of his career. A protégé of Governor Big Jim Folsom (Joe Don Baker), he was a liberal judge who ran for governor promising to improve the lot of Alabama's poor, black and white alike, only to be defeated by the Klan's opposition to any candidate who didn't stand up for the cause of segregation, which was under fire from the Supreme Court decision to integrate public schools. That's when Wallace won office by becoming a virulent segregationist, then went on to campaign three times for president on a tacitly racist platform that found a receptive audience among traditionally Democratic voters in the North, and still does in its current Rovian variant. As Frankenheimer put it in his interview with TNT: "Wallace is the Faust of our generation, a tragic hero who sold his soul." He is also a key figure in the realignment that created the present divided political landscape, although his daughter Peggy supported Barack Obama in 2008 and thinks her father would have, too, had he lived to see that campaign.[9]

This is obviously great dramatic material, and Frankenheimer squeezes out every drop of emotion, showing Wallace's second wife, Cornelia (a young Angelina Jolie), dancing with him in his wheelchair and trying to coax an erection, and the black-prison-trustee servant Archie (Clarence Williams III) bathing his body with its pipe-stem legs and back covered with bed sores. Archie is an invented composite character who seriously considers driving an ice pick into Wallace's skull when they're alone in the kitchen one night. But at the end it's Archie who wheels the governor into the Dexter Avenue Baptist Church to make his speech of repentance and wheels him out again (a deep focus shot of the tiny figure coming up the aisle while members of the congregation reach out to him as he passes by) as the choir sings—appropriately, for once—"Amazing Grace."

Frankenheimer later called his version of Lyndon Johnson (Michael Gambon) in *Path to War* "a modern King Lear," but that's probably because he was reluctant to admit he had created yet another Faust story, although Gambon, who out-roars the storm whenever LBJ is having one of his famous rages, obviously took the *King Lear* analogy to heart. (Among other Frankenheimer films that are Faust stories, the most obvious is *Seconds* [1966].) Another liberal Democrat from the South, Johnson was elected president in 1964 by the biggest majority in history, with plans to complete FDR's New Deal by eradicating racial injustice and poverty in America. Many of his programs were passed into law, including Medicare and the Civil Rights Act of 1964 (Sinise does a cameo as Wallace paying Johnson a visit and meeting his match in the great bull-thrower), but the "Great Society" was derailed—and Johnson's presidency with it—by America's disastrous involvement in the War of Vietnamese Liberation. *George Wallace* and *Path to War* are a diptych about the decline and fall of American liberalism, embodied in bigger-than-life Faustian protagonists whose tempters are, respectively, the Ku Klux Klan and Secretary of Defense Robert McNamara (Alec Baldwin).

Frankenheimer's signature composition: a diminutive Clark Clifford (Donald Sutherland, *left*) remonstrates with a looming Lyndon B. Johnson (Michael Gambon) in *Path to War* (Avenue Pictures Productions, 2002).
Digital frame enlargement.

In *Path to War* Johnson inveighs against McNamara and the generals for telling him to escalate, but he always does what they say, while Undersecretary of State George Ball (Bruce McGill) plays the reproving chorus in every meeting, until the leader of the free world is stumbling from escalation to escalation as his advisors desert or change their minds, and his freedom of action dwindles to zero. The construction recalls Northrop Frye's description of tragedy: the hero is free to do whatever he chooses until he chooses to jump off a cliff, after which gravity takes over. The second half of *Path to War* is a zombie movie, populated by figures drained of life and purpose, in which Johnson mechanically responds with more troops and bombs to the latest optimistic projections from two buffoonish generals, Earle G. Wheeler (Frederic Forrest) and William Westmoreland (Tom Skerritt), until he makes his decision not to seek reelection.

Visually, these are very different films. *George Wallace* is filmed with a Steadicam like *Against the Wall* and sprinkled with punchy baroque compositions, as if Frankenheimer relished the chance to finally remake *Citizen Kane* (1941), although the time scheme is actually pretty straightforward, recounted in double chronological order: beginning with the day of the shooting and following Wallace's downward spiral and eventual redemption while flashing back to show his rise to power. What gives this time scheme its cumulative power is the collision and superimposition of images that it makes possible—repeated premonitory landmarks like King's church and the Edmund Pettus Bridge (in Selma, Alabama, where on March 7, 1965, civil rights demonstrators came under police attack), and eerier juxtapositions: Archie's brother telling him that he "can strike the blow" before Bremer does it for him at the Laurel Shopping Center; Lurleen Wallace (Mare Winningham) meeting the trophy wife who will replace her after her death from cancer when Cornelia is just thirteen, and already sizing up George; or Big Jim stumping around on a bandaged foot and brandishing his crutch during a tirade at the mansion when he comes to ask for a pension increase, just before we see Wallace in his wheelchair for the first time, with spinning wheels of destiny supplying the transition. The film is happening inside Wallace's head, and the repeated black-and-white images of Klansmen in white and marchers under a blazing sun are ghosts, intercut with tight close-ups of his eyes.

The narrative of *Path to War* is lineal but elliptical, and the visuals pass the sobriety test with high marks. Employing very little shaky camerawork, ninety percent of the scenes take place in rooms at the White House with white men sitting around big conference tables earnestly debating their next plan of action while the consequences of their decisions appear on TV screens . . . and once through an office window when a shocked McNamara watches the Quaker protester Norman Morrison (Victor Slezak) set fire to himself on a wall facing the Pentagon. (Baldwin puts his hand over his mouth like a spinster who has heard a four-letter word.) When Johnson impulsively bundles his war cabinet off to Vietnam on a tour of inspection, they are like pale, blinking, wizened school children on a field trip to a hell of their own making.

"The aim was to emotionally involve the audience in the picture, without . . . calling attention to the camera or anything like that," said Frankenheimer at the time. "I wanted to make it as real as I possibly could. And there's a lot of depth-of-focus stuff in there, because there's just so much going on in the background"—much of it involving Johnson's younger aides: Dick Goodwin (James Frain), Bill Moyers (Chris Eigeman), and Jack Valenti, played by the real Valenti's look-alike son John. The "hard-sell" style carried over from television is back where it belongs, shaping the drama unobtrusively through mise-en-scène— "through what you put on the screen," said Frankenheimer. "A two-shot rather than a close-up, a sympathetic portrayal of a character, rather than an unsympathetic one. A flattering camera angle, rather than an unflattering one. . . . Just the design of a set, how you want the set to look. How you want a scene photographed. All kinds of things." *Path to War*, which ends with a high-angle shot of the shaken television crews slowly starting to pack up after covering Johnson's abdication speech, is a brilliant final summation of the esthetic that Frankenheimer carried from television into features.

McNamara in particular is put through visual changes. When he looks up at the portrait of his predecessor James Forrestal and talks about how the man committed suicide after Truman fired him and hung a decoration on him, Alec Baldwin's head swells till it looks like it might pop; when he is about to be fired himself, the portrait looms in the foreground; and when he accepts his medal, the camera stays tight on his sweating face as he flashes back to the dogmatic pronouncements he made while leading the country into a quagmire. Without adopting the avant-garde strategies of the historical films Roberto Rossellini made for television, *Path to War* achieves the same aims: the fact that Johnson and McNamara are portrayed as well-intentioned men (liberals almost always have good intentions) does not spare them being examined like bacteria under a microscope. The airless choreography of talking heads in plush rooms is as expressionistic as the subjective stylings of *George Wallace*, and a marvel to watch.

Oddly enough, it may have been *George Wallace* that enabled Frankenheimer to exorcise the ghost of RFK, by recreating the assassination he only heard about with Wallace as a stand-in for Kennedy. He noted tersely in an interview that the two days he spent filming at the shuttered Ambassador Hotel (a popular L.A. location for period re-creations until it was torn down) were his first visit to the scene of the crime since June 5, 1968.[10] He even brings Kennedy (played by Mark Valley) back to life briefly for a tense confrontation with Wallace, which ends in a tie. After that, in *Path to War*, Bobby is Banquo's ghost on television stoking Johnson's paranoia about the Kennedys, whose advisors he blames for giving him bad advice, then turning on him. The ultimate cause of the war, the film implies, was Johnson's fear that Bobby could use any faltering in his resolve to pursue John Kennedy's policies in Vietnam to destroy him—an interesting motive for the protagonist of a dark tale whose labyrinthine complexity recalls

Middleton and Webster more than Shakespeare. *Path to War* is visually a labyrinth, and Johnson's paranoia is the minotaur at its center.

As a cinematic Jonah who was almost destroyed by the prophecy of *The Manchurian Candidate* coming true the second time (with another U.S. senator from New York getting shot in the kitchen), Frankenheimer was simply recording his own experience in these two films where the invisible destiny pulling the characters' strings occasionally shows its hand in eerie flashes. What remains to be seen is whether the reluctant prophet's last vision, *Path to War*, describes the fate awaiting the country in Afghanistan, but the auguries are not good, and the entrails are starting to give off a nasty smell.

NOTES

1. In denigrating the fictional Iselin (James Gregory), claim Jacobson and González, Senator Jordan (John McGiver) is "recapitulating a most powerful—and common—denunciation of [Senator Joseph] McCarthy." President Truman, they note, once referred to America's Witchfinder General as "the greatest asset the Kremlin has" (96). Jacobson and González have written a very good book, but in my opinion what they call the contradictions of America are mostly the contradictions of cold war liberalism, which continue to ravage the administration of Barack Obama as it keeps on waging Bush's War on Terror under another name, whereas the supposed contradictions of the American Right are simply hypocrisy—the Right is rarely in contradiction with itself.

2. "Eisenstein *delire* la politique stalinienne . . . ," Narboni writes. Jacobson and González could easily adopt Narboni's formulation to sum up their searching interpretation of *The Manchurian Candidate*.

    I know of no other explanation for the incongruous detail of Senator Jordan being shot through a carton of milk, so that he appears to bleed milk rather than blood. In her review of *Yojimbo*, Pauline Kael reads this as a joke about liberals having milk for blood and cites its occurrence at a moment of high tragedy (Raymond killing his future father-in-law and then the woman he loves) as a discord like the comic touches in Kurosawa's samurai western. But the effect of introducing a gag in a serious scene is secondary to the intellectual discord caused by an anti-liberal gag in a film that espouses a liberal worldview.

    In this respect the spurting milk carton is like the ecstatic fountains of milk that bring the scene of the mechanical cream-separator in Eisenstein's *The General Line* (1929) to a climax: they are not a criticism, conscious or otherwise, of the film's politics. On the contrary, says Narboni, Stalin's censors attacked the film because they couldn't stand its "X-ray and *true caricature* of their politics" (25). The Party wanted "graphs showing the surge in dairy production, not unleashed cascades of milk" (24).

    Clearly Frankenheimer intended for the milk to seem to pour out of Jordan's heart—that's why, impossibly, no milk spurts out the back of the carton when Raymond's bullet pierces it. But the image is a euphemism for the blood that isn't shown, a shock effect masked by a metaphor that is, in a way, appropriate to the pathos of the moment. (Raymond murders six people, but *The Manchurian Candidate* is a film without blood, even though it was released two years after *Psycho* [1960].) It's no more a slam at liberals than the climactic words of the fat-headed "better dead than Red" acceptance speech Iselin's running mate is giving at the convention ("My life before my liberty"), which causes Raymond's aim to swerve at the last moment.

But while *The Manchurian Candidate* is as committed to liberalism as *The General Line* is to Stalinism, its firmest commitment is to its own formalism (the crime Eisenstein was forever being taxed with when his approval rating began to decline), which makes it a truer representation of that ideology than the party boss thought he had ordered up: the eagle's wings that sprout from Senator Jordan's head in his first scene are like angels' wings (the opposite of the dark fascist eagle looming over Raymond when he fires at Jordan), and when the liberal father figure is murdered, the milk of human kindness spurts out of his heart instead of blood. I'm sure these images sometimes get laughs that Frankenheimer didn't plan on, like all the crazy sexual imagery in *The General Line*, but his critique of the party line, like Eisenstein's, would not be made until the end of his career.

3. Fans of *The Manchurian Candidate* can be forgiven for thinking that the real authors of the events that fulfilled Frankenheimer's second unintentional prophecy were seeking "powers that will make martial law look like anarchy," to quote Raymond Shaw's mother, powers they already had conveniently drawn up and tagged with a stentorian acronym, the USA PATRIOT Act (Uniting and Strengthening America by Providing Appropriate Tools Required to Intercept and Obstruct Terrorism Act of 2001). That 342-page document, written in the early days of the Bush administration, was an extension of the Antiterrorism Act, which a Democratic president, Bill Clinton, asked Congress to pass in 1996, and it is still the law of the land.

4. The show is fictionalized but hosted by Dick Cavett, who in real life hosted a PBS talk show of some repute at the time, a kind of forum for liberal views of politics and culture.

5. The inconclusive evidence that Lee Harvey Oswald may have seen Frankenheimer's film is summed up in Loken. This controversy of course assumes that Oswald was the assassin.

6. I wrote the production information for the American release of the film, based on the strangest collection of on-set interviews I've ever seen. From what I read there, *The Island of Dr. Moreau* came closer to being a film without an author than *The Manchurian Candidate* (the Greil Marcus hypothesis, deftly skewered by Jacobson and González). That it ended up being a John Frankenheimer film anyway is a tribute to Frankenheimer and a pyrrhic victory for la politique des auteurs.

7. *Reindeer Games* is now available on DVD in the director's cut, with a commentary by Frankenheimer explaining why he let himself be talked into cutting it down.

8. All quotes and other information about these two films come from the production information posted by TNT (http://alt.tnt.tv/movies/tntoriginals/wallace/prod.credits.notes.html) and HBO (www.hbo.com/films/pathtowar/).

9. See http://www.cnn.com/2008/POLITICS/11/03/wallace.kennedy.obama/index.html.

10. "For several scenes, the production took over the famed Ambassador Hotel in Los Angeles, a monument to a tragic moment in history that Frankenheimer remembers well" (TNT production information). But which scenes?

JOHN FRANKENHEIMER'S DIRECTORIAL CAREER: A CHRONOLOGY

1948

dates unknown   Unknown episodes of *Lamp unto My Feet*

1951

September 3   Episode 1.1 of *Search for Tomorrow* airs

1952

dates unknown   Frankenheimer writes and directs *Harvey Howard's Ranch Roundup* on Channel 13 in Los Angeles and various films for the United States Air Force

1953

February 22	"The Capture of John Dillinger (January 25, 1934)" airs on *You Are There*
March 15	"The Hamilton-Burr Duel (July 11, 1804)" airs on *You Are There*
March 22	"The Discovery of Anesthesia (October 16, 1846)" airs on *You Are There*
April 18	Frankenheimer begins stint as floor manager on *Rod Brown of the Rocket Rangers*, averaging several episodes a month
June 30	Frankenheimer leaves U.S.A.F.
date unknown	*The Garry Moore Show*
date unknown	*Person to Person*
date unknown	*See It Now*

1954

February 12	"Dagmar's Braces" airs on *Mama*
February 19	"Katrin at the Exposition" airs on *Mama*
April 27	"Escape Route" airs on *Danger*
May 29	Frankenheimer concludes stint on *Rod Brown of the Rocket Rangers*
November 9	"Padlocks" airs on *Danger* with James Dean
November 28	"The Plot against King Solomon" airs on *You Are There*

December 7	"Knife in the Dark" airs on *Danger*
December 21	"Treasure of the Argo" airs on *Danger*

1955

January 4	"Precinct Girl" airs on *Danger* with Peggy Ann Garner
January 18	"No Passport for Death" airs on *Danger*
February 1	"The Dark Curtain" airs on *Danger*
March 3	"South of the Sun" airs on *Climax!* with Edward Arnold, Margaret O'Brien
March 24	"The Darkest Hour" airs on *Climax!* with Joanne Dru, Zachary Scott
April 7	"Private Worlds" airs on *Climax!* with Claudette Colbert, Lorne Greene
April 28	"The First and the Last" airs on *Climax!* with John Agar, John Carradine
May 19	"No Stone Unturned" airs on *Climax!* with Jeff Donnell, Tom Drake
June 2	"The Unimportant Man" airs on *Climax!* with Macdonald Carey, Ruth Hussey
June 23	"To Wake at Midnight" airs on *Climax!* with Wendell Corey, Akim Tamiroff
August 11	"Edge of Terror" airs on *Climax!* with Lloyd Bridges, Phyllis Kirk
August 25	"Deal a Blow" airs on *Climax!* with Edward Arnold, James MacArthur
September 15	"Silent Decision" airs on *Climax!* with Betty Furness, Franchot Tone
September 29	"Sailor on Horseback" airs on *Climax!* with Mercedes McCambridge, Lloyd Nolan
October 20	"House of Shadows" airs on *Climax!* with James Daly, Diana Lynn
November 10	"Scheme to Defraud" airs on *Climax!* with Marilyn Erskine, Dennis O'Keefe
November 24	"Portrait in Celluloid" airs on *Climax!* with Jack Carson, Kim Hunter
December 8	"The Passport" airs on *Climax!* with Viveca Lindfors, Frank Lovejoy
December 29	"Bail Out at Forty-three Thousand" airs on *Climax!* with Richard Boone, Nancy Davis

1956

January 12	"The Hanging Judge" airs on *Climax!* with John Carradine, Reginald Denny
February 2	"Gamble on a Thief" airs on *Climax!* with Macdonald Carey, Phyllis Kirk
February 23	"Nightmare by Day" airs on *Climax!* with Mary Astor, Katy Jurado
March 8	"The Gay Illiterate: The Louella Parsons Story" airs on *Climax!* with Gracie Allen, Eve Arden, Jean-Pierre Aumont, Lex Barker, Joan Bennett, Jack Benny, Charles Boyer, Joan Fontaine, Susan Hayward
March 22	"Pale Horse, Pale Rider" airs on *Climax!* with Lili Darvas, John Forsythe
April 5	"Spin into Darkness" airs on *Climax!* with Charles Drake, Virginia Grey
April 26	"Sit Down with Death" airs on *Climax!* with Ralph Bellamy, Constance Ford

May 17	"Flame-Out on T-6" airs on *Climax!* with Sidney Blackmer, Richard Carlson
May 31	"Figures in Clay" airs on *Climax!* with Lloyd Bridges, Edmond O'Brien
June 14	"To Scream at Midnight" airs on *Climax!* with Richard Jaeckel, Diana Lynn
July 9	Frankenheimer commences shooting on *The Young Stranger*, his first feature
October 4	"Forbidden Area" airs on *Playhouse 90* with Charlton Heston, Tab Hunter
October 25	"Rendezvous in Black" airs on *Playhouse 90* with Franchot Tone, Viveca Lindfors
November 22	"Eloise" airs on *Playhouse 90* with Evelyn Rudie, Hans Conried, Kay Thompson
December 20	"The Family Nobody Wanted" airs on *Playhouse 90* with Lew Ayres, Nanette Fabray

1957

January 10	"The Ninth Day" airs on *Playhouse 90* with Piper Laurie, Mary Astor
February 14	"The Comedian" airs on *Playhouse 90* with Mickey Rooney, Kim Hunter
March 14	"The Last Tycoon" airs on *Playhouse 90* with Jack Palance, Peter Lorre
April 8	*The Young Stranger* opens with James MacArthur, James Gregory, Kim Stanley, James Daly
April 11	"If You Knew Elizabeth" airs on *Playhouse 90* with Claire Trevor, Gary Merrill
May 23	"Winter Dreams" airs on *Playhouse 90* with John Cassavetes, Dana Wynter
June 13	"Clash by Night" airs on *Playhouse 90* with Kim Stanley, Lloyd Bridges
June 27	"The Fabulous Irishman" airs on *Playhouse 90* with Art Carney, Peter Lorre
September 12	"The Death of Manolete" airs on *Playhouse 90* with Jack Palance, Suzy Parker
October 3	"A Sound of Different Drummers" airs on *Playhouse 90* with Sterling Hayden, Diana Lynn
November 21	"The Troublemakers" airs on *Playhouse 90* with Nick Adams, Mary Astor
December 12	"The Thundering Wave" airs on *Playhouse 90* with Joan Bennett, James Mason

1958

January 9	"The Last Man" airs on *Playhouse 90* with Wallace Ford, Hurd Hatfield
February 6	"The Violent Heart" airs on *Playhouse 90* with Pamela Brown, Ben Gazzara
May 1	"Rumors of Evening" airs on *Playhouse 90* with Barbara Bel Geddes, Billie Burke, Patricia Hitchcock

May 22	"Bomber's Moon" airs on *Playhouse 90* with Martin Balsam, Cliff Robertson
June 19	"A Town Has Turned to Dust" airs on *Playhouse 90* with James Gregory, William Shatner
August 4	"The Last Summer" airs on *Studio One in Hollywood* with Dennis Hopper, Betty Furness
October 2	"The Days of Wine and Roses" airs on *Playhouse 90* with Cliff Robertson, Piper Laurie
November 20	"Old Man" airs on *Playhouse 90* with Malcolm Atterbury, Sterling Hayden

1959

January 1	"Face of a Hero" airs on *Playhouse 90* with Jack Lemmon, Rip Torn
January 15	"The Blue Men" airs on *Playhouse 90* with Eileen Heckart, Eli Wallach
March 12	"For Whom the Bell Tolls: Part 1" airs on *Playhouse 90* with Steven Hill, Sydney Pollack, Jason Robards Jr., Maria Schell
March 19	"For Whom the Bell Tolls: Part 2" airs on *Playhouse 90* with Steven Hill, Sydney Pollack, Jason Robards Jr., Maria Schell
April 23	"The Browning Version" airs on *The DuPont Show of the Month* with John Gielgud, Margaret Leighton
September 30	"People Kill People Sometimes" airs on *The Sunday Showcase* with Geraldine Page, George C. Scott, Jason Robards Jr.
October 20	"The Turn of the Screw" airs on *Ford Startime* with Laurinda Barrett, Ingrid Bergman, Hayward Morse

1960

January 29	"The Fifth Column" airs on *Buick Electra Playhouse* with Richard Burton, Maximilian Schell, Sally Ann Howes
March 25	"The Snows of Kilimanjaro" airs on *Buick Electra Playhouse* with Robert Ryan, Ann Todd, Janice Rule
March 27	"The American" airs on *Sunday Showcase* with Lee Marvin, Steven Hill, Sydney Pollack
April 22	"Journey to the Day" airs on *Playhouse 90* with Mary Astor, Mike Nichols

1961

May 24	*The Young Savages* opens with Burt Lancaster, Dina Merrill, Shelley Winters

1962

March 28	*All Fall Down* opens in Chicago with Warren Beatty, Eva Marie Saint, Brandon De Wilde, Angela Lansbury, Karl Malden
July 3	*Birdman of Alcatraz* opens with Burt Lancaster, Karl Malden, Thelma Ritter, Betty Field

October 24	*The Manchurian Candidate* opens with Frank Sinatra, Laurence Harvey, Angela Lansbury, Janet Leigh, Henry Silva
October 27	"Black Saturday"—the peak of the Cuban Missile Crisis

1964

February 12	*Seven Days in May* opens with Burt Lancaster, Kirk Douglas, Fredric March, Ava Gardner, Edmond O'Brien
September 22	*The Train* opens in France with Burt Lancaster, Paul Scofield, Jeanne Moreau, Michel Simon

1965

March 17	*The Train* opens in the United States

1966

September 14	*Seconds* opens with Rock Hudson, John Randolph, Salome Jens
December 22	*Grand Prix* opens with James Garner, Eva Marie Saint, Yves Montand, Toshirô Mifune

1968

June 5	Frankenheimer drives Robert F. Kennedy to the Ambassador Hotel in Los Angeles where shortly after midnight the presidential hopeful is assassinated
December 8	*The Fixer* opens with Alan Bates, Dirk Bogarde, Georgia Brown

1969

January 22	*The Extraordinary Seaman* opens in Uruguay with David Niven, Faye Dunaway, Alan Alda, Mickey Rooney (no American release)
August 28	*The Gypsy Moths* opens with Burt Lancaster, Deborah Kerr, Gene Hackman

1970

October 12	*I Walk the Line* opens in New York with Gregory Peck, Tuesday Weld, Estelle Parsons, Ralph Meeker

1971

June 23	*The Horsemen* opens in New York with Omar Sharif, Leigh Taylor-Young, Jack Palance

1973

May 18	*The Impossible Object* (*The Story of a Love Story*) opens in Italy with Alan Bates, Dominique Sanda, Michel Auclair, Evans Evans (no American release)

October 29	*The Iceman Cometh* opens in New York, as part of Ely Landau's *American Film Theatre*, with Lee Marvin, Fredric March, Robert Ryan, Jeff Bridges

1974

June 26	*99 and 44/100% Dead* opens in New York with Richard Harris, Edmond O'Brien, Ann Turkel, Constance Ford

1975

May 18	*French Connection II* opens in New York with Gene Hackman, Fernando Rey

1977

January 30	Appears in "Black Marlin Fishing in Australia," airing on *The American Sportsman*
March 31	*Black Sunday* opens with Robert Shaw, Bruce Dern, Marthe Keller

1979

June 15	*Prophecy* opens in New York with Talia Shire, Robert Foxworth, Armand Assante, Richard Dysart

1982

February 6	"The Golden Age of Television" airs on *Playhouse 90* with Frankenheimer, Mickey Rooney, Kim Hunter, and Mel Torme discussing "The Comedian"
July 23	*The Challenge* opens with Scott Glenn, Toshirô Mifune
October 24	*The Rainmaker* airs on *HBO Theatre* with Tommy Lee Jones, Tuesday Weld

1985

September 20	*The Holcroft Covenant* opens in London with Michael Caine, Anthony Andrews, Victoria Tennant, Lilli Palmer
October 18	*The Holcroft Covenant* opens in the United States

1986

November 7	*52 Pick-Up* opens with Roy Scheider, Ann-Margret, John Glover

1987

May 31	*Riviera* opens with Patrick Bauchau, Jon Finch, Elyssa Davalos

1989

March 24	*Dead Bang* opens with Don Johnson, Penelope Ann Miller, William Forsythe

1990

March 23   *The Fourth War* opens in the United States

1991

September 10   *Year of the Gun* opens at the Toronto Film Festival with Andrew McCarthy, Sharon Stone, Valeria Golino

November 1   *Year of the Gun* opens in the United States

1992

August 19   "Maniac at Large" airs on *Tales from the Crypt* with Obba Babatundé, Blythe Danner

1994

March 26   *Against the Wall* (an HBO special) airs with Kyle MacLachlan, Samuel L. Jackson, Frederic Forrest

September 17   *The Burning Season* opens at the Toronto Film Festival with Raúl Julia, Sonia Braga, Luis Guzmán, Nigel Havers

September 17   *The Burning Season* (an HBO special) airs in the United States

1995

November 29   Appears in "Rod Serling: Submitted for Your Approval," airing on *American Masters*

1996

March 3   *Andersonville* airs with Frederic Forrest, William H. Macy

August 23   *The Island of Dr. Moreau* opens with Marlon Brando, Val Kilmer, David Thewlis, Fairuza Balk

1997

August 24   *George Wallace* airs with Gary Sinise, Mare Winningham, Angelina Jolie

1998

September 12   *Ronin* opens at the Venice Film Festival with Robert De Niro, Jean Reno, Natascha McElhone, Stellan Skarsgård

September 13   Appears in "Angela Lansbury: A Balancing Act," airing on *Biography*

September 23   *Ronin* opens in the United States

2000

February 24   *Reindeer Games* opens in San Juan with Ben Affleck, Isaac Hayes, James Frain

October 31   Appears in "'The Contender': The Making of a Political Thriller," airing on *HBO First Look*

2001

April 26 — "The Hire"/"Ambush" (BMW commercial) begins airing worldwide with Tomas Milian, Clive Owen

2002

April 23 — Appears in "Burt Lancaster," airing on *The Hollywood Greats*

May 18 — *Path to War* airs with Michael Gambon, Donald Sutherland, Alec Baldwin, Felicity Huffman

July 6 — John Frankenheimer dies in Los Angeles, age seventy-two

WORKS CITED AND CONSULTED

HER = Margaret Herrick Library, Academy of Motion Picture Arts and Sciences, Beverly Hills

Adler, Renata. "The Fixer Put through Hollywood Mill." *New York Times* 9 December 1968: 59.
"An AFI Seminar with Ralph Woolsey, ASC." *American Cinematographer* (February 1978): 156–57, 166–69, 176–77, 211–12.
Agnew, Jean-Christophe. "Coming Up for Air: Consumer Culture in Historical Perspective." *Consumer Society in American History: A Reader*. Ed. Lawrence B. Glickman. Ithaca, N.Y.: Cornell UP, 1999. 373–97.
Albee, Edward. "The American Dream." *The Collected Plays of Edward Albee, 1958–1965*. Woodstock, N.Y.: Overlook Press, 2007. 95–148.
All Fall Down Pressbook. *All Fall Down* file. Cinema-Television Library, University of Southern California.
Rev. of *All Fall Down*. *Monthly Film Bulletin* 29.336/347 (1962): 74.
"All-Time 100 Movies." *Time*. http://www.time.com/time/2005/100movies/0,23220,the_manchurian_candidate,00.html. Accessed 21 May 2010.
Alter, Robert. "Jewishness as Metaphor." *Bernard Malamud and the Critics*. Ed. Leslie A. and Joyce W. Field. New York: New York UP, 1970. 29–42.
Amos, Lindsay. "Veteran's a Maestro Behind the Wheel of a Thriller." *Moviexpress*. http://moviexpress.tripod.com/id49.htm. Accessed 31 August 2009.
Applebaum, Ralph. "Pop Art Pitfalls." *Films and Filming* (October 1979): 15.
Armstrong, Stephen B. *Pictures about Extremes: The Films of John Frankenheimer*. Jefferson, N.C.: McFarland, 2008.
"Attack of Berry-berry." *Time* 13 April 1962. http://www.time.com/time/magazine/article/0,9171,827301,00.html. Accessed 29 July 2009.
Austvik, Ole Gunnar. "The War Over the Price of Oil: Oil and the Conflict on the Persian Gulf." *International Journal of Global Energy Issues* 5.2/3/4 (January 1997): 134–43.
Badsey, Stephen. *The Manchurian Candidate*. Trowbridge, Wiltshire: Flicks Books, 1998.
Balio, Tino. *United Artists: The Company That Changed the Film Industry*. Madison: U of Wisconsin P, 1985.
Baudrillard, Jean. *The Transparency of Evil: Essays on Extreme Phenomena*. Trans. James Benedict. London: Verso, 1993.
Bazin, André. "The Evolution of the Language of Cinema." *What Is Cinema?* Berkeley: U of California P, 1968.
Beaupre, Lee. "Frankenheimer in Comeback—to H'Wood, That Is—After Disappointments Overseas." *Daily Variety* 28 December 1973: 2.
Beilis, Mendel. *The Story of My Sufferings*. Trans. Harrison Goldberg. New York: Mendel Beilis Publishing, 1926.
Bell, Douglas. "An Oral History with Karl Malden." 2007. HER.

Bell, Malcolm. *The Turkey Shoot*. New York: Grove Press, 1985.
Bell, Matt. "Your Worst Fears Made Flesh: *The Manchurian Candidate*'s Paranoid Delusion and Gay Liberation." *GLQ: A Journal of Lesbian and Gay Studies* 12.1 (2006): 85–116.
Berg, Charles Ramírez. "Manifest Myth-Making: Texas History in the Movies." *The Persistence of Whiteness: Race and Contemporary Hollywood Cinema*. Ed. Daniel Bernardi. New York: Routledge, 2008. 3–20.
Betts, John Rickards. "Technological Revolution and the Rise of Sport, 1850–1900." *Mississippi Valley Historical Review* 40.2 (September 1953): 231–56.
"Big-Bang Bagatelle." *Newsweek* 20 April 1964. 54.
Biskind, Peter. *Seeing Is Believing: How Hollywood Taught Us to Stop Worrying and Love the Fifties*. London: Pluto Press, 1983.
Blaney, Paul H. "Paranoid Conditions." *Oxford Textbook of Psychopathology*. 2nd ed. Ed. Theodore Millon, Paul H. Blaney, and Roger D. Davis. New York: Oxford UP, 1999. 339–61.
Blume, Mary. "A Love Story That Doesn't Die." *Los Angeles Times* 8 October 1972. 31.
Bogard, Travis, and Jackson Bryer, eds. *The Theatre We Worked For: The Letters of Eugene O'Neill to Kenneth Macgowan*. New Haven, Conn.: Yale UP, 1982.
Boime, Albert. "The Prix de Rome: Images of Authority and Threshold of Official Success." *Art Journal* 44.3 (Autumn 1984): 281–89.
Bordwell, David. *Poetics of Cinema*. New York: Routledge, 2008.
Bordwell, David, Janet Staiger, and Kristin Thompson. *The Classical Hollywood Cinema: Film Style & Mode of Production to 1960*. New York: Columbia UP, 1985.
Bouchoux, Corinne. *Rose Valland: La Résistance au Musée*. La Crèche: Geste Editions, 2006.
Bowie, Stephen. "John Frankenheimer." *Senses of Cinema* 41 (October-December 2006). http://archive.sensesofcinema.com/contents/directors/06/frankenheimer.html. Accessed 5 March 2009.
Breitrose, Henry. "On the Search for the Real Nitty-Gritty: Problems & Possibilities in 'Cinéma-Vérité.'" *Film Quarterly* 17.4 (Summer 1964): 36–40.
Brown, Geoff. "The Island of Doctor Moreau." *The Times* 14 November 1996. 41.
Brustein, Robert. *The Theatre of Revolt*. Boston: Little, Brown, 1964.
Bryson, John. "John Frankenheimer, Maker of 'French Connection II,' Makes French Confections, Too." *People* 4 August 1975. 41–42.
Burke, Kenneth. *Permanence and Change: An Anatomy of Purpose*. Indianapolis: Bobbs-Merrill, 1965.
Butler, Judith. *Precarious Life: The Powers of Mourning and Violence*. New York: Verso, 2004.
Caldwell, John Thornton. *Televisuality: Style, Crisis and Authority in American Television*. New Brunswick, N.J.: Rutgers UP, 1995.
Canby, Vincent. "Barnstorming Parachutists." *New York Times* 29 August 1969. 20.
———. "Frankenheimer's 'Prophecy': Mercury, Lukewarm." *New York Times* 15 June 1976. C17
———. "Of Time and Talent: The Growth of Burt Lancaster." *New York Times* 24 May 1981. D1+.
Canetti, Elias. *Crowds and Power*. Trans. Carol Stewart. New York: Farrar, Straus & Giroux, 1984.
Cappell, Ezra. *American Talmud: The Cultural Work of Jewish American Fiction*. Albany: State U of New York P, 2007.
Carroll, Noel. *Comedy Incarnate*. Malden, Mass.: Blackwell, 2007.
Carruthers, Susan L. "Brainwashing." *Propaganda and Mass Persuasion: A Historical Encyclopedia, 1500 to the Present*. Ed. Nicholas J. Cull, David Culbert, and David Welch. Santa Barbara, Calif.: ABC-Clio, 2003. 46–48.
———. "*The Manchurian Candidate* (1962) and the Cold War Brainwashing Scare." *Historical Journal of Film, Radio and Television* 18.1 (March 1998): 75 (20).

———. "Redeeming the Captives: Hollywood and the Brainwashing of America's Prisoners of War in Korea." *Film History* [Australia] 10.3 (1998): 275–94.

Champlin, Charles. *John Frankenheimer: A Conversation.* Burbank, Calif.: Riverwood Press, 1995.

Charbonneau, Stephen. "John Frankenheimer." *Contemporary North American Film Directors.* Ed. Yoram Allon et al. London: Wallflower, 2000. 159–62.

Chow, Rey. *The Age of the World Target: Self-Referentiality in War, Theory, and Comparative Work.* Durham, N.C.: Duke UP, 2006.

Clark, Richard X. *The Brothers of Attica.* New York: Link Books, 1973.

Clarke, Thurston. *The Last Campaign: Robert F. Kennedy and 82 Days That Inspired America.* New York: Henry Holt, 2008.

Coates, Ivan. "Enforcing the Cold War Consensus: McCarthyism, Liberalism, and *The Manchurian Candidate.*" *Australasian Journal of American Studies* 12.1 (1993): 47–64.

Combs, Richard. "How Is It That John Frankenheimer's Brilliant Career Was Over Before It Actually Started?: Richard Combs Explains." *Film Comment* 38.6 (November 2002): 49–52.

Condon, Richard. *The Manchurian Candidate.* 1959. Reprint, New York: Thunder Mouth's Press, 2003.

Conolly, Jez. "Film Reviews: Lost Classic—Seconds (John Frankenheimer 1966)." *The Big Picture* (27 July 2009). http://www.thebigpicturemagazine.com/index.php?option=com_content&view=article&id=146:lost-classic-seconds-john-frankenheimer-1966&catid=34:film-reviews&Itemid=60. Accessed 4 August 2009.

Cornea, Christine. *Science Fiction Cinema: Between Fantasy and Reality.* New Brunswick, N.J.: Rutgers UP, 2007.

Corrigan, Timothy. "Auteurs and the New Hollywood." *The New American Cinema.* Ed. Jon Lewis. Durham, N.C.: Duke UP, 1998. 38–63.

Coursodon, Jean-Pierre. "John Frankenheimer." *American Directors: Volume II.* Ed. Jean-Pierre Coursodon and Pierre Sauvage. New York: McGraw-Hill, 1983. 138–44.

Creed, Barbara. *The Monstrous Feminine: Film, Feminism, Psychoanalysis.* London: Routledge, 1993.

Crist, Judith. "Below Zero." *New York* 4 February 1974. 57.

Crowther, Bosley. "*All Fall Down.*" *New York Times* 12 April 1962. 41.

———. "Burt Lancaster Stars in 'Train,' a Thriller." *New York Times* 18 March 1965. 25.

———. "Familiarity Breeds Content." *New York Times* 21 March 1965. 11.

Danks, Adrian. "Border Crossings: Placing René Clement's *La Bataille du rail.*" *Senses of Cinema* 27 (July-August 2003). http://archive.sensesofcinema.com/contents/cteq/03/27/la_bataille_du_rail.html. Accessed 9 September 2009.

Davis, Doug. "Future-War Storytelling: National Security and Popular Film." *ReThinking Global Security: Media, Popular Culture, and the "War on Terror."* Ed. Andrew Martin and Patrice Petro. New Brunswick, N.J.: Rutgers UP, 2006. 13–44.

Davis, Philip. *Bernard Malamud: A Writer's Life.* Oxford: Oxford UP, 2007.

Deleuze, Gilles. *L'Image-mouvement: Cinéma 1.* Paris: Éditions de Minuit, 1983.

Deleuze, Gilles, and Félix Guattari. *Anti-Oedipus: Capitalism and Schizophrenia.* Trans. Robert Hurley, Mark Seem, and Helen R. Lane. Minneapolis: U of Minnesota P, 1983.

———. *Kafka: Toward a Minor Literature.* Trans. Dana Polan. Minneapolis: U of Minnesota P, 1986.

Dimendberg, Edward. *Film Noir and the Spaces of Modernity.* Cambridge, Mass.: Harvard UP, 2004.

Dirks, Tim. "The Greatest Films: *The Manchurian Candidate* (1962)." *Filmsite.* http://www.filmsite.org/manc.html. Accessed 21 May 2010.

Doane, Mary Ann. "Technophilia: Technology, Representation and the Feminine." *Body/Politics: Women and the Discourses of Science*. Ed. Mary Jacobus et al. London: Routledge, 1990. 163–76.
"Down South in North Korea." *Time* 2 November 1962. http://www.time.com/time/magazine/article/0,9171,874637,00.html?internalid=atm100. Accessed 21 May 2010.
Drought, James. *The Gypsy Moths*. 1955. Reprint, Greenwich, Conn.: Fawcett, 1964.
Dysart, Richard A. Interview with Murray Pomerance. 23 January 2010.
Easton, Nina J. "The Director as Survivor." *Los Angeles Times* 5 November 1989: 24.
Ecksel, Robert. "Faust Goes to Hollywood." *Bright Lights Film Journal* 62 (November 2008). http://www.brightlightsfilm.com/62/62seconds.html. Accessed 4 August 2009.
Ehrenreich, Barbara, and Deirdre English. *For Her Own Good: 150 of the Experts' Advice to Women*. Garden City, N.Y.: Doubleday Anchor, 1978.
Eisenhower, Dwight. "Military-Industrial Complex Speech" (farewell address). *Public Papers of the Presidents*. Washington, D.C.: Federal Register Division, National Archives and Record Service, General Services Administration, 1960. 1035–40.
Ellison, Harlan. "*The Train* by John Frankenheimer." *Cinema* 2 no. 6 (July-August 1965): 48–49. *The Train* scrapbook, John Frankenheimer Collection, HER.
Elsaesser, Thomas. "The Pathos of Failure: American Films in the 1970s: Notes on the Unmotivated Hero." *The Last Great American Picture Show: New Hollywood Cinema in the 1970s*. Ed. Thomas Elsaesser, Alexander Horwath, and Noel King. Amsterdam: Amsterdam UP, 2004. 279–92.
———. "Tales of Sound and Fury: Observations on the Family Melodrama." *Home Is Where the Heart Is: Studies in Melodrama and the Woman's Film*. Ed. Christine Gledhill. London: BFI, 2002. 43–69.
Ely, David. *Seconds*. New York: Signet, 1963.
Emery, Robert J. *The Directors: Take One*. New York: Allworth Press, 2002.
Engle, Karen. *Seeing Ghosts: 9/11 and the Visual Imagination*. Montreal: McGill-Queen's UP, 2009.
Ezard, John. "Sexy Self-Image That Revved Up Dirk Bogarde." *Guardian* 2 October 2004. http://www.guardian.co.uk/ uk/2004/oct/02/books.film. Accessed 20 May 2010.
Faludi, Susan. *Backlash: The Undeclared War against Women*. London: Vintage, 1992.
Farber, Stephen. "Film Reviews: *Seconds*." *Film Quarterly* 20.2 (December 1966): 25–28.
———. "On the Search for the Real Nitty-Gritty: Problems & Possibilities in Cinéma-Vérité." *Film Quarterly* 17.4 (Summer 1964): 11–22.
———. "The Spectacle Film: 1967." *Film Quarterly* 20.4 (Summer 1967): 11–22.
Farrell, Kirby. "Toxic Corps: Rage against the Corporate State." *BAD: Infamy, Darkness, Evil, and Slime on Screen*. Ed. Murray Pomerance. Albany: State U of New York P, 2004. 92–107.
Fauser, Annegret. "*La Guerre en dentelles*: Women and the *Prix de Rome* in French Cultural Politics." *Journal of the American Musicological Society* 5.1 (Spring 1998): 83–129.
Finler, Joel W. *The Hollywood Story*. London: Wallflower Press, 2003.
Fitzgerald, F. Scott. "How to Live on Practically Nothing a Year." *Saturday Evening Post* 20 September 1924: 17, 165–66, 169–70.
Flannagan, Roy. "Nicholas Mosley." *Review of Contemporary Fiction* (Fall 2002): 55–71.
———. "The Way of Seeing the Story: An Interview with Nicholas Mosley." *Review of Contemporary Fiction* (Fall 2002): 87–97.
Foucault, Michel. *Discipline and Punish: The Birth of the Prison*. Trans. Alan Sheridan. New York: Pantheon, 1977.
Francione, Gary L. *Animals, Property, and the Law*. Philadelphia: Temple UP, 1995.
Frankenheimer, John. *A Conversation with Charles Champlin*. Burbank: Riverwood Press, 1995.

———. "Filming *The Iceman Cometh.*" *Action* (Director's Guild of America) (January/February 1974).

———."John Frankenheimer—Archive of American Television Interview." Conducted by Michael Rosen. 21 March and 13 April 2000. http://www.youtube.com/user/TVLEGENDS #g/c/9E773A546D9056F6.

———. "John Frankenheimer: Renaissance Auteur." *Hollywood Interview* 8 February 2008.

"Frankenheimer Replaces Penn at 'Train' Throttle." *Daily Variety* 19 August 1963. *The Train* scrapbook, John Frankenheimer Collection, HER.

Freud, Sigmund. "Psycho-Analytic Notes on an Autobiographical Account of a Case of Paranoia (Dementia Paranoides)." *The Case of Schreber, Papers on Technique, and Other Works. The Standard Edition of the Complete Psychological Works of Sigmund Freud.* Vol. 12 (1911–1913). Ed. James Strachey et al. London: Vintage, 2001. 1–82.

Friedman, Lester. "Darkness Visible: Images of Nazis in American Film." *BAD: Infamy, Darkness, Evil, and Slime on Screen.* Ed. Murray Pomerance. Albany: State U of New York P, 2004. 255–71.

Friedman, Milton. *Capitalism and Freedom.* 3rd ed. Chicago: U of Chicago P, 2002.

Gateward, Frances, and Murray Pomerance. "Introduction." *Sugar, Spice and Everything Nice: Cinemas of Girlhood.* Detroit: Wayne State UP, 2002. 13–21.

Gill, Brendan. "Iron Horses." *New Yorker* 20 March 1965. 152–54. *The Train* scrapbook, John Frankenheimer Collection, HER.

Gomides, Camilo. "Putting a New Definition of Ecocriticism to the Test: The Case of *The Burning Season*, a Film (Mal)Adaptation." *Interdisciplinary Studies in Literature and the Environment* 13.1 (Winter 2006): 13–23.

Goode, Erich. *Paranormal Beliefs: A Sociological Introduction.* Prospect Heights, Ill.: Waveland Press, 2000.

Gould, Jack. "John Frankenheimer's Mounting of 'A Town Has Turned to Dust' [for *Playhouse 90*] was simply superb." *New York Times* 21 June 1958.

———, ed. *Watching Television Come of Age: The New York Times Reviews.* Austin: U of Texas P, 2001.

Gow, Gordon. "Prophecy." *Film and Filming* 13.4 (October 1979): 30.

Gray, Floyd, ed. *Anthologie de la poésie française.* Charlottesville, Va.: Rockwood Texts, 1999.

Gross, Larry, and Robert Avrech. "John Frankenheimer Interview." *Millimeter* 3.7–8 (July-August 1975): 40+.

Grunchec, Philippe. *The Grand Prix de Rome: Paintings from the école des Beaux-Arts 1797–1863.* Washington, D.C: International Exhibitions Foundation, 1984.

———, ed. *Le Grand Prix de Peinture: Les concours des Prix de Rome de 1797 à 1863.* Paris: École Nationale Supérieure des Beaux Arts, 1983.

Guha, Ramachandra. "Radical American Conservation and Wilderness Preservations: A Third World Critique." *The Great New Wilderness Debate.* Ed. Baird Callicott and Michael P. Nelson. Athens: U of Georgia P, 1998. 231–45.

Gunning, Tom. "The Cinema of Attractions: Early Film, Its Spectator and the Avant-Garde." *Wide Angle* 8.3–4 (Fall 1986): 63–70.

Haber, Joyce. "Frankenheimer a Hot Head with an Up-Down Film Record." *Los Angeles Times* 18 July 1971: C17.

Haiken, Elizabeth. *Venus Envy: A History of Cosmetic Surgery.* Baltimore: Johns Hopkins UP, 1997.

Hampton, Howard. "Sympathy for the Devil." *Film Comment* 29.6 (November-December 1993): 36–41.

Haney, Lynn. *Gregory Peck: A Charmed Life.* London: Robson Books, 2003.

Harmetz, Aljean. "'The Manchurian Candidate,' Old Failure, Is Now a Hit." *New York Times* 24 February 1988. http://www.nytimes.com/1988/02/24/movies/manchurian-candidate-old-failure-is-now-a-hit.html?scp=1&sq=harmetz%2C+manchurian&st=nyt. Accessed 29 November 2010.

Hatch, Kristen. "Fille Fatale: Regulating Images of Adolescent Girls, 1962–1996." *Sugar, Spice and Everything Nice: Cinemas of Girlhood*. Ed. Frances Gateward and Murray Pomerance. Detroit: Wayne State UP, 2002. 163–81.

Heidegger, Martin. *Being and Time*. Trans. Joan Stambaugh. Albany: State U of New York P, 1996.

Hentges, Sarah. *Pictures of Girlhood: Modern Female Adolescence on Film*. Jefferson, N.C.: McFarland, 2006.

Hersey, John. *The Algiers Motel Incident*. 1968. Reprint, Baltimore: Johns Hopkins UP, 1998.

Hersh, Seymour. *The Dark Side of Camelot*. Boston: Little, Brown, 1997.

Higashi, Sumiko. "*Walker* and *Mississippi Burning*: Postmodernism versus Illusionist Narrative." *The Historical Film*. Ed. Marcia Landy. New Brunswick, N.J.: Rutgers UP, 2001. 218–34.

Higham, Charles. "Frankenheimer." *Sight and Sound* 37.2 (Spring 1968): 93.

Hinson, Hal. "Review of *The Manchurian Candidate*." *Washington Post* 13 February 1988. http://www.washingtonpost.com/wpsrv/style/longterm/movies/videos/manchuriancandidatehinson.htm. Accessed 21 May 2010.

Hoberman, J. "When Dr. No Met Dr. Strangelove." *Sight and Sound* 3.12 (December 1993): 16–21.

Hofler, Robert. *The Man Who Invented Rock Hudson: The Pretty Boys and Dirty Deals of Henry Willson*. New York: Carroll & Graf, 2005.

Hofstadter, Richard. *The Paranoid Style in American Politics and Other Essays*. New York: Alfred A. Knopf, 1965.

Holland, Eugene W. "Desire." *Gilles Deleuze: Key Concepts*. Ed. Charles J. Stivale. Montreal: McGill-Queen's UP, 2005. 53–62.

Hollinger, Karen. "The Monster as Woman: Two Generations of Cat People." *The Dread of Difference: Gender and the Horror Film*. Ed. Barry Keith Grant. Austin: U of Texas P, 1996. 296–308.

"Hollywood: Will There Ever Be a 21st Century-Fox?" *Time* 9 February 1970. http://www.time.com. Accessed 4 September 2007.

Holmes, Allison. "John Frankenheimer Tribute: Introduction." *DGA Magazine* 27.3 (October 2002): 54–55.

Huddleston, Tom. "*Manchurian Candidate* (1962)." *Time Out* 2069 (April 2010). http://www.timeout.com/film/ reviews/72653/the_manchurian_candidate.html. Accessed 21 May 2010.

Hunter, Stephen. "The Also Ran: Jonathan Demme's *Manchurian Candidate* Trails the Chilling Original." *Washington Post* 30 July 2004: C1. http://www.washingtonpost.com/wp-dyn/articles/A26007-2004Ju129.html. Accessed 21 May 2010.

Inge, William. *All Fall Down*. Script of 28 November 1960. Turner/MGM Script Collection, HER.

———. *All Fall Down*. Script of 23 July 1961 (John Frankenheimer copy). *All Fall Down* Production Code File, HER.

Jackson, Tony. "*The Manchurian Candidate* and the Gender of the Cold War." *Literature-Film Quarterly* 28.1 (2000): 34–40.

Jacobson, Matthew Frye, and Gaspar González. *What Have They Built You to Do?: "The Manchurian Candidate" and Cold War America*. Minneapolis: U of Minnesota P, 2006.

"John Frankenheimer: 'The Man Who Made *Seconds* Deserves a Second Chance.'" *Film and Filming* 353 (1984): 16–18.

Jones, Madison. *An Exile*. Savannah, Ga.: Frederic C. Beil, 2005.

Kael, Pauline. *5001 Nights at the Movies*. New York: Holt, Rinehart and Winston, 1985.
———. *For Keeps: 30 Years at the Movies*. New York: Plume, 1996.
———. "Frightening the Horses." *Going Steady*. Boston: Little, Brown, 1968. 206–13.
———. "'The Innocents,' and What Passes for Experience." *Film Quarterly* 15.4 (Summer 1962): 21–36.
———. "Notes on Evolving Heroes, Morals, Audiences." *New Yorker* 8 November 1975.
Kafka, Franz. "The Metamorphosis." *The Penal Colony: Stories and Short Pieces*. Trans. Willa and Edwin Muir. New York: Schocken Books, 1961. 65–132.
———. *The Trial*. Trans. Willa and Edwin Muir. New York: Modern Library, 1961.
Kates, Robert W., Thomas M. Paris, and Anthony A. Leiserowitz. "What Is Sustainable Development?: Goals, Indicators, Values, and Practice." *Environment: Science and Policy for Sustainable Development* 47.3 (April 2005): 8–21.
Kerr, Deborah. "Decisive Definition: Letter to *Time*." *Time* 2 March 1970. http://www.time.com. Accessed 4 September 2007.
King, Barry. "Stardom as an Occupation." *The Hollywood Film Industry*. Ed. Paul Kerr. London: Routledge & Kegan Paul, 1986. 154–84.
Kirby, Lynne. *Parallel Tracks: The Railroad and Silent Cinema*. Durham, N.C.: Duke UP, 1997.
Kirshner, Jonathan. "Subverting the Cold War in the 1960s: *Dr. Strangelove*, *The Manchurian Candidate*, and *The Planet Of the Apes*." *Film & History* 31.2 (2001): 40–44.
Knebel, Fletcher, and Charles W. Bailey II. *Seven Days in May*. New York: Harper & Row, 1962.
Kolker, Robert. *A Cinema of Loneliness: Penn, Stone, Kubrick, Scorsese, Spielberg, Altman*. 3rd ed. Oxford: Oxford UP, 2000.
Landry, Robert J. "Bradford Sees Frankenheimer's 'Object' Story as 'Narcissism.'" *Daily Variety* 30 January 1974.
Lenoir, Jean-Pierre. "Stalling a Great 'Train' Robbery." *New York Times* 3 November 1963: X7. *The Train* scrapbook, John Frankenheimer Collection, HER.
Leonard, John. "Solipsistic Smog." *New York Times* 14 January 1969: 43.
Lévi-Strauss, Claude. *La Pensée sauvage*. Paris: Plon, 1962.
Levy, Emanuel. "*Manchurian Candidate* 1962: The Politics of Release and Re-release." *Emanuel Levy: Cinema 24/7*. http://www.emanuellevy.com/search/details.cfm?id=16. Accessed 21 May 2010.
Loken, John. *Oswald's Trigger Films: The Manchurian Candidate, We Were Strangers, Suddenly?* San Ramon, Calif.: Falcon, 2000.
Lubin, Milton. "John Frankenheimer's Direction Is Superb." *Hollywood Reporter* 27 June 1955.
Lucanio, Patrick. *Them or Us: Archetypal Interpretations of the Fifties Alien Invasion Films*. Bloomington: Indiana UP, 1987.
Magid, Ron. "Samurai Tactics." *American Cinematographer* 70.10 (October 1998): 34–42.
Malamud, Bernard. *The Fixer*. New York: Farrar, Straus & Giroux, 1966.
———. "Jewishness in American Fiction." *Bernard Malamud on Life and Work*. Ed. Alan Cheuse and Nicholas Delbanco. New York: Columbia UP, 1996.
Maloff, Saul. "Impossible Object." *New York Times* 2 February 1969. BR35.
Rev. of *The Manchurian Candidate*. *New York Times* 25 October 1962. http://movies.nytimes.com/movie/review?res=9E03EFDC113AE53BA15756C2A9669D946391D6CF. Accessed 21 May 21, 2010.
Rev. of *The Manchurian Candidate*. *New Yorker* 3 November 1962: 115.
Rev. of *The Manchurian Candidate*. *New Yorker* 21 October 1967: 147.
Rev. of *The Manchurian Candidate*. *Variety* 17 October 1962. http://www.variety.com/index.asp?layout=Variety100&reviewid=VE1117792904&content=jump&jump=review&category=1935&cs=1. Accessed 21 May 2010.
Marcus, Greil. *The Manchurian Candidate*. London: BFI, 2002.

Marks, John. *The Search for the "Manchurian Candidate": The CIA and Mind Control.* New York: W. W. Norton, 1991.
Marling, Karal Ann. *As Seen on TV: The Visual Culture of Everyday Life in the 1950s.* Cambridge, Mass.: Harvard UP, 1994.
Martin, Steve. *Born Standing Up: A Comic's Life.* New York: Scribner, 2007.
Maslin, Janet. "Real Tough Guys, Real Derring-Do." *New York Times* 25 September 1998.
Mast, Gerald. *A Short History of the Movies.* 2nd ed. New York: Bobbs-Merrill, 1976.
McCrisken, Trevor B., and Andrew Pepper. *American History and Contemporary Hollywood Film.* New Brunswick, N.J.: Rutgers UP, 2005.
McGarry, Eileen. "Documentary Realism and Women's Cinema." *Women and Film* 2.7 (Summer 1975): 50.
McGilligan, Patrick. *Interviews with Screenwriters of the 1960s.* Berkeley: U of California P, 1997.
Meeker, Joseph. "The Comic Mode." *The Eco-criticism Reader: Landmarks in Literary Ecology.* Ed. Cheryll Glotfelty and Harold Fromm. Athens: U of Georgia P, 1996. 155–69.
Melanson, Philip. *The Robert F. Kennedy Assassination: New Revelations on the Conspiracy and Cover-Up, 1968–1991.* New York: Shapolsky Publishers, 1991.
Menand, Louis. "Brainwashed." *New Yorker* 15 September 2003. http://www.newyorker.com/archive/2003/09/15/030915crat_atlarge. Accessed 29 November 2010.
Miller, Stephen. *Johnny Cash: The Life of an American Icon.* London: Omnibus Press, 2005.
Millikan, Jay. "The Conspiracy Thrillers of the 1970s: Paranoid Time." *Stylus* 7 July 2004. http://www.stylusmagazine.com/feature.php?ID=1092. Accessed 6 January 2009.
Millinship, William. "'Train's' On Track." *Washington Post* 26 January 1964: G1. The Train scrapbook, John Frankenheimer Collection, HER.
Mintz, Alan, and Susan Kellogg. *Domestic Revolutions: A Social History of American Family Life.* New York: Free Press, 1988.
Mosley, Nicholas. *Efforts at Truth.* Normal, Ill.: Dalkey Archive Press, 1995.
———. *Impossible Object.* 1969. Reprint, Normal, Ill.: Dalkey Archive Press, 1985.
"Musicals, Great Musicals: The Arthur Freed Unit at MGM." *Great Performances.* PBS. 2 December 1996.
Nabokov, Vladimir. *Lolita.* New York: Vintage, 1991.
Nader, Ralph. *Unsafe at Any Speed.* New York: Grossman Publishers, 1965.
Narboni, Jean. "Le hors-cadre decide de tout." *Cahiers du cinéma* 271 (November 1976): 14–21.
Naremore, James. *More Than Night: Film Noir in Its Contexts.* Berkeley: U of California P, 2008.
Nathans, Benjamin. *Beyond the Pale: The Jewish Encounter with Late Imperial Russia.* Berkeley: U of California P, 2002.
National Library of Medicine. "Paranoid Disorders." *Medical Subject Headings: National Institutes of Health* (15 October 2008). http://www.nlm.nih.gov/cgi/mesh/2009/MB_cgi?field=uid&term=D010259. Accessed 4 May 2009.
Newman, Kim. "The Island of Dr. Moreau." *Sight and Sound* 7.1 (January 1997): 38.
Nicholas, Lynn H. *The Rape of Europa: The Fate of Europe's Treasures in the Third Reich and the Second World War.* New York: Vintage, 1995.
Nietzsche, Friedrich. *Thus Spoke Zarathustra: A Book for All and None.* Trans. Walter Kaufmann. New York: Modern Library, 1995.
Novick, Robert. *The Holocaust in American Life.* Boston: Houghton Mifflin, 1999.
O'Brian, Jack. " . . . 26-Year-old Frankenheimer [is] TV's Best Director." *New York Journal-American* 15 March 1957.
Ohi, Kevin. "Of Red Queens and Garden Clubs: *The Manchurian Candidate,* Cold War Paranoia, and the Historicity of the Homosexual." *Camera Obscura* 20.1 (2005): 149–83.
O'Neill, Eugene. *The Iceman Cometh.* 1947. Foreword by Harold Bloom. New Haven, Conn.: Yale UP, 2006.

O'Neill, James Jr. "'The Train' on Time; It Took a Million Dollars to Blast 30 French Cars." *Washington Daily News* 1 April 1964. *The Train* scrapbook, John Frankenheimer Collection, HER.

Osborn, William C. *The Paper Plantation: Ralph Nader's Study Group Report on the Pulp and Paper Industry in Maine*. New York: Grossman Publishers, 1974.

O'Sullivan, Shane. *Who Killed Bobby? The Unsolved Murder of Robert F. Kennedy*. New York: Union Square Press, 2008.

Paine, Thomas. *The Rights of Man*. 1791. New York: Dover, 1999.

Palmer, R. Barton. "The Hitchcock Romance and the '70s Paranoid Thriller." *After Hitchcock: Influence, Imitation, and Intertextuality*. Ed. David Boyd and R. Barton Palmer. Austin: U of Texas P, 2006. 85–108.

Panofsky, Erwin. "Style and Medium in the Motion Pictures." *The Visual Turn: Classical Film Theory and Art History*. Ed. Angela Dalle Vacche. New Brunswick, N.J.: Rutgers UP, 2003. 69–84.

"Pantless at Armageddon." *Time* (6 July 1959). http://www.time.com/time/magazine/article/0,9171,825787,00.html. Accessed 2 June 2009.

Park, Ed. "Somebody's Watching Me." *Village Voice* 20 August 2002. http://www.villagevoice.com/2002-08-20/film/somebody-s-watching-me. Accessed 20 May 2010.

"Path to War: Interview with John Frankenheimer." http://www.hbo.com/movies. Accessed 29 November 2010.

Perlstein, Rick. *Nixonland: The Rise of a President and the Fracturing of America*. New York: Scribner, 2008.

Peck, Gregory. "Letter to John Frankenheimer Regarding the Editing of *I Walk the Line*." 20 February 1970. Gregory Peck file, HER.

Perkins, Victor F. "Direction and Authorship." *Auteurs and Authorship*. Ed. Barry Keith Grant. New York: Blackwell, 2008. 72.

Pisters, Patricia. "Delirium Cinema or Machines of the Invisible?" *Deleuze and the Schizoanalysis of Cinema*. Ed. Ian Buchanan and Patricia MacCormack. London: Continuum, 2008. 102–15.

Polito, Robert. *Farber on Film*. New York: Library of America, 2009.

Pomerance, Murray. "He Loved What He Did So Much! An Interview with Evans Frankenheimer." *Film International* 51 (May 2011).

Powers, James. "All Fall Down." *Hollywood Reporter* 26 March 1962, n.p.

———. "*Seconds* Class Horror Film with Rock Hudson: Frankenheimer Megs Ed Lewis Pic." *Hollywood Reporter* 192.24 (September 1966): 3.

Pratley, Gerald. *The Cinema of John Frankenheimer*. New York: A. S. Barnes, 1969. San Diego: Oak Tree Publications, 1976.

———. *The Films of John Frankenheimer: Forty Years in Film—John Frankenheimer Talks about His Life in the Cinema to Gerald Pratley*. Bethlehem, Pa.: Lehigh UP, 1998.

Prince, Stephen. *Firestorm: American Film in the Age of Terrorism*. New York: Columbia UP, 2009.

Priore, Domenic, and Becky Ebenkamp. *Look, Listen, Vibrate, Smile*. San Francisco: Last Gasp Printing, 2001.

Rachels, James. *Created from Animals: The Moral Implications of Darwinism*. Oxford: Oxford UP, 2010.

Revkin, Andrew C. *The Burning Season: The Murder of Chico Mendes and the Fight for the Amazon Rainforest*. New York: First Island Press, 1990.

———. "The Uncertain Legacy of Chico Mendes." *New York Times Dot Earth* 22 December 2008. http://community.nytimes.com/comments/dotearth.blogs.nytimes.com/2008/12/22/the-uncertain-legacy-of-chico-mendes/. Accessed 20 May 2010.

Rhys, Tim, and Ian Bage. "John Frankenheimer Survives Hollywood." *MovieMaker: The Art and Business of Making Movies* 1 October 1996.

"The Right Track." *Newsweek* 22 March 1965. The *Train* scrapbook, John Frankenheimer Collection, HER.

Roberts, Jerry. *Great American Playwrights on the Screen*. Milwaukee: Hal Leonard, 2003.

Robertson, Nan. "Mastroianni Picked to Open 25th New York Film Festival." *New York Times* 12 August 1987: C17. http://www.nytimes.com/1987/08/12/movies/mastroianni-picked-to-open-25th-new-york-film-festival.html. Accessed 21 May 2010.

Rodowick, David N. "Madness, Authority and Ideology: The Domestic Melodrama of the 1950s." *Home Is Where the Heart Is: Studies in Melodrama and the Woman's Film*. Ed. Christine Gledhill. London: BFI, 2002. 268–80.

Rogin, Michael. "Kiss Me Deadly: Communism, Motherhood, and Cold War Movies." *Representations* 6 (Spring 1984): 1–36.

Rosenbaum, Jonathan. "The Manchurian Candidate." *Chicago Reader* 26 October 1985. http://www.chicagoreader.com/chicago/the-manchurian-candidate/Film?oid=1048103. Accessed 27 January 2010.

Rushton, Richard. "What Can a Face Do?: On Deleuze and Faces." *Cultural Critique* 51 (Spring 2002): 219–37.

Samuel, Maurice. *Blood Accusation: The Strange History of the Mendel Beilis Case*. New York: Alfred A. Knopf, 1966.

Sarris, Andrew. *The American Cinema: Directors and Directions 1929–1968*. 1968. Reprint, New York: Da Capo Press, 1996.

Schatz, Thomas. "The New Hollywood." *Film Theory Goes to the Movies*. Ed. Jim Collins, Hilary Radner, and Ava Preacher Collins. New York: Routledge, 1993. 8–36.

Schivelbusch, Wolfgang. *Tastes of Paradise: A Social History of Spices, Stimulants, and Intoxicants*. Trans. David Jacobson. New York: Vintage, 1993.

Schreber, Daniel Paul. *Memoirs of My Nervous Illness*. New York: NYRB Classics, 2000.

Scott, Ian. *American Politics in Hollywood Film*. Edinburgh: Edinburgh UP, 2000.

Rev. of *Seconds*. *Daily Cinema* 9292 (November 1966): 9.

Rev. of *Seconds*. *Monthly Film Bulletin* 33.395 (December 1966): 181–82.

Seed, David. "Brainwashing and Cold War Demonology." *Prospects* 22 (1997): 535–73.

Semmerling, Tim Jon. *"Evil" Arabs in American Popular Film: Orientalist Fear*. Austin: U of Texas P, 2006.

Shaheen, Jack G. *Reel Bad Arabs: How Hollywood Vilifies a People*. New York: Olive Branch Press, 2001.

Shary, Timothy. *Generation Multiplex: The Image of Youth in Contemporary American Cinema*. Austin: U of Texas P, 2002.

Shengold, Leonard, M.D. *Soul Murder: The Effects of Childhood Abuse and Deprivation*. New York: Fawcett Columbine, 1991.

———. *Soul Murder Revisited: Thoughts about Therapy, Hate, Love, and Memory*. New Haven, Conn.: Yale UP, 1999.

Shilling, Chris. *The Body and Social Theory*. London: Sage Publications, 1993.

Shurlock, Geoffrey. "Letter to Robert Vogel, March 31, 1961, re *All Fall Down*." *All Fall Down* Production Code file, HER.

Simon, Alex. "John Frankenheimer: The Hollywood Interview." 1998. http://thehollywoodinterview.blogspot.com/2008/02/john-frankenheimer-hollywood-interview.html. Accessed 17 January 2010.

Simpson, David. *9/11: The Culture of Commemoration*. Chicago: U of Chicago P, 2006.

Singer, Peter. *Animal Liberation: A New Ethics for Our Treatment of Animals*. 4th ed. London: Pimlico Press, 1995.

Sinise, Gary. "John Frankenheimer Tribute: Thank You, John." *DGA Magazine* 27.3 (October 2002): 57–59.
6 Tuttt. "Malcolm and Annie." Internet Movie Database. http://www.imdb.com. Message Board for *The Gypsy Moths*. 13 November 2005.
Sloterdijk, Peter. *Terror from the Air*. Trans. Amy Patton and Steve Corcoran. Los Angeles: Semiotext(e), 2009.
Slotkin, Richard. *Gunfighter Nation: The Myth of the Frontier in Twentieth-Century America*. New York: Harper Perennial, 1993.
Smithpeter, Jeffrey Neal. "To the Latest Generation: Cold War and Post Cold War U.S. Civil War Novels in Their Social Context." Ph.D. diss., Louisiana State University, 2005.
Sobchack, Vivian. *Screening Space: The American Science Fiction Film*. New Brunswick, N.J.: Rutgers UP, 1997.
Sontag, Susan. "Film and Theatre." *Theater and Film: A Comparative Anthology*. Ed. Robert Knopf. New Haven, Conn.: Yale UP, 2005. 134–51.
Spiegel, Simon. "Things Made Strange: On the Concept of 'Estrangement' in Science Fiction Theory." *Science Fiction Studies* 35 (2008): 369–85.
Spoto, Donald. *Otherwise Engaged: The Life of Alan Bates*. London: Hutchinson, 2007.
Stam, Robert. *Reflexivity in Film and Literature: From Don Quixote to Jean-Luc Godard*. New York: Columbia UP, 1992.
Sterritt, David. "Films That People Can Talk About." *Christian Science Monitor* 15 September 1975: 26.
———. "What Have They Built You to Do?: The Manchurian Candidate and Cold War America." *PopMatters* 8 January 2007. http://www.popmatters.com/pm/review/what-have-they-built-you-to-do-by-matthew-frye-jacobson-and-gaspar-gonz. Accessed 25 June 2009.
Stewart, Garrett. "Digital Fatigue: Imaging War in Recent American Film." *Film Quarterly* 62.4 (2009): 45–55.
Stewart, Robert M. "Prophecy." *Cinefantastique* 1 (October 1979): 43.
Svetkey, Benjamin. "Rain-Forest Crunch: TV's Chico Mendes Eco-Pic Hacks through the Jungle of Hollywood." *Entertainment Weekly* 16 September 1994. http://www.ew.com/ew/article/0,,303681,00.html. Accessed 20 May 2010.
Tasker, Yvonne. *Spectacular Bodies: Gender, Genre, and the Action- Cinema*. London: Routledge, 1993.
Taylor, John Russell. "All Fall Down." *Sight and Sound* 31.3 (Summer 1962): 144.
Telotte, J. P. *Replications: A Robotic History of the Science Fiction Film*. Urbana: U of Illinois P, 1995.
Thomas, John. "John Frankenheimer: The Smile on the Face of the Tiger." *Film Quarterly* 19.2 (Winter 1965–66): 2–13.
Thomas, Kevin. "MGM Presents Comedy 'Extraordinary Seaman.'" *Los Angeles Times* 4 July 1969: C9.
Thullier, Jacques. "L'artiste et l'institution: l'école des Beaux-Arts et le Prix de Rome." *Le Grand Prix de Peinture: Les concours des Prix de Rome de 1797 à 1863* Ed. Philippe Grunchec. Paris: École Nationale Supérieure des Beaux Arts, 1983. 59–86.
Thurber, Jon, and Susan King. "John Frankenheimer, 72; Director Was Master of the Political Thriller." *Los Angeles Times* 7 July 2002: B16.
Tobias, Scott. "John Frankenheimer Interview." *A.V. Club* 16 February 2000. http://www.avclub.com/articles/john-frankenheimer,13639/. Accessed 20 May 2010.
Rev. of *The Train*. *Hollywood Reporter* 26 February 1965: n.p. *The Train* scrapbook, John Frankenheimer Collection, HER.
Tucker, Ken. "The Burning Season." *Entertainment Weekly* 16 September 1994. http://www.ew.com/ew/article/0,,303742,00.html. Accessed 20 May 2010.

Turan, Kenneth. "The Manchurian Candidate." *Los Angeles Times* 30 July 2004. http://www.calendarlive.com/movies/turan/cl-et-turan30ju130,2,1369411.story. Accessed 21 May 2010.

Turner, Bryan S. *The Body & Society*. London: Sage Publications, 1996.

Tynan, Kenneth. "Missing the Connection." *Observer*. 1 November 1964. In *The Train* scrapbook, John Frankenheimer Collection, HER.

Useem, Bert, and Peter Kimball. *States of Siege: U.S. Prison Riots 1971–1986*. New York: Oxford UP, 1991.

Valland, Rose. *Le Front de l'art: défense des collections françaises, 1939–1945*. Paris: Plon, 1961.

Virilio, Paul. *War and Cinema: The Logistics of Perception*. Trans. Patrick Camiller. New York: Verso, 1989.

Vizzard, J. A. "Memorandum, January 29, 1962, Regarding Issuing Code Certificate for *All Fall Down*." *All Fall Down* Production Code file, HER.

Westcombe, Roger. "The Manchurian Candidate (1962)." *Crimeculture*. http://www.crimeculture.com/Contents/FilmReviews/ ManchurianCand.htm. Accessed 18 May 2009.

Wexman, Virginia Wright. *A History of Film*. 7th ed. Boston: Allyn & Bacon, 2010.

Wheeler, L. Kip. "Freytag's Pyramid." http://web.cn.edu/kwheeler/freytag.html. Accessed 21 May 2010.

White, Edmund. "The Inner Burroughs." *Burroughs Live: The Collected Interviews of William S. Burroughs, 1960–1997*. Ed. Sylvère Lotringer. Los Angeles: Semiotext(e), 2001. 473–78.

White, Hayden. "The Modernist Event." *The Persistence of History*. Ed. Vivian Sobchack. New York: Routledge, 1996.

Wicker, Tom. *A Time to Die*. Lincoln: U of Nebraska P, 1975.

Wildermuth, Mark E. "Electronic Media and the Feminine in the National Security Regime." *Journal of Popular Film and Television* 35.3 (2008): 121–26.

Williams, Alan. *Republic of Images: A History of French Filmmaking*. Cambridge, Mass.: Harvard UP, 1992

Williams, Linda Ruth. *The Erotic Thriller in Contemporary Cinema*. Edinburgh: Edinburgh UP, 2005.

———. "A Woman Scorned: The Neo-noir Erotic Thriller as Revenge Drama." *Neo-Noir*. Ed. Mark Bould, Kathrina Glitre, and Greg Tuck. London: Wallflower Press, 2009. 168–85.

Wilson, Colin. "An Introduction to James Drought." *James Drought—American Author* (1966). http://www.drought.com/index.htm. Accessed 6 December 2009.

———. *The Outsider*. 1956. Reprint, New York: Putnam, 1982.

Wilson, David. "Review of *Seconds*." *Sight and Sound* 36.1 (December 1966): 46.

Winston, Archer. "Reviewing Stand: 'The Train' Rolls into Astor & Plaza." *New York Post* 18 March 1965: 20.

Woldu, Gail Hilson, and Sophie Queuniet. "Au-delà du scandale de 1905: Propos sur le Prix de Rome au début du XXe siècle." *Revue de Musicologie* 82.2e (1996): 245–26.

Woodward, Steven. "She's Murder, Pretty Poisons and Bad Seeds." *Sugar, Spice and Everything Nice: Cinemas of Girlhood*. Ed. Frances Gateward and Murray Pomerance. Detroit: Wayne State UP, 2002. 303–21.

Wylie, Phillip. *Generation of Vipers*. 1955. Ed. Curtis White. Reprint, Champaign, Ill.: Dalkey Archive Press, 2007.

Žižek, Slavoj. *Looking Awry: An Introduction to Jacques Lacan through Popular Culture*. Cambridge, Mass.: MIT Press, 1991.

———. "The Superego and the Act: A Lecture by Slavoj Žižek." *European Graduate School* (August 1999). http://www.egs.edu/faculty/zizek/zizek-superego-and-the-act-1999.html. Accessed 4 May 2009.

———. *Welcome to the Desert of the Real*. New York: Verso, 2002.

CONTRIBUTORS

REBECCA BELL-METEREAU, professor of film at Texas State University, directs the Media Studies Minor Program there and is the author of *Hollywood Androgyny* and *Simone Weil* and essays in *Cinema and Modernity*; *American Cinema of the 1950s*; *Film and Television after 9/11*; *Bad: Infamy, Darkness, Evil, and Slime on Screen*; *The Family in America*; *Ladies and Gentlemen, Boys and Girls*; *Writing With*; *Cultural Conflicts in 20th Century Literature*; *Technological Imperatives*; *Women Worldwalkers*; *College English*; *Quarterly Review of Film and Video*; *Journal of Popular Film & Television*; and *Cinema Journal*.

CHARLES RAMÍREZ BERG is University Distinguished Teaching Professor in the Department of Radio-Television-Film at the University of Texas at Austin. He is the author of *Latino Images in Film*; *Cinema of Solitude: A Critical Study of Mexican Film*; and *Posters from the Golden Age of Mexican Cinema*. His articles have appeared in journals such as *CineAction*, *Film Criticism*, *Aztlan*, *The Howard Journal of Communications*, and *Jump Cut*. He has published numerous book chapters and encyclopedia entries on film history, theory, and criticism, and provided onscreen commentary for *The Bronze Screen*, *Twin Peaks: The First Season*, and audio commentary (with Thomas Schatz) for the DVD of Hitchcock's *Spellbound*.

MATTHEW H. BERNSTEIN teaches at Emory University, where he currently chairs the Department of Film Studies. His publications include *Screening a Lynching: Leo Frank on Film and TV*; *Walter Wanger, Hollywood Independent*; and edited collections on Hollywood censorship, John Ford sound westerns, and Michael Moore.

DENNIS BINGHAM teaches English and film studies in the Indiana University School of Liberal Arts at Indiana University Purdue University Indianapolis. He is the author of *Whose Lives Are They Anyway? The Biopic as Contemporary Film Genre* and numerous writings on stardom, acting, genre, and gender in cinema.

TOM CONLEY is Lowell Professor of Romance Languages and Visual and Environmental Studies at Harvard University, author of *Cartographic Cinema*, and translator of Christian Jacob's *The Sovereign Map* and Marc Augé's *Casablanca*:

Movies and Memory. He has completed *An Errant Eye* and a forthcoming new edition of *The Self-Made Map: Cartographic Writing in Early Modern France*.

CHRISTINE CORNEA is a lecturer with the School of Film and Television at the University of East Anglia. She has published extensively on science fiction in film and television, including her book *Science Fiction Cinema: Between Fantasy and Reality*. She has also published on screen performance and theory, including her most recent, edited book, *Genre and Performance: Film and Television*. At present, she is working on *Post-Apocalypse on the Small Screen*.

COREY K. CREEKMUR is associate professor of English and Film Studies at the University of Iowa, where he also directs the Institute for Cinema and Culture. His publications and research focus on popular Hindi cinema, film genres, film music, comics, and representations of race, gender, and sexuality in popular culture. He is the co-editor of *Out in Culture: Gay, Lesbian, and Queer Essays on Popular Culture, Cinema, Law, and the State in Asia* and *The International Film Musical*, and the author of forthcoming studies of gender and sexuality in the western and of the neglect of Indian cinema by film studies.

VICTORIA DUCKETT is a lecturer in film and the arts in the Centre for Ideas, Victorian College of the Arts and Music, University of Melbourne. In 2006 she curated the film series "Performing Passions: Sarah Bernhardt and the Silent Screen" for the Cinema Ritrovato Festival (Bologna). She has recently published in *Senses of Cinema* and contributed to the anthologies *Reclaiming the Archive: Feminism and Film History* and *Méliès' Trip to the Moon: Fantastic Voyages of the Cinematic Imagination*. An early participant in the Women and the Silent Screen conference (Utrecht, 1999), she is currently completing a book on Sarah Bernhardt and silent film as well as editing an issue on gender and early film for the journal *Nineteenth Century Theatre and Film*.

BILL KROHN has been the Los Angeles correspondent for *Cahiers du cinéma* since 1978. He co-wrote, co-directed, and co-produced *It's All True: Based on an Unfinished Film by Orson Welles*. His books include *Hitchcock at Work*; *Luis Buñuel: Chimera*; the French monographs *Stanley Kubrick* and *Alfred Hitchcock* (published in English in 2010); and *Serial Killer Dreams*, forthcoming in 2011. Besides publishing regularly in the *Cahiers*, he writes for *Cineaste*, *Cinema Scope* and *Trafic*, and reviews films for *The Economist*.

DOUGLAS McFARLAND is professor of Liberal Arts and director of General Education at Flagler College in St. Augustine, Florida. He has published pieces on the Coen brothers, Peter Bogdanovich, and Hitchcock, as well as Montaigne and Rabelais.

CONTRIBUTORS

JAMES MORRISON is professor of Literature and Film Studies at Claremont McKenna College. He has published several books on film, most recently *Roman Polanski* and, as editor, *Hollywood Reborn: Movie Stars of the 1970s*.

JERRY MOSHER is an assistant professor in the Department of Film and Electronic Arts at California State University, Long Beach. His research focuses on American cinema and its representation of the body. He has published essays on film and culture in numerous anthologies.

ROBIN L. MURRAY is professor of English and coordinator of the film studies minor at Eastern Illinois University. She is the co-author, with Joseph Heumann, of *Ecology and Popular Film: Cinema on the Edge* and two forthcoming volumes, *That's All Folks? Ecocritical Readings of American Animated Features* and *Gunfight at the Eco-Corral: Western Film and the Environment*.

R. BARTON PALMER is Calhoun Lemon Professor of Literature and director of film studies at Clemson University. He is the author, editor, or general editor of more than forty books on various literary and cinematic subjects, including most recently *To Kill a Mockingbird: From Page to Screen* and (with Robert Bray) *Hollywood's Tennessee: The Williams Films and Postwar America*. He serves with Linda Badley as general editor of the Traditions in World Cinema series (Edinburgh University Press) and is the founding general editor, with Tison Pugh, of New Perspectives on Medieval Literature (University Press of Florida).

MURRAY POMERANCE is professor of sociology at Ryerson University and the author of *Michelangelo Red Antonioni Blue: Eight Reflections on Cinema*, *The Horse Who Drank the Sky: Film Experience Beyond Narrative and Theory*, *Johnny Depp Starts Here*, and *An Eye for Hitchcock*, as well as editor or co-editor of numerous volumes, including *Cinema and Modernity*; *Enfant Terrible! Jerry Lewis in American Film*; *A Family Affair: Cinema Calls Home*; and the forthcoming volumes *Stars of David: The Jewish Experience in American Cinema* and *Shining in Shadows: Movie Stars of the 2000s*. He edits the Horizons of Cinema series at SUNY Press and the Techniques of the Moving Image series at Rutgers University Press, and, with Lester D. Friedman and Adrienne L. McLean, respectively, co-edits the Screen Decades and Star Decades series at Rutgers. In 2009 he appeared on Broadway in conjunction with *The 39 Steps*.

STEPHEN PRINCE is professor of communication at Virginia Tech and the author of *Firestorm: American Film in the Age of Terrorism*; *Movies and Meaning*; *Classical Film Violence*; *The Warrior's Camera: The Cinema of Akira Kurosawa*; *A New Pot of Gold: Hollywood under the Electronic Rainbow*; *Screening Violence*; *Savage Cinema: Sam Peckinpah and the Rise of Ultraviolent Movies*; and other works. He has edited *Sam Peckinpah's "The Wild Bunch"*; *The Horror Film*; and *American Cinema of the 1980s: Themes and Variations*. His audio commentaries have appeared on the DVDs of films by Peckinpah and Kurosawa.

DAVID STERRITT is chairman of the National Society of Film Critics, adjunct professor at Columbia University and the Maryland Institute College of Art, chief book critic of *Film Quarterly*, film critic of *Tikkun*, and a regular contributor to *Cineaste*. He was film critic and cultural correspondent of the *Christian Science Monitor* for decades, and his writing has appeared in *Cahiers du cinéma*, the *New York Times*, *Journal of French Philosophy*, *Journal of Aesthetics and Art Criticism*, and many other publications. His books include *Mad to Be Saved: The Beats, the '50s, and Film*; *The Films of Jean-Luc Godard: Seeing the Invisible*; *Guiltless Pleasures: A David Sterritt Film Reader*; *The B List*; and *The Honeymooners*.

LINDA RUTH WILLIAMS is professor of film in the English Department at the University of Southampton, UK. She is author and editor of four books, including *The Erotic Thriller in Contemporary Cinema* (2005) and *Contemporary American Cinema* (2006, with Michael Hammond), and has written numerous articles on contemporary cinema, gender, sexuality, and censorship. She is now writing Ken Russell's biography and a monograph on Spielberg and childhood.

INDEX

Abyss, The (James Cameron, 1989), 84
Académie Royale de Peintre, 131
Accident (Joseph Losey, 1967), 200, 204, 206–207, 210
Ace in the Hole (Billy Wilder, 1951), 224
Addy, Wesley, 58
Adler, Renata, 260, 287
Aeschylus, 266
Affleck, Ben, 271
Against The Wall (John Frankenheimer, 1994), 4, 8, 91–94, 96–100, 102, 229, 244, 265, 267–271, 274, 285
AIDS, 211
Alamo, The (John Wayne, 1960), 43
Albee, Edward, 171, 185, 188, 287
Alcatraz Prison, 102, 146–149, 153–156, 158
Aldrich, Robert, 9
Algiers Motel Incident, The (John Hersey), 96, 292
Alien (Ridley Scott, 1979), 231, 235–237
All About Eve (Joseph L. Mankiewicz, 1950), 152
All Fall Down (John Frankenheimer, 1962), 2–3, 6, 78, 184–187, 190, 193–194, 196, 204, 215, 282, 287, 289, 292, 295–298
All That Heaven Allows (Douglas Sirk, 1955), 56
Alter, Robert, 258–259, 287
Altman, Robert, 171–172, 293
Alvarez Kelly (Edward Dmytryk, 1966), 77
Ambassador Hotel (Los Angeles), 91, 200, 275, 277, 283
Ambush (John Frankenheimer, 2001), 271, 286
American Academy of Motion Picture Arts and Sciences, 131, 133, 196, 287
American Civil Liberties Union, 50, 53
American Film Theatre, 170, 284
American-International Pictures, 219
Anderson, Lindsay, 172
Andersonville (John Frankenheimer, 1996), 2, 4, 78, 100, 229, 244, 268–269, 285
Andersonville Trial, The (Sol Levitt), 268–269
Antonioni, Michelangelo, 210, 301
Apocalypse Now (Francis Ford Coppola, 1979), 270
Arles, France, 84, 87, 115
Armendariz, Pedro, 270
Armstrong, Stephen B., 29, 129, 134, 167–168, 173, 244, 252, 255, 260, 287

Arnold, Edward, 1, 280
Assante, Armand, 237, 284
Assassination of Trotsky, The (Joseph Losey, 1972), 207
Assistant, The (Bernard Malamud), 257–258
Astor, Mary, 1, 280, 281, 282
Atlanta, 30, 73
Attica State Penitentiary, 4, 91–100, 102, 266–267, 269, 271, 289
Aubrey, James, 219–220, 224
Auclair, Michel, 202, 209, 283
Aumont, Tina, 206, 280
Axelrod, George, 15, 42–47, 50

Bach, Johann Sebastian, 70
Badsey, Stephen, 29, 31, 105, 287
Bailey, Charles W. III, 18, 293
Baker, Carroll, 161
Baker, Joe Don, 272
Baldwin, Alec, 273–275, 286
Balk, Fairuza, 241, 270, 285
Bandini, Lorenzo, 138
Bardamu, Ferdinand, 153
Barton, James, 170
Bass, Saul, 41, 54
Bates, Alan, 200–202, 204–209, 212, 244, 249, 283, 297
Battle of Algiers, The (Gillo Pontecorvo, 1966), 83
Baudrillard, Jean, 103–104, 287
Baxley, Barbara, 193
Bazin, André, 40, 287
Bean, Sean, 79, 271
Beatty, Warren, 6, 184–186, 189, 194, 196, 282
Bedelia, Bonnie, 225, 227
Bedford, Brian, 137, 141
Behra, Jean, 139
Beilis, Menachem Mendel, case, 246
Belges, Jean Lemaire de, 145, 156
Benjamin, Walter, 75
Bennett, Joan, 1, 280, 281
Berge, Richard, 63, 74
Bergman, Ingrid, 174, 282
Bernstein, Walter, 63
Bertolucci, Bernardo, 201
Best Years of Our Lives, The (William Wyler, 1946), 252
Beverly Hillbillies, The (television series), 219–220
Bible, The (John Huston, 1966), 129

303

Big House, The (George W. Hill, 1930), 97, 150
Big House USA (Howard W. Koch, 1955), 150
Biograph, 1
Birdman of Alcatraz (John Frankenheimer, 1962), 2, 3, 8, 71–72, 78, 96–97, 102, 133, 145, 147–149, 151, 153, 155–156, 158, 215, 244, 262, 282
Birth of a Nation, The (D. W. Griffith, 1915), 270
Biskind, Peter, 235, 288
Blackboard Jungle (Richard Brooks, 1955), 184
Black Gunn (Robert Hartford-Davis, 1972), 77
Black Hundreds, 246–248, 252
Black Panthers, 100, 266
Black Power movement, 97–99
Black Sunday (John Frankenheimer, 1977), 7–8, 104–105, 107–115, 264–265, 284
Blade Runner (Ridley Scott, 1982), 237
Blume in Love (Paul Mazursky, 1973), 212
Body of Lies (Ridley Scott, 2008), 115
Boenisch, Carl, 217
Bogarde, Dirk, 204, 250, 253, 283, 290
Boime, Albert, 131–133, 288
Bonnie and Clyde (Arthur Penn, 1967), 165, 221
Booker Prize, 203
Boorman, John, 157
Bosco, Philip, 267
Boston, 30, 288, 292–294, 298
Bourne Ultimatum, The (Paul Greengrass, 2007), 115
Boutet de Monvel, Violaine, 65, 77
Bowie, Stephen, 13, 75, 173, 221, 226–227 231
Boys in the Band, The (William Friedkin, 1970), 172
Bradford, Barbara Taylor, 204
Bradford, Robert, 204, 212, 293
Brando, Marlon, 133, 239, 241–242, 269–270, 285
Brands Hatch, 136
Brazil, 117, 120–121, 126–127, 268
Brecht, Bertolt, 171, 209, 213
Bremer, Arthur, 272, 274
Bresson, Robert, 150–153, 156
Bricken, Jules, 71
Bridges, Jess, 177, 183, 284
Bright, Matthew, 162
Brood, The (David Cronenberg, 1979), 237
Brooks, Richard, 184
Brussels World's Fair (1958), 140
Brustein, Robert, 177, 288
Brute Force (Jules Dassin, 1947), 150
Bullitt (Peter Yates, 1968), 3, 84
Burning Season, The (John Frankenheimer, 1994), 3–4, 117–123, 124, 127, 229, 268–269, 285, 291, 295, 297
Burroughs, William S., 16, 298
Bury, Sean, 211
Bush, George W., 19, 21, 28, 276–277, 286
Butch Cassidy and the Sundance Kid (George Roy Hill, 1969), 214
Butley (Simon Gray), 204–206
Butterfield 8 (Daniel Mann, 1960), 43

Cabaret (Bob Fosse, 1972), 172
Cagney, James, 149, 152
Caldwell, John Thornton, 173, 288

Cameron, James, 84, 231
Cammell, Donald, 231
Camus, Albert, 266
Canby, Vincent, 221, 254, 288
Cannes Film Festival, 57, 202, 235
Capitalism and Freedom (Milton Friedman), 231, 291
Cappell, Ezra, 259–260, 288
"Capture of John Dillinger, The" (John Frankenheimer, 1953), 4, 279
Carlino, Lewis John, 56
Carradine, John, 1, 280
Carroll, Noël, 74, 288
Cash, Johnny, 158, 294
Cassavetes, John, 171, 281
Catcher in the Rye, The (J. D. Salinger), 217
Cavett, Dick, 112, 277
Central Intelligence Agency, 49
Challenge, The (John Frankenheimer, 1982), 78, 129, 284
Champlin, Charles, 29, 47, 168, 180, 263, 268, 289–290
Charbonneau, Stephen, 7, 289
Chariots of Fire (Hugh Hudson, 1981), 268
Château de Compiègne, 132
Chermont, Isabelle le Masne de, 63
Chessman, Caryl, 259
Chicago Times-Herald, 136
Chinatown (Roman Polanski, 1974), 45
Chow, Rey, 107, 289
Chushingura (Hiroshi Inagaki, 1962), 82
Cinema of Loneliness, A (Robert Kolker), 159, 293
Circuit de Monaco, 136
Circuit Zandvoort, 136
Citizen Kane (Orson Welles, 1941), 36, 40, 274
Civil Rights Act of 1964, 273
Clark, Richard X., 101
Clarke, Thurston, 91, 289
Clayton, Jack, 174
Clement, René, 66–70, 72, 74–75, 289
Clermont-Ferrand, France, 336
Climax! (television anthology series), 1, 31, 280, 281
Clover, Carol, 167
Coen, Franklin, 63, 66, 77
Cohen, Bonni, 63, 74
Colbert, Claudette, 1, 280
Colbert, Jean-Baptiste, 131–132
Colbert, Stephen, 18
Collector, The (William Wyler, 1965), 204
Collins, Peter, 139
Columbia Pictures, 160–161, 200, 288, 293, 295, 297, 302
Comden, Betty, 220
Come Back Little Sheba (Daniel Mann, 1952), 221
Comedian, The (John Frankenheimer, 1957), 32–36, 38, 47, 173, 281, 284
Coombs, Richard, 159
Condon, Richard, 15, 17–18, 50, 53–54, 56, 48, 261, 265, 289
Conrad, Barnaby, 272
Conversation, The (Francis Ford Coppola, 1974), 13

INDEX 305

Conway, Thom, 223
Coppola, Francis Ford, 13, 264
Corrigan, Lloyd, 52
Coursodon, Jean-Pierre, 73, 289
Cowan, Jerome, 155
Crank (Neveldine/Taylor, 2006), 115
Creed, Barbara, 237–238, 289
Cronenberg, David, 237–238
Crowther, Bosley, 68, 186, 189, 260, 289
Cruel Intentions (Roger Kumble, 1999), 166
Crush, The (Alan Shapiro, 1993), 163
Cuban missile crisis, 49, 283
Culver City, 135, 219

Daddy Long Legs (Jean Negulesco, 1955), 152
Dahl, John, 166
Daily Mail, 161, 168
Daily Mirror, 161, 168
Daily Variety, 202, 287, 291, 293
Dance Girl Dance (Dorothy Arzner, 1940), 77
Danger (television anthology series), 31, 262, 279–280
Daniel, Gordon, 138
Danks, Adrian, 66, 289
Dassin, Jules, 184
Davis, Doug, 106, 289
Davis, Frank, 63, 66, 77
Dawson, Kamala, 120, 122
Day of the Jackal, The (Fred Zinnemann, 1973), 111
Days of Heaven (Terrence Malick, 1978), 171
Days of Wine and Roses (John Frankenheimer, 1958), 2, 174, 282
Dean, James, 1, 184, 279
"Death of Manolete, The" (John Frankenheimer, 1957), 272, 281
Deer Hunter, The (Michael Cimino, 1978), 171
De Gaulle, Charles, 70, 111
Deleuze, Gilles, 22–24, 28, 156, 289, 292, 295–296
Delicate Balance, A (Tony Richardson, 1973), 172
Deliverance (John Boorman, 1972), 157, 159, 167
Demme, Jonathan, 13, 292
Democratic National Convention (1968), 100
Demon Seed (Donald Cammell, 1977), 231
Deneuve, Catherine, 204
De Niro, Robert, 2, 13, 79, 81, 84, 113, 271, 285
Denny, Reginald, 97, 280
Dern, Bruce, 8, 109, 284
De Wilde, Brandon, 6, 186–187, 195–196, 282
Dhiege, Khigh, 15, 37, 51, 55
Dightam, Marc, 211
DiMaggio, Joe, 93
Dimendberg, Edward, 156, 289
Dirty Dozen, The (Robert Aldrich, 1967), 80
Discipline and Punish (Michel Foucault), 146, 153, 290
D.O.A (Rudolph Maté, 1950), 149
Doane, Mary Ann, 237–238, 290
Doctor Zhivago (David Lean, 1965), 130
Double Elvis (Andy Warhol), 140
Douglas, Kirk, 18, 21, 283
Douglas, Michael, 166

Dreyer, Carl Theodore, 174
Dreyfus, Alfred, 259
Dreyfus affair, 246
Drought, James, 215–219, 222, 227–228, 261, 290, 298
Dylan, Bob, 98
Dysart, Richard, 2, 8, 236, 284, 290

Each Dawn I Die (William Keighley, 1939), 150
Eagle Eye (D. J. Caruso, 2008), 115
Eames, Charles, 139
Easy Rider (Dennis Hopper, 1969), 214, 219
École des Beaux Arts, 132, 291, 297
Eigeman, Chris, 275
8 ½ (Federico Fellini, 1963), 201
Eisenhower, Dwight, 49, 76, 190, 290
Eisenstein, Sergei, 265, 276–277
Ellison, Harlan, 69, 71, 290
Elmer Gantry (Richard Brooks, 1960), 71, 221
Elsaesser, Thomas, 159, 167, 193–194, 290
Ely, David, 21, 54, 56
Embarcadero (San Francisco), 147–148
Emmy Awards, 4, 31, 47, 102, 127
Environmental Protection Agency, 236
Epton, Dick, 97
Eraserhead (David Lynch, 1977), 171
Evans (Frankenheimer), Evans, 8, 193, 199–202, 209, 283, 295
Evans, Walker, 168
Exile, An (Madison Jones), 157, 164, 292
Exorcist: The Beginning (Renny Harlin, 2004), 229
Extraordinary Seaman, The (John Frankenheimer, 1969), 3, 129, 200, 283, 297
Eyes of Laura Mars, The (Irvin Kershner, 1978), 157

Fahrenheit 9/11 (Michael Moore, 2004), 13
Faludi, Susan, 165, 290
Fanon, Frantz, 239
Farber, Manny, 264, 271
Farber, Stephen, 129, 130, 134–135, 142, 235, 290
Farm Workers Union, 266
Farocki, Harun, 107
Farrell, Kirby, 234, 290
Fatal Attraction (Adrian Lyne, 1988), 163, 165–166
Faulkner, William, 216
Fellini, Federico, 201, 210
52 Pick Up (John Frankenheimer, 1986), 78, 284
Film Quarterly, 129, 288, 290, 292–293, 297, 302
Financial Times, 159, 161, 164, 168
Firestone, Cinda, 267
Fitzgerald, F. Scott, 57, 199, 216, 290
Five Easy Pieces (Bob Rafelson, 1970), 159, 171
Fixer, The (John Frankenheimer, 1968), 3, 135, 200, 204, 244–247, 249, 251–253, 255–261, 283, 287, 293
Flon, Suzanne, 65–66
Fonda, Peter, 214
Ford, Constance, 191, 280, 284
Ford, John, 1, 40, 98, 299

Forrest, Frederick, 267, 274, 285
Forsyth, Frederick, 111
Fort Leavenworth, Kansas, 149–153
Foucault, Michel, 146, 153, 155, 290
Four Horsemen of the Apocalypse, The (Vincent Minnelli, 1962), 193
Fowles, John, 204
Foxworth, Robert, 236, 238, 284
Frady, Marshall, 272
Frain, James, 275, 285
Fraisse, Robert, 84
France, 62–65, 67–68, 129, 131–132, 134–136, 199–200, 202, 204, 210, 212, 246, 283, 291–292, 298, 300
Francis of Assisi, 258
Franco London Film, 204, 212
Frankenstein (James Whale, 1931), 230
Fraser, Elisabeth, 59
Freeway (Matthew Bright, 1996), 163
French Connection, The (William Friedkin, 1972), 3, 226, 271
French Connection II, The (John Frankenheimer, 1975), 3, 5–6, 262, 264, 284, 288
French New Wave, 7, 172, 211, 226, 233, 264
Freud, Sigmund, 17, 22, 52, 152, 191, 291
Freytag, Gustav, 41, 298
Friedkin, William, 3, 262
Friedman, Lester D., 70, 291, 301
Friedman, Milton, 231–232, 291
From Here to Eternity (Fred Zinnemann, 1953), 217
Front, The (Martin Ritt, 1976), 93
Frost, Robert, 210

Gaddis, Thomas, 146, 148–150, 155
Galileo (Joseph Losey, 1975), 172
Gambon, Michael, 273, 286
Garfinkel, Eric, 77
Garland, Judy, 54
Garner, James, 134, 136–139, 141, 280, 283
Geer, Will, 22, 56, 234
General, The (Buster Keaton, 1926), 67, 69, 71–72
General Line, The (Sergei Eisenstein, 1929), 265, 276–277
Genet, Jean, 171
Gentleman's Agreement (Elia Kazan, 1947), 160
George Wallace (John Frankenheimer, 1997), 4, 8, 78, 102, 229, 263, 271–275, 285
Georgia, 167, 268, 283, 291, 294
Gertrud (Carl Theodore Dreyer, 1964), 174
Gettysburg (Ronald F. Maxwell, 1973), 268
Gibney, Alex, 13
Gielgud, John, 1, 282
Gilroy, Tony, 13
Ginsberg, Allen, 93
Ginther, Richie, 139
Giraud-Carrier, Isabelle, 211
Glengarry Glen Ross (James Foley, 1992), 83
Goering, Hermann, 63
Goethe, Johann Wolfgang von, 70
Golden Gate Bridge (San Francisco), 147
Golden Globes, 127
Goldman, Emma, 177
Goldsmith, Jerry, 55, 58

Golino, Valeria, 111, 285
Goode, Erich, 16, 291
Good Shepherd, The (Robert De Niro, 1996), 13
González, Gaspar, 26, 28–29, 49–50, 105, 263, 276–277, 292
Graduate, The (Mike Nichols, 1967), 171
Grand Central Station (New York City), 55
Grande Illusion, La (Jean Renoir, 1937), 68
Grant, Cary, 219
Gray, Simon, 204
Green, Adolph, 220
Green, Guy, 204
Green, Walon, 270
Greene, Graham, 46
Gregory, James, 15, 39, 52, 276, 281–282
Grierson, John, 66
Griffith, D. W., 1, 9, 215
Griffith, Hugh, 248
Grand Prix (John Frankenheimer, 1968), 2–3, 5–7, 41, 78, 84, 87, 129–142, 199, 201, 215, 264, 283, 291, 297
Grand Prix de Rome, 129–135, 139, 140, 142, 291, 297
Guattari, Félix, 22–23, 28, 289
Guerard, Michael, 199
Gulf War (1990–91), 240; Gulf War Syndrome, 240
Gunn, Moses, 180
Guns of Navarone, The (J. Lee Thompson, 1961), 160
Guzmán, Luis, 121, 285
Gypsy Moths, The (John Frankenheimer, 1969), 2–3, 6–7, 8, 83–84, 87, 129, 135, 167, 200, 214–216, 218–221, 223, 225, 228, 253–254, 261, 283, 290, 297

Haber, Joyce, 204, 291
Hackman, Gene, 5–6, 160, 215–216, 221, 226–227, 262, 282–284
Haiken, Elizabeth, 233, 291
Hall, Peter, 172
Hallelujah Trail, The (John Sturges, 1965), 221
Harlem (New York City), 97, 260
Hatch, Kristin, 161–162, 164, 168, 292
Handel, George Frideric, 70
Hard Candy (David Slade, 2005), 163
Hardy, Françoise, 134
Harlin, Renny, 229
Hartman, Elizabeth, 248–249
Harvey, Laurence, 15, 30, 43, 48, 50–51, 53–54, 254, 283
Havers, Nigel, 125, 285
Hawaii (George Roy Hill, 1966), 129
Haworth, Ted, 235
Hawthorne, Mike, 139
HBO, 3–4, 14, 78, 87, 91, 94, 97, 118, 127, 171, 229, 268, 272, 277, 284–285, 295
Heidegger, Martin, 27, 292
Heiress, The (William Wyler, 1949), 177
Henderson, Douglas, 34
Henry VIII (king of England), 134
Herlihy, James Leo, 184
Herr, Michael, 270
Hersey, John, 96, 100, 292
Heston, Charlton, 1, 281

INDEX

Hicks, Granville, 260
Higashi, Sumiko, 96, 292
High Sierra (Raoul Walsh, 1941), 155
Hill, Phil, 138–139
Hitchcock, Alfred, 8, 26, 40, 79, 174, 219, 281, 295, 299–300
Hofstadter, Richard, 14, 21, 292
Holcroft Covenant, The (John Frankenheimer, 1985), 3, 213, 284
Hollywood from Vietnam to Reagan (Robin Wood), 159
Hollywood Reporter, 31, 74, 195, 209, 235, 293, 295, 297
Holm, Ian, 250
Holocaust, 247, 259–260, 294
Homecoming, The (Peter Hall, 1973), 172
Hoover, J. Edgar, 53
Hopper, Dennis, 214, 282
Horsemen, The (John Frankenheimer, 1971), 3, 8, 129, 193, 199–201, 204, 283
House of Games (David Mamet, 1987), 83
House Un-American Activities Committee, 49, 235
Howe, James Wong, 54–55, 235
How Green Was My Valley (John Ford, 1941), 98
Hudson, Rock, 2, 22, 24, 28, 48, 54–60, 233, 283, 292, 295
Hunter, Kim, 1, 33, 281, 284
Hunter, Tab, 57, 264, 281
Hussein, Saddam, 240
Hutchinson, Ron, 120, 269, 271, 297

I Am a Fugitive from a Chain Gang (Mervyn LeRoy, 1932), 150
Iceman Cometh, The (John Frankenheimer, 1973), 3, 170–183
Images (Robert Altman, 1972), 171
Impossible Object (John Frankenheimer, 1973), 3, 199–206, 209–212, 283, 293–294
Ionesco, Eugène, 171
Inagaki, Hiroshi, 82
In Celebration (Lindsay Anderson, 1975), 172
Information Machine, The (Charles Eames, 1958), 139
Inge, William, 1, 184, 196, 280
In the Heat of the Night (Norman Jewison, 1967), 218
Island of Dr. Moreau, The (Don Taylor, 1977), 239
Island of Dr. Moreau, The (John Frankenheimer, 1996), 3, 5, 78, 127, 229–230, 239–241, 265, 269–270, 277, 285, 294
Island of Lost Souls (Erle C. Kenton, 1932), 230, 239
It's Always Fair Weather (Stanley Donen, 1955), 220
I Walk the Line (John Frankenheimer, 1970), 3, 6, 157–164, 166–168, 200, 283, 295
I Want to Live! (Robert Wise, 1958), 224

Jackie III (Andy Warhol), 140
Jackson, Samuel L., 95, 266, 269, 285
Jacobson, Matthew Frye, 26, 28–29, 49–50, 105, 263, 276–277, 292, 297
James, Clifton, 178
Japan, 81–83, 139, 141, 237
Jarre, Maurice, 65, 75, 138
Jaws (Steven Spielberg, 1975), 9, 265
Jazz Singer, The (Michael Curtiz, 1952), 77
Jennings, Humphrey, 66
Jens, Salome, 59, 234, 283
Jeu de Paume (Paris), 65, 68, 73
JFK (Oliver Stone, 1991), 99
Jim Thorpe—All American (Michael Curtiz, 1951), 77
Johnson, Lyndon B., 4, 14, 102, 272–273
Johnson, Stella, 152
Jolie, Angelina, 272, 285
Jolson Sings Again (Henry Levin, 1949), 216
Jolson Story, The (Alfred E. Green, 1946), 216
Jones, Madison, 157, 162, 168, 292
Judgment at Nuremberg (Stanley Kramer, 1961), 121, 264
Julia, Raul, 117, 120, 123, 268, 285
Jurassic Park (Steven Spielberg, 1993), 84

Kael, Pauline, 6, 9, 157–158, 171–172, 189, 191, 276, 293
Kafka, Franz, 23, 28, 289, 293
Kant, Emmanuel, 70
Kantor, MacKinlay, 268
Keaton, Buster, 67, 69, 71, 74
Keller, Marthe, 109, 284
Kellogg, Susan, 191–192, 294
Kennedy, John F., 29–30, 49–50, 53, 105, 190, 231, 263, 275
Kennedy, Robert F., 7, 91, 93, 102, 105, 200, 229, 263, 264–268, 277, 283, 289, 294–295
Kenton, Erle C., 230, 239
Kent State University, 93, 271
Kerkorian, Kirk, 220
Kerr, Deborah, 6, 215, 217, 219–223, 226–227, 253, 283, 293
KGB, 79, 81, 114
Khartoum (Basil Dearden, 1966), 129
Kids (Larry Clark, 1995), 252
Kiev, Ukraine, 247–248
Killers, The (Robert Siodmak, 1946), 149
Killing of Sister George, The (Robert Aldrich, 1968), 172
Kill Me Again (John Dahl, 1989), 166
Kilmer, Val, 241, 269–270, 285
Kimball, Peter, 92, 100, 298
Kinberg, Jud, 204, 207
King and I, The (Walter Lang, 1956), 219
King, Louise, 139
King, Martin Luther Jr., 93, 271–272
King, Rodney, 97
Kirby, Lynne, 67–68, 293
Kissinger, Henry, 93
Kleeb, Helen, 51
Knebel, Fletcher, 18, 293
Kohlsaat, Herman H., 136
Kolker, Robert, 159, 293
Kramer, Stanley, 9
Kring, Tim, 127
Kristeva, Julia, 237
Kubrick, Stanley, 161, 293, 300
Kumble, Roger, 166

Kurosawa, Akira, 5, 276, 301–302
Kuwait, 240

Lady in the Lake, The (Robert Montgomery, 1947), 145
Lancaster, Burt, 2, 6, 18, 21, 62, 65–66, 68, 71–72, 76, 83, 96, 145, 154, 215, 217–219, 221–226, 252–253, 282–283, 286, 288–289
Landau, Ely, 170, 284
Lansbury, Angela, 15–16, 39, 187–188, 194, 196, 282–283, 285
Last Tango in Paris (Bernardo Bertolucci, 1972), 201
Last Year at Marienbad (Alain Resnais, 1961), 204
Lean, David, 9, 210
Le Brun, Charles, 131
Le Carré, John, 105
Le Clainche, Charles, 151
Legrand, Michel, 201
Leigh, Janet, 27, 44, 283
Lenny (Bob Fosse, 1974), 172
Leonard, John, 203–204, 211–212, 293, 296
Leterrier, François, 150
Levinson, Barry, 272
Lévi-Strauss, Claude, 156, 293
Lewis, Edward, 135, 216, 260
Lewis, Joseph L., 40
Lindon, Lionel, 190
Lindsay, Kenneth, 63
Little Foxes, The (William Wyler, 1941), 40, 177
Little Murders (Alan Arkin, 1971), 172
Lolita (Stanley Kubrick, 1962), 161, 163, 165, 168, 294
Looking for Mr. Goodbar (Richard Brooks, 1977), 157
Lonsdale, Michael, 82
Lorre, Peter, 1, 281
Los Angeles, 30, 58, 97, 200, 213, 263, 277, 279, 283, 286, 288, 290–291, 297–298, 300
Los Angeles Times, 200, 204, 209, 288, 290–291, 297–298
Losey, Joseph, 172, 200, 203–204, 207, 210, 212
Louis XI (king of France), 135
Louis XIV (king of France), 131–132
Love Story (Arthur Hiller, 1970), 202
Loving (Irvin Kershner, 1970), 212
Lucanio, Patrick, 230, 293
Lumet, Sidney, 9, 170, 173, 178–179, 182, 260
Lupino, Ida, 155
Lusitania (ship), 149, 156
Lynch, David, 171
Lyne, Adrian, 165

MacLachlan, Kyle, 94, 266–267, 285
Magnificent Obsession (Douglas Sirk, 1954), 56
Magnificent Seven, The (John Sturges, 1960), 80
Magus, The (Guy Green, 1968), 204
Malamud, Bernard, 3, 200, 244–247, 255, 257–260, 287, 289, 293
Malamut, Leonard, 70
Malcolm X, 93
Malden, Karl, 153, 187, 194, 196, 282, 287–288
Malraux, André, 130
Maltese Falcon, The (John Huston, 1941), 45

Mamet, David, 79–80, 82–83
Manchurian Candidate, The (Richard Condon), 15, 17–18, 48, 50, 53–54, 261, 265, 289
Manchurian Candidate, The (John Frankenheimer, 1962), 3, 6, 8, 13–15, 18–19, 26–52, 55–56, 58–59, 61–62, 72, 75, 78, 95, 105, 108, 135, 158, 188, 215–216, 231, 233, 254–255, 261–262, 264–266, 276–277, 283, 287–289, 292–294, 296–298
Manchurian Candidate, The (Jonathan Demme, 2004), 13, 292
Man Escaped, A (Robert Bresson, 1956), 150, 151, 152–153
Man for All Seasons, A (Fred Zinnemann, 1966), 134
Mangold, James, 158
Mann, Anthony, 8
Mann, Thomas, 70
Manulis, Martin, 264
Man with a Movie Camera, The (Dziga Vertov, 1929), 41
March, Fredric, 18, 21, 177, 183, 283–284
Margaret of Austria, 145
Marilyn Diptych (Andy Warhol), 140
Marquand, Christian, 206
Marseilles, France, 5
Martin, Steve, 213
Marty (Delbert Mann, 1955), 252
Marvin, Lee, 171, 175, 179, 183, 282, 284
Maslin, Janet, 5–6, 294
Mason, James, 1, 281
Massari, Lea, 203
Mating Season, The (Mitchell Leisen, 1951), 152
Mayer, Louis B., 133
McCarthy, Andrew, 111–112, 266, 285
McCarthy, Eugene, 91, 266, 268
McCarthy, Joseph, 15, 18, 48–50, 53, 56, 93, 216, 235, 276
McDowell, Roddy, 57
McElhone, Natascha, 79, 114, 285
McGill, Bruce, 274
McGiver, John, 276
McNaughton, John, 166
Meeker, Joseph, 118–119, 153, 294
Melville, Jean Pierre, 83
Mendes, Chico, 4, 117, 119–123, 127–128, 268, 297
Mendez Filho, Francisco Alves, 117
Mengolini, Aldo, 266
Metamorphosis, The (Franz Kafka), 23, 293
Metro Goldwyn Mayer (MGM), 134–135, 138, 193, 200, 219–220, 292, 294, 297
Michael Clayton (Tony Gilroy, 2007), 13
Mifune, Toshirô, 139, 141, 283–284
Milian, Tomas, 123, 286
Miller, Arthur, 6, 276
Miller, J. P., 2
Millikan, Jay, 13, 294
Milliniship, William, 73, 75, 294
Millot, Charles, 70
Minnelli, Vincente, 193
Mintz, Alan, 191–192, 294
Misfits, The (John Huston, 1961), 152
Mississippi Burning (Alan Parker, 1988), 96, 292
Mitchell, Joni, 99

Monaco, 114, 136
Monash, Paul, 272
Monroe, Marilyn, 93
Montand, Yves, 6, 134, 137–138, 141, 283
Monte Carlo, Monaco, 138
Montgomery, Robert, 145
Montmartre (Paris), 80, 84
Monza, 136, 141
Moore, Michael, 13, 299
Moreau, Jeanne, 62, 283
Moro, Aldo, 111, 265–266
Morrison, Temuera, 270
Morrow, Vic, 184
Mosley, Nicolas, 200–201, 203–204, 206–212, 290, 294
Moss, Stirling, 138
Mount Whitney, 155
Mount Tamalpais, 147
MPAA Ratings System, 220
Mulligan, Robert, 9
Museum of Modern Art (New York), 19
Museum of Television and Radio (New York), 19
Music Man, The (Morton DaCosta, 1962), 178
My Lai massacre, 100

Nader, Ralph, 232, 237, 294–295
National Book Award, 258
Nazi Germany, 62–64, 66, 68–70, 72–77, 80, 246, 252, 259–260, 291
Nesbitt, Cathleen, 6
Newnham, Nicole, 63, 74
Newsweek, 65, 71, 265, 288, 296
New York, 7, 9, 19, 30–31, 55, 92–95, 100, 125, 133, 139, 170–171, 201, 203, 264, 267, 276, 283–284, 287–298, 302
New Yorker, The, 6, 67, 157, 291, 293–294
New York Film Festival, 30, 296
New York Journal-American, 31, 294
New York Post, 69, 298
New York School, 9, 264
New York Times, 5, 31, 203, 254, 287–289, 291–296, 302
New York World's Fair (1964), 139
Nice, France, 5, 84, 86, 114–115
Nietzsche, Friedrich, 21, 23, 26, 70, 200, 294
Night and Fog (Alain Resnais, 1955), 153
Night and the City (Jules Dassin, 1950), 184
Night of the Quarter Moon (Hugo Haas, 1959), 77
Nixon, Richard M., 21, 93, 190, 295
Nixon, Tricia, 93
North, Sheree, 216, 227
North by Northwest (Alfred Hitchcock, 1959), 26, 45, 219
Novick, Robert, 259, 294

Obama, Barack, 272, 276–277
O'Brian, Edmond, 35, 147–148, 173, 281, 283–284
O'Casey, Sean, 178
Ochs, Phil, 267
Odyssey, The (Homer), 118
O'Horgan, Tom, 172
Olmos, Edward James, 121

One Hundred Cans (Andy Warhol), 140
O'Neill Eugene, 170–171, 175, 177–178, 180, 182–183, 202, 288, 294
O'Neill, James, 73, 295
Ophuls, Marcel, 153
Ophuls, Max, 174
Opatoshu, David, 247
Orange Bowl, 110, 115
Orange Car Crash Fourteen Times (Andy Warhol), 140
Oswald, Lee Harvey, 50, 61, 277, 293
Oswald, Russell, 100, 267
Outsider, The (Colin Wilson), 256, 298

Pakula, Alan J., 9, 13
Palance, Jack, 1, 9, 281, 283
Palestine, 105, 107–108, 246
Paley, William, 219
Palme d'Or, 135
Palmer, R. Barton, 13, 77, 244
Pankow, John, 111
Panofsky, Erwin, 135, 142, 175, 295
Parallax View, The (Alan J. Pakula, 1974), 13
Paris, 21, 32, 63–67, 69, 70–71, 291, 293, 297–298
Parks, Larry, 216
Parrish, Leslie, 35, 53
Parsons, Estelle, 160, 164–165, 280, 283
Path to War (John Frankenheimer, 2002), 4, 8, 102, 265, 271–276, 286, 295
Pawnbroker, The (Sidney Lumet, 1964), 260
Peacemaker, The (Mimi Leder, 1997), 106
Pearlman, Ron, 269
Peck, Gregory, 3, 6, 157–158, 160–161, 164–165, 168, 283, 291, 295
Pedi, Tom, 180
Penn, Arthur, 71, 291, 293
Pensée Sauvage, Le (Claude Lévi-Strauss), 156, 293
Perkins, Anthony, 57
Pickup on South Street (Samuel Fuller, 1953), 152
Picnic (Joshua Logan, 1955), 215, 217
Pillow Talk (Michael Gordon, 1959)
Pinter, Harold, 171, 201, 203–204, 210, 212
Plana, Tony, 75, 79, 122, 124, 238, 276
Playhouse 90 (television anthology series), 1, 2, 31–33, 264, 272, 281–282, 284, 291
Play Misty for Me (Clint Eastwood, 1971), 157
Play of the Week, The (television anthology series), 170
Poison Ivy (Kait Shea Ruben, 1992), 163, 166
Pomerance, Murray, 6, 8, 77
Pontecorvo, Gillo, 83
Powers, James, 235, 295
Pratley, Gerald, 22, 29, 32, 36, 47, 78, 80, 86, 107–108, 117, 135–139, 142, 158–160, 167–168, 181, 199–200, 202, 208–212, 235, 258–259, 261, 295
Premiere Epistre de l'amant vert, La (Jean Lemaire de Belges), 145
Presley, Elvis, 184
Pretty Poison (Noel Black, 1968), 162
Prince, Stephen, 107, 301
Production Code, 188, 201, 222, 292, 296, 298

INDEX

Professionals, The (Richard Brooks, 1966), 80, 221
Prophecy (John Frankenheimer, 1979), 7, 78, 127, 229–230, 235–236, 238–239, 241–243, 266, 276–277, 284, 288, 291, 297
Pryce, Jonathan, 79, 84, 113
Psycho (Alfred Hitchcock, 1960), 26–27
Pulitzer Prize, 104, 258, 268
Puttnam, David, 127, 268

Racimo, Victoria, 237–238
Radio City Music Hall (New York City), 220
Rainmaker, The (Joseph Anthony, 1956), 121
Randolf, Tim, 139
Randolph, John, 22, 55–56, 232–233, 283
Rape of Europa, The (book, Lynn H. Nicholas; film, Richard Berge, Bonni Cohen, and Nicole Newnham, 2006), 63, 70, 74, 76, 294
Ray, Nicholas, 2, 8
Rear Window (Alfred Hitchcock, 1954), 152
Rebel Without a Cause (Nicholas Ray, 1955), 2, 217
Redacted (Brian De Palma, 2007), 106
Red Rock West (John Dahl, 1993), 166
Reindeer Games (John Frankenheimer, 2000), 78, 105, 271, 277, 285
Remember the Day (Henry King, 1941), 77
Rémy, Albert, 70
Reno, Jean, 78, 81, 285
Renoir, Claude, 201
Renoir, Jean, 40, 68, 74, 86
Resnais, Alain, 204, 210
Revkin, Andrew, 119, 122–123, 127, 295
Rey, Fernando, 262, 284
Rhinoceros (Tom O'Horgan, 1974), 172
Rice, Milton, 137
Richardson, Tony, 172
Rigney, Daniel, 270
Rintels, David, 268
Riot in Cell Block 11 (Don Siegel, 1954), 154
Ritt, Martin, 93–94
Ritter, Thelma, 151–152, 282
Robards, Jason, 170–171, 176, 178–179, 282
Roberts Commission, 76
Rockefeller, Nelson, 92, 98, 100, 267
Rocky (John G. Avildsen, 1976), 9
Rogin, Michael, 50, 296
Ronin (John Frankenheimer, 1998), 2–3, 5, 7, 33, 78–85, 87–88, 93, 95, 97, 99, 101, 105, 107, 109, 111–116, 229, 271, 285
Rooney, Mickey, 33–34, 173, 281, 283–284
Rope (Alfred Hitchcock, 1948), 174
Rosen, Michael, 30, 291
Rosenbergs, Julius and Ethel, 93
Rossellini, Roberto, 275
Roughing It (Mark Twain), 123
Ruben, Kait Shea, 163
Ryan, Robert, 175, 183, 282, 284

Sabato, Antonio, 134, 137
Sacco and Vanzetti case, 259
Saint, Eva Marie, 134, 139, 186–187, 194, 196, 282–283
Salinger, J. D., 216–217
Salkind, Alexander, 212

Salvador (Oliver Stone, 1986), 111
Samourai, Le (Jean-Pierre Melville, 1967), 83
Sanda, Dominique, 201–202, 204–206, 209, 283
Sand Pebbles, The (Robert Wise, 1966), 129
San Francisco, 30, 146–148, 153, 295
Sarris, Andrew, 202, 233, 243, 296
Saudi Arabia, 240
Sauvage, Pierre, 73, 289
Scalphunters, The (Sydney Pollack, 1968), 221
Schivelbusch, Wolfgang, 191–192, 296
Schreber, Daniel Paul, 17, 291, 296
Scofield, Paul, 62, 64–65, 70, 283
Scorned (Andrew Stevens, 1994), 165
Scorsese, Martin, 264, 293
Scott, Ian, 105, 296
Scott, Ridley, 231, 237
Scott, Zachary, 1, 280
Seattle, 30
Seconds (David Ely, 1962), 21, 54, 56
Seconds (John Frankenheimer, 1966), 2–3, 7, 13–14, 21–28, 48, 54–61, 78, 95, 129, 135, 215, 229, 230–236, 239, 241–243, 273, 283, 289–290, 292, 295–296, 298
Segal, George, 212
Semmerling, Tim Jon, 108, 296
Serling, Rod, 1, 18, 264, 285
Seven Days in May (John Frankenheimer, 1964), 3, 6, 13–14, 18–19, 25, 56, 78, 105–106, 127, 135, 158, 215, 231, 283, 293
Shaheen, Jack G., 105, 296
Shane (George Stevens, 1953), 122
Shapiro, Alan, 163
Sharif, Omar, 8, 283
Shary, Timothy, 163, 296
Shaw, Robert, 108, 110, 264, 284
Shengold, Leonard, 296
Shire, Talia, 236, 238, 284
Shurlock, Geoffrey, 190, 296
Siege, The (Edward Zwick, 1998), 104
Siegel, Don, 154
Sight and Sound, 159, 235, 292, 294, 297–298
Simon, Alex, 91, 119, 296
Simon, Michel, 62, 283
Sinatra, Frank, 15, 27, 30, 34, 43, 46–47, 49–50, 52, 54, 61, 93, 254, 263, 283
Sinise, Gary, 243, 263, 272–273, 285, 297
Sirhan, Sirhan, 91
Sirk, Douglas, 56
Skarsgård, Stellan, 79, 114–115, 285
Skerritt, Tom, 274
Slade, David, 163
Slezak, Victor, 274
Slotkin, Richard, 117–118, 123, 297
Sloterdijk, Peter, 107, 297
Smith, Michael, 94, 99, 101–102
Sobchack, Vivian, 230–231, 297–298
Some Came Running (Vincente Minnelli, 1958), 215
Sontag, Susan, 172, 174, 297
Sorcerer (William Friedkin, 1977), 3
Sorrow and the Pity, The (Marcel Ophuls, 1969), 153
Sound and the Fury, The (William Faulkner), 216

INDEX

Sound of Music, The (Robert Wise, 1965), 130
South Carolina, 167
Spielberg, Steven, 84, 172, 293, 302
Spinoza, Baruch, 245–246, 248, 250, 254, 258
Spivy, Madame, 51, 193
Splendor in the Grass (Elia Kazan, 1961), 184
Spock, Benjamin, 192
Spoto, Donald, 205–206, 297
Springfield Rifle (André de Toth, 1952), 77
Stalin, Josef, 265, 276–277
Stam, Robert, 211, 297
Stanley, Richard, 239, 269–270
Star Wars (George Lucas, 1977), 9, 266
Sterritt, David, 48, 302
Stevens, Andrew, 165
Stewart, Garrett, 113–114, 297
Stewart, Jackie, 138
Stone, Oliver, 99, 215
Stone, Sharon, 112, 266, 285
Story of My Sufferings, The (Menachem Mendel Beilis) 247, 287
Strangers on a Train (Alfred Hitchcock, 1951), 26
Stratford International Film Festival, 209
Sudduth, Skip, 79
Sum of All Fears, The (Phil Alden Robinson, 2002), 106
Sunset Blvd. (Billy Wilder, 1950), 152
Sutherland, Donald, 273, 286
Swanson, Gloria, 152
Sylbert, Paul, 257
Syriana (Stephen Gaghan, 2005), 106, 115

Taxi Driver (Martin Scorsese, 1976), 171
Taxi to the Dark Side (Alex Gibney, 2007), 13
Taylor, Don, 239
Taylor, Elizabeth, 43, 54
Taylor, James Russell, 188, 192, 297
Telotte, J. P., 230–231, 297
Tennant, Victoria, 213, 284
Terminator, The (James Cameron, 1984), 231
Thewlis, David, 240, 271, 285
Thieves Like Us (Robert Altman, 1974), 159
Thompson, Francis, 139
Time, 18, 286, 290, 295
To Be Alive (Francis Thompson, 1964), 139
To Kill a Mockingbird (Robert Mulligan, 1962), 160, 301
Tormé, Mel, 33, 284
Touch of Class, A (Melvin Frank, 1973), 212
Tournier, Jean, 73
Train, The (John Frankenheimer, 1964), 2, 3, 6–8, 55–56, 62–80, 83–84, 87, 199, 201, 215, 252, 283, 290–291, 293–294, 295–298
Tree Grows in Brooklyn, A (Elia Kazan, 1947), 77
Trial, The (Franz Kafka), 23, 293
Triple Elvis (Andy Warhol), 140
Trumbo, Dalton, 6, 204, 258, 261
Trumbo, Mitsy, 204, 213
Tsiantis, Lee, 77
Tucker, Ken, 120, 297
Turner, Bryan S., 242, 298
Turner, Ted, 78, 117, 229, 230, 263, 268, 292, 298

Turn of the Screw, The (John Frankenheimer, 1959), 174, 282
Twain, Mark, 123
Twenty-five Colored Marilyns (Andy Warhol), 140
Twilight Zone, The (television series), 18, 28
Two Lane Blacktop (Monte Hellman, 1971), 159

Under Fire (Roger Spottiswoode, 1983), 111
Useem, Bert, 92, 100, 298

Valente, Jack, 275
Valente, John, 275
Valland, Rose, 63–70, 74, 76–77, 288, 298
Valley, Mark, 275
V-Effekt (Bertolt Brecht), 209, 213
Vertov, Dziga, 41
Vietnam, 4, 93–94, 96, 100, 109, 112, 159, 214, 265–266, 268, 272–275
Virilio, Paul, 107, 110, 298
von Sternberg, Josef, 174
von Tripps, Wolfgang, 139
Voyage au bout de la nuit (Louis Ferdinand Céline), 153

Wag the Dog (Barry Levinson, 1998), 83
Walker, Jessica, 134
Wallant, Edward Lewis, 260
Walsh, David, 167
Walsh, Raoul, 5
Warner Brothers, 127, 220
Washington, DC, 30, 125, 236, 290
Washington Post, 73, 75, 292, 294
Waterloo Station (London), 115
Watkins Glen Grand Prix, 136
Wayne, John, 43
Weld, Tuesday, 6, 157, 160–164, 283–284
Welles, Orson, 1, 36, 40, 177, 264, 300
Wells, H. G., 239–240, 242, 269, 271, 275
Wexman, Virginia Wright, 220, 298
Whale, James, 230
White, Hayden, 95, 298
White Heat (Raoul Walsh, 1949), 149, 152
Who's Afraid of Virginia Woolf (Mike Nichols, 1966), 172
Wicker, Tom, 93, 95, 298
Widmark, Richard, 43, 184
Wild Bunch, The (Sam Peckinpah, 1969), 214, 270, 302
Wilder, Billy, 5, 224
Wild Things (John McNaughton, 1998), 166
Wilhelm II (emperor of Germany), 149
Williams, Clarence III, 98, 270, 273
Williams, Tennessee, 1
Willson, Henry, 57, 292
Wilson, Colin, 218, 256, 298
Wilson, Scott, 215, 227, 253
Windom, William, 215
Winningham, Mare, 274, 285
Wise, Robert, 224
Witt, Katarina, 87
Wolper, David, 267
Woman on the Beach, The (Jean Renoir, 1947), 77
Woman Under the Influence, A (John Cassavetes, 1974), 171

Wood, Robin, 159
Woodstock Music Festival, 99
Woodward, Steven, 163, 298
Woolsey, Ralph, 173, 178, 287
Wottitz, Walter, 73
Wright, Lawrence, 104
Wyler, William, 1, 40, 177, 204
Wylie, Philip, 52, 298

Yates, Peter, 3
Year of Living Dangerously, The (Peter Weir, 1982), 111

Year of the Gun (John Frankenheimer, 1991), 107, 111–114, 265, 285
Young, Nathan, 56
Young Savages, The (John Frankenheimer, 1961), 71, 282
Young Strangers, The (John Frankenheimer, 1957) 2, 174, 204, 271, 281
You Are There (television anthology series), 4, 31, 279

Zinnemann, Fred, 9, 111, 134
Žižek, Slavoj, 19, 22, 27, 103, 298